spdri

srlhn

kprhnv

dcgre

JOE M. PULLIS, Ed.D.
Professor, Department of Office Administration
and Business Communication
College of Administration and Business
Louisiana Tech University

Glencoe Publishing Company/Bobbs-Merrill Division

*SPEEDWRITING
SHORTHAND
COMPREHENSIVE
DICTIONARY

Cheryl D. Pullis, M.Ed.
System Consultant

Send all inquiries to:
Glencoe Publishing Company
15319 Chatsworth Street
Mission Hills, California 91345

Printed in the United States of America

ISBN 0-02-685152-0

1 2 3 4 5 6 7 8 9 93 92 91 90 89 88

CONTENTS

Word Division Rules   v

Comprehensive Dictionary   1

Appendix

     Speedwriting Shorthand Principles by System Category   479

     Index of Brief Forms (alphabetical)   486

     Index of Abbreviations (alphabetical)   490

     Index of Phrases   492

     Identification Initials for United States and Territories   496

     Identification Initials for Canadian Provinces and Territories   498

     Index of American and Canadian Cities   499

     Metric Terms   502

WORD DIVISION RULES

The *Speedwriting Shorthand Comprehensive Dictionary* contains more than 22,000 shorthand outlines for the most frequently used words in business communications. All places where these words can correctly be divided in transcription applications are shown. The rules used for these word divisions are as follows:

1. Divide words only between syllables: dis•play, con•scious.
   Thus, one-syllable words cannot be divided: strength, through.

2. Do not divide a word of five or fewer letters: ideas, refer.

3. Do not divide a proper noun, a contraction, an abbreviation, or a figure: America, shouldn't, A.S.P.C.A., $10,234.75.

4. Do not divide a one- or two-letter syllable at the end of a word: ready, lively.

5. Retain as much of a word as possible on the first line; otherwise, retain at least two letters of a word on the first line.

6. Whenever possible, divide a word after its prefix or before its suffix: dis•or•gan•ize, set•tle•ment.
   Preferred: dis•organize, settle•ment

7. Whenever possible, divide a compound word between the elements of the compound: busi•ness•woman, over•pro•duc•tion.
   Preferred: business•woman, over•production

8. Divide hyphenated words at the hyphen only: self-assured, sister-in-law.

9. Divide words between double consonants when a suffix is added unless the root word itself ends in double letters, in which case division is made after the double letters: small•est, fill•ing, miss•ing, big•gest, con•trol•ling.

10. Divide a word between two consecutive single-vowel syllables: con•tinu•ation, situ•ation.

11. In general, retain an internal single-vowel syllable with the first part of the word: sepa•rate, elimi•nate.

    But divide before a single-vowel syllable if that syllable is part of the word-ending forms of *able* or *ible, icle* or *ical, ity* or *ety:* pay•able, med•ical, abil•ity.

    Also, divide before a single-vowel syllable if that syllable is part of a root word that contains a prefix: dis•agree, dis•avow.

12. Retain the single vowel *i* with *za* in nouns ending in *ization*: or•gan•iza•tion, au•thor•iza•tion.

The basic reference for syllabication of words is *The American Heritage Dictionary, Second College Edition* (Houghton Mifflin Company, Boston). When the pronunciation of a word changes with its part of speech usage, the specified part of speech and the appropriate outline are presented. When a shorthand outline for a given word might be written in more than one way, the most frequently used pronunciation is the basis for outline construction.

A

a	
aback	*abc*
aban·don	*abNn*
aban·doned	*abNn-*
aban·don·ing	*abNn*
aban·don·ment	*abNnm*
abase	*abs*
abase·ment	*absm*
abate	*aba*
abated	*aba-*
abate·ment	*abam*
ab·bre·vi·ate	*abrva*
ab·bre·vi·ated	*abrva-*
ab·bre·via·tion	*abrvej*
ab·bre·via·tions	*abrvejs*
ab·di·cate	*abdca*
ab·do·men	*abdm*
ab·domi·nal	*abdml*
ab·duct	*abdc*
ab·ducted	*abdc-*
ab·duc·tion	*abdcj*

ab·er·ra·tion	*abry*
abet	*abt*
abet·ted	*abt-*
abey·ance	*abaN*
ab·hor·rent	*abhrN*
abide	*abd*
abid·ing	*abd*
abil·ities	*Bls*
abil·ity	*Bl*
ab·ject	*abjc*
able	*B*
ably	*Bl*
ab·nor·mal	*abnr l*
ab·nor·mal·ities	*abnr lls*
ab·nor·mal·ity	*abnr ll*
ab·nor·mally	*abnr ll*
aboard	*abrd*
abode	*abd*
abol·ish	*abls*
abol·ished	*abls-*
abol·ish·ing	*abls*
abol·ish·ment	*ablsm*
abo·li·tion	*ablj*

Word	Shorthand	Word	Shorthand
abomi·na·ble	*abmß*	ab·scess	*abss*
abomi·nate	*abma*	ab·scond	*abscn*
abomi·na·tion	*abmy*	ab·sence	*absn*
abort	*abrt*	ab·sences	*absns*
aborted	*abrt-*	ab·sent	*absn*
abort·ing	*abrt̲*	ab·sen·tee	*absnte*
abor·tion	*abry*	ab·sen·tee·ism	*absntez*
abor·tions	*abrys*	ab·sent·ing	*absn̲*
aborts	*abrts*	ab·so·lute	*abslu*
abound	*abon*	ab·so·lutely	*abslul*
abounds	*abons*	ab·so·lutes	*abslus*
about	*ab*	ab·so·lu·tion	*absly*
above	*abv*	ab·solve	*abzlv*
above·board	*abvbrd*	ab·solved	*abzlv-*
ab·ra·sion	*abry*	ab·sorb	*absrb*
ab·ra·sions	*abrys*	ab·sorbed	*absrb-*
ab·ra·sive	*abrsv*	ab·sorb·ing	*absrb̲*
abreast	*abrß*	ab·sorp·tion	*absrpy*
abridge	*abry*	ab·stain	*abßn*
abridged	*abry-*	ab·sten·tion	*abßny*
abridg·ment	*abrym*	ab·sti·nence	*abßnn*
abroad	*abrd*	ab·sti·nent	*abßnn*
abrupt	*abrpt*	ab·stract	*abßrc*

ab·stract·ing	*abSrc*	acade·mies	*acd es*
ab·stracts	*abSrcs*	academy	*acd e*
ab·surd	*absrd*	ac·cede	*vd*
ab·surd·ity	*absrd ͨ*	ac·ceded	*vd-*
abun·dance	*abNN*	ac·ced·ing	*vd*
abun·dant	*abNN*	ac·cel·er·ate	*lra*
abuse (v.)	*abz*	ac·cel·er·ated	*lra-*
abuse (n.)	*abs*	ac·cel·er·at·ing	*lra_*
abused	*abz-*	ac·cel·era·tion	*lry*
abuses (v.)	*abzs*	ac·cel·era·tor	*lrar*
abuses (n.)	*abss*	ac·cel·er·ome·ter	*lr lr*
abus·ing	*abz_*	ac·cent	*VN*
abu·sive	*absv*	ac·cented	*VN-*
abu·sively	*absvl*	ac·cen·tu·ate	*vnCa*
abu·sive·ness	*absv ͨ*	ac·cen·tua·tion	*vnCuy*
abut·ment	*ablm*	ac·cept	*ac*
abut·ments	*ablms*	ac·cept·abil·ity	*acB ͨ*
abyss	*abs*	ac·cept·able	*acB*
aca·de·mia	*acd a*	ac·cept·ably	*acB*
aca·demic	*acd c*	ac·cep·tance	*acN*
aca·dem·ically	*acd cl*	ac·cep·tances	*acNs*
aca·de·mi·cian	*acd y*	ac·cep·tant	*acN*
aca·de·mi·cians	*acd ys*	ac·cepted	*ac-*

Word	Shorthand		Word	Shorthand
ac·cept·ing	*ac_*		ac·com·mo·da·tions	*akdys*
ac·cepts	*acs*		ac·com·pa·nied	*aco-*
ac·cess	*vs*		ac·com·pa·nies	*acos*
ac·ces·si·bil·ity	*vsβl*		ac·com·pa·ni·ment	*acom*
ac·ces·si·ble	*vsβ*		ac·com·pa·nist	*acoδ*
ac·cess·ing	*vs_*		ac·com·pany	*aco*
ac·ces·sion	*vsy*		ac·com·pa·ny·ing	*aco_*
ac·ces·sions	*vsys*		ac·com·plice	*akpls*
ac·ces·so·ries	*vsres*		ac·com·plish	*ak*
ac·ces·sory	*vsre*		ac·com·plished	*ak-*
ac·ci·dent	*vdN*		ac·com·plishes	*aks*
ac·ci·den·tal	*vdNl*		ac·com·plish·ing	*ak_*
ac·ci·den·tally	*vdNll*		ac·com·plish·ment	*akm*
ac·ci·dents	*vdNs*		ac·com·plish·ments	*akms*
ac·claim	*acl*		ac·cord	*acrd*
ac·cli·mate	*acla*		ac·cord·ance	*acrdN*
ac·cli·ma·tize	*acltz*		ac·corded	*acrd-*
ac·co·lade	*acld*		ac·cord·ing	*acrd_*
ac·com·mo·date	*akda*		ac·cord·ingly	*acrdl*
ac·com·mo·dated	*akda-*		ac·cor·dion	*acrden*
ac·com·mo·dates	*akdas*		ac·cost	*acδ*
ac·com·mo·dat·ing	*akda_*		ac·count	*ak*
ac·com·mo·da·tion	*akdy*		ac·count·abil·ity	*akβl*

Word	Shorthand	Word	Shorthand
ac·count·able		ac·cu·mu·la·tor	
ac·count·ancy		ac·cu·ra·cies	
ac·count·ant		ac·cu·racy	
ac·count·ants		ac·cu·rate	
ac·counted		ac·cu·rately	
ac·count·ing		ac·cu·sa·tion	
ac·counts		ac·cu·sa·tions	
ac·credit		ac·cuse	
ac·credi·ta·tion		ac·cused	
ac·cred·ited		ac·cus·ing	
ac·cred·it·ing		ac·cus·tom	
ac·cred·its		ac·cus·tomed	
ac·crual		ace	
ac·cru·als		ac·er·bate	
ac·crue		ace·tate	
ac·crued		ace·tone	
ac·cu·mu·late		ache	
ac·cu·mu·lated		aches	
ac·cu·mu·lat·ing		achiev·able	
ac·cu·mu·la·tion		achieve	
ac·cu·mu·la·tions		achieved	
ac·cu·mu·la·tive		achieve·ment	
ac·cu·mu·la·tively		achieve·ments	

Word	Shorthand	Word	Shorthand
achiever		ac·quaint·ing	
achiev·ers		ac·qui·esce	
achieves		ac·quire	
achiev·ing		ac·quired	
ach·ing		ac·quir·ing	
acid		ac·qui·si·tion	
acidic		ac·qui·si·tional	
acid·ity		ac·qui·si·tions	
acids		ac·quit	
ac·knowl·edge		ac·quit·tal	
ac·knowl·edged		acre	
ac·knowl·edges		acre·age	
ac·knowl·edg·ing		acres	
ac·knowl·edg·ment		acrid	
ac·knowl·edg·ments		ac·ri·mo·ni·ous	
acme		ac·ri·mony	
acne		ac·ro·bat	
acous·tic		ac·ro·batic	
acous·ti·cal		ac·ro·bat·ics	
ac·quaint		ac·ro·nym	
ac·quain·tance		acropo·lis	
ac·quain·tances		across	
ac·quainted		acrylic	

act	*ac*	ac·tu·ate	*acCa*
acted	*ac-*	acu·men	*acm*
act·ing	*ac*	acute	*acu*
ac·tion	*acq*	acutely	*acul*
ac·tions	*acqs*	acute·ness	*acu'*
ac·ti·vate	*acva*	ad	*a*
ac·ti·vated	*acva-*	adage	*aq*
ac·ti·vates	*acvas*	adapt	*adpl*
ac·ti·vat·ing	*acva*	adapt·abil·ity	*adplB'*
ac·ti·va·tion	*acvq*	adapt·able	*adplB*
ac·tive	*acv*	ad·ap·ta·tion	*Aplq*
ac·tively	*acvl*	adapted	*adpl-*
ac·tiv·ities	*acv'ls*	adapter	*adplr*
ac·tiv·ity	*acv'*	adapt·ers	*adplrs*
actor	*acr*	adapt·ing	*adpl*
ac·tors	*acrs*	adap·tion	*adpq*
acts	*acs*	adap·tive	*adpv*
ac·tual	*acCul*	adap·tor	*adplr*
ac·tu·al·ity	*acCul'*	add	*a*
ac·tu·ally	*acCull*	added	*a-*
ac·tu·arial	*acCurel*	ad·denda	*adNa*
ac·tu·ar·ies	*acCures*	ad·den·dum	*adN*
ac·tu·ary	*acCure*	ad·dict (v.)	*adc*

ad·dict (n.)	*Ac*	adds	*As*
ad·dicted	*adc-*	ade·noid	*Anyd*
ad·dic·tion	*adcy*	ade·noids	*Anyds*
add·ing	*A_*	adept	*adpt*
ad·di·tion	*ady*	ade·quacy	*Aqse*
ad·di·tional	*adyl*	ade·quate	*Aqt*
ad·di·tion·ally	*adyll*	ade·quately	*Aqll*
ad·di·tions	*adys*	ad·here	*Ahr*
ad·di·tive	*Av*	ad·hered	*Ahr-*
ad·di·tives	*Avs*	ad·her·ence	*Ahrn*
addle	*Al*	ad·her·ent	*Ahrn*
add-on	*A = o*	ad·her·ing	*Ahr_*
add-ons	*A = os*	ad·he·sion	*Ahy*
ad·dress (v. or n.)	*adrs*	ad·he·sive	*Ahsv*
ad·dress (n.)	*Ars*	ad·he·sive·ness	*Ahsv'*
ad·dressed	*adrs-*	ad·he·sives	*Ahsvs*
ad·dressee	*adrse*	ad hoc	*Ahc*
ad·dress·ees	*adrses*	ad in·fi·ni·tum	*Anfnt*
ad·dresser	*adrsr*	ad·ja·cent	*ajsn*
ad·dress·ers	*adrsrs*	ad·jec·tive	*ajcv*
ad·dresses (v. or n.)	*adrss*	ad·join	*ajyn*
ad·dresses (n.)	*Arss*	ad·join·ing	*ajyn_*
ad·dress·ing	*adrs_*	ad·joins	*ajyns*

ad·journ		ad·min·is·ter·ing	
ad·journed		ad·min·is·ters	
ad·journ·ment		ad·min·is·trate	
ad·judge		ad·min·is·trates	
ad·judged		ad·min·is·trat·ing	
ad·ju·di·cate		ad·min·is·tra·tion	
ad·ju·di·cated		ad·min·is·tra·tions	
ad·ju·di·ca·tion		ad·min·is·tra·tive	
ad·junct		ad·min·is·tra·tively	
ad·juncts		ad·min·is·tra·tor	
ad·just		ad·min·is·tra·tors	
ad·just·able		ad·min·is·tra·trix	
ad·justed		ad·mi·ra·ble	
ad·juster		ad·mi·ra·bly	
ad·just·ers		ad·mi·ral	
ad·just·ing		ad·mi·rals	
ad·just·ment		ad·mi·ralty	
ad·just·ments		ad·mi·ra·tion	
ad·jus·tor		ad·mire	
ad·jus·tors		ad·mired	
ad lib		ad·mirer	
ad·min·is·ter		ad·mis·si·bil·ity	
ad·min·is·tered		ad·mis·si·ble	

ad·mis·sion	*Aŋ*	adore	*adr*
ad·mis·sions	*Aŋs*	adorn	*adrn*
admit	*Aɩ*	adorn·ment	*adrnm*
ad·mits	*Aɩs*	ad·re·nal	*adrnl*
ad·mit·tance	*AɩM*	ad·rena·line	*adrnln*
ad·mit·ted	*Aɩ-*	adrift	*adrfl*
ad·mit·tedly	*Aɩ-l*	adroit	*adryl*
ad·mit·ting	*Aɩ_*	adroitly	*adryll*
ad·mon·ish	*Amɩ*	ads	*As*
ad·mo·ni·tion	*Amŋ*	adu·la·tion	*aɟl*
adobe	*adbe*	adult	*adll*
ado·les·cence	*AlsM*	adul·tery	*adllre*
ado·les·cent	*AlsM*	adult·hood	*adllh*
ado·les·cents	*AlsMs*	adults	*adlls*
adopt	*adpl*	ad·vance	*AvM*
adopted	*adpl-*	ad·vanced	*AvM-*
adopt·ing	*adpl_*	ad·vance·ment	*AvMm*
adop·tion	*adpŋ*	ad·vances	*AvMs*
adop·tions	*adpŋs*	ad·vanc·ing	*AvM_*
adop·tive	*adpv*	ad·van·tage	*Avŋ*
adopts	*adpls*	ad·van·ta·geous	*Avŋs*
ador·able	*adrß*	ad·van·ta·geously	*Avŋsl*
ado·ra·tion	*Arŋ*	ad·van·tages	*Avŋs*

ad·vent		ad·vise·ment	
ad·ven·ture		ad·viser	
ad·ven·tures		ad·vis·ers	
ad·ven·tur·ous		ad·vises	
ad·verb		ad·vis·ing	
ad·ver·bial		ad·vi·sor	
ad·ver·sary		ad·vi·sors	
ad·verse		ad·vi·sory	
ad·versely		ad·vo·cacy	
ad·ver·sity		ad·vo·cate (v.)	
ad·ver·tise		ad·vo·cate (n.)	
ad·ver·tised		ad·vo·cated	
ad·ver·tise·ment		ad·vo·cates (v.)	
ad·ver·tise·ments		ad·vo·cates (n.)	
ad·ver·tiser		ad·vo·cat·ing	
ad·ver·tis·ers		aegis	
ad·ver·tises		aera·tion	
ad·ver·tis·ing		aerial	
ad·vice		aero·bal·lis·tics	
ad·vis·abil·ity		aero·dy·nam·ics	
ad·vis·able		aero·nau·ti·cal	
ad·vise		aer·onomy	
ad·vised		aero·sol	

aero·sols		af·fili·at·ing	
aero·space		af·fili·ation	
aes·thetic		af·fili·ations	
aes·thet·ically		af·fin·ity	
aes·thet·ics		af·firm	
afar		af·fir·ma·tion	
af·fa·ble		af·firma·tive	
af·fair		af·firma·tively	
af·fairs		af·firmed	
af·fect		af·firm·ing	
af·fected		af·firms	
af·fect·ing		affix	
af·fec·tion		af·fixed	
af·fec·tion·ate		af·fix·ing	
af·fec·tive		af·flict	
af·fects		af·flicted	
af·fi·da·vit		af·flic·tion	
af·fi·da·vits		af·flu·ence	
af·fili·ate (v.)		af·flu·ent	
af·fili·ate (n.)		af·ford	
af·fili·ated		af·ford·able	
af·fili·ates (v.)		af·forded	
af·fili·ates (n.)		af·ford·ing	

af·fords	*afds*	aged	*aj-*
af·front	*afrN*	age·less	*ajls*
af·ghan	*afgn*	agen·cies	*ajNes*
afield	*afld*	agency	*ajNe*
afloat	*aflo*	agenda	*ajNa*
afore·men·tioned	*afmj-*	agen·das	*ajNas*
afore·said	*afsd*	agent	*ajN*
afraid	*afrd*	agents	*ajNs*
aft	*aft*	ages	*ajs*
after	*af*	ag·gra·vate	*agrva*
af·ter·burner	*afbrns*	ag·gra·vated	*agrva-*
af·ter·care	*afcr*	ag·gra·va·tion	*agrvj*
af·ter·ef·fect	*afefc*	ag·gre·gate (adj. or n.)	*agrgl*
af·ter·math	*af~l*	ag·gre·gate (v.)	*agrga*
af·ter·noon	*afnn*	ag·gre·gates (n.)	*agrgls*
af·ter·noons	*afnns*	ag·gre·gates (v.)	*agrgas*
af·ter·taste	*afl8*	ag·gre·ga·tion	*agrgj*
af·ter·thought	*aflt*	ag·gres·sion	*agrj*
af·ter·ward	*afw*	ag·gres·sive	*agrsv*
af·ter·wards	*afws*	ag·gres·sively	*agrsvl*
again	*aq*	ag·gres·sive·ness	*agrsv'*
against	*aq*	ag·gres·sor	*agrsr*
age	*aj*	agile	*ajl*

agil·ity	*ajl͘*	aides	*ads*
aging	*aɤ_*	aid·ing	*ad̠*
agi·tate	*ajta*	aids	*ads*
agi·ta·tion	*ajⱦ*	ail·ment	*alm*
agi·ta·tor	*ajtar*	aim	*a⌒*
ago	*aq*	aimed	*a⌒ -*
ago·nize	*agnz*	aim·ing	*a⌒ _*
agony	*agne*	aim·less	*a⌒ls*
agree	*agre*	aims	*a⌒s*
agree·able	*agreß*	air	*ar*
agreed	*agre -*	air·borne	*arbrn*
agree·ing	*agre_*	air conditioner	*ar kdɟr*
agree·ment	*agrem*	air conditioners	*ar kdɟrs*
agree·ments	*agrems*	air conditioning	*ar kdɟ_*
agrees	*agres*	air·craft	*arcrfl*
ag·ri·busi·ness	*agrbs*	air·drop	*ardrp*
ag·ri·cul·tural	*agrl*	aired	*ar -*
ag·ri·cul·tur·ally	*agrll*	air·ing	*ar_*
ag·ri·cul·ture	*agr*	air·lift	*arlfl*
ahead	*ahd*	air·line	*arln*
aid	*ad*	air·liner	*arlnr*
aide	*ad*	air·lines	*arlns*
aided	*ad-*	air·mail	*ar⌒l*

air·mailed	*ar l-*	alarms	*alr s*
air·man	*ar n*	al·beit	*Abel*
air·plane	*arpln*	al·bino	*Abno*
air·planes	*arplns*	album	*Ab*
air·port	*arpl*	al·bu·min	*Abm*
air·ports	*arpls*	al·bums	*Ab s*
air·space	*arsps*	al·co·hol	*Achl*
air·strip	*arSrp*	al·co·holic	*Achlc*
air·strips	*arSrps*	al·co·hol·ics	*Achlcs*
air·tight	*arli*	al·co·hol·ism	*Achlz*
air·wave	*ar v*	al·cove	*Acv*
air·waves	*ar vs*	alder	*Adr*
air·way	*ar a*	al·der·man	*Adr n*
air·ways	*ar as*	al·der·men	*Adrm*
air·wor·thi·ness	*ar rle'*	ale	*al*
aisle	*il*	alert	*alrl*
aisles	*ils*	alerted	*alrl-*
akin	*acn*	alert·ing	*alrl*
a la carte	*a la crl*	alert·ness	*alrl'*
alarm	*alr*	alerts	*alrls*
alarmed	*alr -*	al·falfa	*Aflfa*
alarm·ing	*alr*	al·ge·bra	*Aybra*
alarm·ist	*alr S*	al·ge·braic	*Aybrac*

al·go·rithm	*agrt*	al·leges	*alys*
alias	*ales*	al·le·giance	*alyn*
alibi	*abi*	al·leg·ing	*aly*
alien	*alen*	al·le·gor·ical	*agrcl*
ali·en·ate	*alena*	al·le·gory	*agre*
ali·en·ated	*alena-*	al·ler·gic	*alryc*
ali·ena·tion	*aleny*	al·ler·gies	*aryes*
align	*aln*	al·lergy	*arye*
align·ing	*aln*	al·le·vi·ate	*alva*
align·ment	*alnm*	al·le·vi·ated	*alva -*
aligns	*alns*	al·le·vi·ates	*alvas*
alike	*alc*	al·le·vi·at·ing	*alva*
ali·mony	*a ne*	alley	*ae*
alive	*alv*	al·li·ance	*alin*
al·kali	*acli*	al·lied	*ai-*
al·ka·line	*acln*	al·li·ga·tor	*agtr*
all	*a*	al·lo·cate	*aca*
allay	*ala*	al·lo·cated	*aca-*
al·le·ga·tion	*agy*	al·lo·cat·ing	*aca*
al·le·ga·tions	*agys*	al·lo·ca·tion	*acy*
al·lege	*aly*	al·lo·ca·tions	*acys*
al·leged	*aly-*	allot	*all*
al·leg·edly	*aly-l*	al·lot·ment	*allm*

al·lot·ments	*allms*	aloof	*alf*
al·lot·ted	*alt-*	aloud	*alod*
allow	*alo*	alpha	*afa*
al·low·able	*alob*	al·pha·bet	*afbl*
al·low·ance	*aloN*	al·pha·bet·ical	*afblcl*
al·low·ances	*aloNs*	al·pha·bet·ically	*afblcll*
al·lowed	*alo-*	al·pha·bet·ize	*afblz*
al·low·ing	*alo_*	al·pha·bet·ized	*afblz-*
al·lows	*alos*	al·pha·nu·meric	*afn rc*
alloy	*Ay*	al·pine	*Apn*
al·loys	*Ays*	al·ready	*Ar*
al·lude	*ald*	also	*Aso*
al·luded	*ald-*	altar	*Alr*
al·lure	*alr*	alter	*Alr*
al·lu·vium	*alve*	al·tera·tion	*Alry*
ally	*Au*	al·tera·tions	*Alrys*
al·ma·nac	*A mc*	al·ter·ca·tion	*Alrcy*
al·mighty	*A ie*	al·ter·ca·tions	*Alrcys*
al·mond	*amd*	al·tered	*Alr-*
al·most	*A S*	al·ter·ing	*Alr_*
alone	*aln*	al·ter·nate (v.)	*Alrna*
along	*alg*	al·ter·nate (n. or adj.)	*Alrnl*
along·side	*algsd*	al·ter·nated	*Alrna-*

Word	Shorthand	Word	Shorthand
al·ter·nately	*Alrnll*	alum·nus	*al ms*
al·ter·nates (v.)	*Alrnas*	al·ways	*a*
al·ter·nates (n.)	*Alrnls*	am	*⌐*
al·ter·na·tion	*Alrn*	a.m.	*a*
al·ter·na·tions	*Alrns*	amass	*a s*
al·ter·na·tive	*Alrnv*	amassed	*a s-*
al·ter·na·tively	*Alrnvl*	ama·teur	*a dr*
al·ter·na·tives	*Alrnvs*	ama·teurs	*a drs*
al·ter·na·tor	*Alrnar*	amaze	*a z*
al·ters	*Alrs*	amazed	*a z-*
al·though	*Alo*	amaz·ing	*a z-*
al·time·ter	*Al dr*	amaz·ingly	*a zl*
al·ti·tude	*Alld*	am·bas·sa·dor	*a bsdr*
al·ti·tudes	*Allds*	amber	*a br*
alto	*Alo*	am·bi·ent	*a beN*
al·to·gether	*Alglr*	am·bi·gu·ity	*a bgul*
al·tru·ism	*Alruz*	am·bigu·ous	*a bgus*
al·tru·is·tic	*Alrusc*	am·bi·tion	*a by*
alu·mi·nous	*alms*	am·bi·tions	*a bys*
alu·mi·num	*alm*	am·bi·tious	*a bss*
alumna	*al na*	am·biva·lent	*a bvelN*
alum·nae	*al ne*	amble	*a B*
alumni	*al ni*	am·bu·lance	*a belN*

am·bu·la·tory		am·mu·ni·tion	
am·bush		am·ne·sia	
ame·lio·rate		among	
amen		amongst	
ame·na·ble		amoral	
amend		amo·rous	
amend·able		am·or·ti·za·tion	
amended		am·or·tize	
amend·ing		am·or·tized	
amend·ment		amount	
amend·ments		amounted	
amends		amount·ing	
amen·ities		amounts	
amen·ity		amp	
America		am·pere	
American		am·peres	
Americanization		am·per·sand	
Americans		am·phibian	
ami·able		am·phibi·ans	
ami·ca·ble		am·phi·thea·ter	
amid		ample	
amino		am·pli·fi·ca·tion	
am·mo·nia		am·pli·fied	

Word	Shorthand	Word	Shorthand
am·pli·fier		ana·lyt·ical	
am·pli·fi·ers		ana·lyt·ically	
am·plify		ana·lyze	
am·pu·tate		ana·lyzed	
am·pu·ta·tion		ana·lyzer	
am·pu·ta·tions		ana·lyzes	
am·pu·tee		ana·lyz·ing	
am·pu·tees		anatomy	
amuse		an·ces·tor	
amused		an·ces·tors	
amuse·ment		an·ces·try	
amus·ing		an·chor	
an		an·chored	
an·al·ge·sia		an·chor·man	
an·al·ge·sic		an·chors	
ana·log		an·cient	
analo·gous		an·cil·lary	
analogy		and	
analy·ses		an·ec·do·tal	
analy·sis		an·ec·dote	
ana·lyst		an·ec·dotes	
ana·lysts		ane·mia	
ana·lytic		ane·mic	

an·es·the·sia	*astza*	ani·mos·ity	*a—sı*
an·es·the·si·olo·gist	*astzelğ*	ankle	*aql*
an·es·thetic	*asttc*	an·kles	*aqls*
anes·the·tist	*anstt8*	annex (v.)	*anx*
anes·the·tize	*ansttz*	annex (v. or n.)	*ax*
an·eu·rysm	*arz*	an·nexed	*ax -*
anew	*anu*	an·nexes	*axs*
angel	*anğl*	an·ni·hi·late	*anıla*
an·gels	*anğls*	an·ni·hi·la·tion	*anıl*
anger	*agr*	an·ni·ver·sa·ries	*avrsres*
angle	*agl*	an·ni·ver·sary	*avrsre*
an·gler	*aglr*	an·no·tate	*ala*
an·glers	*aglrs*	an·no·tated	*ala -*
an·gles	*agls*	an·no·ta·tion	*alı*
an·grily	*agrl*	an·nounce	*anoⁿ*
angry	*agre*	an·nounced	*anoⁿ -*
an·guish	*ag 4*	an·nounce·ment	*anoⁿm*
an·guished	*ag 4-*	an·nounce·ments	*anoⁿms*
an·gu·lar	*aglr*	an·nouncer	*anoⁿr*
ani·mal	*a—l*	an·nounces	*anoⁿs*
ani·mals	*a—ls*	an·nounc·ing	*anoⁿ_*
ani·mated	*a—a-*	annoy	*any*
ani·ma·tion	*a—ɣ*	an·noy·ance	*anyⁿ*

an·noyed	*any-*	an·tago·nism	*algnz*
an·nual	*aul*	an·tago·nize	*algnz*
an·nu·ally	*aull*	an·te·ce·dent	*atsdN*
an·nu·als	*auls*	an·te·lope	*allp*
an·nu·ities	*anuls*	an·tenna	*alna*
an·nu·ity	*anul*	an·ten·nas	*alnas*
annul	*anl*	an·te·rior	*alrer*
an·nu·lar	*alr*	an·te·ri·orly	*alrerl*
an·nul·ment	*anlm*	an·them	*al*
anode	*ad*	an·thology	*allje*
ano·dize	*adz*	an·thro·pology	*alrplje*
anoint	*anyN*	an·ti·bi·otic	*albrlc*
anoma·lies	*an—ls*	an·ti·bi·ot·ics	*albrlcs*
anomaly	*an—l*	an·ti·body	*albde*
anony·mous	*ann—s*	antic	*alc*
an·other	*aol*	an·tici·pate	*alspa*
an·swer	*asr*	an·tici·pated	*alspa-*
an·swer·able	*asrB*	an·tici·pates	*alspas*
an·swered	*asr-*	an·tici·pat·ing	*alspa_*
an·swer·ing	*asr_*	an·tici·pa·tion	*alspj*
an·swers	*asrs*	an·tics	*alcs*
ant	*aN*	an·ti·dis·crimi·na·tion	*alDcrmy*
ant·acid	*aNasd*	an·ti·dote	*aldo*

Word	Shorthand	Word	Shorthand
an·ti·freeze	*alfrz*	any·place	*nepls*
an·ti·grav·ity	*algrv*	any·thing	*ne_*
an·ti·his·ta·mine	*aths̲m*	any·way	*ne a*
an·ti·quate	*alqa*	any·where	*ne r*
an·ti·quated	*alqa-*	aorta	*arta*
an·tique	*alc*	aor·tic	*artc*
an·tiques	*alcs*	apart	*apt*
an·ti·so·cial	*alssl*	apart·heid	*apthi*
an·tithe·sis	*allss*	apart·ment	*aptm*
an·ti·trust	*allrs*	apart·ments	*aptms*
ant·ler	*aNlr*	apa·thy	*aple*
an·to·nym	*aln*	ape	*ap*
an·to·nyms	*alns*	apex	*apx*
anvil	*avl*	apiece	*aps*
anxi·eties	*agzils*	aplomb	*apt*
anxi·ety	*agzi*	apoca·lypse	*apclps*
anx·ious	*agss*	apoca·lyp·tic	*apclptc*
anx·iously	*agssl*	apolo·getic	*apljtc*
any	*ne*	apolo·gies	*apljes*
any·body	*nebde*	apolo·gize	*apljz*
any·how	*neho*	apolo·gized	*apljz-*
any·more	*ne*	apology	*aplje*
any·one	*ne /*	apos·tasy	*apsse*

apos·tle	*apsl*	ap·pend	*apN*
apos·tles	*apsls*	ap·pend·age	*apNy*
apos·tro·phe	*apSrfe*	ap·pended	*apN-*
apothe·cary	*aptcre*	ap·pen·di·ci·tis	*apNsts*
ap·pall	*apl*	ap·pen·dix	*apNx*
ap·palled	*apl-*	ap·pe·tite	*apti*
ap·pa·ra·tus	*aprts*	ap·pe·tizer	*aptzr*
ap·parel	*aprl*	ap·pe·tiz·ing	*aptz_*
ap·par·ent	*aprN*	ap·plaud	*apld*
ap·par·ently	*aprNl*	ap·plauded	*apld-*
ap·peal	*apl*	ap·plaud·ing	*apld_*
ap·pealed	*apl-*	ap·plause	*aplz*
ap·peal·ing	*apl_*	apple	*apl*
ap·peals	*apls*	ap·ples	*apls*
ap·pear	*apr*	ap·pli·ance	*aplN*
ap·pear·ance	*aprN*	ap·pli·ances	*aplNs*
ap·pear·ances	*aprNs*	ap·pli·ca·bil·ity	*aplcB^l*
ap·peared	*apr-*	ap·pli·ca·ble	*aplcB*
ap·pear·ing	*apr_*	ap·pli·cant	*aplcN*
ap·pears	*aprs*	ap·pli·cants	*aplcNs*
ap·pease	*apz*	ap·pli·ca·tion	*aplcy*
ap·peases	*apzs*	ap·pli·ca·tions	*aplcys*
ap·pel·late	*aplt*	ap·pli·ca·tor	*aplcar*

ap·plied	*apli-*	ap·pre·ci·ate	*ap*
ap·plies	*aplis*	ap·pre·ci·ated	*ap-*
apply	*apli*	ap·pre·ci·ates	*aps*
ap·ply·ing	*apli̲*	ap·pre·ci·at·ing	*ap̲*
ap·point	*apy*	ap·pre·cia·tion	*apy*
ap·pointed	*apy-*	ap·pre·cia·tive	*apv*
ap·pointee	*apye*	ap·pre·hen·sion	*aprhny*
ap·point·ees	*apyes*	ap·pre·hen·sive	*aprhNv*
ap·point·ing	*apy̲*	ap·pren·tice	*aprNs*
ap·point·ment	*apym*	ap·pren·tices	*aprNss*
ap·point·ments	*apyms*	ap·pren·tice·ship	*aprNst*
ap·points	*apys*	ap·prise	*aprz*
ap·por·tion	*apry*	ap·prised	*aprz-*
ap·por·tion·ment	*aprym*	ap·pris·ing	*aprz̲*
ap·praisal	*aprzl*	ap·proach	*aprC*
ap·prais·als	*aprzls*	ap·proached	*aprC-*
ap·praise	*aprz*	ap·proaches	*aprCs*
ap·praised	*aprz-*	ap·proach·ing	*aprC̲*
ap·praiser	*aprzr*	ap·pro·pri·ate	*apo*
ap·prais·ers	*aprzrs*	ap·pro·pri·ated	*apo-*
ap·prais·ing	*aprz̲-*	ap·pro·pri·ately	*apol*
ap·pre·cia·ble	*apB*	ap·pro·pri·ate·ness	*apo'*
ap·pre·cia·bly	*apB*	ap·pro·pri·at·ing	*apo̲*

ap·pro·pria·tion	*apoy*	aquarium	*aqre*
ap·pro·pria·tions	*apoys*	aquatic	*aqlc*
ap·prov·able	*apvß*	aque·ous	*aqes*
ap·proval	*apvl*	aq·ui·fer	*aqfr*
ap·prov·als	*apvls*	aq·ui·fers	*aqfrs*
ap·prove	*apv*	Arabic	*arbç*
ap·proved	*apv-*	ar·able	*arß*
ap·proves	*apvs*	ar·bi·ter	*arblr*
ap·prov·ing	*apv̲*	ar·bi·tra·ble	*arblrß*
ap·proxi·mate	*apx*	ar·bi·trary	*arblrre*
ap·proxi·mated	*apx-*	ar·bi·tra·tion	*arblry*
ap·proxi·mately	*apxl*	ar·bi·tra·tor	*arblrar*
ap·proxi·mat·ing	*apx̲*	ar·bi·tra·tors	*arblrars*
ap·proxi·ma·tion	*apxy*	arbor	*arbr*
ap·proxi·ma·tions	*apxys*	ar·bors	*arbrs*
apri·cot	*aprcl*	arc	*arc*
April	*Ap*	ar·cade	*arcd*
apron	*aprn*	arch	*arC*
aprons	*aprns*	ar·chaeo·log·ical	*arcelycl*
apt	*apl*	ar·chae·olo·gist	*arcelyß*
ap·ti·tude	*aplld*	ar·chae·ology	*arcelye*
aqua	*aqa*	ar·chaic	*arcac*
aq·ua·ma·rine	*aq rn*	arch·ery	*arCre*

arches	*arCs*	ar·gues	*argus*
ar·chi·tect	*arclc*	ar·gu·ing	*argu_*
ar·chi·tects	*arclcs*	ar·gu·ment	*argum*
ar·chi·tec·tural	*arclcCrl*	ar·gu·men·ta·tive	*argumv*
ar·chi·tec·tur·ally	*arclcCrll*	ar·gu·ments	*argums*
ar·chi·tec·ture	*arclcCr*	arid	*ard*
ar·chi·val	*arcvl*	arise	*arz*
ar·chive	*arcv*	arisen	*arzn*
ar·chives	*arcvs*	arises	*arzs*
ar·chi·vist	*arcvS*	aris·ing	*arz_*
arc·tic	*arclc*	aris·to·crat	*arScrl*
ar·dent	*ardN*	arith·me·tic	*art⌐lc*
ar·du·ous	*arjus*	arm	*ar⌐*
are	*r*	ar·ma·ment	*ar⌐m*
area	*ara*	arm·chair	*ar⌐Cr*
areas	*aras*	armed	*ar⌐-*
area·wide	*ara⌐d*	ar·mi·stice	*ar⌐Ss*
arena	*arna*	armor	*ar⌐r*
are·nas	*arnas*	ar·mory	*ar⌐re*
aren't	*rN*	arm·rest	*ar⌐rS*
ar·gu·able	*arguß*	arms	*ar⌐s*
argue	*argu*	army	*ar⌐e*
ar·gued	*argu-*	aroma	*ar⌐a*

arose	*arz*	ar·ri·vals	*arvls*
around	*aroN*	ar·rive	*arv*
arouse	*aroz*	ar·rived	*arv-*
ar·raign	*arn*	ar·rives	*arvs*
ar·raign·ment	*arnm*	ar·riv·ing	*arv_*
ar·range	*ar*	ar·ro·gance	*argN*
ar·ranged	*ar-*	ar·ro·gant	*argN*
ar·range·ment	*arm*	arrow	*aro*
ar·range·ments	*arms*	ar·row·head	*arohd*
ar·ranger	*arr*	ar·rows	*aros*
ar·ranges	*ars*	ar·se·nal	*arsnl*
ar·rang·ing	*ar_*	arson	*arsn*
array	*ara*	art	*art*
ar·rear	*arr*	ar·te·rial	*artrel*
ar·rear·age	*arry*	ar·ter·ies	*artres*
ar·rear·ages	*arrys*	ar·tery	*artre*
ar·rears	*arrs*	ar·thri·tis	*artrts*
ar·rest	*arS*	ar·ti·cle	*artcl*
ar·rested	*arS-*	ar·ti·cles	*artcls*
ar·rester	*arSr*	ar·ticu·late (adj.)	*artcll*
ar·rest·ers	*arSrs*	ar·ticu·late (v.)	*artcla*
ar·rests	*arSs*	ar·ticu·lated	*artcla-*
ar·ri·val	*arvl*	ar·ticu·lat·ing	*artcla_*

ar·ticu·la·tion	*artcly*	ash	*as*
ar·ti·fact	*artfc*	ashamed	*as —*
ar·ti·facts	*artfcs*	ashes	*ass*
ar·ti·fi·cial	*artfsl*	ashore	*asr*
ar·ti·fi·cially	*artfsll*	ash·tray	*astra*
ar·til·lery	*artlre*	ash·trays	*astras*
art·ist	*artS*	Asian	*aj*
ar·tis·tic	*artSc*	aside	*asd*
art·istry	*artSre*	ask	*asc*
art·ists	*artSs*	asked	*asc-*
arts	*arts*	ask·ing	*asc_*
art·work	*arto*	asks	*ascs*
as	*3*	asleep	*aslp*
as·bes·tos	*asbSs*	as·pect	*aspc*
as·cend	*asN*	as·pects	*aspcs*
as·cender	*asNr*	aspen	*aspn*
as·cend·ing	*asN_*	as·per·sion	*aspry*
as·cen·sion	*asny*	as·phalt	*asfll*
as·cent	*asN*	as·phyxi·ate	*asfxa*
as·cer·tain	*asrln*	as·pi·rant	*asprN*
as·cer·tained	*asrln-*	as·pi·rants	*asprNs*
as·cer·tain·ing	*asrln_*	as·pi·rate	*aspra*
as·cribe	*aS*	as·pi·rat·ing	*aspra_*

as·pi·ra·tion	*aspry*	as·sent	*asN*
as·pi·ra·tions	*asprys*	as·sert	*asrt*
as·pire	*aspr*	as·serted	*asrt-*
as·pi·rin	*asprn*	as·ser·tion	*asry*
as·pir·ing	*aspr*	as·ser·tive	*asrv*
as·sail	*asl*	as·serts	*asrts*
as·sail·ant	*aslN*	as·sess	*ass*
as·sail·ants	*aslNs*	as·sess·able	*assB*
as·sas·sin	*assn*	as·sessed	*ass-*
as·sas·si·nate	*assna*	as·sesses	*asss*
as·sas·si·nated	*assna-*	as·sess·ing	*ass_*
as·sas·si·na·tion	*assny*	as·sess·ment	*assm*
as·sault	*asll*	as·sess·ments	*assms*
as·saults	*aslls*	as·ses·sor	*assr*
assay	*asa*	as·ses·sors	*assrs*
as·sem·blage	*as B1*	asset	*ast*
as·sem·ble	*as B*	as·sets	*asts*
as·sem·bled	*as B-*	as·sign	*asn*
as·sem·bler	*as Br*	as·sign·abil·ity	*asnBl*
as·sem·bles	*as Bs*	as·sign·able	*asnB*
as·sem·blies	*as Bs*	as·sig·na·tion	*asgny*
as·sem·bling	*as B*	as·signed	*asn-*
as·sem·bly	*as B*	as·sign·ing	*asn_*

as·sign·ment	*asnm*	as·sort·ment	*asrlm*
as·sign·ments	*asnms*	as·sort·ments	*asrlms*
as·signs	*asns*	as·suage	*as⌐*
as·simi·late	*as la*	as·sume	*as*
as·simi·lated	*as la-*	as·sumed	*as -*
as·simi·lat·ing	*as la*	as·sumes	*as s*
as·sist	*ass*	as·sum·ing	*as _*
as·sis·tance	*assN*	as·sump·tion	*as y*
as·sis·tant	*assN*	as·sump·tions	*as ys*
as·sis·tants	*assNs*	as·sur·ance	*asrN*
as·sis·tant·ship	*assNs*	as·sur·ances	*asrNs*
as·sis·tant·ships	*assNss*	as·sure	*asr*
as·sisted	*ass-*	as·sured	*asr-*
as·sist·ing	*ass_*	as·sures	*asrs*
as·sists	*asss*	as·sur·ing	*asr_*
as·so·ci·ate	*aso*	as·ter·isk	*asrsc*
as·so·ci·ated	*aso-*	as·ter·isks	*asrscs*
as·so·ci·ates	*asos*	asthma	*az a*
as·so·ci·at·ing	*aso_*	asth·matic	*az lc*
as·so·cia·tion	*asoy*	aston·ish	*asns*
as·so·cia·tions	*asoys*	aston·ish·ing	*asns*
as·sort	*asrl*	astound	*asoN*
as·sorted	*asrl-*	astray	*asra*

Word	Shorthand	Word	Shorthand
as·tro·naut		at·ro·phy	
as·tro·nauts		at·tach	
as·trono·mer		at·ta·ché	
as·tronomy		at·tached	
as·tute		at·taches	
as·tute·ness		at·tach·ing	
asy·lum		at·tach·ment	
asym·met·ri·cal		at·tach·ments	
asyn·chro·nous		at·tack	
at		at·tacked	
ate		at·tacks	
athe·ist		at·tain	
ath·lete		at·tain·able	
ath·letes		at·tained	
ath·letic		at·tain·ing	
ath·let·ics		at·tain·ment	
Atlantic		at·tains	
atlas		at·tempt	
at·mos·phere		at·tempted	
at·mos·pheric		at·tempt·ing	
atom		at·tempts	
atomic		at·tend	
atro·cious		at·ten·dance	

at·ten·dant	*alMM*	at·tor·neys	*alrnes*
at·ten·dants	*alMMs*	at·tract	*alrc*
at·tended	*alM-*	at·tracted	*alrc-*
at·tendee	*alMe*	at·tract·ing	*alrc̠*
at·tend·ees	*alMes*	at·trac·tion	*alrcy*
at·tend·ing	*alM̠*	at·trac·tions	*alrcys*
at·tends	*alMs*	at·trac·tive	*alrcv*
at·ten·tion	*all*	at·tracts	*alrcs*
at·ten·tive	*alnv*	at·trib·ut·able	*alrbuß*
at·ten·tive·ness	*alnv´*	at·trib·ute (v.)	*alrbu*
at·tenu·ate	*alna*	at·tri·bute (n.)	*alrbu*
at·tenu·at·ing	*alna̠*	at·trib·uted	*alrbu-*
at·tenu·ation	*alnuy*	at·trib·utes (v.)	*alrbus*
at·test	*al8*	at·tri·butes (n.)	*alrbus*
at·tested	*al8-*	at·tri·tion	*alry*
at·test·ing	*al8̠*	at·tune	*aln*
at·tests	*al8s*	atyp·ical	*alpcl*
attic	*alc*	auc·tion	*acy*
at·tire	*alr*	auc·tions	*acys*
at·ti·tude	*alld*	au·dac·ity	*ads'*
at·ti·tudes	*allds*	au·di·ble	*adß*
at·ti·tu·di·nal	*alldnl*	au·di·bly	*adß*
at·tor·ney	*alrne*	au·di·ence	*adeM*

Word	Outline	Word	Outline
au·di·ences	*adeNs*	aura	*ara*
audio	*ado*	aus·pice	*asps*
audio-visual	*ado = vzul*	aus·pices	*aspss*
audit	*adl*	aus·pi·cious	*aspɫs*
au·dited	*adl-*	aus·ter·ity	*aSrɫ*
au·ditee	*adle*	au·then·tic	*alNc*
au·dit·ing	*adl̲*	au·then·ti·cate	*alNca*
au·di·tion	*adȷ*	au·then·ti·cated	*alNca-*
au·di·tions	*adȷs*	au·then·ti·cat·ing	*alNca̲*
au·di·tor	*adlr*	au·then·ti·ca·tion	*alNcȷ*
au·di·to·rium	*adlre*	au·then·tic·ity	*alnlsɫ*
au·di·to·ri·ums	*adlres*	au·thor	*alr*
au·di·tors	*adlrs*	au·thored	*alr-*
au·di·tory	*adlre*	au·thori·ta·tive	*alrlv*
au·dits	*adls*	au·thor·ities	*alrɫs*
auger	*agr*	au·thor·ity	*alrɫ*
au·gers	*agrs*	au·thor·iza·tion	*alrȝȷ*
aug·ment	*agm*	au·thor·iza·tions	*alrȝȷs*
aug·mented	*agm-*	au·thor·ize	*alrȝ*
augur	*agr*	au·thor·ized	*alrȝ-*
au·gust	*ag8*	au·thor·izes	*alrȝs*
August	*Aq*	au·thor·iz·ing	*alrȝ̲*
aunt	*aN*	au·thors	*alrs*

au·tis·tic	*alsc*	aux·il·iary	*agzlre*
auto	*alo*	avail	*avl*
au·to·bi·og·ra·phy	*albrgrfe*	avail·abil·ities	*avlʒᶦs*
au·to·cratic	*alcrlc*	avail·abil·ity	*avlʒᶦ*
au·to·graph	*algrf*	avail·able	*avlʒ*
au·to·graphs	*algrfs*	ava·rice	*avrs*
au·to·mate	*al a*	avenge	*avny*
au·to·mated	*al a-*	ave·nue	*ave*
au·to·matic	*al lc*	ave·nues	*aves*
au·to·mat·ically	*al lcl*	aver	*avr*
au·to·mat·ics	*al lcs*	av·er·age	*avry*
au·to·mat·ing	*al a_*	av·er·aged	*avry-*
au·to·ma·tion	*al y*	av·er·ages	*avrys*
au·toma·tize	*al lz*	av·er·ag·ing	*avry_*
au·to·mo·bile	*alo ʒ*	averse	*avrs*
au·to·mo·biles	*alo ʒs*	aver·sion	*avry*
au·to·mo·tive	*al v*	avert	*avrl*
au·tono·mous	*aln s*	avia·tion	*avey*
au·to·pi·lot	*alpll*	avid	*avd*
au·top·sies	*alpses*	av·idly	*avdl*
au·topsy	*alpse*	avi·on·ics	*avencs*
autos	*aloo*	avo·ca·tion	*avcy*
au·tumn	*al*	avoid	*avyd*

avoid·able	*avyd3*	awhile	*a l*
avoid·ance	*avydn*	awk·ward	*acw*
avoided	*avyd-*	awn·ing	*an*
avoid·ing	*avyd_*	awn·ings	*an=*
avoids	*avyds*	awoke	*a c*
avow	*avo*	ax	*ax*
await	*a a*	axial	*el*
awaited	*a a-*	axiom	*e*
await·ing	*a a_*	axis	*s*
awaits	*a as*	axle	*l*
awake	*a c*	axles	*ls*
awak·en·ing	*a cn*	aye	*l*
award	*aw*	ayes	*is*
awarded	*aw-*		
award·ing	*aw_*		
awards	*aws*	**B**	
aware	*a r*		
aware·ness	*a r'*	bab·ble	*b3*
away	*a a*	bab·bled	*b3-*
awe	*a*	ba·bies	*bbes*
awe·some	*as*	baby	*bbe*
awful	*af*	ba·by·ish	*bbe4*
aw·fully	*afl*	ba·by·sit·ting	*bbesl_*
		bac·ca·lau·re·ate	*bclrel*

bache·lor	*bClr*	back-up (adj.)	*bc =p*
bache·lors	*bClrs*	backup (n.)	*bcp*
back	*bc*	back·ward	*bcw*
back·ache	*bcac*	back·wards	*bcws*
back·aches	*bcacs*	back·yard	*bcyd*
back·bone	*bcbn*	bacon	*bk*
back·drop	*bcdrp*	bac·te·ria	*bclra*
backed	*bc-*	bac·te·rial	*bclrel*
backer	*bcr*	bac·te·ri·ology	*bclrelje*
back·fire	*bcfr*	bad	*bd*
back·ground	*bcgroN*	badge	*bj*
back·grounds	*bcgroNs*	badger	*bjr*
back·hand	*bchN*	badges	*bjs*
back·handed	*bchN-*	badly	*bdl*
back·hoe	*bcho*	baf·fle	*bfl*
back·ing	*bc_*	baf·fles	*bfls*
back·lash	*bcls*	bag	*bg*
back·log	*bclg*	bag·gage	*bgj*
back·logs	*bclgs*	bags	*bgs*
back·pack	*bcpc*	bail	*bl*
back·pack·ing	*bcpc_*	bailed	*bl-*
backs	*bcs*	bail·iff	*blf*
back·stop	*bcSp*	bait	*ba*

baits	*bas*	bal·loons	*blns*
bake	*bc*	bal·lot	*bel*
baked	*bc-*	bal·lots	*bels*
bak·ery	*bcre*	ball·room	*blr*
bak·ing	*bc̱*	balls	*bls*
bal·ance	*bēn*	balmy	*bre*
bal·anced	*bēn-*	ban	*bn*
bal·ances	*bēns*	banal	*bnl*
bal·anc·ing	*bēṉ*	ba·nal·ity	*bnlˡ*
bal·co·nies	*blkes*	ba·nana	*bnna*
bal·cony	*blke*	band	*bn*
bald	*bld*	band·age	*bny*
bale	*bl*	ban·danna	*bndna*
bales	*bls*	banded	*bn-*
balk	*bc*	ban·died	*bne-*
balked	*bc-*	band·ing	*bn*
ball	*bl*	bands	*bn̄s*
bal·last	*bls*	bandy	*bne*
bal·lasts	*blss*	bane	*bn*
bal·let	*bla*	bang	*bq*
bal·lis·tic	*blsc*	bang·ing	*bq̱*
bal·lis·tics	*blscs*	ban·ish	*bns*
bal·loon	*bln*	ban·is·ter	*bnsr*

bank	*bq*	bar·baric	*brbrc*
bank·able	*bq8*	bar·be·cue	*brbcu*
bank·book	*bqbc*	barbed	*brb-*
bank·card	*bqcrd*	bar·ber	*brbr*
banked	*bq-*	bar·bi·tu·rate	*brbCrl*
banker	*bqr*	bare	*br*
bank·ers	*bqrs*	barely	*brl*
bank·ing	*bq_*	bar·gain	*brgn*
bank·rupt	*bqrpl*	bar·gained	*brgn-*
bank·rupt·cies	*bqrpses*	bar·gain·ing	*brgn_*
bank·ruptcy	*bqrpse*	bar·gains	*brgns*
bank·rupts	*bqrpts*	barge	*brj*
banks	*bqs*	barges	*brjs*
banned	*bn-*	bark	*brc*
ban·ner	*bnr*	barker	*brcr*
ban·ners	*bnrs*	barn	*brn*
ban·quet	*bnql*	barn·yard	*brnyd*
ban·quets	*bnqls*	ba·rome·ter	*br—lr*
ban·ter	*bNr*	baro·met·ric	*br—lrc*
Baptist	*bpl8*	bar·rack	*brc*
bap·tize	*bplz*	bar·racks	*brcs*
bar	*br*	bar·rage	*brz*
barb	*brb*	barred	*br-*

bar·rel	*brl*	ba·si·cally	*bscl*
bar·rels	*brls*	ba·sics	*bscs*
bar·ren	*brn*	basin	*bsn*
bar·ri·cade	*brcd*	bas·ing	*bs_*
bar·ri·caded	*brcd-*	ba·sins	*bsns*
bar·rier	*brer*	basis	*bss*
bar·ri·ers	*brers*	bask	*bsc*
bar·ring	*br_*	bas·ket	*bscl*
bars	*brs*	bas·ket·ball	*bsclbl*
bar·tender	*brlNr*	bas·kets	*bscls*
bar·tend·ers	*brlNrs*	bass	*bs*
bar·ter	*brlr*	bas·si·net	*bsnl*
basal	*bsl*	bas·si·nets	*bsnls*
base	*bs*	baste	*bS*
base·ball	*bsbl*	bas·tion	*bsy*
based	*bs-*	bat	*bl*
base·line	*bsln*	batch	*bC*
base·ment	*bsm*	batches	*bCs*
base·ments	*bsms*	bates	*bas*
bases (n. or v.)	*bss*	bath	*bl*
bases (n.)	*bsz*	bathe	*bl*
bash·ful	*bsf*	bath·house	*blhos*
basic	*bsc*	bath·ing	*bl_*

bath·room	*blr*	bea·con	*bk*
bath·rooms	*blrs*	bead	*bd*
baths	*bls*	beads	*bds*
bats	*bls*	beak	*bc*
bat·tal·ion	*bllyn*	beam	*b*
bat·ted	*bl-*	beamed	*b-*
bat·tered	*blr-*	beam·ing	*b‿*
bat·ter·ies	*blres*	beams	*bs*
bat·tery	*blre*	bean	*bn*
bat·tle	*bll*	beans	*bns*
bat·tled	*bll-*	bear	*br*
bat·tle·field	*bllfld*	beard	*brd*
bat·tles	*blls*	bearer	*brr*
bau·ble	*bB*	bear·ers	*brrs*
baud	*bd*	bear·ing	*br‿*
baux·ite	*bxi*	bear·ings	*br≈*
bawl	*bl*	bears	*brs*
bay	*ba*	beast	*bS*
bayou	*bu*	beastly	*bSl*
ba·zaar	*bzr*	beat	*be*
be	*b*	beaten	*ben*
beach	*bC*	beat·ing	*be‿*
beaches	*bCs*	beats	*bes*

beau·ti·cian	*bly*	been	*b*
beau·ti·fi·ca·tion	*blfy*	beer	*br*
beau·ti·ful	*blef*	beet	*be*
beau·ti·fully	*blefl*	bee·tle	*bll*
beauty	*ble*	beets	*bes*
bea·ver	*bvr*	be·fall	*bfl*
be·came	*bk*	be·fit·ting	*bfl̲*
be·cause	*bcz*	be·fore	*bf*
beck	*bc*	be·fore·hand	*bfhN*
beckon	*bcn*	be·friend	*bfrN*
be·come	*bk*	be·friended	*bfrN-*
be·comes	*bks*	beg	*bg*
be·com·ing	*bk̲*	began	*bgn*
bed	*bd*	beg·gar	*bgr*
bed·ding	*bd̲*	beg·gars	*bgrs*
bed·room	*bdr*	begin	*bgn*
bed·rooms	*bdrs*	be·gin·ner	*bgnr*
beds	*bds*	be·gin·ners	*bgnrs*
bed·side	*bdsd*	be·gin·ning	*bgn̲*
bed·time	*bdt*	be·gins	*bgns*
bee	*b*	be·grudge	*bgrj*
beef	*bf*	begun	*bgn*
bee·hive	*bhv*	be·half	*bhf*

be·have	*bhv*	bell	*bl*
be·hav·ing	*bhv̲*	bel·lig·er·ent	*blgrN*
be·hav·ior	*bhvr*	bells	*bls*
be·hav·ioral	*bhvrl*	belly	*ble*
be·hav·iors	*bhvrs*	be·long	*blg*
be·hind	*bhN*	be·longed	*blg-*
be·hold	*bhld*	be·long·ing	*blg̲*
be·hoove	*bhv*	be·long·ings	*blg̳*
be·hooves	*bhvs*	be·longs	*blgs*
beige	*bz*	be·loved	*blv-*
being	*b̄*	below	*blo*
be·ings	*b̳*	belt	*bll*
be·la·bor	*b̄lbr*	belt·ing	*bll*
be·lated	*bla-*	belts	*bl̄s*
be·lief	*blf*	bench	*bnC*
be·liefs	*blfs*	benches	*bnCs*
be·lieve	*blv*	bend	*bN*
be·lieved	*blv-*	bend·ing	*bN̲*
be·liever	*blvr*	bends	*bN̄s*
be·liev·ers	*blvrs*	be·neath	*bnl*
be·lieves	*blvs*	bene·dic·tion	*bndcy*
be·liev·ing	*blv*	bene·fac·tor	*bnfcr*
be·lit·tle	*bltl*	bene·fac·tors	*bnfcrs*

bene·fi·cial	_bnfsl_	best	_bS_
bene·fi·ci·ar·ies	_bnfseres_	be·stow	_bSo_
bene·fi·ci·ary	_bnfsere_	be·stowed	_bSo-_
bene·fit	_bnfl_	bests	_bSs_
bene·fited	_bnfl-_	bet	_bl_
bene·fit·ing	_bnfl_	be·tray	_blra_
bene·fits	_bnfls_	be·trayal	_blral_
be·nevo·lent	_bnvlN_	be·tray·ing	_blra_
be·nign	_bnn_	bet·ter	_blr_
bent	_bN_	bet·ter·ment	_blrm_
ben·zene	_bnzn_	bet·ting	_bl_
be·quest	_bqS_	be·tween	_bln_
be·quests	_bqSs_	bevel	_bvl_
be·reave	_brv_	bev·er·age	_bvy_
be·reaved	_brv-_	bev·er·ages	_bvys_
berm	_br_	bevy	_bve_
berry	_bre_	be·ware	_br_
ber·serk	_brsrc_	be·wil·der	_bldr_
berth	_brl_	be·wil·der·ing	_bldr_
berths	_brls_	be·yond	_beN_
be·side	_bsd_	bi·an·nual	_baul_
be·sides	_bsds_	bi·an·nu·ally	_baull_
be·smirch	_bs rC_	bias	_brs_

bi·ased	*brs-*	big	*bg*
bib	*bb*	biga·mist	*bg s*
Bible	*bB*	bigamy	*bg e*
bib·lio·graphic	*bblegrfc*	big·ger	*bgr*
bib·li·og·ra·phies	*bblegrfes*	big·gest	*bgs*
bib·li·og·ra·phy	*bblegrfe*	bigot	*bgt*
bibs	*bbs*	big·otry	*bgtre*
bi·car·bon·ate	*bcrbnt*	bike	*bc*
bick·er·ing	*bcr*	bi·kini	*bcne*
bi·cy·cle	*bscl*	bi·lat·eral	*bltrl*
bi·cy·cles	*bscls*	bi·lat·er·ally	*bltrll*
bi·cy·cling	*bscl*	bile	*bl*
bid	*bd*	bi·lin·gual	*blgl*
bid·der	*bdr*	bilk	*blc*
bid·ders	*bdrs*	bill	*bl*
bid·ding	*bd*	bill·board	*blbrd*
bide	*bd*	bill·boards	*blbrds*
bids	*bds*	billed	*bl-*
bi·en·nial	*brnel*	bil·let	*blt*
bi·en·ni·ally	*brnell*	bil·let·ing	*blt*
bi·en·nium	*brne*	bil·lets	*blts*
bi·fo·cal	*bfcl*	bill·fold	*blfld*
bi·fo·cals	*bfcls*	bil·liard	*blrd*

Word	Shorthand
bil·liards	blrds
bill·ing	bl
bill·ings	bl̄
bil·lion	B
bil·lion·aire	Br
bil·lions	Bs
bil·lionth	BL
bills	bls
bi·monthly	b⌐ol
bin	bn
bi·nary	bnre
bind	bN
binder	bNr
bind·ers	bNrs
bind·ery	bNre
bind·ing	bN̲
bingo	bgo
bin·ocu·lars	bnclrs
bins	bns
bio·chem·ical	brc⌐cl
bio·chem·is·try	brc⌐Sre
bio·feed·back	brfdbc
bio·graphic	brgrfc
bio·graph·ical	brgrfcl
bi·og·ra·phy	brgrfe
bio·log·ical	brlycl
bi·ology	brlye
bi·opsy	brpse
bi·otic	brlc
bi·par·ti·san	bplzn
bi·po·lar	bplr
birch	brc
bird	brd
birds	brds
birth	brl
birth·day	brld
birth·days	brlds
birth·mark	brl⌐rc
birth·place	brlpls
birth·stone	brlSn
bis·cuit	bscl
bi·sect	bsc
bishop	bsp
bit	bl
bite	br
bites	brs

bit·ing	*br̄*	blame·less	*bl__ls*
bits	*br̄s*	blam·ing	*bl__*
bit·ter	*br̄r*	blanch	*blnc̄*
bit·ter·ness	*br̄r´*	bland	*bln*
bi·tu·men	*brm*	blank	*blq*
bi·tu·mi·nous	*brms*	blan·ket	*blqt*
bi·weekly	*bcl*	blan·kets	*blqts*
bi·zarre	*bzr*	blank·ness	*blq´*
black	*blc*	blanks	*blqs*
black·board	*blcbrd*	blare	*blr*
blacken	*blcn*	blasé	*blza*
black·en·ing	*blcn̲*	blas·pheme	*blsf*
black·jack	*blgc*	blast	*bls*
black·mail	*blc__l*	blaster	*blsr*
black·out	*blcol*	blast·ing	*bls*
black·outs	*blcols*	bla·tant	*bltn*
blacks	*blcs*	blaze	*blz*
black·top	*blclp*	blazer	*blzr*
blad·der	*bldr*	blaz·ers	*blzrs*
blade	*bld*	blaz·ing	*blz̲*
blades	*blds*	bleach	*blc̄*
blame	*bl__*	bleacher	*blcr*
blamed	*bl__ -*	bleak	*blc*

bled	*bld*	bliss	*bls*
bleed	*bld*	bliss·ful	*blsf*
bleed·ing	*bld*	blis·ter	*blsr*
blem·ish	*bls*	blis·ters	*blsrs*
blem·ishes	*blss*	blitz	*blls*
blend	*ben*	bliz·zard	*blzrd*
blended	*ben-*	blob	*blb*
blend·ing	*ben*	block	*blc*
blends	*bens*	block·ade	*blcd*
bless	*bls*	block·ades	*blcds*
blessed	*bls-*	block·age	*blcg*
bless·ing	*bls*	block·buster	*blcbsr*
bless·ings	*bls*	blocked	*blc-*
blew	*blu*	block·ing	*blc*
blight	*bli*	blocks	*blcs*
blind	*ben*	blond	*ben*
blind·ing	*ben*	blonde	*ben*
blindly	*benl*	blond·ish	*bens*
blind·ness	*ben'*	blood	*bld*
blinds	*bens*	blood·shed	*bldsd*
blink	*blg*	blood·shot	*bldst*
blinker	*blgr*	blood·stain	*bldsn*
blinks	*blgs*	bloody	*blde*

bloom	_bl_	boarded	_brd-_
blos·som	_bls_	board·ing	_brd_
blot	_blt_	boards	_brds_
blot·ter	_bltr_	board·walk	_brdc_
blouse	_bloz_	boast	_bs_
blow	_blo_	boast·ful	_bsf_
blower	_blor_	boasts	_bss_
blow·ing	_blo_	boat	_bo_
blown	_bln_	boater	_bor_
blow·out	_blool_	boat·ers	_bors_
blows	_blos_	boat·ing	_bo_
blowup	_blop_	boats	_bos_
blue	_blu_	bob	_bb_
blue·print	_bluprN_	bob·bin	_bbn_
blue·prints	_bluprNs_	bob·bins	_bbns_
bluff	_blf_	bode	_bd_
blun·der	_blNr_	bodes	_bds_
blunt	_blN_	bod·ies	_bdes_
bluntly	_blNl_	bodily	_bdl_
blur	_blr_	body	_bde_
blurred	_blr-_	body·guard	_bdegrd_
blush	_bls_	bog	_bq_
board	_brd_	bogged	_bq-_

Word	Shorthand	Word	Shorthand
bogus	*bgs*	bond·holder	*bNhldr*
boil	*byl*	bond·hold·ers	*bNhldrs*
boiled	*byl-*	bond·ing	*bN*
boiler	*bylr*	bonds	*b̄ns*
boil·er·plate	*bylrpla*	bone	*bn*
boil·ers	*bylrs*	bones	*bns*
boils	*byls*	bon·fire	*bnfr*
bois·ter·ous	*bySrs*	bonus	*bns*
bold	*bld*	bo·nuses	*bnss*
bolder	*bldr*	book	*bc*
bold·face	*bldfs*	book·case	*bccs*
boldly	*bldl*	book·cases	*bccss*
bold·ness	*bld'*	booked	*bc-*
bol·ster	*blSr*	book·ing	*bc_*
bolt	*bll*	book·ings	*bc=*
bolted	*bll-*	book·keeper	*bccpr*
bolts	*blls*	book·keep·ers	*bccprs*
bomb	*b⌐*	book·keep·ing	*bccp_*
bom·bard	*b⌐brd*	book·let	*bcll*
bomb·ing	*b⌐*	book·lets	*bclls*
bo·nanza	*bnnza*	book·mak·ing	*bc⌐c*
bond	*bN*	book·mo·bile	*bc⌐B*
bonded	*bN-*	books	*bcs*

book·seller	*bcslr*	bor·der·ing	*brdr*
book·sell·ers	*bcslrs*	bor·der·line	*brdrln*
book·shelf	*bcslf*	bor·ders	*brdrs*
book·store	*bcsr*	bore	*br*
book·stores	*bcsrs*	bored	*br-*
boom	*b*	bore·dom	*brd*
boom·ing	*b*	bor·ing	*br*
booms	*bs*	born	*brn*
boon	*bn*	borne	*brn*
boor	*br*	bor·ough	*bro*
boor·ish	*brs*	bor·row	*bro*
boors	*brs*	bor·rowed	*bro-*
boost	*bs*	bor·rower	*bror*
boosted	*bs-*	bor·row·ers	*brors*
booster	*bsr*	bor·row·ing	*bro*
boost·ers	*bsrs*	bor·row·ings	*bro*
boost·ing	*bs*	boss	*bs*
boot	*bu*	bosses	*bss*
booth	*bl*	bo·tan·ical	*blncl*
booths	*bls*	botany	*blne*
boots	*bus*	botch	*bC*
bor·der	*brdr*	both	*bo*
bor·dered	*brdr-*	bother	*blr*

both·ered	bounded	
both·ers	bound·ing	
both·er·some	bound·less	
bot·tle	bounty	
bot·tle·neck	bou·quet	
bot·tle·necks	bout	
bot·tler	bou·tique	
bot·tles	bow	
bot·tling	bowel	
bot·tom	bow·els	
bot·tomed	bowl	
bot·tom·ing	bowler	
bot·tom·less	bowl·ers	
bot·toms	bowl·ing	
bought	bowls	
boul·der	bows	
boule·vard	box	
boule·vards	boxed	
bounce	boxes	
bounced	box·ing	
bound	boy	
bounda·ries	boy·cott	
boundary	boy·hood	

boy·ish	*bys*	branch	*brnC*
boys	*bys*	branches	*brnCs*
brace	*brs*	branch·ing	*brnC*
brace·let	*brsll*	brand	*brN*
braces	*brss*	branded	*brN-*
bracket	*brcl*	brands	*brNs*
brack·eted	*brcl-*	brass	*brs*
brack·ets	*brcls*	brat	*brl*
brad	*brd*	brave	*brv*
brag	*brq*	brav·ery	*brvre*
brag·gart	*brgrl*	brawl	*brl*
brag·ging	*brq_*	bra·zen	*brzn*
braid	*brd*	braz·ing	*brz_*
braille	*brl*	breach	*brC*
brain	*brn*	breaches	*brCs*
brains	*brns*	bread	*brd*
brain·storm·ing	*brnSr_*	breads	*brds*
brain·wash	*brn_*	breadth	*brdl*
braise	*brz*	bread·win·ner	*brd nr*
braised	*brz-*	break	*brc*
brake	*brc*	break·able	*brcB*
brakes	*brcs*	break·age	*brcq*
bran	*brn*	break·down	*brcdon*

break·downs	*brcdons*	brew	*bru*
breaker	*brcr*	brew·ery	*brure*
break·ers	*brcrs*	brew·ing	*bru_*
break·fast	*brcfs*	bribe	*brb*
break·ing	*brc_*	brib·ery	*brbre*
break·out	*brcol*	brick	*brc*
breaks	*brcs*	bricks	*brcs*
break·through	*brclru*	brick·yard	*brcyd*
break·throughs	*brclrus*	bri·dal	*brdl*
breast	*brs*	bride	*brd*
breath	*brl*	bridge	*bry*
breathe	*brl*	bridges	*brys*
breather	*brlr*	bridg·ing	*bry_*
breath·ing	*brl_*	brief	*brf*
breath·less	*brlls*	brief·case	*brfcs*
breath·tak·ing	*brllc_*	briefed	*brf-*
bred	*brd*	brief·ing	*brf_*
breech	*brC*	brief·ings	*brf=*
breed	*brd*	briefly	*brfl*
breeder	*brdr*	briefs	*brfs*
breeds	*brds*	bri·gade	*brgd*
breeze	*brz*	bright	*bri*
brev·ity	*brv ¹*	brighten	*brin*

brighter	*brir*	broad·cast·ing	*brdcs̲*
bright·est	*bris*	broad·casts	*brdcss*
brightly	*bril*	broaden	*brdn*
bright·ness	*bri'*	broad·ened	*brdn-*
bril·liance	*brlyn*	broad·en·ing	*brdn̲*
bril·liant	*brlyn*	broad·ens	*brdns*
bril·liantly	*brlynl*	broader	*brdr*
brim·ming	*br͜*	broad·est	*brds*
brine	*brn*	broadly	*brdl*
bring	*brq*	broad·side	*brdsd*
bring·ing	*brq̲*	bro·cade	*brcd*
brings	*brqs*	broc·coli	*brcl*
brink	*brq*	bro·chure	*brsr*
brisk	*brsc*	bro·chures	*brsrs*
briskly	*brscl*	broil	*bryl*
bris·tle	*brsl*	broiled	*bryl-*
bris·tles	*brsls*	broiler	*brylr*
British	*brls*	broke	*brc*
brit·tle	*brll̆*	bro·ken	*brcn*
broad	*brd*	bro·ker	*brcr*
broad·cast	*brdcs*	bro·ker·age	*brcry*
broad·caster	*brdcsr*	bro·kers	*brcrs*
broad·cast·ers	*brdcsrs*	bron·chial	*brqel*

bron·chi·tis	*brqls*	brunt	*brN*
bronze	*brnz*	brush	*brs*
brood	*brd*	brushed	*brs-*
brood·ing	*brd*	brushes	*brss*
brook	*brc*	brush·ing	*brs*
broom	*br*	brusque	*brsc*
broth	*brl*	bru·tal	*brul*
brother	*brlr*	bru·tal·ity	*brll'*
broth·er·hood	*brlrh*	bru·tally	*brull*
brother-in-law	*brlr = n = la*	brute	*bru*
broth·erly	*brlrl*	bub·ble	*bB*
broth·ers	*brlrs*	bub·bles	*bBs*
brought	*brl*	buck	*bc*
brow	*bro*	bucket	*bcl*
brow·beat	*brobe*	buck·ets	*bcls*
brown	*bron*	buckle	*bcl*
browse	*broz*	buck·les	*bcls*
bruise	*brz*	buck·ling	*bcl*
bruises	*brzs*	bucks	*bcs*
bruis·ing	*brz-*	bud	*bd*
brunch	*brnC*	bud·dies	*bdes*
bru·net	*brnl*	bud·ding	*bd*
bru·nette	*brnl*	buddy	*bde*

budge	*by*	buildup	*bldp*
budget	*byl*	built	*bll*
budg·et·ary	*bylre*	built-in	*bll = n*
budg·eted	*byl-*	bulb	*blb*
budg·et·ing	*byl_*	bulbs	*blbs*
budg·ets	*byls*	bulge	*bly*
buff	*bf*	bulg·ing	*bly_*
buffed	*bf-*	bulk	*blc*
buffer	*bfr*	bulk·head	*blchd*
buff·ered	*bfr-*	bulky	*blce*
buff·ers	*bfrs*	bull	*bl*
buf·fet	*bfa*	bull·dozer	*bldzr*
buff·ing	*bf_*	bull·doz·ing	*bldz_*
buffs	*bfs*	bul·let	*bll*
bug	*bq*	bul·le·tin	*blln*
bugle	*bgl*	bul·le·tins	*bllns*
bugs	*bqs*	bul·lets	*blls*
build	*bld*	bul·lion	*blyn*
builder	*bldr*	bulls	*bls*
build·ers	*bldrs*	bully	*ble*
build·ing	*bld*	bum	*b*
build·ings	*bld_*	bump	*bp*
builds	*blds*	bumped	*bp-*

bumper	*b̆pr*	bu·reau·crats	*brcrts*
bump·ing	*b̆p̱*	bu·reaus	*bros*
bumps	*b̆ps*	bur·geon	*brjn*
bumpy	*b̆pe*	bur·geoned	*brjn-*
bun	*bn*	bur·geon·ing	*brjṉ*
bunch	*bnC*	bur·glar	*brglr*
bun·dle	*bnl*	bur·gla·ries	*brglres*
bun·dled	*bnl-*	bur·glar·ize	*brglrz*
bun·dles	*bnls*	bur·glary	*brglre*
bun·ga·low	*bglo*	burial	*brel*
bun·gle	*bgl*	bur·ied	*bre-*
bun·ion	*bnyn*	burn	*brn*
bunk	*bq*	burned	*brn-*
bun·ker	*bqr*	burner	*brnr*
bun·kers	*bqrs*	burn·ers	*brnrs*
buoy·ant	*byM*	burn·ing	*brṉ*
bur·den	*brdn*	burn·out	*brnot*
bur·dened	*brdn-*	burns	*brns*
bur·dens	*brdns*	burnt	*brM*
bur·den·some	*brdns—*	burr	*br*
bu·reau	*bro*	bur·sar	*brsr*
bu·reauc·racy	*brcrse*	bur·si·tis	*brsls*
bu·reau·cratic	*brcrlc*	burst	*brS*

burst·ing	*brs*	busy	*bze*
bury	*bre*	but	*b*
bus	*bs*	bu·tane	*btn*
buses	*bss*	butcher	*bCr*
bush	*bsh*	but·ler	*btlr*
bushel	*bshl*	but·ter	*btr*
bush·els	*bshls*	but·tered	*btr-*
bushes	*bshs*	but·ter·fat	*btrft*
bush·ing	*bsh*	but·ton	*btn*
bush·ings	*bsh*	but·toned	*btn-*
busier	*bzer*	but·ton·ing	*btn*
busi·est	*bzes*	but·tons	*btns*
busily	*bzl*	buy	*b*
busi·ness	*bs*	buyer	*br*
busi·nesses	*bss*	buy·ers	*brs*
busi·ness·like	*bslc*	buy·ing	*b*
busi·ness·man	*bs m*	buys	*bs*
busi·ness·men	*bsm*	buzz	*bz*
busi·ness·woman	*bs m*	by	*b*
busi·ness·women	*bs m*	bylaw	*bla*
bus·ing	*bs*	by·laws	*blas*
bust	*bs*	by·line	*bln*
bus·tle	*bsl*	by·pass	*bps*

by·passed	*bps-*	ca·dence	*cdN*
by·passes	*bpss*	cadet	*cdl*
by·stander	*bSNr*	cad·mium	*cd e*
byte	*br*	cadre	*cdre*
		cafe	*cfa*

C

		cafe·te·ria	*cflra*
		cafe·te·rias	*cflras*
cab	*cb*	cafe·to·rium	*cflre*
cab·bage	*cby*	caf·feine	*cfn*
cabin	*cbn*	cage	*cy*
cabi·net	*cbnl*	ca·jole	*cyl*
cabi·nets	*cbnls*	cake	*cc*
cable	*cB*	cakes	*ccs*
ca·ble·gram	*cBq*	cake·walk	*cc c*
ca·ble·grams	*cBqs*	cak·ing	*cc‾*
ca·bles	*cBs*	ca·lam·ity	*cl‾*
ca·bling	*cB‾*	cal·cium	*clse*
ca·boose	*cbs*	cal·cu·late	*clcla*
cabs	*cbs*	cal·cu·lated	*clcla-*
cache	*cA*	cal·cu·lates	*clclas*
ca·cophony	*ccfne*	cal·cu·lat·ing	*clcla‾*
cac·tus	*ccls*	cal·cu·la·tion	*clclj*
ca·daver	*cdvr*	cal·cu·la·tions	*clcljs*

cal·cu·la·tor	*clclar*	calm	*c*
cal·cu·la·tors	*clclars*	calmly	*cl*
cal·cu·lus	*clcls*	calo·rie	*clre*
cal·en·dar	*clNr*	calo·ries	*clres*
cal·en·dars	*clNrs*	calve	*cv*
calf	*cf*	calves	*cvs*
cali·ber	*clbr*	cam	*c*
cali·brate	*clbra*	ca·ma·ra·de·rie	*crdre*
cali·brated	*clbra-*	came	*k*
cali·bra·tion	*clbry*	cam·era	*cra*
cali·bra·tions	*clbrys*	cam·era·man	*cram*
cali·pers	*clprs*	cam·eras	*cras*
cal·is·then·ics	*clstncs*	cam·ou·flage	*cflz*
call	*cl*	camp	*cp*
call·back	*clbc*	cam·paign	*cpn*
call·backs	*clbcs*	cam·paigned	*cpn-*
called	*cl-*	cam·paigner	*cpnr*
caller	*clr*	cam·paign·ers	*cpnrs*
call·ers	*clrs*	cam·paigns	*cpns*
cal·lig·ra·phy	*clgrfe*	camper	*cpr*
call·ing	*cl*	camp·ers	*cprs*
cal·lous	*cls*	camp·ground	*cpgroN*
calls	*cls*	camp·grounds	*cpgroNs*

camp·ing	_c p_	can·dle	_cdl_
camps	_c ps_	can·dles	_cdls_
camp·site	_c psı_	can·dor	_cdr_
cam·pus	_c ps_	candy	_cde_
cam·puses	_c pss_	cane	_cn_
cams	_c s_	ca·nine	_cnn_
can	_c_	can·is·ter	_cSr_
Canada	_cda_	canned	_c-_
Canadian	_cnden_	can·ning	_c_
canal	_cnl_	can·not	_cn_
ca·nals	_cnls_	canny	_ce_
can·cel	_csl_	canoe	_cnu_
can·celed	_csl-_	canopy	_cpe_
can·cel·ing	_csl_	cans	_cs_
can·cel·la·tion	_csly_	can't	_cM_
can·cel·la·tions	_cslgs_	can·tan·ker·ous	_clqrs_
can·cer	_csr_	can·teen	_cln_
can·de·la·bra	_cdlbra_	can·vas	_cvs_
can·did	_cdd_	can·vass	_cvs_
can·di·dacy	_cddse_	can·vassed	_cvs-_
can·di·date	_cddl_	can·yon	_cyn_
can·di·dates	_cddls_	cap	_cp_
can·dies	_cdes_	ca·pa·bil·ities	_cpßᴸˢ_

Word	Shorthand	Word	Shorthand
ca·pa·bil·ity	cpβ^l	cap·sule	cpsl
ca·pa·ble	cpβ	cap·sules	cpsls
ca·pa·bly	cpβ	cap·tain	cpln
ca·pac·ities	cps^ls	cap·tains	cplns
ca·paci·tor	cpstr	cap·tion	cpj
ca·paci·tors	cpstrs	cap·tioned	cpj-
ca·pac·ity	cps^l	cap·tions	cpjs
cape	cp	cap·ti·vate	cplva
caper	cpr	cap·ti·va·tion	cplvj
cap·il·lary	cplre	cap·tive	cpv
capi·tal	cpll	cap·tiv·ity	cpv^l
capi·tal·ism	cpllz	cap·ture	cpCr
capi·tal·ist	cplls	cap·tured	cpCr-
capi·tal·iza·tion	cpllzj	cap·tures	cpCrs
capi·tal·ize	cpllz	cap·tur·ing	cpCr_
capi·tal·ized	cpllz-	car	cr
capi·tol	cpll	cara·mel	cr—l
ca·pitu·late	cpCla	car·bide	crbd
capped	cp-	car·bo·hy·drate	crbhdrl
cap·ping	cp_	car·bon	crbn
ca·pri·cious	cprΛs	car·bon·ate	crbna
caps	cps	car·bu·re·tor	crbrar
cap·size	cpsz	car·bu·re·tors	crbrars

car·cino·genic	*crsnjnc*	care·less	*crls*
car·ci·noma	*crsn a*	care·lessly	*crlsl*
card	*crd*	care·less·ness	*crls´*
card·board	*crdbrd*	cares	*crs*
card·holder	*crdhldr*	ca·ress	*crs*
card·hold·ers	*crdhldrs*	cargo	*crq*
car·diac	*crdec*	car·goes	*crgs*
car·di·nal	*crdnl*	car·ing	*cr*
card·ing	*crd*	car·load	*crld*
car·di·olo·gist	*crdeljs*	car·loads	*crlds*
car·dio·res·pi·ra·tory	*crdersprtre*	car·nal	*crnl*
car·dio·vas·cu·lar	*crdevsclr*	car·na·tion	*crny*
card·less	*crdls*	car·ni·val	*crnvl*
cards	*crds*	car·nivo·rous	*crnvrs*
care	*cr*	carol	*crl*
ca·reer	*crr*	car·ols	*crls*
ca·reer·ist	*crr8*	car·ou·sel	*crsl*
ca·reer·ists	*crr8s*	car·pen·ter	*crpNr*
ca·reers	*crrs*	car·pen·ters	*crpNrs*
care·free	*crfre*	car·pet	*crpt*
care·ful	*crf*	car·peted	*crpt-*
care·fully	*crfl*	car·pet·ing	*crpt_*
care·ful·ness	*crf´*	car·pets	*crpts*

Word	Shorthand	Word	Shorthand
car·pool	crpl	car·ton	crln
car·pooler	crplr	car·tons	crlns
car·pool·ers	crplrs	car·toon	crln
car·pool·ing	crpl	car·toons	crlns
car·port	crpl	car·tridge	crlr
car·rel	crl	car·tridges	crlrs
car·rels	crls	carts	crls
car·riage	cry	carve	crv
car·ried	cre-	cas·cade	cscd
car·rier	crer	case	cs
car·ri·ers	crers	cased	cs-
car·ries	cres	cases	css
car·rot	crl	case·work	cs o
carry	cre	case·worker	cs or
car·ry·all	creA	case·work·ers	cs ors
car·ry·ing	cre	cash	cA
car·ry·over	creO	cashed	cA-
cars	crs	cashes	cAs
cart	crl	cash·ier	cAr
cart·age	crly	cash·iers	cArs
carte blanche	crl blns	cash·ing	cA
car·tel	crll	cas·ing	cs
car·ti·lage	crllj	ca·sino	csno

cask	*csc*	cata·lyst	* clls*
cas·ket	*cscl*	cata·lytic	*clllc*
cas·se·role	*csrl*	ca·tas·tro·phe	*clsrfe*
cas·sette	*csl*	cata·strophic	*clsrfc*
cas·settes	*csls*	catch	*cC*
cast	*cS*	catch·all	*cCA*
cast·away	*cSa a*	catches	*cCs*
cas·ti·gate	*cSga*	catch·ing	*cC*
cast·ing	*cS*	cate·go·ries	*clgres*
cast·ings	*cS*	cate·go·rized	*clgrz*
cas·tle	*csl*	cate·go·riz·ing	*clgrz*
cast-off (adj.)	*cS = of*	cate·gory	*clgre*
cast·off (n.)	*cSof*	cater	*clr*
cas·trate	*cSra*	ca·tered	*clr*
casts	*cSs*	ca·terer	*clrr*
casual	*czul*	ca·ter·ers	*clrrs*
casu·ally	*czull*	ca·ter·ing	*clr*
casu·al·ties	*czulles*	cat·er·pil·lar	*clrplr*
casu·alty	*czulle*	cat·er·pil·lars	*clrplrs*
cat	*cl*	ca·the·dral	*cldrl*
cata·log	*cal*	cathe·ter	*cllr*
cata·log·ing	*cal*	cath·ode	*cld*
cata·logs	*cals*	cath·odes	*clds*

ca·thodic	*cldc*	cav·ern	*cvrn*
catho·lic	*cllc*	caviar	*cver*
Catholic	*cllc*	cav·ities	*cv ls*
cats	*cls*	cav·ity	*cv l*
cat·tle	*cll*	cease	*ss*
Caucasian	*ccq*	ceased	*ss-*
cau·cus	*ccs*	cease·less	*ssls*
caught	*cl*	cedar	*sdr*
caulk	*cc*	cede	*sd*
caulked	*cc-*	ceded	*sd-*
caulk·ing	*cc_*	ced·ing	*sd_*
cause	*cz*	ceil·ing	*slg*
caused	*cz-*	ceil·ings	*slgs*
causes	*czs*	cele·brate	*slbra*
cause·way	*cz_a*	cele·brat·ing	*slbra_*
caus·ing	*cz_*	cele·bra·tion	*slbrj*
caus·tic	*csc*	ce·leb·ri·ties	*slbrles*
cau·ter·ize	*clrz*	ce·leb·rity	*slbrle*
cau·tion	*cq*	cel·ery	*slre*
cau·tioned	*cq-*	ce·les·tial	*slsCl*
cau·tious	*cas*	celi·bate	*slbl*
cau·tiously	*casl*	cell	*sl*
cave	*cv*	cello	*Clo*

cel·lo·phane	*slfn*	cen·ti·me·ter	*cm*
cells	*sls*	cen·ti·me·ters	*cms*
cel·lu·lar	*sllr*	cen·tral	*sNrl*
Celsius	*slses*	cen·tral·iza·tion	*sNrlz*
ce·ment	*sm*	cen·tral·ize	*sNrlz*
ce·mented	*sm-*	cen·tral·ized	*sNrlz-*
ce·ment·ing	*sm_*	cen·tral·izes	*sNrlzs*
ce·ments	*sms*	cen·tral·iz·ing	*sNrlz_*
ceme·ter·ies	*s⎯lres*	cen·trally	*sNrll*
ceme·tery	*s⎯lre*	cen·trifu·gal	*sNlrfgl*
cen·sor	*sNr*	cen·tri·fuge	*sNrff*
cen·sored	*sNr-*	cents	*¢*
cen·sor·ship	*sNrs*	cen·tu·ries	*snCres*
cen·sus	*sNs*	cen·tury	*snCre*
cent	*¢*	ce·ramic	*S⎯c*
cen·ten·nial	*sntnel*	ce·ram·ics	*S⎯cs*
cen·ter	*sNr*	ce·real	*srel*
cen·tered	*sNr-*	ce·re·als	*srels*
cen·ter·ing	*sNr_*	ce·re·bral	*srbrl*
cen·ter·piece	*sNrps*	cere·mo·nies	*sr⎯nes*
cen·ter·pieces	*sNrpss*	cere·mony	*sr⎯ne*
cen·ters	*sNrs*	cer·tain	*Sln*
cen·ti·grade	*sNgrd*	cer·tainly	*Slnl*

cer·tainty	*Slnle*	chair·per·son	*CrPsn*
cer·tifi·cate (n.)	*Slfcl*	chair·per·sons	*CrPsns*
cer·tifi·cate (v.)	*Slfca*	chairs	*Crs*
cer·tifi·cated	*Slfca-*	chair·woman	*Cr——m*
cer·tifi·cates (n.)	*Slfcls*	chair·women	*Cr_m*
cer·tifi·cates (v.)	*Slfcas*	chalk	*Cc*
cer·ti·fi·ca·tion	*Slf*	chalk·board	*Ccbrd*
cer·ti·fi·ca·tions	*Slfs*	chalk·boards	*Ccbrds*
cer·ti·fied	*Slf-*	chal·lenge	*Clnj*
cer·ti·fies	*Slfs*	chal·lenged	*Clnj-*
cer·tify	*Slf*	chal·lenges	*Clnjs*
cer·ti·fy·ing	*Slf_*	chal·leng·ing	*Clnj_*
cer·vi·cal	*Svcl*	cham·ber	*C—br*
cer·vix	*Svx*	cham·bers	*C—brs*
ces·sa·tion	*ssj*	champ	*C—p*
cha·grin	*Agrn*	cham·pagne	*A—pn*
chain	*Cn*	cham·pion	*C—pen*
chains	*Cns*	cham·pion·ship	*C—pens*
chair	*Cr*	chance	*CN*
chaired	*Cr-*	chan·cel·lor	*CNlr*
chair·man	*Cr——m*	chan·cery	*CNre*
chair·man·ship	*Crms*	chances	*CNs*
chair·men	*Crm*	change	*Cnj*

change·able	*Cnjß*	char·ac·ter·is·tics	*crcs*
changed	*Cnj-*	char·ac·ter·iza·tion	*crczſ*
change·over	*CnjO*	char·ac·ter·iza·tions	*crczſs*
change·overs	*CnjOs*	char·ac·ter·ize	*crcz*
changes	*Cnjs*	char·ac·ter·ized	*crcz-*
chang·ing	*Cnj_*	char·ac·ter·iz·ing	*crcz_*
chan·nel	*Cnl*	char·ac·ters	*crcs*
chan·neled	*Cnl-*	char·coal	*Crcl*
chan·nels	*Cnls*	charge	*G*
chant	*CN*	charge·able	*Gß*
chaos	*cas*	charged	*G-*
cha·otic	*calc*	charger	*Gr*
chap	*Cp*	charges	*Gs*
chapel	*Cpl*	charg·ing	*G_*
chap·eron	*sprn*	chari·ta·ble	*CrlB*
chap·lain	*Cpln*	char·ities	*Cr ls*
chap·lains	*Cplns*	char·ity	*Cr l*
chap·ter	*Cplr*	char·la·tan	*srlln*
chap·ters	*Cplrs*	charm	*Cr*
char	*Cr*	charm·ing	*Cr _*
char·ac·ter	*crc*	chart	*Crl*
char·ac·ter·is·tic	*crc*	charted	*Crl-*
char·ac·ter·is·ti·cally	*crcl*	char·ter	*Crlr*

Word	Shorthand	Word	Shorthand
char·tered		check	
char·ter·ing		check·book	
char·ters		checked	
chart·ing		checker	
charts		check·er·board	
chase		check·ers	
chases		check·ing	
chas·ing		check·list	
chas·sis		check·off	
chaste		check-out (adj.)	
chas·tise		check·out (n.)	
chas·tised		check·point	
chat		checks	
chat·tel		checkup	
chat·ter		cheek	
chauf·feur		cheeks	
chau·vin·ist		cheer	
cheap		cheered	
cheaper		cheer·ful	
cheap·est		cheer·fully	
cheaply		cheer·leader	
cheat		cheer·lead·ers	
cheat·ing		cheers	

cheese	*(shorthand)*	chiefly	*(shorthand)*
chef	*(shorthand)*	chiefs	*(shorthand)*
chefs	*(shorthand)*	child	*(shorthand)*
chem·ical	*(shorthand)*	child·birth	*(shorthand)*
chem·ically	*(shorthand)*	child·hood	*(shorthand)*
chem·icals	*(shorthand)*	child·ish	*(shorthand)*
chem·ist	*(shorthand)*	chil·dren	*(shorthand)*
chem·is·tries	*(shorthand)*	chili	*(shorthand)*
chem·is·try	*(shorthand)*	chill	*(shorthand)*
chem·ists	*(shorthand)*	chilled	*(shorthand)*
chemo·therapy	*(shorthand)*	chilly	*(shorthand)*
cher·ish	*(shorthand)*	chim·ney	*(shorthand)*
cher·ries	*(shorthand)*	chim·neys	*(shorthand)*
cherry	*(shorthand)*	chin	*(shorthand)*
chess	*(shorthand)*	china	*(shorthand)*
chest	*(shorthand)*	China	*(shorthand)*
chew	*(shorthand)*	chink	*(shorthand)*
chew·ing	*(shorthand)*	chip	*(shorthand)*
chic	*(shorthand)*	chipped	*(shorthand)*
chi·can·ery	*(shorthand)*	chip·per	*(shorthand)*
chicken	*(shorthand)*	chip·ping	*(shorthand)*
chide	*(shorthand)*	chips	*(shorthand)*
chief	*(shorthand)*	chi·ro·prac·tic	*(shorthand)*

chi·ro·prac·tor	*crprclr*	choppy	*Cpe*
chi·ro·prac·tors	*crprclrs*	cho·ral	*crl*
chisel	*Czl*	chord	*crd*
chlo·ride	*clrd*	chore	*Cr*
chlo·rin·ate	*clrna*	cho·re·og·ra·pher	*cregrfr*
chlo·rin·ated	*clrna-*	cho·re·og·ra·phy	*cregrfe*
chlo·ri·na·tion	*clrny*	cho·rus	*crs*
chlo·rine	*clrn*	chose	*Cz*
choco·late	*Ccll*	cho·sen	*Czn*
choice	*Cys*	Christian	*crsj*
choices	*Cyss*	Christmas	*X—s*
choir	*q*	Christmases	*X—ss*
choirs	*qs*	chrome	*cr*
choke	*Cc*	chro·mium	*cr e*
choked	*Cc-*	chro·mo·so·mal	*cr s l*
chok·ing	*Cc_*	chro·mo·some	*cr s*
cho·les·terol	*clSrl*	chronic	*crnc*
choose	*Cz*	chron·ically	*crncl*
chooses	*Czs*	chron·icle	*crncl*
choos·ing	*Cz-*	chron·icles	*crncls*
chop	*Cp*	chrono·log·ical	*crnlycl*
chopped	*Cp-*	chrono·log·ically	*crnlycll*
chop·per	*Cpr*	chro·nology	*crnlye*

chubby	*Cbe*	cir·cuitry	*Sclre*
chuckle	*Ccl*	cir·cuits	*Scls*
chum	*C*	cir·cu·lar	*Sclr*
chunk	*Cq*	cir·cu·late	*Scla*
church	*CrC*	cir·cu·lated	*Scla-*
churches	*CrCs*	cir·cu·lates	*Sclas*
chute	*Au*	cir·cu·lat·ing	*Scla̱*
cider	*sdr*	cir·cu·la·tion	*Sclj*
cigar	*sgr*	cir·cu·la·tory	*Scltre*
ciga·rette	*sgrl*	cir·cum·cise	*Sksz*
ciga·rettes	*sgrls*	cir·cum·scribe	*Sk S*
ci·gars	*sgrs*	cir·cum·spect	*Skspc*
cinch	*snC*	cir·cum·stance	*Sk*
cin·der	*sNr*	cir·cum·stances	*Sks*
cin·ders	*sNrs*	cir·cum·stan·tial	*Sksl*
cinema	*sn a*	cir·cum·vent	*SkvN*
cin·na·mon	*snm*	cir·cum·vented	*SkvN-*
ci·pher	*sfr*	cir·cus	*Scs*
cir·cle	*Scl*	cir·rho·sis	*Sss*
cir·cled	*Scl-*	ci·ta·tion	*slj*
cir·cles	*Scls*	ci·ta·tions	*sljs*
cir·cling	*Scḻ*	cite	*si*
cir·cuit	*Scl*	cited	*si-*

cites	*sis*	clam	*cl*
cit·ies	*sies*	clamor	*clr*
cit·ing	*si*	clamp	*clp*
citi·zen	*slzn*	clamp·ing	*clp-*
citi·zenry	*slznre*	clamps	*clps*
citi·zens	*slzns*	clams	*cls*
citi·zen·ship	*slzns*	clan	*cln*
cit·ric	*strc*	clan·des·tine	*clndSn*
cit·rus	*strs*	clap	*clp*
city	*sle*	clapped	*clp-*
civic	*svc*	clari·fi·ca·tion	*clrf*
civ·ics	*svcs*	clari·fi·ca·tions	*clrfs*
civil	*svl*	clari·fied	*clrf-*
ci·vil·ian	*svlyn*	clari·fies	*clrfs*
ci·vil·ians	*svlyns*	clarify	*clrf*
civi·li·za·tion	*svlz*	clari·fy·ing	*clrf-*
civi·lized	*svlz-*	clar·ity	*clr*
claim	*cl*	clash	*cl4*
claim·ant	*cl M*	class	*cls*
claim·ants	*cl Ms*	classed	*cls-*
claimed	*cl -*	classes	*clss*
claim·ing	*cl -*	clas·sic	*clsc*
claims	*cls*	clas·sics	*clscs*

clas·si·fi·ca·tion	*clsfg*	cleanup	*clnp*
clas·si·fi·ca·tions	*clsfgs*	clear	*clr*
clas·si·fied	*clsf-*	clear·ance	*clrN*
clas·sify	*clsf*	clear·ances	*clrNs*
clas·si·fy·ing	*clsf_*	cleared	*clr-*
class·mate	*cls~a*	clearer	*clrr*
class·mates	*cls~as*	clear·ing	*clr_*
class·room	*clsr~*	clear·ing·house	*clrghos*
class·rooms	*clsr~s*	clearly	*clrl*
clause	*clz*	clear·ness	*clr´*
clauses	*clzs*	clears	*clrs*
claus·tro·pho·bia	*clSrfba*	clem·ency	*clmse*
claw	*cla*	clergy	*clrge*
claws	*clas*	cler·ical	*clrcl*
clay	*cla*	clerk	*clrc*
clean	*cln*	clerks	*clrcs*
cleaned	*cln-*	clerk·ship	*clrcA*
cleaner	*clnr*	clever	*clvr*
clean·ers	*clnrs*	clev·erly	*clvrl*
clean·ing	*cln_*	cli·ché	*clAa*
clean·li·ness	*clnl´*	click	*clc*
cleanse	*clnz*	clicks	*clcs*
cleansed	*clnz-*	cli·ent	*clN*

Word	Outline	Word	Outline
cli·en·tele	*clintl*	clips	*clps*
cli·ents	*cliNs*	clique	*clc*
cliff	*clf*	clock	*clc*
cli·mate	*clt*	clock·ing	*clc‾*
cli·mates	*clts*	clocks	*clcs*
cli·max	*clx*	clock·wise	*clcᵣ*
climb	*cl*	clog	*clq*
climbed	*cl –*	clogged	*clq–*
climb·ing	*cl ‾*	close (adj.)	*cls*
clinch	*clnC*	close (v.)	*clz*
clinched	*clnC –*	closed	*clz–*
cling	*clq*	closely	*clsl*
clinic	*clnc*	close·ness	*cls´*
clin·ical	*clncl*	close-out	*clz = ot*
clin·ically	*clncll*	closer	*clsr*
cli·ni·cian	*clny*	closes	*clzs*
cli·ni·cians	*clnys*	clos·est	*clsS*
clin·ics	*clncs*	closet	*clzt*
clip	*clp*	clos·ets	*clzts*
clipped	*clp–*	close-up	*cls = p*
clip·per	*clpr*	clos·ing	*clz‾*
clip·ping	*clp_*	clos·ings	*clz=*
clip·pings	*clp=*	clo·sure	*clzr*

clo·sures	*clzrs*	clut·tered	*cllr-*
clot	*cll*	coach	*cC*
cloth	*cll*	coached	*cC-*
clothe	*cll*	coaches	*cCs*
clothes	*clls*	coach·ing	*cC*
cloth·ing	*cll*	co·agu·late	*cogla*
clots	*clls*	co·agu·lated	*cogla-*
cloud	*clod*	co·agu·la·tion	*cogly*
clouds	*clods*	coal	*cl*
cloudy	*clode*	coa·li·tion	*coly*
clout	*clol*	coarse	*crs*
clo·ver	*clvr*	coarsen	*crsn*
clown·ing	*clon*	coars·ened	*crsn-*
club	*clb*	coarse·ness	*crs'*
club·house	*clbhos*	coast	*cS*
clubs	*clbs*	coastal	*cSl*
clum·si·ness	*clnze'*	coaster	*cSr*
clumsy	*clnze*	coast·ers	*cSrs*
clus·ter	*clSr*	coast·line	*cSln*
clus·ters	*clSrs*	coat	*co*
clutch	*clC*	coated	*co-*
clutched	*clC-*	coat·ing	*co*
clut·ter	*cllr*	coat·ings	*co*

coats		coded	
coat·tail		co·de·fen·dant	
co·au·thor		co·deine	
coax		codes	
cob		codi·cil	
co·balt		codi·fied	
cob·bler		codify	
cob·blers		cod·ing	
cob·ble·stone		cod·ings	
cob·web		co·di·rec·tor	
cob·webs		coed	
co·caine		co·edu·ca·tional	
co·chair·man		co·ef·fi·cient	
cockle		co·ef·fi·cients	
cock·les		co·er·cion	
cock·pit		co·ex·ist	
cock·tail		cof·fee	
cock·tails		cof·fee·pot	
cocoa		cof·fer	
co·co·nut		cof·fers	
co·coon		cof·fin	
cod·dle		co·foun·der	
code		cog	

cogi·tate	*cgta*	coke	*cc*
cog·ni·tion	*cgny*	cold	*cld*
cog·ni·tive	*cgnv*	colder	*cldr*
cog·ni·zance	*cgnzn*	cold·est	*clds*
cog·ni·zant	*cgnzn*	colds	*clds*
co·her·ence	*chrn*	coli·seum	*clse*
co·her·ent	*chrn*	co·li·tis	*clls*
co·he·sion	*chy*	col·labo·rate	*clbra*
co·he·sive	*chsv*	col·labo·rated	*clbra-*
co·host	*chs*	col·labo·ra·tion	*clbry*
coil	*cyl*	col·labo·ra·tive	*clbrav*
coiled	*cyl-*	col·labo·ra·tor	*clbrar*
coils	*cyls*	col·lage	*clz*
coin	*cyn*	col·lapse	*clps*
co·in·cide	*consd*	col·lapsed	*clps-*
co·in·cided	*consd-*	col·laps·ible	*clpsB*
co·in·ci·dence	*ndn*	col·laps·ing	*clps_*
co·in·ci·den·tal	*ndnl*	col·lar	*clr*
co·in·ci·den·tally	*ndnll*	col·lars	*clrs*
co·in·cides	*consds*	col·late	*cla*
co·in·cid·ing	*consd_*	col·lated	*cla-*
coins	*cyns*	col·lat·eral	*cltrl*
co·in·sur·ance	*cins*	col·lat·ing	*cla_*

col·league	*clq*	co·logne	*cln*
col·leagues	*clgs*	colon	*cln*
col·lect	*clc*	colo·nel	*crnl*
col·lected	*clc-*	co·lo·nial	*clnel*
col·lect·ible	*clcB*	colony	*clne*
col·lect·ibles	*clcBs*	color	*clr*
col·lect·ing	*clc*	col·ora·tion	*clry*
col·lec·tion	*clq*	col·ored	*clr-*
col·lec·tions	*clqs*	col·or·ful	*clrf*
col·lec·tive	*clcv*	col·or·ing	*clr*
col·lec·tively	*clcvl*	col·ors	*clrs*
col·lec·tor	*clcr*	co·los·sal	*clsl*
col·lec·tors	*clcrs*	colt	*cll*
col·lects	*clcs*	colts	*clls*
col·lege	*cly*	col·umn	*cl*
col·leges	*clys*	co·lum·nar	*cl mr*
col·le·giate	*clyl*	col·um·nist	*cl nS*
col·lide	*cld*	col·umns	*cl s*
col·lided	*cld-*	coma	*c a*
col·li·sion	*cly*	comb	*c*
col·lo·quium	*clqe*	com·bat	*kbl*
col·lo·qui·ums	*clqes*	com·bat·ing	*kbl*
col·lu·sion	*cly*	com·bi·na·tion	*kbny*

com·bi·na·tions	*kbnys*	com·ics	*kcs*
com·bine	*kbn*	com·ing	*k̠*
com·bined	*kbn-*	comma	*ka*
com·bines	*kbns*	com·mand	*kN*
com·bin·ing	*kbn̠*	com·manded	*kN-*
combo	*kbo*	com·mander	*kNr*
com·bus·ti·ble	*kbℓℓ*	com·mand·ing	*kN*
com·bus·tion	*kbsy*	com·mand·ment	*kN̄m*
come	*k*	com·mands	*kNs*
come·back	*kbc*	com·memo·rate	*k ⌣ra*
co·me·dian	*kden*	com·memo·rat·ing	*k ⌣ra̠*
come·dies	*kdes*	com·memo·ra·tion	*k ⌣ry*
comedy	*kde*	com·memo·ra·tive	*k ⌣rv*
comes	*ks*	com·mence	*kN*
comet	*kl*	com·menced	*kN-*
com·fort	*kfl*	com·mence·ment	*kNm*
com·fort·able	*kflB*	com·mences	*kNs*
com·fort·ably	*kflB*	com·menc·ing	*kN*
com·forter	*kflr*	com·mend	*kN̄*
com·fort·ing	*kfl̠*	com·mend·able	*kNB*
com·forts	*kfls*	com·men·da·tion	*kNy*
comic	*kc*	com·men·da·tions	*kNys*
com·ical	*kcl*	com·mended	*kN-*

com·mend·ing	*kɳ*	com·mis·sioner	*kjr*
com·men·su·rate	*kɳrl*	com·mis·sion·ers	*kjrs*
com·ment	*kɳ*	com·mis·sion·ing	*kj-*
com·men·tar·ies	*kɳres*	com·mis·sions	*kjs*
com·men·tary	*kɳre*	com·mit	*kl*
com·men·ta·tor	*kɳar*	com·mit·ment	*klm*
com·mented	*kɳ-*	com·mit·ments	*klms*
com·ment·ing	*kɳ*	com·mits	*kls*
com·ments	*kɳs*	com·mit·ted	*kl-*
com·merce	*krs*	com·mit·tee	*k*
com·mer·cial	*krsl*	com·mit·tees	*ks*
com·mer·cial·iza·tion	*krslz*	com·mit·ting	*kl*
com·mer·cial·ize	*krslz*	com·mode	*kd*
com·mer·cial·ized	*krslz-*	com·mod·ities	*kd^{ls}*
com·mer·cially	*krsll*	com·mod·ity	*kd^{l}*
com·mer·cials	*krsls*	com·mon	*kn*
com·min·gle	*kgl*	com·monly	*knl*
com·min·gled	*kgl-*	com·mon·place	*knpls*
com·mis·er·ate	*kzra*	com·mons	*kns*
com·mis·sar·ies	*ksres*	com·mon·wealth	*kn ll*
com·mis·sary	*ksre*	com·mo·tion	*kj*
com·mis·sion	*kj*	com·mune	*kn*
com·mis·sioned	*kj-*	com·mu·ni·ca·ble	*kncß*

com·mu·ni·cate	*knca*	com·pa·nies	*cos*
com·mu·ni·cated	*knca-*	com·pan·ion	*kpnyn*
com·mu·ni·cates	*kncas*	com·pan·ions	*kpnyns*
com·mu·ni·cat·ing	*knca_*	com·pan·ion·ship	*kpnyns*
com·mu·ni·ca·tion	*kncy*	com·pany	*co*
com·mu·ni·ca·tions	*kncys*	com·pa·ra·ble	*kprß*
com·mu·ni·ca·tive	*kncav*	com·para·tive	*kprv*
com·mu·ni·ca·tively	*kncavl*	com·para·tively	*kprvl*
com·mu·ni·ca·tor	*kncar*	com·pare	*kpr*
com·mu·ni·qué	*knca*	com·pared	*kpr-*
com·mu·nism	*knz*	com·pares	*kprs*
com·mu·ni·ties	*kn's*	com·par·ing	*kpr_*
com·mu·nity	*kn'*	com·pari·son	*kprsn*
com·mu·ta·tion	*kly*	com·pari·sons	*kprsns*
com·mute	*ku*	com·part·ment	*kplm*
com·muter	*kur*	com·part·ments	*kplms*
com·mut·ing	*ku_*	com·pass	*kps*
com·pact	*kpc*	com·pas·sion	*kpy*
com·pact·ing	*kpc_*	com·pas·sion·ate	*kpyl*
com·pac·tion	*kpcy*	com·pat·ibil·ity	*kplß'*
com·pact·ness	*kpc'*	com·pat·ible	*kplß*
com·pac·tor	*kpcr*	com·pel	*kpl*
com·pacts	*kpcs*	com·pelled	*kpl-*

com·pel·ling	*kpl*	com·pi·la·tion	*kply*
com·pen·sate	*kpNa*	com·pile	*kpl*
com·pen·sated	*kpNa-*	com·piled	*kpl-*
com·pen·sates	*kpNas*	com·piler	*kplr*
com·pen·sat·ing	*kpNa_*	com·pil·ers	*kplrs*
com·pen·sa·tion	*kpNy*	com·piles	*kpls*
com·pen·sa·tor	*kpNar*	com·pil·ing	*kpl_*
com·pen·sa·tors	*kpNars*	com·pla·cent	*kplsN*
com·pen·sa·tory	*kpNlre*	com·plain	*kpln*
com·pete	*kpe*	com·plain·ant	*kplnN*
com·peted	*kpe-*	com·plained	*kpln-*
com·pe·tence	*kplN*	com·plainer	*kplnr*
com·pe·ten·cies	*kplNes*	com·plain·ing	*kpln_*
com·pe·tency	*kplNe*	com·plains	*kplns*
com·pe·tent	*kplN*	com·plaint	*kplN*
com·petes	*kpes*	com·plaints	*kplNs*
com·pet·ing	*kpe_*	com·ple·ment	*kplm*
com·pe·ti·tion	*kply*	com·ple·men·tary	*kplmre*
com·peti·tive	*kplv*	com·ple·mented	*kplm-*
com·peti·tively	*kplvl*	com·ple·ments	*kplms*
com·peti·tive·ness	*kplv´*	com·plete	*kp*
com·peti·tor	*kpllr*	com·pleted	*kp-*
com·peti·tors	*kpllrs*	com·pletely	*kpl*

Word	Shorthand	Word	Shorthand
com·plete·ness	kp´	com·po·nents	kpnNs
com·pletes	kps	com·pose	kpz
com·plet·ing	kp_	com·posed	kpz-
com·ple·tion	kpy	com·pos·ing	kpz_
com·plex	kplx	com·pos·ite	kpzl
com·plexes	kplxs	com·pos·ites	kpzls
com·plex·ion	kplcy	com·po·si·tion	kpzy
com·plex·ity	kplx´	com·po·sure	kpzr
com·pli·ance	kplN	com·pound	kpoN
com·pli·cate	kplca	com·pounded	kpoN-
com·pli·cated	kplca-	com·pound·ing	kpoN_
com·pli·cat·ing	kplca_	com·pounds	kpoNs
com·pli·ca·tion	kplcy	com·pre·hend	kprhN
com·pli·ca·tions	kplcys	com·pre·hen·si·ble	kprhNB
com·plied	kpli-	com·pre·hen·sion	kprhny
com·plies	kplis	com·pre·hen·sive	kprhNv
com·pli·ment	kplm	com·pre·hen·sively	kprhNvl
com·pli·men·tary	kplmre	com·press	kprs
com·pli·mented	kplm-	com·pressed	kprs-
com·pli·ments	kplms	com·presses	kprss
com·ply	kpli	com·press·ible	kprsB
com·ply·ing	kpli_	com·pres·sion	kpry
com·po·nent	kpnN	com·pres·sor	kprsr

com·pres·sors	*kprsrs*	com·put·er·iz·ing	*kpurz-*
com·prise	*kprz*	com·put·ers	*kpurs*
com·prised	*kprz-*	com·put·ing	*kpu*
com·prises	*kprzs*	com·rade	*krd*
com·pris·ing	*kprz-*	con	*k*
com·pro·mise	*kpr~z*	con·ceal	*ksl*
com·pro·mises	*kpr~zs*	con·cealed	*ksl-*
com·pro·mis·ing	*kpr~z-*	con·ceal·ment	*kslm*
comp·trol·ler	*klr*	con·cede	*ksd*
comp·trol·lers	*klrs*	con·ceded	*ksd-*
com·pul·sion	*kpl*	con·ceit	*kse*
com·pul·sions	*kpls*	con·ceited	*kse-*
com·pul·sory	*kplsre*	con·ceiv·able	*ksvß*
com·put·able	*kpuß*	con·ceiv·ably	*ksvß*
com·pu·ta·tion	*kpl*	con·ceive	*ksv*
com·pu·ta·tional	*kpll*	con·ceived	*ksv-*
com·pu·ta·tions	*kpls*	con·cen·trate	*ksNra*
com·pute	*kpu*	con·cen·trated	*ksNra-*
com·puted	*kpu-*	con·cen·trates	*ksNras*
com·puter	*kpur*	con·cen·trat·ing	*ksNra*
com·put·er·iza·tion	*kpurzl*	con·cen·tra·tion	*ksNry*
com·put·er·ize	*kpurz*	con·cen·tra·tions	*ksNrys*
com·put·er·ized	*kpurz-*	con·cen·tric	*ksNrc*

con·cept	*kspt*	con·cluded	*kcld-*
con·cep·tion	*kspy*	con·cludes	*kclds*
con·cepts	*kspts*	con·clud·ing	*kcld_*
con·cep·tual	*kspCul*	con·clu·sion	*kcly*
con·cep·tu·al·ize	*kspCulz*	con·clu·sions	*kclys*
con·cep·tu·al·iz·ing	*kspCulz_*	con·clu·sive	*kclsv*
con·cep·tu·ally	*kspCull*	con·clu·sively	*kclsvl*
con·cern	*ksrn*	con·coct	*kcc*
con·cerned	*ksrn-*	con·coc·tion	*kccy*
con·cern·ing	*ksrn_*	con·comi·tant	*kklN*
con·cerns	*ksrns*	con·comi·tantly	*kklNl*
con·cert	*ksrt*	con·cor·dance	*kcrdN*
con·certed	*ksrt-*	con·course	*kcrs*
con·certs	*ksrts*	con·crete	*kcre*
con·ces·sion	*ksy*	con·cur	*kcr*
con·ces·sion·aire	*ksyr*	con·curred	*kcr-*
con·ces·sions	*ksys*	con·cur·rence	*kcrN*
con·cili·ation	*ksley*	con·cur·rent	*kcrN*
con·cili·ations	*ksleys*	con·cur·rently	*kcrNl*
con·cili·ator	*kslar*	con·cur·ring	*kcr_*
con·cili·atory	*ksletre*	con·curs	*kcrs*
con·cise	*kss*	con·cus·sion	*kcy*
con·clude	*kcld*	con·demn	*kd~*

con·dem·na·tion	*kd⌣ny*	con·done	*kdn*
con·demned	*kd⌣-*	con·doned	*kdn-*
con·demn·ing	*kd⌣*	con·dos	*kdoo*
con·den·sa·tion	*kdNy*	con·du·cive	*kdsv*
con·dense	*kdN*	con·duct	*kdc*
con·densed	*kdN-*	con·ducted	*kdc-*
con·denser	*kdNr*	con·duct·ing	*kdc̲*
con·dens·ers	*kdNro*	con·duc·tion	*kdcy*
con·dens·ing	*kdN̲*	con·duc·tive	*kdcv*
con·de·scend·ing	*kdsN̲*	con·duc·tor	*kdcr*
con·di·tion	*kdy*	con·duc·tors	*kdcro*
con·di·tional	*kdyl*	con·ducts	*kdcs*
con·di·tion·ally	*kdyll*	con·duit	*kdul*
con·di·tioned	*kdy-*	con·duits	*kduls*
con·di·tioner	*kdyr*	cone	*cn*
con·di·tion·ers	*kdyrs*	cones	*cns*
con·di·tion·ing	*kdy_*	con·fabu·la·tion	*kfbly*
con·di·tions	*kdyo*	con·fec·tion	*kfcy*
condo	*kdo*	con·fed·era·tion	*kfdry*
con·do·lence	*kdlN*	con·fer	*kfr*
con·do·lences	*kdlNo*	con·feree	*kfre*
con·do·minium	*kdme⌣*	con·fer·ees	*kfres*
con·do·mini·ums	*kdme⌣s*	con·fer·ence	*kfrN*

con·fer·ences	*kfrNs*	con·firm·ing	*kfr_*
con·ferred	*kfr-*	con·firms	*kfrs*
con·fers	*kfrs*	con·fis·cate	*kfsca*
con·fess	*kfs*	con·fis·cated	*kfsca-*
con·fes·sion	*kfj*	con·flict	*kflc*
con·fetti	*kfle*	con·flict·ing	*kflc_*
con·fide	*kfd*	con·flicts	*kflcs*
con·fi·dence	*kfdN*	con·form	*kf_*
con·fi·dent	*kfdN*	con·for·mance	*kf_M*
con·fi·den·tial	*kfdnsl*	con·formed	*kf_-*
con·fi·den·ti·al·ity	*kfdnsel*	con·form·ing	*kf__*
con·fi·den·tially	*kfdnsll*	con·form·ity	*kf_ı*
con·fi·dently	*kfdNl*	con·forms	*kf_s*
con·figu·ra·tion	*kfgry*	con·front	*kfrN*
con·figu·ra·tions	*kfgrys*	con·fron·ta·tion	*kfrNy*
con·fine	*kfn*	con·fron·ta·tions	*kfrNys*
con·fined	*kfn-*	con·fronted	*kfrN-*
con·fine·ment	*kfnm*	con·front·ing	*kfrN_*
con·fines	*kfns*	con·fuse	*kfz*
con·fin·ing	*kfn_*	con·fused	*kfz-*
con·firm	*kfr*	con·fuses	*kfzs*
con·fir·ma·tion	*kfry*	con·fus·ing	*kfz_*
con·firmed	*kfr-*	con·fu·sion	*kfj*

Word	Shorthand	Word	Shorthand
con·gen·ial	*kjnyl*	coni·fer	*kfr*
con·geni·tal	*kjnll*	con·jec·ture	*kjcCr*
con·gested	*kjS-*	con·ju·ga·tion	*kjgj*
con·ges·tion	*kjsy*	con·junc·tion	*kjgj*
con·ges·tive	*kjSv*	con·junc·tions	*kjgjs*
con·gratu·late	*kq*	con·junc·tive	*kjgv*
con·gratu·lated	*kq-*	con·jure	*kjr*
con·gratu·lat·ing	*kq_*	con·jured	*kjr-*
con·gratu·la·tion	*kgj*	con·nect	*kc*
con·gratu·la·tions	*kgjs*	con·nected	*kc-*
con·gratu·la·tory	*kgre*	con·nect·ing	*kc_*
con·gre·gate (v.)	*kgrga*	con·nec·tion	*kcj*
con·gre·gate (adj.)	*kgrgl*	con·nec·tions	*kcjs*
con·gre·ga·tion	*kgrgj*	con·nec·tor	*kcr*
con·gre·ga·tional	*kgrgjl*	con·nec·tors	*kcrs*
con·gress	*kgrs*	con·nects	*kcs*
con·gres·sional	*kgrjl*	con·niv·ance	*kvN*
con·gress·man	*kgrs m*	con·nive	*kv*
con·gress·men	*kgrsm*	con·nived	*kv-*
con·gress·woman	*kgrs m*	con·no·ta·tion	*kly*
con·gress·women	*kgrs m*	con·quer	*kcr*
con·gru·ence	*kgruN*	con·quest	*kqS*
con·ical	*kcl*	con·quests	*kqSs*

cons	*ks*	con·ser·va·tive	*ksrvv*
con·science	*ksN*	con·ser·va·tor	*ksrvlr*
con·sci·en·tious	*ksenss*	con·serve	*ksrv*
con·sci·en·tiously	*ksenssl*	con·served	*ksrv-*
con·scious	*kss*	con·serv·ing	*ksrv̲*
con·scious·ness	*kss'*	con·sider	*ks*
con·script	*kS*	con·sid·er·able	*ksß*
con·scrip·tion	*kSı*	con·sid·er·ably	*ksß*
con·se·crated	*kscra-*	con·sid·er·ate	*ksl*
con·secu·tive	*kscv*	con·sid·era·tion	*ksı*
con·secu·tively	*kscvl*	con·sid·era·tions	*ksıs*
con·sen·sus	*ksNs*	con·sid·ered	*ks-*
con·sent	*ksN*	con·sid·er·ing	*ks̲*
con·sented	*ksN-*	con·sid·ers	*kss*
con·sent·ing	*ksN̲*	con·sign	*ksn*
con·sents	*ksNs*	con·signed	*ksn-*
con·se·quence	*ksqN*	con·signee	*ksne*
con·se·quences	*ksqNs*	con·sign·ees	*ksnes*
con·se·quent	*ksqN*	con·sign·ing	*ksn̲*
con·se·quen·tial	*ksqnsl*	con·sign·ment	*ksnm*
con·se·quently	*ksqNl*	con·sign·ments	*ksnms*
con·ser·va·tion	*ksrvı*	con·signor	*ksnı*
con·ser·va·tion·ist	*ksrvıs*	con·sist	*ksß*

con·sisted	*kss-*	con·spiracy	*ksprse*
con·sis·tency	*kssne*	con·sta·ble	*kss*
con·sis·tent	*kssn*	con·stant	*ksn*
con·sis·tently	*kssne*	con·stantly	*ksne*
con·sist·ing	*kss*	con·stel·la·tion	*ksly*
con·sists	*ksss*	con·stitu·ency	*kscune*
con·sole	*ksl*	con·stitu·ent	*kscun*
con·soles	*ksls*	con·stitu·ents	*kscuns*
con·soli·date	*kslda*	con·sti·tute	*kslu*
con·soli·dated	*kslda-*	con·sti·tuted	*kslu-*
con·soli·dates	*ksldas*	con·sti·tutes	*kslus*
con·soli·dat·ing	*kslda*	con·sti·tut·ing	*kslu*
con·soli·da·tion	*ksldy*	con·sti·tu·tion	*ksly*
con·soli·da·tions	*ksldys*	con·sti·tu·tional	*kslyl*
con·soli·da·tor	*ksldar*	con·sti·tu·tions	*kslys*
con·soli·da·tors	*ksldars*	con·strain	*ksrn*
con·so·nance	*ksnn*	con·strained	*ksrn-*
con·so·nant	*ksnn*	con·straint	*ksrn*
con·sort	*ksrt*	con·straints	*ksrns*
con·sor·tia	*ksrsa*	con·strict	*ksrc*
con·sor·tium	*ksrse*	con·stricted	*ksrc-*
con·spicu·ous	*kspcus*	con·stric·tion	*ksrcy*
con·spicu·ously	*kspcusl*	con·struct	*ksrc*

con·structed	$k\mathcal{S}rc\text{-}$	con·sum·ing	$ks\frown$
con·struct·ing	$k\mathcal{S}rc\text{_}$	con·sum·mate (v.)	$ks\frown a$
con·struc·tion	$k\mathcal{S}rc\gamma$	con·sum·mate (adj.)	$ks\frown \lambda$
con·struc·tions	$k\mathcal{S}rc\gamma s$	con·sum·mated	$ks\frown a\text{-}$
con·struc·tive	$k\mathcal{S}rcv$	con·sum·ma·tion	$ks\frown \gamma$
con·struc·tively	$k\mathcal{S}rcvl$	con·sump·tion	$ks\frown \gamma$
con·struc·tor	$k\mathcal{S}rcr$	con·tact	klc
con·struc·tors	$k\mathcal{S}rcrs$	con·tacted	$klc\text{-}$
con·strue	$k\mathcal{S}ru$	con·tact·ing	$klc\text{_}$
con·strued	$k\mathcal{S}ru\text{-}$	con·tacts	$klcs$
con·sult	$ksll$	con·ta·gious	$klys$
con·sult·ant	$ksll\mathcal{N}$	con·tain	kln
con·sult·ants	$ksll\mathcal{N}s$	con·tained	$kln\text{-}$
con·sul·ta·tion	$kslly$	con·tainer	$klnr$
con·sul·ta·tions	$kslly s$	con·tain·er·iza·tion	$klnr_\jmath$
con·sul·ta·tive	$ksllv$	con·tain·er·ize	$klnr_\zeta$
con·sulted	$ksll\text{-}$	con·tain·er·ized	$klnr_\zeta\text{-}$
con·sult·ing	$ksll\text{_}$	con·tain·ers	$klnrs$
con·sum·able	$ks\frown \mathcal{B}$	con·tain·ing	$kln\text{_}$
con·sume	$ks\frown$	con·tain·ment	$klnm$
con·sumed	$ks\frown \text{-}$	con·tain·ments	$klnms$
con·sumer	$ks\frown r$	con·tains	$klns$
con·sum·ers	$ks\frown rs$	con·tami·nant	$klm\mathcal{N}$

con·tami·nants	*klmNs*	con·tes·tant	*klSN*
con·tami·nate	*klma*	con·tes·tants	*klSNs*
con·tami·nated	*klma-*	con·tested	*klS-*
con·tami·nat·ing	*klma_*	con·test·ing	*klS_*
con·tami·na·tion	*klmy*	con·tests	*klSs*
con·tem·plate	*kt pla*	con·text	*klxl*
con·tem·plated	*kt pla-*	con·texts	*klxls*
con·tem·plates	*kt plas*	con·tigu·ous	*klgus*
con·tem·plat·ing	*kt pla_*	con·ti·nent	*klnN*
con·tem·po·ra·ne·ously	*kt prnesl*	con·ti·nen·tal	*klnNl*
con·tem·po·rary	*kt prre*	con·tin·gen·cies	*klnyNes*
con·tempt	*kt l*	con·tin·gency	*klnyNe*
con·tend	*klN*	con·tin·gent	*klnyN*
con·tended	*klN-*	con·tinual	*kul*
con·tender	*klNr*	con·tinu·ally	*kull*
con·tend·ers	*klNrs*	con·tinu·ance	*kuN*
con·tend·ing	*klN_*	con·tinu·ances	*kuNs*
con·tends	*klNs*	con·tinu·ation	*kuy*
con·tent	*klN*	con·tinue	*ku*
con·ten·tion	*klny*	con·tin·ued	*ku-*
con·tent·ment	*klNm*	con·tin·ues	*kus*
con·tents	*klNs*	con·tinu·ing	*ku_*
con·test	*klS*	con·ti·nu·ities	*ku ls*

con·ti·nu·ity	*ku'*	con·trast	*klrS*
con·tinu·ous	*kus*	con·trasted	*klrS-*
con·tinu·ously	*kusl*	con·trast·ing	*klrS̲*
con·tinuum	*ku⌢*	con·tra·vene	*klrvn*
con·tour	*klr*	con·tra·ven·tion	*klrvny*
con·tours	*klrs*	con·trib·ut·able	*kbB*
con·tra·cep·tion	*klrspy*	con·trib·ute	*kb*
con·tract	*kc*	con·trib·uted	*kb-*
con·tracted	*kc-*	con·trib·utes	*kbs*
con·tract·ible	*kcB*	con·trib·ut·ing	*kb̲*
con·tract·ing	*kc̲*	con·tri·bu·tion	*kby*
con·trac·tion	*kcy*	con·tri·bu·tions	*kbys*
con·trac·tor	*kcr*	con·tribu·tor	*kbr*
con·trac·tors	*kcrs*	con·tribu·tors	*kbrs*
con·tracts	*kcs*	con·tribu·tory	*kbre*
con·trac·tual	*kcul*	con·trite	*klru*
con·trac·tu·ally	*kcull*	con·trive	*klrv*
con·tra·dict	*klrdc*	con·trol	*kl*
con·tra·dic·tion	*klrdcy*	con·trol·la·ble	*klB*
con·tra·dic·tory	*klrdcre*	con·trolled	*kl-*
con·trari·ness	*klrre'*	con·trol·ler	*klr*
con·trari·wise	*klrre ʒ*	con·trol·lers	*klrs*
con·trary	*klrre*	con·trol·ling	*kl̲*

con·trols	*kls*	con·verge	*kvrg*
con·tro·ver·sial	*klrvrsl*	con·ver·sant	*kvrsN*
con·tro·versy	*klrvrse*	con·ver·sa·tion	*kvrsj*
con·tu·sion	*klj*	con·ver·sa·tional	*kvrsjl*
con·tu·sions	*kljs*	con·ver·sa·tions	*kvrsjs*
con·va·les·cence	*kvlsN*	con·verse	*kvrs*
con·va·les·cent	*kvlsN*	con·versely	*kvrsl*
con·va·lesc·ing	*kvls̲*	con·ver·sion	*kvrj*
con·vec·tion	*kvcj*	con·ver·sions	*kvrjs*
con·vene	*kvn*	con·vert	*kvrt*
con·vened	*kvn-*	con·verted	*kvrt-*
con·vener	*kvnr*	con·verter	*kvrtr*
con·venes	*kvns*	con·vert·ible	*kvrtß*
con·ven·ience	*kv*	con·vert·ing	*kvrt̲*
con·ven·iences	*kvs*	con·verts	*kvrts*
con·ven·ient	*kv*	con·vey	*kva*
con·ven·iently	*kvl*	con·vey·ance	*kvaN*
con·ven·ing	*kvn̲*	con·veyed	*kva-*
con·vent	*kvN̲*	con·veyer	*kvar*
con·ven·tion	*kvrj*	con·vey·ing	*kva̲*
con·ven·tional	*kvrjl*	con·veyor	*kvar*
con·ven·tion·ally	*kvrjll*	con·veys	*kvas*
con·ven·tions	*kvrjs*	con·vict	*kvc*

con·vic·tion	*kvcy*	cool·ing	*cl_*
con·vic·tions	*kvcys*	coop	*cp*
con·vince	*kvɲ*	co-op	*co = op*
con·vinced	*kvɲ-*	co·op·er·ate	*cop*
con·vinces	*kvɲs*	co·op·er·ated	*cop-*
con·vinc·ing	*kvɲ_*	co·op·er·ates	*cops*
con·vo·ca·tion	*kvcy*	co·op·er·at·ing	*cop_*
con·vul·sion	*kvly*	co·op·era·tion	*copy*
con·vul·sive	*kvlsv*	co·op·era·tive	*copv*
cook	*cc*	co·op·era·tively	*copvl*
cookie	*cce*	co·op·era·tive·ness	*copv'*
cook·ies	*cces*	co·op·era·tives	*copvs*
cook·ing	*cc_*	co·op·era·tor	*copr*
cook·out	*ccol*	co·or·di·nate (adj. or n.)	*cordnl*
cook·outs	*ccols*	co·or·di·nate (v.)	*cordna*
cooks	*ccs*	co·or·di·nated	*cordna-*
cook·ware	*cc r*	co·or·di·nates (n.)	*cordnls*
cool	*cl*	co·or·di·nates (v.)	*cordnas*
cool·ant	*clɲ*	co·or·di·nat·ing	*cordna_*
cooled	*cl-*	co·or·di·na·tion	*cordny*
cooler	*clr*	co·or·di·na·tor	*cordnar*
cool·ers	*clrs*	co·or·di·na·tors	*cordnars*
cool·est	*cls*	cop	*cp*

cope	*cp*	cork	*crc*
cop·ied	*cpe-*	corn	*crn*
copier	*cper*	cor·ner	*crnr*
copi·ers	*cpers*	cor·nered	*crnr-*
cop·ies	*cpes*	cor·ner·ing	*crnr_*
co·pi·lot	*cpll*	cor·ners	*crnrs*
co·pi·lots	*cplls*	cor·ner·stone	*crnrSn*
cop·ing	*cp_*	co·rona	*crna*
cop·per	*cpr*	coro·nar·ies	*crnres*
copy	*cpe*	coro·nary	*crnre*
copy·ing	*cpe_*	coro·ner	*crnr*
copy·right	*cperi*	cor·po·ral	*crprl*
copy·righted	*cperi-*	cor·po·rate	*crprl*
cord	*crd*	cor·po·ra·tion	*corp*
cord·age	*crdy*	cor·po·ra·tions	*corps*
cor·dial	*cryl*	corps	*cr*
cor·dially	*cryll*	corpse	*crps*
cord·less	*crdls*	cor·rect	*crc*
cords	*crds*	cor·rected	*crc-*
cor·du·roy	*crdry*	cor·rect·ing	*crc_*
core	*cr*	cor·rec·tion	*crcy*
core·less	*crls*	cor·rec·tional	*crcyl*
cor·ing	*cr_*	cor·rec·tions	*crcys*

cor·rec·tive	$crcv$	cor·ro·sion	cry
cor·rectly	$crcl$	cor·ru·gated	$crga\text{-}$
cor·rect·ness	crc'	cor·ru·ga·tion	$crgf$
cor·rects	$crcs$	cor·rupt	$crpt$
cor·re·late	$crla$	cor·rupt·ible	$crpt\beta$
cor·re·lated	$crla\text{-}$	cor·rup·tion	$crpf$
cor·re·lat·ing	$crla\underline{}$	cor·sage	$crsz$
cor·re·la·tion	$crlf$	cor·ti·sone	$crtsn$
cor·re·la·tions	$crlys$	cos·metic	$cz\text{-}tc$
cor·re·spond	cor	cos·met·ics	$cz\text{-}tcs$
cor·re·sponded	$cor\text{-}$	cos·me·tology	$cz\text{-}tlje$
cor·re·spon·dence	cor	cos·mo·poli·tan	$cz\text{-}pltn$
cor·re·spon·dent	$corN$	co·spon·sor	$cspNr$
cor·re·spon·dents	$corNs$	cost	$c8$
cor·re·spond·ing	$cor\underline{}$	cost·ing	$c\underline{8}$
cor·re·spond·ingly	$corf$	costly	$c8l$
cor·re·sponds	$cors$	costs	$c8s$
cor·ri·dor	$crdr$	cos·tume	cst
cor·ri·dors	$crdrs$	cos·tumes	$csts$
cor·robo·rate	$crbra$	cost·wise	$c8z$
cor·robo·rat·ing	$crbra\underline{}$	cot	ct
cor·robo·ra·tion	$crbry$	co·ten·ant	$ctnN$
cor·roded	$crd\text{-}$	co·ten·ants	$ctnNs$

cot·tage	*cy*	coun·ter·bal·anc·ing	*krblN*
cot·tages	*clys*	count·ered	*kr-*
cot·ton	*cln*	coun·ter·feit	*krfl*
couch	*coC*	count·er·ing	*kr*
cough	*cf*	coun·ter·mea·sure	*kr zr*
could	*cd*	coun·ter·part	*krpl*
couldn't	*cdN*	coun·ter·parts	*krpls*
coun·cil	*ksl*	coun·ter·point	*krpy*
coun·cil·man	*ksl m*	coun·ter·pro·duc·tive	*krPdcv*
coun·cil·men	*kslm*	count·ers	*krs*
coun·cilor	*kslr*	coun·ter·sue	*krsu*
coun·cil·ors	*kslrs*	coun·ter·sued	*krsu-*
coun·cils	*ksls*	coun·ties	*kes*
coun·sel	*ksl*	count·ing	*k*
coun·seled	*ksl-*	count·less	*kls*
coun·sel·ing	*ksl*	coun·tries	*cNres*
coun·selor	*kslr*	coun·try	*cNre*
coun·sel·ors	*kslrs*	counts	*ks*
count	*k*	county	*ke*
count·down	*kdon*	cou·ple	*cpl*
counted	*k-*	cou·pled	*cpl-*
counter	*kr*	cou·pler	*cplr*
coun·ter·act	*krac*	cou·ples	*cpls*

cou·pling	*cpl*	cov·er·age	*cvry*
cou·plings	*cpl*	cov·er·ages	*cvrys*
cou·pon	*cpn*	cov·ered	*cvr-*
cou·pons	*cpns*	cov·er·ing	*cvr*
cour·age	*cry*	cov·ers	*cvrs*
cou·ra·geous	*crys*	cov·ert	*cvrt*
cou·rier	*crer*	covey	*cve*
course	*crs*	cow	*co*
coursed	*crs-*	cow·ard	*cord*
courses	*crss*	co·worker	*c_or*
court	*crt*	co·work·ers	*c_ors*
cour·te·ous	*crtes*	coy	*cy*
cour·te·ously	*crtesl*	cozy	*cze*
cour·te·sies	*crtses*	crab	*crb*
cour·tesy	*crtse*	crack	*crc*
court·house	*crthos*	cracked	*crc-*
court·room	*crtr*	cracker	*crcr*
courts	*crts*	crack·ers	*crcrs*
court·yard	*crtyd*	crack·ing	*crc*
cousin	*czn*	crackle	*crcl*
cove·nant	*cvnN*	crack·les	*crcls*
cove·nants	*cvnNs*	cracks	*crcs*
cover	*cvr*	craft	*crft*

crafts	*crfls*	crazy	*crze*
crafts·man	*crfls⁓n*	cream	*cr⁓*
crafts·man·ship	*crflsms*	creamer	*cr⁓r*
crafts·men	*crflsm*	creamy	*cr⁓e*
cram	*cr⁓*	crease	*crs*
crammed	*cr⁓ -*	creased	*crs -*
cramp	*cr⁓p*	creases	*crss*
cramped	*cr⁓p-*	cre·ate	*cra*
cramps	*cr⁓ps*	cre·ated	*cra-*
crane	*crn*	cre·ates	*cras*
cranes	*crns*	cre·at·ing	*cra_*
cra·nial	*crnel*	crea·tion	*crej*
crank	*crq*	crea·tive	*crav*
crank·case	*crqcs*	crea·tively	*cravl*
cranky	*crqe*	crea·tiv·ity	*crevl*
crash	*crʃ*	crea·tor	*crar*
crashed	*crʃ-*	crea·ture	*crCr*
crashes	*crʃs*	cre·dence	*crdN*
crash·ing	*crʃ_*	cre·den·tial	*crdnʃl*
crater	*crar*	cre·den·tials	*crdnʃls*
crave	*crv*	cred·ibil·ity	*crdßl*
crawl	*crl*	cred·ible	*crdß*
crawl·ing	*crl_*	credit	*cr*

cred·it·able	_crβ_	crimi·nal·ity	_crmlʳ_
cred·ited	_cr-_	crimi·nally	_crmll_
cred·it·ing	_cṛ_	crimi·nology	_crmlye_
credi·tor	_crr_	crimp	_cr p_
credi·tors	_crrs_	crimped	_cr p-_
cred·its	_crs_	crimp·ing	_cr p̱_
creed	_crd_	cringe	_crny_
creek	_crc_	cringed	_crny-_
creep	_crp_	crip·ple	_crpl_
creo·sote	_creso_	crip·pled	_crpl-_
cres·cent	_crsM_	crip·ples	_crpls_
crest	_crδ_	crip·pling	_crpḻ_
crew	_cru_	cri·ses	_crsʒ_
crew·man	_cru m_	cri·sis	_crss_
crew·men	_crum_	crisp	_crsp_
crews	_crus_	cri·te·ria	_crlra_
crib	_crb_	cri·te·rion	_crlren_
cribbed	_crb-_	critic	_crlc_
cried	_cru-_	crit·ical	_crlcl_
cries	_crus_	crit·ically	_crlcll_
crime	_cr_	criti·cism	_crlsʒ_
crimes	_cr s_	criti·cisms	_crlsʒ s_
crimi·nal	_crml_	criti·cize	_crlsʒ_

criti·cized	*crlsz-*	crow	*cro*
criti·ciz·ing	*crlsz_*	crowd	*crod*
crit·ics	*crlcs*	crowded	*crod-*
cri·tique	*crlc*	crowd·ing	*crod_*
cri·tiqued	*crlc-*	crowds	*crods*
cri·tiques	*crlcs*	crown	*cron*
crook	*crc*	crowned	*cron-*
crooked	*crc-*	cru·cial	*crsl*
crop	*crp*	cru·ci·fix·ion	*crsfcy*
crops	*crps*	cru·cify	*crsf*
cross	*crs*	crude	*crd*
crossed	*crs-*	cruel	*crul*
cross·ing	*crs_*	cruise	*crz*
cross·ings	*crs_*	crumb	*cr*
cross·over	*crsO*	crum·ble	*cr B*
cross·road	*crsrd*	crum·bled	*cr B-*
cross·roads	*crsrds*	crum·bling	*cr B_*
cross·walk	*crs c*	crumbs	*cr s*
cross·wise	*crs z*	crum·ple	*cr pl*
cross·word	*crs rd*	crum·pled	*cr pl-*
crotch	*crC*	crunch	*crnC*
crouch	*croC*	cru·sade	*crsd*
croup	*crp*	cru·sader	*crsdr*

crushed		cul·mi·nat·ing	
crusher		cul·prit	
crush·ers		cult	
crush·ing		cul·ti·vate	
crust		cul·ti·va·tion	
crutches		cul·tural	
cry		cul·ture	
cry·ing		cul·tures	
crys·tal		cul·vert	
crys·tals		cum·ber·some	
cube		cu·mu·la·tive	
cubes		cup	
cubic		cups	
cu·bi·cle		cur·able	
cud·dle		curb	
cudgel		cure	
cue		cured	
cues		cur·few	
cuff		cur·ing	
cuffs		cu·ri·os·ity	
cu·li·nary		cu·ri·ous	
cul·mi·nate		curl	
cul·mi·nated		curled	

curl·ing	$\mathcal{crl}$	curves	$\mathcal{crvs}$
cur·ren·cies	$\mathcal{crNes}$	cush·ion	$\mathcal{cy}$
cur·rency	$\mathcal{crNe}$	cush·ioned	$\mathcal{cy}-$
cur·rent	$\mathcal{crN}$	cus·tard	$\mathcal{cSrd}$
cur·rently	$\mathcal{crNl}$	cus·to·dial	$\mathcal{cSdel}$
cur·rents	$\mathcal{crNs}$	cus·to·dian	$\mathcal{cSden}$
cur·ricula	$\mathcal{crcla}$	cus·to·di·ans	$\mathcal{cSdens}$
cur·ricu·lar	$\mathcal{crclr}$	cus·tody	$\mathcal{cSde}$
cur·ricu·lum	$\mathcal{crcl}$	cus·tom	$\mathcal{cS}$
cur·ricu·lums	$\mathcal{crcls}$	cus·tom·arily	$\mathcal{cSrl}$
curse	$\mathcal{crs}$	cus·tom·ary	$\mathcal{cSre}$
cur·sive	$\mathcal{crsv}$	cus·tomer	$\mathcal{K}$
cur·sor	$\mathcal{crsr}$	cus·tom·ers	$\mathcal{Ks}$
cur·sory	$\mathcal{crsre}$	cus·toms	$\mathcal{cSs}$
curt	$\mathcal{crl}$	cut	$\mathcal{cl}$
cur·tail	$\mathcal{crll}$	cut·back	$\mathcal{clbc}$
cur·tailed	$\mathcal{crll}-$	cut·backs	$\mathcal{clbcs}$
cur·tail·ment	$\mathcal{crllm}$	cute	$\mathcal{cu}$
cur·tail·ments	$\mathcal{crllms}$	cut·lery	$\mathcal{cllre}$
cur·tain	$\mathcal{crln}$	cut·off	$\mathcal{clof}$
cur·tains	$\mathcal{crlns}$	cut·offs	$\mathcal{clofs}$
cur·va·ture	$\mathcal{crvCr}$	cuts	$\mathcal{cls}$
curve	$\mathcal{crv}$	cut·ter	$\mathcal{clr}$

cut·ters	*clrs*	daft	*dfl*
cut·ting	*cl_*	da·guerreo·type	*dgrlp*
cya·nide	*sind*	dai·lies	*dls*
cycle	*scl*	daily	*dl*
cy·cled	*scl-*	dainty	*dNe*
cy·cles	*scls*	dair·ies	*dres*
cy·cli·cal	*sclcl*	dairy	*dre*
cyl·in·der	*slNr*	daisy	*dze*
cyl·in·ders	*slNrs*	dam	*d*
cynic	*snc*	dam·age	*d y*
cyn·ical	*sncl*	dam·aged	*d y-*
cy·press	*sprs*	dam·ages	*d ys*
cyst	*sß*	dam·ag·ing	*d y-*
cys·tic	*ssc*	dame	*d*
		damn	*d*
		damned	*d -*

D

		damp	*d p*
		dampen	*d pn*
		damper	*d pr*
		dams	*d s*
dab	*db*	dance	*dN*
dab·ble	*dß*	dancer	*dNr*
dad	*dd*	danc·ers	*dNrs*
daddy	*dde*		
daf·fo·dil	*dfdl*		
daf·fo·dils	*dfdls*		

dances	*dNs*	data	*dla*
danc·ing	*dN*	da·ta·base	*dlabs*
dan·druff	*dNrf*	da·ta·bases	*dlabss*
dandy	*dNe*	da·ta·link	*dlalq*
dan·ger	*dnjr*	da·ta·links	*dlalqs*
dan·ger·ous	*dnjrs*	da·ta·set	*dlasl*
dan·ger·ously	*dnjrsl*	da·ta·sets	*dlasls*
dan·gers	*dnjrs*	date	*da*
dan·gle	*dgl*	dated	*da-*
dare	*dr*	date·line	*daln*
dares	*drs*	dates	*das*
dar·ing	*dr*	dat·ing	*da*
dark	*drc*	datum	*dl*
darken	*drcn*	daugh·ter	*dlr*
darker	*drcr*	daughter-in-law	*dlr = n = la*
dark·ness	*drc'*	daugh·ters	*dlrs*
dark·room	*drcr*	daunt·less	*dNls*
dar·ling	*drlq*	dawn	*dn*
darn	*drn*	dawned	*dn-*
dart	*drl*	day	*d*
dash	*ds*	day·break	*dbrc*
dash·board	*dsbrd*	day·dream	*ddr*
dashed	*ds -*	day·dream·ing	*ddr*

day·light	*dli*	deals	*dls*
days	*ds*	dealt	*dlt*
day·time	*dt*	dean	*dn*
daze	*dz*	deans	*dns*
daz·zle	*dzl*	dear	*dr*
daz·zling	*dzl*	dearly	*drl*
dea·con	*dk*	dearth	*drt*
de·ac·ti·vate	*dacva*	death	*dt*
de·ac·ti·vated	*dacva-*	deathly	*dtl*
dead	*dd*	deaths	*dts*
dead·line	*ddln*	de·ba·cle	*dbcl*
dead·lines	*ddlns*	debar	*dbr*
dead·lock	*ddlc*	de·base	*dbs*
dead·locked	*ddlc-*	de·bat·able	*dbaß*
deadly	*ddl*	de·bate	*dba*
deaf	*df*	de·bated	*dba-*
deaf·ness	*df'*	de·bat·ing	*dba*
deal	*dl*	de·ben·ture	*dbnCr*
dealer	*dlr*	de·ben·tures	*dbnCrs*
deal·ers	*dlrs*	de·bili·tate	*dblla*
deal·er·ship	*dlrs*	de·bili·tated	*dblla-*
deal·ing	*dl*	debit	*dbl*
deal·ings	*dl*	deb·ited	*dbl-*

deb·it·ing	*dbl*	de·ceive	*dsv*
deb·its	*dbīs*	de·ceived	*dsv-*
de·bris	*dbre*	de·ceiv·ing	*dsv*
debt	*dl*	de·cel·era·tion	*dslrj*
debtor	*dlr*	December	*Dc*
debt·ors	*dlrs*	de·cency	*dsNe*
debts	*dls*	de·cent	*dsN*
debug	*dbq*	de·cen·tral·ized	*dsNlrz-*
de·bug·ging	*dbq_*	de·cen·tral·iz·ing	*dsNlrz_*
debut	*dbu*	de·cep·tion	*dspj*
dec·ade	*dcd*	de·cep·tive	*dspv*
dec·ades	*dcds*	de·ci·bel	*dsB*
decal	*dcl*	de·cide	*dsd*
de·cals	*dcls*	de·cided	*dsd-*
de·cant	*dcN*	de·cid·edly	*dsd-l*
de·canter	*dcNr*	de·cides	*dsds*
de·capi·tate	*dcpla*	de·cid·ing	*dsd_*
de·cath·lon	*dclln*	deci·mal	*ds—l*
decay	*dca*	deci·mals	*ds—ls*
de·ceased	*dss-*	de·ci·pher	*dsfr*
de·ce·dent	*dsdN*	de·ci·sion	*dsj*
de·ceit	*dse*	de·ci·sions	*dsjs*
de·ceit·ful	*dsef*	de·ci·sive	*dssv*

de·ci·sively	*dssvl*	deco·ra·tion	*dcry*
deck	*dc*	deco·ra·tions	*dcrys*
deck·ing	*dc_*	deco·ra·tive	*dcrv*
decks	*dcs*	deco·ra·tor	*dcrar*
dec·la·ra·tion	*dclry*	deco·rous	*dcrs*
dec·la·ra·tions	*dclrys*	deco·rum	*dcr*
de·clara·tory	*dclrtre*	decoy	*dcy*
de·clare	*dclr*	de·crease	*dcrs*
de·clared	*dclr-*	de·creased	*dcrs-*
de·clares	*dclrs*	de·creases	*dcrss*
de·clar·ing	*dclr_*	de·creas·ing	*dcrs_*
dec·li·na·tion	*dclny*	de·cree	*dcre*
de·cline	*dcln*	de·creed	*dcre-*
de·clined	*dcln-*	de·crees	*dcres*
de·clines	*dclns*	de·crimi·nal·iza·tion	*dcrmlzy*
de·clin·ing	*dcln_*	dedi·cate	*ddca*
de·code	*dcd*	dedi·cated	*ddca-*
de·com·pose	*dkpz*	dedi·ca·tion	*ddcy*
de·con·tami·nate	*dklma*	de·duct	*ddc*
decor	*dcr*	de·ducted	*ddc-*
deco·rate	*dcra*	de·duct·ibil·ity	*ddcßl*
deco·rated	*dcra-*	de·duct·ible	*ddcß*
deco·rat·ing	*dcra_*	de·duct·ibles	*ddcßs*

Word	Shorthand	Word	Shorthand
de·duct·ing	*ddc̲*	de·faults	*dflls*
de·duc·tion	*ddcy*	de·feat	*dfe*
de·duc·tions	*ddcys*	de·feated	*dfe-*
deed	*dd*	de·fect	*dfc*
deeds	*dds*	de·fec·tive	*dfcv*
deem	*d⌐*	de·fec·tor	*dfcr*
deemed	*d⌐-*	de·fects	*dfcs*
deems	*d⌐s*	de·fend	*dfn*
deep	*dp*	de·fen·dant	*dfnn*
deepen	*dpn*	de·fen·dants	*dfnns*
deeper	*dpr*	de·fended	*dfn-*
deep·est	*dps*	de·fender	*dfnr*
deeply	*dpl*	de·fend·ers	*dfnrs*
deer	*dr*	de·fend·ing	*dfn̲*
de-escalation	*descly*	de·fense	*dfn̄*
de·face	*dfs*	de·fenses	*dfns*
de·fac·ing	*dfs̲*	de·fen·si·ble	*dfnß*
de·fal·ca·tion	*dflcy*	de·fen·sive	*dfnv*
de·fal·ca·tions	*dflcys*	de·fen·sively	*dfnvl*
defa·ma·tion	*dfⴰy*	defer	*dfr*
de·fault	*dfll*	def·er·ence	*dfrn*
de·faulted	*dfll-*	de·fer·ment	*dfrm*
de·fault·ing	*dfll̲*	de·fer·ral	*dfrl*

de·ferred	*dfr-*	de·fla·tor	*dflar*
de·fer·ring	*dfr*	defog	*dfq*
de·fi·ance	*dfin*	de·form	*df*
de·fi·ant	*dfin*	de·for·ma·tion	*df⌐*
de·fi·cien·cies	*df∆nes*	de·for·ma·tions	*df⌐s*
de·fi·ciency	*df∆ne*	de·formed	*df-*
de·fi·cient	*dfsn*	de·form·ing	*df_*
defi·cit	*dfsl*	de·form·ity	*df‾ı*
defi·cits	*dfsls*	de·forms	*df⌐s*
de·fies	*dfis*	de·fraud	*dfrd*
de·file	*dfl*	de·fraud·ing	*dfrd_*
de·fin·able	*dfnB*	de·fray	*dfra*
de·fine	*dfn*	de·frost	*dfrS*
de·fined	*dfn-*	de·frosted	*dfrS-*
de·fines	*dfns*	de·funct	*dfq*
de·fin·ing	*dfn_*	defy	*dfi*
defi·nite	*dfnl*	de·gen·er·ate (v.)	*dgnra*
defi·nitely	*dfnll*	de·gen·er·ate (adj. or n.)	*dgnrl*
defi·ni·tion	*dfnɣ*	deg·ra·da·tion	*dgrdɣ*
defi·ni·tions	*dfnɣs*	de·grade	*dgrd*
de·fini·tive	*dfnv*	de·graded	*dgrd-*
de·fini·tively	*dfnvl*	de·grades	*dgrds*
de·fla·tion	*dflɣ*	de·greaser	*dgrsr*

de·gree	*dgre*	de·le·tion	*dly*
de·grees	*dgres*	de·le·tions	*dlys*
de·hu·midi·fi·ca·tion	*dh dfy*	de·lib·er·ate (adj.)	*dlbrl*
de·hy·drate	*dhdra*	de·lib·er·ate (v.)	*dlbra*
deify	*def*	de·lib·er·ately	*dlbrll*
deign	*dn*	de·lib·era·tion	*dlbry*
deity	*de^l*	de·lib·era·tions	*dlbrys*
de·jec·tion	*dycy*	deli·cacy	*dlcse*
delay	*dla*	deli·cate	*dlcl*
de·layed	*dla-*	deli·ca·tes·sen	*dlclsn*
de·lay·ing	*dla_*	de·li·cious	*dlss*
de·lays	*dlas*	de·light	*dli*
dele·gate (n.)	*dlgl*	de·lighted	*dli-*
dele·gate (v.)	*dlga*	de·light·ful	*dlf*
dele·gated	*dlga-*	de·lights	*dlis*
dele·gates (n.)	*dlgls*	de·line·ate	*dlna*
dele·gates (v.)	*dlgas*	de·line·ated	*dlna-*
dele·ga·tion	*dlgy*	de·line·at·ing	*dlna_*
de·lete	*dle*	de·line·ation	*dlney*
de·leted	*dle-*	de·lin·quen·cies	*dlg Nes*
dele·te·ri·ous	*dllres*	de·lin·quency	*dlg Ne*
de·letes	*dles*	de·lin·quent	*dlg N*
de·let·ing	*dle_*	de·liri·ous	*dllres*

de·lirium	*dlre*	de·mean	*d m*
de·liver	*dl*	de·meanor	*d mr*
de·liv·er·able	*dlß*	de·merit	*d rl*
de·liv·er·ance	*dlN*	de·min·er·al·izer	*dmrlzr*
de·liv·ered	*dl -*	de·mise	*d z*
de·liv·erer	*dlr*	de·mised	*d z-*
de·liv·er·ers	*dlrs*	demo	*d o*
de·liv·er·ies	*dles*	de·mo·bil·iza·tion	*d ßzl*
de·liv·er·ing	*dl*	de·moc·racy	*d vcrse*
de·liv·ers	*dls*	demo·crat	*d vcrl*
de·liv·ery	*dle*	Demo·crat	*d vcrl*
delta	*dlla*	demo·cratic	*d vcrlc*
de·lude	*dld*	Demo·crats	*d vcrls*
de·luge	*dlg*	de·modu·la·tors	*d glars*
de·lu·sion	*dlg*	demo·graphic	*d grfc*
de·luxe	*dlx*	demo·graph·ics	*d grfcs*
delve	*dlv*	de·mol·ish	*d ls*
de·mag·net·ize	*d gnlz*	de·mol·ished	*d ls-*
de·mand	*dm*	demo·li·tion	*d lg*
de·manded	*dm -*	demon	*dm*
de·mand·ing	*dm*	de·mon·stra·ble	*dmSrß*
de·mands	*dms*	de·mon·stra·bly	*dmSrß*
de·mar·ca·tion	*d rcy*	dem·on·strate	*dmSra*

dem·on·strated	*dmSra-*	den·ims	*dn s*
dem·on·strates	*dmSras*	de·nomi·na·tional	*dnmjl*
dem·on·strat·ing	*dmSra*	de·nomi·na·tor	*dnmar*
dem·on·stra·tion	*dmSry*	de·note	*dnl*
dem·on·stra·tions	*dmSrys*	de·notes	*dnls*
de·mon·stra·tive	*dmSrv*	de·not·ing	*dnl*
dem·on·stra·tor	*dmSrar*	de·nounce	*dnoN*
dem·on·stra·tors	*dmSrars*	dense	*dN*
de·mor·al·ize	*d rlz*	den·sity	*dNl*
de·mor·al·ized	*d rlz-*	dent	*dN*
de·mo·tion	*d y*	den·tal	*dNl*
de·mo·tions	*d ys*	dented	*dN-*
de·mount·able	*d oNB*	den·tist	*dNS*
demur	*d r*	den·tists	*dNSs*
de·mure	*d r*	den·ture	*dnCr*
de·mur·rage	*d ry*	den·tures	*dnCrs*
den	*dn*	deny	*dni*
de·nial	*dnil*	de·ny·ing	*dni*
de·ni·als	*dnils*	de·odor·ant	*dodrN*
de·nied	*dni-*	de·part	*dpl*
de·nier	*dnir*	de·parted	*dpl-*
de·nies	*dnis*	de·part·ing	*dpl*
denim	*dn*	de·part·ment	*dpl*

de·part·men·tal	*dptl*	de·pleted	*dple-*
de·part·men·tal·iza·tion	*dptlzj*	de·ple·tion	*dplj*
de·part·men·tal·ize	*dptllz*	de·plor·able	*dplrB*
de·part·men·tal·izes	*dptllzs*	de·ploy	*dply*
de·part·ments	*dpts*	de·ployed	*dply-*
de·parts	*dpts*	de·ploy·ment	*dplym*
de·par·ture	*dptr*	de·po·nent	*dpnN*
de·par·tures	*dptrs*	de·popu·la·tion	*dpplj*
de·pend	*dpN*	de·port	*dpt*
de·pend·able	*dpNB*	de·por·ta·tion	*dptj*
de·pend·ant	*dpNN*	de·por·ta·tions	*dptjs*
de·pend·ants	*dpNNs*	de·ported	*dpt-*
de·pended	*dpN-*	de·port·ing	*dpt̲*
de·pend·ence	*dpNN*	de·port·ment	*dptm*
de·pend·ency	*dpNNe*	de·ports	*dpts*
de·pend·ent	*dpNN*	de·pose	*dpz*
de·pend·ing	*dpN̄*	de·poses	*dpzs*
de·pends	*dpN̄s*	de·posit	*dpzt*
de·pict	*dpc*	de·pos·ited	*dpzt-*
de·picted	*dpc-*	de·pos·it·ing	*dpzt̲*
de·pict·ing	*dpc̲*	depo·si·tion	*dpzj*
de·picts	*dpcs*	depo·si·tions	*dpzjs*
de·plete	*dple*	de·posi·tor	*dpztr*

de·posi·to·ries	*dpztres*	de·regu·late	*drgla*
de·posi·tors	*dpztrs*	de·regu·lated	*drgla-*
de·posi·tory	*dpztre*	de·regu·la·tion	*drgly*
de·pos·its	*dpzts*	de·ride	*drd*
depot	*dpo*	de·rided	*drd-*
de·pre·cia·ble	*dprsB*	deri·va·tion	*drvy*
de·pre·ci·ate	*dprsa*	de·riva·tive	*drvv*
de·pre·ci·ated	*dprsa-*	de·riva·tives	*drvvs*
de·pre·cia·tion	*dprsey*	de·rive	*drv*
de·press	*dprs*	de·rived	*drv-*
de·pressed	*dprs-*	de·rives	*drvs*
de·press·ing	*dprs̲*	de·riv·ing	*drv̲*
de·pres·sion	*dpry*	de·roga·tory	*drgtre*
de·pres·sions	*dprys*	der·rick	*drc*
de·pres·sur·ize	*dprsrz*	de·scend	*dsN*
dep·ri·va·tion	*dprvy*	de·scen·dant	*dsNN*
de·prive	*dprv*	de·scender	*dsNr*
de·prived	*dprv-*	de·scend·ing	*dsN̲*
depth	*dpt*	de·scribe	*dS̄*
depths	*dpts*	de·scribed	*dS-*
depu·ties	*dptes*	de·scribes	*dSs*
deputy	*dpte*	de·scrib·ing	*dS̲*
de·rail·ment	*drlm*	de·scrip·tion	*dSy*

de·scrip·tions	*dSjs*	des·ig·nees	*dzgnes*
de·scrip·tive	*dSv*	de·signer	*dznr*
de·scrip·tor	*dSr*	de·sign·ers	*dznrs*
de·scrip·tors	*dSrs*	de·sign·ing	*dzn_*
des·ert (n.)	*dzrt*	de·signs	*dzns*
de·sert (v.)	*dzrt*	de·sir·abil·ity	*dzrβˡ*
de·serted	*dzrt-*	de·sir·able	*dzrβ*
de·ser·tion	*dzry*	de·sire	*dzr*
de·serve	*dzrv*	de·sired	*dzr-*
de·served	*dzrv-*	de·sires	*dzrs*
de·serves	*dzrvs*	de·sir·ing	*dzr_*
de·serv·ing	*dzrv_*	de·sir·ous	*dzrs*
des·ic·cate	*dsca*	de·sist	*dzs*
de·sign	*dzn*	desk	*dsc*
des·ig·nate (v.)	*dzgna*	desks	*dscs*
des·ig·nate (adj.)	*dzgnt*	deso·late (adj.)	*dsll*
des·ig·nated	*dzgna-*	deso·late (v.)	*dsla*
des·ig·nates	*dzgnas*	de·spair	*dspr*
des·ig·nat·ing	*dzgna_*	des·per·ate	*dsprt*
des·ig·na·tion	*dzgny*	des·per·ately	*dsprtl*
des·ig·na·tions	*dzgnjs*	des·pera·tion	*dspry*
de·signed	*dzn-*	des·pi·ca·ble	*dspcβ*
des·ig·nee	*dzgne*	de·spise	*dspz*

de·spite		de·tails	
de·spon·dent		de·tain	
des·pot		de·tainer	
des·potic		de·tain·ers	
des·sert		de·tain·ing	
des·serts		de·tect	
des·ti·na·tion		de·tect·able	
des·ti·na·tions		de·tected	
des·tine		de·tec·tion	
des·tined		de·tec·tive	
des·tiny		de·tec·tives	
des·ti·tute		de·tec·tor	
de·stroy		de·tec·tors	
de·stroyed		de·ten·tion	
de·stroy·ing		deter	
de·struc·tion		de·ter·gent	
de·struc·tive		de·te·rio·rate	
de·tach		de·te·rio·rated	
de·tached		de·te·rio·rates	
de·tach·ment		de·te·rio·rat·ing	
de·tail		de·te·rio·ra·tion	
de·tailed		de·ter·mi·nant	
de·tail·ing		de·ter·mi·na·tion	

de·ter·mi·na·tions	*dlys*	de·vel·op·ers	*dvrs*
de·ter·mine	*dl*	de·vel·op·ing	*dv̲*
de·ter·mined	*dl-*	de·vel·op·ment	*dvm*
de·ter·mines	*dls*	de·vel·op·men·tal	*dvml*
de·ter·min·ing	*dl̲*	de·vel·op·men·tally	*dvmll*
de·terred	*dlr-*	de·vel·op·ments	*dvms*
de·ter·rent	*dlrN*	de·vel·ops	*dvs*
de·test	*dlS*	de·vi·ate	*dva*
de·test·able	*dlSB*	de·via·tion	*dvej*
deto·na·tion	*dlny*	de·via·tions	*dvejs*
de·tour	*dlr*	de·vice	*dvs*
de·tract	*dlrc*	de·vices	*dvss*
de·trac·tion	*dlrcy*	devil	*dvl*
de·tracts	*dlrcs*	de·vi·ous	*dves*
det·ri·ment	*dlrm*	de·vise	*dvz*
det·ri·men·tal	*dlrml*	de·vised	*dvz-*
de·valu·ation	*dvluy*	de·vises	*dvzs*
dev·as·tate	*dvSa*	de·void	*dvyd*
dev·as·tat·ing	*dvSa̲*	de·vote	*dvo*
dev·as·ta·tion	*dvSy*	de·voted	*dvo-*
de·velop	*dv*	de·votes	*dvos*
de·vel·oped	*dv-*	de·vot·ing	*dvo̲*
de·vel·oper	*dvr*	de·vo·tion	*dvy*

de·vo·tional	*dvzl*	di·al·ing	*dil_*
de·vour	*dvor*	dia·logue	*dilg*
de·vout	*dvol*	dials	*dils*
dew	*du*	di·aly·sis	*dilss*
dex·ter·ity	*dxlz*	di·ame·ter	*di lr*
dia·be·tes	*dibls*	di·ame·ters	*di lrs*
dia·betic	*diblc*	dia·mond	*dmd*
dia·bet·ics	*diblcs*	dia·phragm	*difr*
di·ag·nose	*digns*	di·ar·rhea	*dira*
di·ag·nosed	*digns-*	diary	*dire*
di·ag·no·sis	*dignss*	dice	*ds*
di·ag·nos·tic	*dignSc*	diced	*ds-*
di·ag·nos·ti·cian	*dignSj*	dic·tate	*dcla*
di·ag·nos·tics	*dignScs*	dic·tated	*dcla-*
di·ago·nal	*dignl*	dic·tates	*dclas*
dia·gram	*dig*	dic·tat·ing	*dcla_*
dia·gram·matic	*diglc*	dic·ta·tion	*dclj*
dia·grams	*digs*	dic·ta·tor	*dclar*
dial	*dil*	dic·ta·tors	*dclars*
dia·lect	*dilc*	dic·tion	*dcj*
dia·lects	*dilcs*	dic·tion·ar·ies	*dcjres*
di·aled	*dil-*	dic·tion·ary	*dcjre*
di·aler	*dilr*	did	*dd*

didn't	*ddN*	dif·fer·ing	*dfr_*
die	*du*	dif·fers	*dfrs*
died	*du -*	dif·fi·cult	*dfc*
dies	*dus*	dif·fi·cul·ties	*dfces*
die·sel	*dsl*	dif·fi·culty	*dfce*
diet	*dul*	dif·fuse	*dfz*
die·tary	*dulre*	dif·fused	*dfz -*
die·tetic	*dullc*	dif·fuser	*dfzr*
die·tet·ics	*dullcs*	dif·fus·ers	*dfzrs*
die·ti·tian	*duly*	dif·fus·ing	*dfz -*
die·ti·tians	*dulys*	dif·fu·sion	*dfy*
diets	*duls*	dig	*dg*
dif·fer	*dfr*	di·gest	*dgs*
dif·fered	*dfr -*	di·ges·tion	*dgsy*
dif·fer·ence	*dfrN*	di·ges·tive	*dgsv*
dif·fer·ences	*dfrNs*	di·gests	*dgss*
dif·fer·ent	*dfrN*	dig·ging	*dg_*
dif·fer·en·tial	*dfrNsl*	digit	*dgl*
dif·fer·en·tials	*dfrNsls*	digi·tal	*dgll*
dif·fer·en·ti·ate	*dfrNsa*	digi·talis	*dglls*
dif·fer·en·ti·ated	*dfrNsa-*	dig·its	*dgls*
dif·fer·en·tia·tion	*dfrNsey*	dig·ni·tary	*dgnlre*
dif·fer·ently	*dfrNl*	dig·ni·tar·ies	*dgnlres*

dig·nity	*dgnle*	dine	*dn*
di·gress	*dgrs*	diner	*dnr*
di·gres·sion	*dgry*	din·ers	*dnrs*
dike	*dc*	dingy	*dnje*
di·lapi·dated	*dlpda-*	din·ing	*dn_*
di·late	*dla*	din·ner	*dnr*
di·lemma	*dl_a*	din·ners	*dnrs*
dili·gence	*dlyn*	din·ner·ware	*dnr_r*
dili·gent	*dlyn*	dino·saur	*dnsr*
dili·gently	*dlynl*	di·oce·san	*dessn*
di·lute	*dlu*	dio·cese	*diss*
di·lu·tion	*dly*	diode	*did*
dim	*d_*	di·ox·ide	*dxd*
dime	*d_*	dip	*dp*
di·men·sion	*dmy*	diph·the·ria	*dflra*
di·men·sional	*dmyl*	di·ploma	*dpl_a*
di·men·sions	*dmys*	di·plo·macy	*dpl_se*
di·min·ish	*dms*	di·plo·mas	*dpl_as*
di·min·ished	*dms-*	dip·lo·mat	*dpl_l*
di·min·ish·ing	*dms_*	dip·lo·matic	*dpl_lc*
di·min·ish·ment	*dmsm*	dip·lo·mat·ically	*dpl_lcl*
dimly	*d_l*	dipped	*dp-*
din	*dn*	dip·ping	*dp_*

dips	*dps*	dis·abil·ity	*DBᶜ*
dire	*dr*	dis·able	*DB*
di·rect	*dr*	dis·abled	*DB-*
di·rected	*dr-*	dis·ables	*DBs*
di·rect·ing	*dr̲*	dis·abling	*DB̲*
di·rec·tion	*dry*	dis·ad·van·tage	*Davy*
di·rec·tional	*dryl*	dis·ad·van·taged	*Davy-*
di·rec·tions	*drys*	dis·ad·van·tages	*Davys*
di·rec·tive	*drv*	dis·agree	*Dagre*
di·rec·tives	*drvs*	dis·agree·able	*DagreB*
di·rectly	*drl*	dis·agreed	*Dagre-*
di·rec·tor	*drr*	dis·agree·ment	*Dagrem*
di·rec·tor·ate	*drrl*	dis·agree·ments	*Dagrems*
di·rec·tor·ates	*drrls*	dis·agrees	*Dagres*
di·rec·to·ries	*drres*	dis·al·low	*Dalo*
di·rec·tors	*drrs*	dis·al·low·ance	*DaloN*
di·rec·tor·ship	*drrʃ*	dis·al·lowed	*Dalo-*
di·rec·tor·ships	*drrʃs*	dis·ap·pear	*Dapr*
di·rec·tory	*drre*	dis·ap·pear·ance	*DaprN*
di·rects	*drs*	dis·ap·peared	*Dapr-*
dirt	*drl*	dis·ap·pears	*Daprs*
dirty	*drle*	dis·ap·point	*Dapy*
dis·abil·ities	*DBᶫs*	dis·ap·pointed	*Dapy-*

dis·ap·point·ing	*Dapy_*	dis·bursed	*Dbrs-*
dis·ap·point·ment	*Dapym*	dis·burse·ment	*Dbrsm*
dis·ap·point·ments	*Dapyms*	dis·burse·ments	*Dbrsms*
dis·ap·proval	*Dapvl*	dis·burs·ing	*Dbrs_*
dis·ap·prove	*Dapv*	disc	*Dc*
dis·ap·proved	*Dapv-*	dis·card	*Dcrd*
dis·ap·proves	*Dapvs*	dis·carded	*Dcrd-*
dis·ap·prov·ing	*Dapv_*	dis·cern	*Drn*
dis·arm	*Dar*	dis·cerned	*Drn-*
dis·ar·ray	*Dara*	dis·charge	*DCj*
dis·as·sem·ble	*Das B*	dis·charged	*DCj-*
dis·as·sem·bled	*Das B-*	dis·charges	*DCjs*
dis·as·sem·bly	*Das B*	dis·charg·ing	*DCj_*
dis·as·so·ci·ate	*Daso*	dis·ci·ple	*dspl*
dis·as·ter	*dzSr*	dis·ci·ples	*dspls*
dis·as·ters	*dzSrs*	dis·ci·ple·ship	*dsplf*
dis·as·trous	*dzSrs*	dis·ci·pli·nary	*Dplnre*
dis·band	*DbN*	dis·ci·pline	*Dpln*
dis·banded	*DbN-*	dis·ci·plined	*Dpln-*
dis·bar	*Dbr*	dis·ci·plines	*Dplns*
dis·be·lief	*Dblf*	dis·ci·plin·ing	*Dpln_*
dis·be·lieve	*Dblv*	dis·claimer	*Dclr*
dis·burse	*Dbrs*	dis·claim·ers	*Dclrs*

dis·close	*Dclz*	dis·count	*Dk*
dis·closed	*Dclz-*	dis·counted	*Dk-*
dis·closes	*Dclzs*	dis·counter	*Dkr*
dis·clos·ing	*Dclz_*	dis·count·ers	*Dkrs*
dis·clo·sure	*Dclzr*	dis·count·ing	*Dk_*
dis·clo·sures	*Dclzrs*	dis·counts	*Dks*
disco	*Dco*	dis·cour·age	*Dcry*
dis·color	*Dclr*	dis·cour·aged	*Dcry-*
dis·col·ored	*Dclr-*	dis·cour·ages	*Dcrys*
dis·com·fort	*Dkfl*	dis·course	*Dcrs*
dis·com·forts	*Dkfls*	dis·cour·te·ous	*Dcrtes*
dis·con·nect	*Dkc*	dis·cover	*Dcvr*
dis·con·nected	*Dkc-*	dis·cov·ered	*Dcvr-*
dis·con·nect·ing	*Dkc_*	dis·cov·er·ies	*Dcvres*
dis·con·nec·tion	*Dkcy*	dis·cov·er·ing	*Dcvr_*
dis·con·nects	*Dkcs*	dis·cov·ers	*Dcvrs*
dis·con·tent	*DklM*	dis·cov·ery	*Dcvre*
dis·con·tinu·ance	*DkuM*	dis·credit	*Dcr*
dis·con·tinue	*Dku*	dis·cred·ited	*Dcr-*
dis·con·tin·ued	*Dku-*	dis·creet	*Dcre*
dis·con·tinu·ing	*Dku_*	dis·creetly	*Dcrel*
dis·con·ti·nu·ity	*Dku'*	dis·crep·an·cies	*DcrpMes*
dis·cord	*Dcrd*	des·crep·ancy	*DcrpMe*

dis·crete	*Dcre*	dis·guise	*Dgz*
dis·cre·tion	*Dcry*	dis·gust	*DgS*
dis·cre·tion·ary	*Dcryre*	dis·gusted	*DgS-*
dis·crimi·nant	*DcrmN*	dish	*dA*
dis·crimi·nate	*Dcrma*	dis·hearten	*DhrLn*
dis·crimi·nates	*Dcrmas*	dis·heart·en·ing	*DhrLn_*
dis·crimi·na·tion	*Dcrmy*	dished	*dA-*
dis·crimi·na·tive	*Dcrmav*	dishes	*dAs*
dis·crimi·na·tory	*Dcrmlre*	dis·hon·est	*DonS*
dis·cuss	*Dcs*	dis·honor	*Donr*
dis·cussed	*Dcs-*	dis·hon·ored	*Donr-*
dis·cusses	*Dcss*	dish·washer	*dA Ar*
dis·cuss·ing	*Dcs_*	dish·wash·ers	*dA Ars*
dis·cus·sion	*Dcy*	dis·il·lu·sion	*Dily*
dis·cus·sions	*Dcys*	dis·il·lu·sioned	*Dily-*
dis·ease	*dzz*	dis·in·cen·tive	*Dnsnv*
dis·eased	*dzz-*	dis·in·cen·tives	*Dnsnvs*
dis·eases	*dzzs*	dis·in·fect	*Dnfc*
dis·fa·vor	*Dfvr*	dis·in·fected	*Dnfc-*
dis·fig·ure·ment	*Dfgrm*	dis·in·herit	*Dnhrl*
dis·grace	*Dgrs*	dis·in·te·grate	*DNgra*
dis·grun·tle	*DgrNl*	dis·in·te·gra·tion	*DNgry*
dis·grun·tled	*DgrNl-*	dis·in·ter·est	*DNS*

dis·in·ter·ested		dis·missed	
dis·join		dis·misses	
dis·junc·tive		dis·obe·di·ence	
disk		dis·obey	
disk·ette		dis·or·der	
disks		dis·or·derly	
dis·like		dis·or·ders	
dis·likes		dis·or·gan·iza·tion	
dis·lo·cate		dis·or·gan·ize	
dis·lo·cat·ing		dis·or·gan·ized	
dis·lo·ca·tion		dis·own	
dis·lo·ca·tions		dis·par·ities	
dis·loyal		dis·par·ity	
dis·mal		dis·patch	
dis·man·tle		dis·patched	
dis·man·tle·ment		dis·patcher	
dis·may		dis·patch·ing	
dis·mem·ber		dis·pel	
dis·mem·bered		dis·pen·sary	
dis·mem·ber·ment		dis·pense	
dis·miss		dis·pensed	
dis·missal		dis·penser	
dis·miss·als		dis·pens·ing	

dis·per·sal	$\mathcal{Dprsl}$	dis·pose	$\mathcal{Dpz}$
dis·perse	$\mathcal{Dprs}$	dis·posed	$\mathcal{Dpz}-$
dis·persed	$\mathcal{Dprs}-$	dis·pos·ing	$\mathcal{Dpz}\_$
dis·perser	$\mathcal{Dprsr}$	dis·po·si·tion	$\mathcal{Dpzl}$
dis·pers·ers	$\mathcal{Dprsrs}$	dis·po·si·tions	$\mathcal{Dpzjs}$
dis·pers·ing	$\mathcal{Dprs}\_$	dis·pro·por·tion	$\mathcal{DPpry}$
dis·per·sion	$\mathcal{Dpry}$	dis·pro·por·tion·ate	$\mathcal{DPpryl}$
dis·place	$\mathcal{Dpls}$	dis·prove	$\mathcal{Dpv}$
dis·placed	$\mathcal{Dpls}-$	dis·proved	$\mathcal{Dpv}-$
dis·place·ment	$\mathcal{Dplsm}$	dis·proves	$\mathcal{Dpvs}$
dis·place·ments	$\mathcal{Dplsms}$	dis·pute	$\mathcal{Dpu}$
dis·play	$\mathcal{Dpla}$	dis·puted	$\mathcal{Dpu}-$
dis·played	$\mathcal{Dpla}-$	dis·putes	$\mathcal{Dpus}$
dis·player	$\mathcal{Dplar}$	dis·put·ing	$\mathcal{Dpu}$
dis·play·ing	$\mathcal{Dpla}\_$	dis·quali·fi·ca·tion	$\mathcal{Dqlfj}$
dis·plays	$\mathcal{Dplas}$	dis·quali·fied	$\mathcal{Dqlf}-$
dis·please	$\mathcal{Dp}$	dis·qualify	$\mathcal{Dqlf}$
dis·pleased	$\mathcal{Dp}-$	dis·quali·fy·ing	$\mathcal{Dqlf}\_$
dis·pleases	$\mathcal{Dps}$	dis·re·gard	$\mathcal{Dre}$
dis·pleas·ure	$\mathcal{Dplzr}$	dis·re·garded	$\mathcal{Dre}-$
dis·pos·able	$\mathcal{Dpz\beta}$	dis·re·gard·ing	$\mathcal{Dre}\_$
dis·pos·ables	$\mathcal{Dpz\beta s}$	dis·re·gards	$\mathcal{Dres}$
dis·posal	$\mathcal{Dpzl}$	dis·re·pair	$\mathcal{Drpr}$

dis·re·spect	*Drspc*	dis·solve	*dzlv*
dis·rupt	*Drpt*	dis·solved	*dzlv-*
dis·rupt·ing	*Drpt_*	dis·solv·ing	*dzlv_*
dis·rup·tion	*Drpj*	dis·taff	*Dtf*
dis·rup·tions	*Drpjs*	dis·tance	*Dtn*
dis·rup·tive	*Drpv*	dis·tances	*Dtns*
dis·sat·is·fac·tion	*Dsatj*	dis·tant	*Dtn*
dis·sat·is·fied	*Dsat-*	dis·taste·ful	*Dtsf*
dis·sect	*dsc*	dis·tem·per	*Dt_pr*
dis·sem·ble	*D-B*	dis·ten·tion	*Dtnj*
dis·semi·nate	*D-na*	dis·till	*Dtl*
dis·semi·nated	*D-na-*	dis·til·late	*Dtla*
dis·semi·nat·ing	*D-na_*	dis·til·la·tion	*Dtlj*
dis·semi·na·tion	*D-nj*	dis·tilled	*Dtl-*
dis·sen·sion	*Dnj*	dis·tiller	*Dtlr*
dis·sent	*DN*	dis·tinct	*Dtq*
dis·ser·ta·tion	*Drtj*	dis·tinc·tion	*Dtqj*
dis·serv·ice	*DSvo*	dis·tinc·tions	*Dtqjs*
dis·simi·lar	*D-lr*	dis·tinc·tive	*Dtqv*
dis·si·pate	*Dpa*	dis·tinctly	*Dtql*
dis·si·pated	*Dpa-*	dis·tin·guish	*Dtq- 4*
dis·si·pa·tion	*Dpj*	dis·tin·guished	*Dtq- 4-*
dis·so·lu·tion	*Dlj*	dis·tin·guish·ing	*Dtq- 4_*

dis·tort	*Dtrt*	dis·tur·bances	*Dtrbns*
dis·torted	*Dtrt-*	dis·turbed	*Dtrb-*
dis·tor·tion	*Dtry*	dis·turb·ing	*Dtrb_*
dis·tor·tions	*Dtrys*	dis·use	*Dus*
dis·torts	*Dtrts*	ditch	*dC*
dis·tract	*Dtrc*	ditches	*dCs*
dis·tress	*Dtrs*	dither	*dtr*
dis·tressed	*Dtrs-*	ditto	*dto*
dis·trib·ut·able	*DB*	dive	*dv*
dis·trib·ute	*D*	di·verge	*dvry*
dis·trib·uted	*D-*	di·verg·ing	*dvry_*
dis·trib·utes	*Ds*	di·verse	*dvrs*
dis·trib·ut·ing	*D_*	di·ver·si·fi·ca·tion	*dvrsfy*
dis·tri·bu·tion	*Dy*	di·ver·si·fi·ca·tions	*dvrsfys*
dis·tri·bu·tions	*Dys*	di·ver·si·fied	*dvrsf-*
dis·tribu·tive	*Dv*	di·ver·sify	*dvrsf*
dis·tribu·tor	*Dr*	di·ver·sion	*dvry*
dis·tribu·tors	*Drs*	di·ver·sity	*dvrs'*
dis·tribu·tor·ship	*Drs*	di·vert	*dvrt*
dis·trict	*Dtrc*	di·verted	*dvrt-*
dis·tricts	*Dtrcs*	di·vert·ing	*dvrt_*
dis·turb	*Dtrb*	dives	*dvs*
dis·tur·bance	*DtrbN*	di·vest	*dv8*

di·vide	dvd	do	du
di·vided	$dvd-$	doc·ile	dsl
divi·dend	$dvdN$	dock	dc
divi·dends	$dvdNs$	docket	dcl
di·vider	$dvdr$	dock·eted	$dcl-$
di·vid·ers	$dvdrs$	dock·ets	$dcls$
di·vides	$dvds$	dock·ing	$dc\underline{\ }$
di·vid·ing	$dvd\underline{\ }$	docks	dcs
di·vine	dvn	dock·side	$dcsd$
div·ing	$dv\underline{\ }$	doc·tor	dr
di·vin·ity	dvn^l	doc·toral	drl
di·vis·ibil·ity	$dvz\beta^l$	doc·tor·ate	drl
di·vis·ible	$dvz\beta$	doc·tored	$dr-$
di·vi·sion	$dv\gamma$	doc·tor·ing	$dr\underline{\ }$
di·vi·sional	$dv\gamma l$	doc·tors	drs
di·vi·sions	$dv\gamma s$	doc·tri·nal	$dclrnl$
di·vi·sive·ness	$dvsv\,'$	doc·trine	$dclrn$
di·vi·sor	$dvzr$	doc·trines	$dclrns$
di·vorce	$dvrs$	docu·ment	dcm
di·vorces	$dvrss$	docu·men·tary	$dcmre$
di·vulge	$dvl\gamma$	docu·men·ta·tion	$dcm\gamma$
diz·zi·ness	$dze\,'$	docu·mented	$dcm-$
dizzy	dze	docu·ment·ing	$dcm\underline{\ }$

docu·ments	*dcms*	domi·nant	*dmN*
dodge	*dj*	domi·nate	*dma*
does	*dz*	domi·na·tion	*dmy*
doesn't	*dzN*	don	*dn*
dog	*dg*	do·nate	*dna*
dog·house	*dghos*	do·nated	*dna-*
dogma	*dg a*	do·nat·ing	*dna_*
dog·matic	*dg lc*	do·na·tion	*dny*
dogs	*dgs*	do·na·tions	*dnys*
doing	*du_*	done	*dn*
do·ings	*du_*	donor	*dnr*
dole	*dl*	do·nors	*dnrs*
dole·ful	*dlf*	don't	*dN*
doll	*dl*	doom	*d*
dol·lar	*$*	door	*dr*
dol·lars	*$*	doors	*drs*
do·main	*d m*	door·way	*dr a*
dome	*d*	dor·mant	*dr N*
do·mes·tic	*d Sc*	dor·mi·tory	*dr lre*
do·mes·ti·cally	*d Scl*	dos·age	*dsy*
do·mes·ti·cated	*d Sca-*	dos·ages	*dsys*
domi·cile	*d sl*	dose	*ds*
domi·ciled	*d sl-*	dot	*dl*

do·tage	*doɣ*	down·graded	*dongrd-*
dote	*do*	down·grad·ing	*dongrd_*
dots	*dᴸs*	down·hill	*donhl*
dou·ble	*dℬ*	down·pour	*donpr*
dou·bled	*dℬ-*	down·right	*donᵣᵢ*
dou·bles	*dℬs*	downs	*dons*
dou·bling	*dℬ_*	down·side	*donsd*
dou·bly	*dℬ*	down·stairs	*donᔕrs*
doubt	*dol*	down·stream	*donᔕr*
doubted	*dol-*	down·time	*dont*
doubt·ful	*dolɣ*	down·town	*donton*
doubt·less	*dolls*	down·turn	*dontrn*
doubts	*dols*	down·ward	*donw*
dough	*do*	dozen	*dzn*
dough·nut	*donl*	doz·ens	*dzns*
dough·nuts	*donls*	draft	*drfl*
dove	*dv*	drafted	*drfl-*
doves	*dvs*	draft·ing	*drfl_*
dower	*doɣ*	drafts	*drfls*
down	*don*	drag	*drg*
down·cast	*doncᔕ*	dragged	*drg-*
downed	*don-*	dragon	*drgn*
down·fall	*donfl*	drag·ons	*drgns*

drain	*drn*	draw	*dra*
drain·age	*drny*	draw·back	*drabc*
drained	*drn-*	draw·backs	*drabcs*
drain·ing	*drn_*	draw·bridge	*drabry*
drains	*drns*	drawer	*drar*
drama	*dr͜a*	draw·ing	*dra_*
dra·matic	*dr͜tc*	draw·ings	*dra͇*
dra·mat·ically	*dr͜tcl*	drawn	*drn*
drama·tist	*dr͜tS*	draws	*dras*
drama·tists	*dr͜tSs*	dread	*drd*
drama·ti·za·tion	*dr͜tzy*	dread·ful	*drdf*
drama·ti·za·tions	*dr͜tzys*	dream	*dr͜*
drama·tize	*dr͜tz*	dreamed	*dr͜-*
drama·tized	*dr͜tz-*	dreamer	*dr͜r*
drank	*drq*	dreams	*dr͜s*
drape	*drp*	dreary	*drre*
draped	*drp-*	drench	*drnC*
drap·er·ies	*drpres*	drenched	*drnC-*
drap·ery	*drpre*	dress	*drs*
drapes	*drps*	dressed	*drs-*
drap·ing	*drp_*	dresses	*drss*
dras·tic	*drSc*	dress·ing	*drs_*
dras·ti·cally	*drScl*	dress·ings	*drs͇*

drew	*dru*	drive·ways	*drv as*
dried	*dri-*	driv·ing	*drv_*
drier	*drir*	drone	*drn*
drift	*drft*	drool	*drl*
drill	*drl*	drool·ing	*drl_*
drilled	*drl-*	droop	*drp*
driller	*drlr*	drop	*drp*
drill·ers	*drlrs*	drop·let	*drpll*
drill·ing	*drl_*	drop·out	*drpol*
drill·ings	*drl_*	dropped	*drp-*
drills	*drls*	drop·ping	*drp_*
drink	*drq*	drops	*drps*
drink·able	*drqß*	drought	*drol*
drinker	*drqr*	drove	*drv*
drink·ing	*drq_*	drown	*dron*
drinks	*drqs*	drow·si·ness	*droze'*
dripped	*drp-*	drowsy	*droze*
drive	*drv*	drudg·ery	*dryre*
driven	*drvn*	drug	*drq*
driver	*drvr*	drug·gist	*drqß*
driv·ers	*drvrs*	drugs	*drqs*
drives	*drvs*	drug·store	*drqßr*
drive·way	*drv a*	drum	*dr*

drum·mer		dumped	
drums		dump·ing	
drunk		dun	
drunk·en·ness		dun·geon	
dry		dun·geons	
dryer		dunk	
dry·ers		dupe	
dry·ing		du·plex	
dry·ness		du·pli·cate (adj. or n.)	
dual		du·pli·cate (v.)	
du·bi·ous		du·pli·cated	
duck		du·pli·cates (n.)	
duct		du·pli·cates (v.)	
ducts		du·pli·cat·ing	
due		du·pli·ca·tion	
duel		du·pli·ca·tions	
dues		du·pli·ca·tor	
dug		du·pli·ca·tors	
dull		du·plic·ity	
duly		du·ra·bil·ity	
dumb		du·ra·ble	
dummy		du·ra·bles	
dump		du·ra·tion	

du·ra·tions	*drys*
dur·ing	*du̱*
dusk	*dsc*
dust	*dS*
dusted	*dS-*
dust·ing	*dS̱*
dusts	*dŠs*
dusty	*dSe*
du·ties	*dles*
du·ti·ful	*dlef*
duty	*dle*
dwarf	*drf*
dwell	*dl*
dwelled	*dl-*
dweller	*dlr*
dwell·ers	*dlrs*
dwell·ing	*dḻ*
dwell·ings	*dḻ=*
dwin·dle	*dnl*
dye	*du*
dyed	*du-*
dyes	*dus*
dye·stuff	*duSf*

dying	*du̱*
dy·namic	*dn c*
dy·nam·ics	*dn cs*
dy·nasty	*dnSe*
dys·en·tery	*Dntre*
dys·func·tion	*Dfq1*
dys·func·tional	*Dfqsl*

E

each	*eC*
eager	*egr*
ea·gerly	*egrl*
ea·ger·ness	*egr'*
eagle	*egl*
ear	*er*
ear·ache	*erac*
ear·drum	*erdr*
ear·lier	*erlr*
ear·li·est	*erlS*
early	*erl*
ear·mark	*er rc*
ear·marked	*er rc-*

earn	*ern*	easi·est	*ezes*
earned	*ern-*	easily	*ezl*
earner	*erns*	eas·ing	*ez-*
earn·ers	*ernrs*	east	*E*
ear·nest	*erns*	Easter	*Er*
ear·nestly	*ernsl*	east·erly	*Erl*
earn·ing	*ern*	east·ern	*Ern*
earn·ings	*ern*	east·ward	*Ew*
earns	*erns*	easy	*eze*
ear·ring	*errq*	easy·go·ing	*ezeq-*
ears	*ers*	eat	*el*
ear·shot	*ersl*	eaten	*eln*
earth	*erl*	eater	*elr*
earthly	*erll*	eat·ing	*el*
earth·quake	*erlqc*	eats	*els*
earth·quakes	*erlqcs*	ebb	*eb*
ease	*ez*	ebony	*ebne*
eased	*ez-*	ec·cen·tric	*Nrc*
easel	*ezl*	eche·lon	*esln*
ease·ment	*ezm*	echo	*eco*
ease·ments	*ezms*	eclipse	*eclps*
eases	*ezs*	eco·log·ical	*eclycl*
easier	*ezer*	eco·log·ically	*eclycll*

ecology	*eclje*	edit	*edl*
eco·nomic	*eco*	ed·ited	*edl-*
eco·nom·ical	*ecol*	ed·it·ing	*edl*
eco·nom·ically	*ecoll*	edi·tion	*edj*
eco·nom·ics	*ecos*	edi·tions	*edjs*
econo·mies	*ecos*	edi·tor	*edlr*
econo·mist	*ecoS*	edi·to·rial	*edlrel*
econo·mists	*ecoSs*	edi·to·ri·als	*edlrels*
econo·mizer	*ecozr*	edi·tors	*edlrs*
econo·miz·ers	*ecozrs*	edits	*edls*
econo·miz·ing	*ecoz-*	edu·ca·ble	*ejcB*
economy	*eco*	edu·cate	*ejca*
ec·stasy	*Vse*	edu·cated	*ejca-*
ec·static	*Vllc*	edu·cat·ing	*ejca*
ecu·men·ical	*ecmcl*	edu·ca·tion	*ejcj*
ec·zema	*a*	edu·ca·tional	*ejcjl*
eddy	*ede*	edu·ca·tions	*ejcjs*
edema	*ed a*	edu·ca·tor	*ejcar*
edge	*ej*	edu·ca·tors	*ejcars*
edged	*ej-*	ef·fect	*efc*
edges	*ejs*	ef·fected	*efc-*
ed·ible	*edB*	ef·fect·ing	*efc*
edi·fi·ca·tion	*edfj*	ef·fec·tive	*efcv*

ef·fec·tively	*efcvl*	egg·plant	*egplN*
ef·fec·tive·ness	*efcv'*	eggs	*egs*
ef·fects	*efcs*	ego	*eq*
ef·fec·tual	*efcCul*	ego·tis·ti·cal	*eglScl*
ef·fec·tu·ated	*efcCa-*	egress	*egrs*
ef·femi·nate	*efml*	eight	*8*
ef·fer·ves·cent	*efrvsN*	eight·een	*18*
ef·fi·ca·ciously	*efcAsl*	eighth	*8L*
ef·fi·cacy	*efcse*	eight·ies	*80s*
ef·fi·cien·cies	*efsNes*	eighty	*80*
ef·fi·ciency	*efsNe*	ei·ther	*elr*
ef·fi·cient	*efsN*	eject	*eyc*
ef·fi·ciently	*efsNl*	ejec·tion	*eycy*
ef·figy	*efje*	eject·ment	*eycm*
ef·flu·ent	*efluN*	eke	*ec*
ef·fort	*efl*	elabo·rate (adj.)	*elbrl*
ef·forts	*efls*	elabo·rate (v.)	*elbra*
ef·front·ery	*efrNre*	elabo·rated	*elbra-*
ef·fu·sive	*efsv*	elabo·rately	*elbrll*
e.g.	*eq*	elabo·rates	*elbras*
egg	*eq*	elapse	*elps*
egg·head	*eghd*	elapsed	*elps-*
egg·nog	*egnq*	elas·tic	*elSc*

elate	
elated	
elbow	
el·bows	
elder	
eld·erly	
elect	
elected	
elect·ing	
elec·tion	
elec·tions	
elec·tive	
elec·tives	
elec·tor	
elec·toral	
elec·tors	
elec·tric	
elec·tri·cal	
elec·tri·cally	
elec·tri·cian	
elec·tri·cians	
elec·tric·ity	
elec·tri·fi·ca·tion	
elec·trify	
elec·tro·car·dio·gram	
elec·tro·cute	
elec·trode	
elec·trodes	
elec·tro·dy·nam·ics	
elec·tro·lyte	
elec·tro·mag·netic	
elec·tro·me·chan·ical	
elec·tron	
elec·tronic	
elec·tron·ically	
elec·tron·ics	
elec·tro·plat·ing	
elec·tro·scope	
elec·tro·static	
elects	
ele·gant	
ele·gantly	
ele·ment	
ele·men·tal	
ele·men·tary	
ele·ments	

ele·phant	*elfN*	elon·gated	*elga-*
ele·phants	*elfNs*	elon·ga·tion	*elgj*
ele·vate	*elva*	elope	*elp*
ele·vated	*elva-*	elo·quent	*elqN*
ele·va·tion	*elvj*	else	*els*
ele·va·tions	*elvjs*	else·where	*els r*
ele·va·tor	*elvar*	elu·sive	*elsv*
ele·va·tors	*elvars*	ema·ci·ate	*e Aa*
elicit	*elsl*	ema·ci·ated	*e Aa-*
elic·ited	*elsl-*	ema·nate	*na*
elic·it·ing	*elsl_*	ema·nat·ing	*na_*
eli·gi·bil·ity	*eljß'*	eman·ci·pate	*e Npa*
eli·gi·ble	*eljß*	eman·ci·pated	*e Npa-*
elimi·nate	*elma*	eman·ci·pa·tion	*e Npj*
elimi·nated	*elma-*	emas·cu·late	*e scla*
elimi·nates	*elmas*	em·balm	*b*
elimi·nat·ing	*elma_*	em·bank·ment	*bqm*
elimi·na·tion	*elmj*	embar	*br*
elimi·na·tive	*elmav*	em·bargo	*brq*
elite	*ele*	em·bar·goes	*brqs*
el·lip·sis	*elpss*	em·bark	*brc*
el·lip·ti·cal	*elplcl*	em·barked	*brc-*
elm	*el*	em·bar·rass	*brs*

em·bar·rassed	_brs-_	em·er·ald	_rld_
em·bar·rass·ing	_brs_	emerge	_ry_
em·bar·rass·ment	_brsm_	emerged	_ry-_
em·bar·ring	_br_	emer·gen·cies	_ryNes_
em·bassy	_bse_	emer·gency	_ryNe_
em·bel·lish	_bls_	emer·gent	_ryN_
ember	_br_	emerg·ing	_ry_
em·bers	_brs_	emeri·tus	_rts_
em·bez·zle	_bzl_	emi·grant	_grN_
em·blem	_bl_	emi·gra·tion	_gry_
em·blems	_bls_	emi·nent	_nN_
em·bod·ied	_bde-_	emi·nently	_nNl_
em·bodi·ment	_bdem_	emis·sion	_y_
em·body	_bde_	emis·sions	_ys_
em·boss	_bs_	emit	_l_
em·bossed	_bs-_	emit·ting	_l_
em·brace	_brs_	emolu·ment	_lm_
em·braced	_brs-_	emolu·ments	_lms_
em·brit·tle	_brll_	emo·tion	_y_
em·brit·tled	_brll-_	emo·tional	_yl_
em·broi·der	_brydr_	emo·tion·ally	_yll_
em·broil	_bryl_	emo·tions	_ys_
em·bryo	_bro_	em·pa·thy	_ple_

em·peror	*prr*	em·pow·er·ing	*por*
em·pha·ses	*fsz*	emp·tied	*le-*
em·pha·sis	*fss*	emp·ties	*les*
em·pha·size	*fsz*	empty	*le*
em·pha·sized	*fsz-*	emp·ty·ing	*le*
em·pha·sizes	*fszs*	emu·late	*la*
em·pha·siz·ing	*fsz-*	emul·si·fied	*e lsf-*
em·phatic	*flc*	emul·sify	*e lsf*
em·pire	*pr*	emul·sion	*e ly*
em·pir·ical	*prcl*	en·able	*nß*
em·piri·cism	*prsz*	en·abled	*nß-*
em·ploy	*p*	en·ables	*nßs*
em·ploy·able	*pß*	en·abling	*nß*
em·ployed	*p-*	enact	*nac*
em·ployee	*pe*	en·acted	*nac-*
em·ploy·ees	*pes*	en·act·ing	*nac*
em·ployer	*pr*	en·act·ment	*nacm*
em·ploy·ers	*prs*	en·amel	*en l*
em·ploy·ing	*p-*	en·am·el·ing	*en l*
em·ploy·ment	*pm*	en·case	*ncs*
em·ploys	*ps*	en·cased	*ncs-*
em·power	*por*	en·chant	*nCN*
em·pow·ered	*por-*	en·chant·ment	*nCNm*

en·cir·cle	_nScl_	en·cour·ages	_ncrys_
en·clave	_nclv_	en·cour·ag·ing	_ncry_
en·close	_enc_	en·croach	_ncrC_
en·closed	_enc-_	en·croach·ment	_ncrCm_
en·closes	_encs_	en·cum·ber	_nkbr_
en·clos·ing	_enc_	en·cum·bered	_nkbr-_
en·clo·sure	_enc_	en·cum·brance	_nkbrN_
en·clo·sures	_encs_	en·cum·brances	_nkbrNs_
en·code	_ncd_	en·cy·clo·pe·dia	_nsclpda_
en·coded	_ncd-_	en·cy·clo·pe·dic	_nsclpdc_
en·cod·ing	_ncd_	end	_n_
en·com·pass	_nkps_	en·dan·ger	_ndnjr_
en·com·passed	_nkps-_	en·dan·gered	_ndnjr-_
en·com·passes	_nkpss_	en·dear	_ndr_
en·com·pass·ing	_nkps_	en·dear·ing	_ndr_
en·core	_ancr_	en·deavor	_ndvr_
en·coun·ter	_nkr_	en·deav·or·ing	_ndvr_
en·coun·tered	_nkr-_	en·deav·ors	_ndvrs_
en·coun·ter·ing	_nkr_	ended	_n-_
en·coun·ters	_nkrs_	end·ing	_n_
en·cour·age	_ncry_	end·less	_nls_
en·cour·aged	_ncry-_	en·dorse	_ndrs_
en·cour·age·ment	_ncrym_	en·dorsed	_ndrs-_

en·dorse·ment	*ndrsm*	en·gage	*ngs*
en·dorse·ments	*ndrsms*	en·gaged	*ngs-*
en·dorser	*ndrsr*	en·gage·ment	*ngsm*
en·dorses	*ndrss*	en·gage·ments	*ngsms*
en·dow·ment	*ndom*	en·gages	*ngss*
ends	*Ns*	en·gag·ing	*ngs_*
en·dur·ance	*ndrN*	en·gen·der	*nyNr*
en·dured	*ndr-*	en·gen·dered	*nyNr-*
ene·mies	*n es*	en·gine	*nyn*
enemy	*n e*	en·gi·neer	*nynr*
en·er·getic	*nrgtc*	en·gi·neered	*nynr-*
en·er·gies	*nrges*	en·gi·neer·ing	*nynr_*
en·er·gize	*nryz*	en·gi·neers	*nynrs*
en·er·gized	*nryz-*	en·gines	*nyns*
en·er·giz·ing	*nryz_*	English	*egls*
en·ergy	*nrye*	en·grave	*ngrv*
en·force	*nfs*	en·graved	*ngrv-*
en·force·able	*nfsB*	en·grav·ing	*ngrv_*
en·forced	*nfs-*	en·gross	*ngrs*
en·force·ment	*nfsm*	en·grossed	*ngrs-*
en·forces	*nfss*	en·gulf	*nglf*
en·forc·ing	*nfs_*	en·gulfed	*nglf-*
en·fran·chise	*nfrnCz*	en·hance	*nhN*

en·hanced	*nhN-*	en·listed	*nlS-*
en·hance·ment	*nhNm*	en·list·ing	*nlS_*
en·hance·ments	*nhNms*	en·lists	*nlSs*
en·hances	*nhNs*	en·liven	*nlvn*
en·hanc·ing	*nhN_*	en·mity	*n~le*
en·join	*nyyn*	enor·mous	*enr~s*
en·joined	*nyyn-*	enor·mously	*enr~sl*
en·join·ing	*nyyn_*	enough	*enf*
enjoy	*nyy*	en·rage	*nry*
en·joy·able	*nyyB*	en·rich	*nrC*
en·joyed	*nyy-*	en·riched	*nrC-*
en·joy·ing	*nyy_*	en·rich·ing	*nrC_*
en·joy·ment	*nyym*	en·rich·ment	*nrCm*
en·joys	*nyys*	en·roll	*nrl*
en·large	*nlry*	en·rolled	*nrl-*
en·larged	*nlry-*	en·rollee	*nrle*
en·large·ment	*nlrym*	en·roll·ees	*nrles*
en·larg·ing	*nlry_*	en·roll·ing	*nrl_*
en·lighten	*nlin*	en·roll·ment	*nrlm*
en·light·ened	*nlin-*	en·roll·ments	*nrlms*
en·light·en·ing	*nlin_*	en·rolls	*nrls*
en·light·en·ment	*nlinm*	en route	*n ru*
en·list	*nlS*	en·sem·ble	*ans~B*

en·sign	*Nn*	en·ter·tain·ment	*Nlnm*
ensue	*nsu*	en·thuse	*nlz*
en·sued	*nsu-*	en·thused	*nlz-*
en·sues	*nsus*	en·thu·si·asm	*nlzez*
en·su·ing	*nsu*	en·thu·si·as·tic	*nlzeSc*
en·sure	*nAr*	en·thu·si·as·ti·cally	*nlzeScl*
en·sures	*nArs*	en·tice	*nls*
en·sur·ing	*nAr*	en·tire	*nlr*
en·tail	*nll*	en·tirely	*nlrl*
en·tails	*nlls*	en·tirety	*nlr*
en·tan·gle·ment	*nlglm*	en·ti·ties	*N*
en·tan·gle·ments	*nlglms*	en·ti·tle	*nlll*
enter	*N*	en·ti·tled	*nlll-*
en·tered	*N-*	en·ti·tle·ment	*nlllm*
en·ter·ing	*N*	en·ti·tle·ments	*nlllms*
en·ter·prise	*Nprz*	en·ti·tles	*nllls*
en·ter·prises	*Nprzs*	en·tity	*Nl*
en·ter·pris·ing	*Nprz-*	en·to·molo·gist	*Nlys*
en·ters	*Ns*	en·to·mology	*Nlye*
en·ter·tain	*Nln*	en·trance (n.)	*NrN*
en·ter·tained	*Nln-*	en·trance (v.)	*nlrN*
en·ter·tainer	*Nlnr*	en·trances (n.)	*NrNs*
en·ter·tain·ing	*Nln*	en·trances (v.)	*nlrNs*

en·trant	*Nrʃ*	en·vi·ron·ment	*nvrnm*
en·tree	*antra*	en·vi·ron·men·tal	*nvrnml*
en·trees	*antras*	en·vi·ron·men·tally	*nvrnmll*
en·trench	*nlrnC*	en·vi·ron·ments	*nvrnms*
en·trenched	*nlrnC-*	en·vi·rons	*nvrns*
en·tre·pre·neur	*anlrprnr*	en·vi·sion	*nvj*
en·tre·pre·neurs	*anlrprnrs*	en·vi·sioned	*nvj-*
en·tries	*Nres*	en·vi·sions	*nvjs*
en·trust	*nlr8*	envoy	*nvy*
en·trusted	*nlr8-*	envy	*nve*
en·trust·ing	*nlr8_*	en·zyme	*nz*
entry	*Nre*	epic	*epc*
en·try·way	*Nre a*	epi·demic	*epdc*
enu·mer·able	*en rB*	epi·dem·ics	*epdcs*
enu·mer·ate	*en ra*	epi·lepsy	*eplpse*
enu·mer·ated	*en ra-*	epi·logue	*eplq*
enu·mera·tion	*en ry*	epis·co·pal	*epscpl*
enun·ci·ate	*enNa*	epi·sode	*epsd*
en·ve·lope	*env*	epi·taph	*eplf*
en·ve·lopes	*envs*	epitome	*epte*
en·vied	*nve-*	equal	*eql*
en·vi·ous	*nves*	equaled	*eql-*
en·vi·ron	*nvrn*	equal·ity	*eql*

equal·iza·tion	*eqlz*	equiva·lent	*eqvlN*
equal·ize	*eqlz*	equiva·lents	*eqvlNs*
equal·iz·ing	*eqlz_*	equivo·cal	*eqvcl*
equally	*eqll*	equivo·cate	*eqvca*
equals	*eqls*	era	*era*
equate	*eqa*	eradi·cate	*erdca*
equated	*eqa-*	eradi·cat·ing	*erdca_*
equates	*eqas*	eradi·ca·tion	*erdcy*
equa·tion	*eqy*	erase	*ers*
equa·tions	*eqys*	eraser	*ersr*
equa·tor	*eqar*	eras·ers	*ersrs*
equi·lat·eral	*eqltrl*	erases	*erss*
equi·lib·rium	*eqlbre*	era·sure	*ersr*
equip	*eqp*	era·sures	*ersrs*
equip·ment	*eqpm*	ere	*er*
equipped	*eqp-*	erect	*erc*
equip·ping	*eqp_*	erected	*erc-*
eq·ui·ta·ble	*eqlB*	erect·ing	*erc_*
eq·ui·ta·bly	*eqlB*	erec·tion	*ercy*
eq·ui·ties	*eqles*	erode	*erd*
eq·uity	*eqle*	eroded	*erd-*
equiva·len·cies	*eqvlNes*	ero·sion	*ery*
equiva·lency	*eqvlNe*	erotic	*erlc*

err	*er*	es·chewed	*esCu-*
er·rand	*erN*	es·cort	*escrt*
er·rands	*erNs*	es·corted	*escrt-*
er·rant	*erN*	es·crow	*escro*
er·ratic	*ertc*	es·crows	*escros*
er·ro·ne·ous	*ernes*	esopha·gus	*esfgs*
er·ro·ne·ously	*ernesl*	es·pe·cially	*esp*
error	*err*	es·pio·nage	*espenz*
er·rors	*errs*	es·pouse	*espoz*
erupt	*erpl*	es·pous·ing	*espoz-*
erup·tion	*erpj*	es·prit de corps	*espre d cr*
erup·tions	*erpjs*	es·quire	*esq*
es·ca·late	*escla*	essay	*esa*
es·ca·lated	*escla-*	es·sence	*esN*
es·ca·lates	*esclas*	es·sen·tial	*esnsl*
es·ca·lat·ing	*escla_*	es·sen·tially	*esnsll*
es·ca·la·tion	*esclj*	es·sen·tials	*esnsls*
es·ca·la·tions	*escljs*	es·tab·lish	*esl*
es·ca·la·tor	*esclar*	es·tab·lished	*esl-*
es·cape	*escp*	es·tab·lishes	*esls*
es·capee	*escpe*	es·tab·lish·ing	*esl_*
es·cap·ees	*escpes*	es·tab·lish·ment	*eslm*
es·chew	*esCu*	es·tab·lish·ments	*eslms*

es·tate	*eSa*	eter·nal	*etrnl*
es·tates	*eSas*	ethic	*etc*
es·teem	*eS*	eth·ical	*etcl*
es·thetic	*esttc*	eth·ics	*etcs*
es·ti·mate (v.)	*eS a*	eth·nic	*etnc*
es·ti·mate (n.)	*eS l*	eth·nic·ity	*etns*
es·ti·mated	*eS a-*	eth·yl·ene	*elln*
es·ti·mates (v.)	*eS as*	etio·log·ical	*etelycl*
es·ti·mates (n.)	*eS ls*	eu·logy	*ulje*
es·ti·mat·ing	*eS a*	eu·phe·mism	*uf z*
es·ti·ma·tion	*eS y*	eu·pho·ria	*ufa*
es·ti·ma·tor	*eS ar*	Europe	*urp*
es·ti·ma·tors	*eS ars*	evacu·ate	*evca*
estop	*eSp*	evacu·ated	*evca-*
es·topped	*eSp-*	evacu·ation	*evcuy*
es·top·pel	*eSpl*	evade	*evd*
es·trange	*eSrny*	evalu·ate	*evla*
es·tranged	*eSrny-*	evalu·ated	*evla-*
es·tro·gen	*eSryn*	evalu·ates	*evlas*
etc.	*etc*	evalu·at·ing	*evla*
et cet·era	*etc*	evalu·ation	*evluy*
etch	*eC*	evalu·ations	*evluys*
etch·ing	*eC*	evalu·ative	*evlav*

evalu·ator	*evlar*	ev·er·greens	*Egrns*
evalu·ators	*evlars*	ev·er·last·ing	*Els*
evan·gel·ism	*evnjlz*	ev·er·last·ingly	*Elsl*
evan·gel·ists	*evnjlss*	ev·er·more	*E*
evapo·rate	*evpra*	every	*E*
evapo·rated	*evpra-*	eve·ry·body	*Ebde*
evapo·ra·tor	*evprar*	eve·ry·day	*Ed*
evapo·ra·tors	*evprars*	eve·ry·one	*El*
eva·sion	*evj*	eve·ry·thing	*E*
eva·sive	*evsv*	eve·ry·where	*Er*
eve	*ev*	evict	*evc*
even	*evn*	evic·tion	*evcj*
eve·ning	*evn*	evic·tions	*evcjs*
eve·nings	*evn*	evi·dence	*evdN*
evenly	*evnl*	evi·denced	*evdN-*
evens	*evns*	evi·dences	*evdNs*
event	*evN*	evi·denc·ing	*evdN*
event·ful	*evNf*	evi·dent	*evdN*
events	*evNs*	evi·dently	*evdNl*
even·tual	*evNCul*	evil	*evl*
even·tu·ally	*evNCull*	evoke	*evc*
ever	*E*	evoked	*evc-*
ev·er·green	*Egrn*	evo·lu·tion	*evlj*

evo·lu·tion·ary	
evolve	
evolved	
evolv·ing	
exact	
ex·act·ing	
ex·actly	
ex·ag·ger·ate	
ex·ag·ger·ated	
exalt	
ex·alted	
exam	
ex·ami·na·tion	
ex·ami·na·tions	
ex·am·ine	
ex·am·ined	
ex·am·iner	
ex·am·in·ers	
ex·am·ines	
ex·am·in·ing	
ex·am·ple	
ex·am·ples	
exams	

ex·as·per·ate	
ex·as·per·ated	
ex·ca·vate	
ex·ca·vated	
ex·ca·vat·ing	
ex·ca·va·tion	
ex·ceed	
ex·ceeded	
ex·ceed·ing	
ex·ceed·ingly	
ex·ceeds	
excel	
ex·cel·lence	
ex·cel·lent	
ex·cels	
ex·cept	
ex·cepted	
ex·cept·ing	
ex·cep·tion	
ex·cep·tional	
ex·cep·tion·ally	
ex·cep·tions	
ex·cerpt	

ex·cerpts	*rpls*	ex·clud·ing	*vcld_*
ex·cess	*vs*	ex·clu·sion	*vcly*
ex·cesses	*vss*	ex·clu·sions	*vclys*
ex·ces·sive	*vsv*	ex·clu·sive	*vclsv*
ex·ces·sively	*vsvl*	ex·clu·sively	*vclsvl*
ex·change	*vCny*	ex·clu·sive·ness	*vclsv'*
ex·change·able	*vCnyß*	ex·clu·siv·ity	*vclsv ͷ*
ex·changed	*vCny-*	ex·cru·ci·ate	*vcrsa*
ex·changer	*vCnyr*	ex·cru·ci·at·ing	*vcrsa_*
ex·chang·ers	*vCnyrs*	ex·cur·sion	*vcry*
ex·changes	*vCnys*	ex·cur·sions	*vcrys*
ex·cise	*v3*	ex·cus·able	*vczß*
ex·ci·sion	*vsy*	ex·cuse (v.)	*vcz*
ex·cit·able	*vß*	ex·cuse (n.)	*vcs*
ex·cite	*vl*	ex·cused	*vcz-*
ex·cited	*vl -*	ex·cuses (v.)	*vczs*
ex·cite·ment	*vlm*	ex·cuses (n.)	*vcss*
ex·cit·ing	*vl_*	ex·cus·ing	*vcz_*
ex·claim	*vcl*	exe·cute	*vcu*
ex·cla·ma·tion	*vcly*	exe·cuted	*vcu-*
ex·clude	*vcld*	exe·cutes	*vcus*
ex·cluded	*vcld-*	exe·cut·ing	*vcu_*
ex·cludes	*vclds*	exe·cu·tion	*vcy*

ex·ecu·tive	*ex*	ex·hausted	*S-*
ex·ecu·tives	*exs*	ex·haust·ing	*S_*
ex·ecu·tor	*clr*	ex·haus·tion	*Sq*
ex·ecu·tors	*clrs*	ex·haus·tive	*Sv*
ex·ecu·tory	*clre*	ex·hibit	*bl*
ex·ecu·trix	*clrx*	ex·hib·ited	*bl-*
ex·em·plary	*plre*	ex·hib·it·ing	*bl_*
ex·em·plify	*plfi*	ex·hi·bi·tion	*by*
ex·empt	*l*	ex·hi·bi·tions	*bys*
ex·empted	*l-*	ex·hibi·tor	*blr*
ex·emp·tion	*q*	ex·hibi·tors	*blrs*
ex·emp·tions	*ys*	ex·hib·its	*bls*
ex·empts	*ls*	ex·hila·rate	*lra*
ex·er·cise	*rsz*	ex·hila·rat·ing	*lra_*
ex·er·cised	*rsz-*	ex·hort	*rl*
ex·er·cises	*rszs*	ex·horts	*rls*
ex·er·cis·ing	*rsz_*	exile	*l*
exert	*rl*	exist	*S*
ex·erted	*rl-*	ex·isted	*S-*
ex·ert·ing	*rl_*	ex·is·tence	*SN*
ex·er·tion	*ry*	ex·is·tent	*SN*
ex·hale	*hl*	ex·ist·ing	*S_*
ex·haust	*S*	ex·ists	*Ss*

exit		ex·pe·di·ently	
ex·ited		ex·pe·dite	
ex·it·ing		ex·pe·dited	
exits		ex·pe·dit·ing	
ex·or·bi·tant		ex·pe·di·tious	
ex·otic		ex·pe·di·tiously	
ex·pand		ex·pe·di·tor	
ex·pand·able		expel	
ex·panded		ex·pelled	
ex·pand·ing		ex·pend	
ex·pands		ex·pend·able	
ex·pan·sion		ex·pended	
ex·pan·sive		ex·pend·ing	
ex parte		ex·pen·di·ture	
ex·pect		ex·pen·di·tures	
ex·pec·tancy		ex·pense	
ex·pec·tant		ex·pensed	
ex·pec·ta·tion		ex·penses	
ex·pec·ta·tions		ex·pens·ing	
ex·pected		ex·pen·sive	
ex·pect·ing		ex·pe·ri·ence	
ex·pects		ex·pe·ri·enced	
ex·pe·di·ent		ex·pe·ri·ences	

Word	Shorthand	Word	Shorthand
ex·pe·ri·enc·ing	✓p_	ex·pla·na·tion	✓plnɋ
ex·peri·ment	✓prm	ex·pla·na·tions	✓plnɋs
ex·peri·men·tal	✓prml	ex·plana·tory	✓plntre
ex·peri·men·tally	✓prmll	ex·ple·tive	✓plv
ex·peri·men·ta·tion	✓prmɋ	ex·plicit	✓plst
ex·peri·mented	✓prm–	ex·plic·itly	✓plstl
ex·peri·ment·ing	✓prm_	ex·plic·it·ness	✓plst´
ex·peri·ments	✓prms	ex·plode	✓pld
ex·pert	✓prt	ex·ploded	✓pld–
ex·per·tise	✓prts	ex·ploit	✓plyt
ex·pertly	✓prtl	ex·ploi·ta·tion	✓plytɋ
ex·perts	✓prts	ex·ploited	✓plyt–
ex·pi·ra·tion	✓prɋ	ex·ploits	✓plyts
ex·pira·tory	✓prtre	ex·plo·ra·tion	✓plrɋ
ex·pire	✓pr	ex·plora·tory	✓plrtre
ex·pired	✓pr–	ex·plore	✓plr
ex·pires	✓prs	ex·plored	✓plr–
ex·pir·ing	✓pr_	ex·plorer	✓plrr
ex·piry	✓pre	ex·plor·ers	✓plrrs
ex·plain	✓pln	ex·plor·ing	✓plr_
ex·plained	✓pln–	ex·plo·sion	✓plɋ
ex·plain·ing	✓pln_	ex·plo·sive	✓plsv
ex·plains	✓plns	ex·po·nent	✓pnN

ex·port	↗pt	ex·press·ways	↗prs as
ex·ported	↗pt–	ex·pul·sion	↗plg
ex·port·ers	↗ptrs	ex·qui·site	↗qzt
ex·port·ing	↗pt_	ex·tem·po·ra·ne·ous	↗t prnes
ex·ports	↗pts	ex·tend	↗n
ex·pose	↗pз	ex·tended	↗n–
ex·posé	↗pзa	ex·tend·ing	↗n_
ex·posed	↗pз–	ex·tends	↗ñs
ex·pos·ing	↗pз_	ex·ten·sion	↗ng
ex·po·si·tion	↗pзj	ex·ten·sions	↗ngs
ex·po·si·tions	↗pзjs	ex·ten·sive	↗nv
ex·po·sure	↗pзr	ex·ten·sively	↗nvl
ex·po·sures	↗pзrs	ex·tent	↗n
ex·pound	↗poɴ	ex·tenu·ate	↗na
ex·press	↗prs	ex·tenu·at·ing	↗na_
ex·pressed	↗prs–	ex·te·rior	↗rer
ex·presses	↗prss	ex·ter·mi·nate	↗rma
ex·press·ing	↗prs_	ex·ter·mi·nat·ing	↗rma_
ex·pres·sion	↗prg	ex·ter·mi·na·tion	↗rmg
ex·pres·sions	↗prgs	ex·ter·mi·na·tor	↗rmar
ex·pres·sive	↗prsv	ex·ter·nal	↗rnl
ex·pressly	↗prsl	ex·ter·nally	↗rnll
ex·press·way	↗prs a	ex·tinct	↗q

ex·tinc·tion		ex·tremely	
ex·tin·guish		ex·tremes	
ex·tin·guished		ex·trem·ist	
ex·tin·guisher		ex·trem·ities	
ex·tin·guish·ers		ex·trem·ity	
ex·tor·tion		ex·tri·cate	
extra		ex·trin·sic	
ex·tract		ex·tro·vert	
ex·tracted		ex·trud·able	
ex·tra·cur·ricu·lar		ex·truded	
ex·tra·dite		ex·tru·sion	
ex·tra·di·tion		exu·ber·ant	
ex·tra·mu·ral		eye	
ex·tra·ne·ous		eye·brow	
ex·traor·di·narily		eye·brows	
ex·traor·di·nary		eye·glass	
ex·trapo·late		eye·glasses	
ex·trapo·lated		eye·lash	
ex·tras		eye·let	
ex·tra·sen·sory		eye·lets	
ex·tra·ter·ri·to·rial		eye·lid	
ex·trava·gance		eyes	
ex·treme		eye·sight	

eye·sore	
eye·sores	

F

fable	
fab·ric	
fab·ri·cate	
fab·ri·cated	
fab·ri·cat·ing	
fab·ri·ca·tion	
fab·ri·ca·tions	
fab·ri·ca·tor	
fab·ri·ca·tors	
fab·rics	
fa·cade	
fa·cades	
face	
faced	
faces	
facet	
fa·ce·tious	
fac·ets	

fa·cial	
fa·cili·tate	
fa·cili·tated	
fa·cili·tates	
fa·cili·tat·ing	
fa·cili·ta·tion	
fa·cili·ta·tor	
fa·cil·ities	
fa·cil·ity	
fac·ing	
fac·ings	
fac·simile	
fact	
fac·tion	
fac·tor	
fac·tored	
fac·to·ries	
fac·tors	
fac·tory	
facts	
fac·tual	
fac·ul·ties	
fac·ulty	

fad	*fd*	fake	*fc*
fade	*fd*	fak·ing	*fc̄*
faded	*fd-*	fall	*fl*
Fahrenheit	*frnht*	fal·lacy	*flse*
fail	*fl*	fallen	*fln*
failed	*fl-*	fall·ing	*fl̄*
fail·ing	*fl̄*	fall·out	*flot*
fails	*fls*	falls	*fls*
fail·ure	*flr*	false	*fls*
fail·ures	*flrs*	false·hood	*flsh*
faint	*fm*	fal·si·fi·ca·tion	*flsf*
faint·ing	*fm*	fal·si·fied	*flsf-*
faintly	*fm̄l*	fal·sify	*flsf*
fair	*fr*	fal·ter	*fltr*
fairly	*frl*	fame	*f*
fair·ness	*fr'*	fa·mil·iar	*flr*
fairs	*frs*	fa·mil·iar·ity	*flr'*
fair·way	*fra*	fa·mil·iar·iza·tion	*lrz*
faith	*fl*	fa·mil·iar·ize	*lrz*
faith·ful	*flf*	fami·lies	*ls*
faith·fully	*flfl*	family	*l*
faith·ful·ness	*flf'*	fam·ine	*fm*
faiths	*fls*	fa·mous	*fs*

fan	*fn*	farm·stead	*fr͞sd*
fa·natic	*fnlc*	far·see·ing	*frse͟*
fan·ci·ful	*fNef*	far·sighted	*frsi-*
fancy	*fNe*	far·ther	*frlr*
fan·fare	*fnfr*	far·thest	*frlS*
fang	*fg*	fas·ci·nate	*fsna*
fans	*fns*	fas·ci·nates	*fsnas*
fan·tas·tic	*fnlSc*	fas·ci·nat·ing	*fsna͟*
fan·tasy	*fNse*	fas·ci·na·tion	*fsnj*
far	*fr*	fash·ion	*bj*
far·away	*fra a*	fash·ion·able	*bjß*
farce	*frs*	fash·ioned	*bj-*
fare	*fr*	fash·ions	*bjs*
fared	*fr-*	fast	*fS*
fares	*frs*	fas·ten	*fsn*
fare·well	*frl*	fas·tened	*fsn-*
far·ing	*fr͟*	fas·tener	*fsnr*
farm	*fr⁀*	fas·ten·ers	*fsnrs*
farmer	*fr⁀r*	faster	*fSr*
farm·ers	*fr⁀rs*	fast·est	*fSS*
farm·house	*fr⁀hos*	fas·tidi·ous	*fSdes*
farm·ing	*fr⁀͟*	fat	*fl*
farms	*fr⁀s*	fatal	*fll*

fa·tal·ities	*fllᵇ*	fa·vor·able	*fvrB*
fa·tal·ity	*fllⁱ*	fa·vor·ably	*fvrB*
fa·tally	*flll*	fa·vored	*fvr-*
fate	*fa*	fa·vor·ing	*fvr_*
fate·ful	*faf*	fa·vor·ite	*fvrl*
fa·ther	*flr*	fa·vor·ites	*fvrlo*
father-in-law	*flr = n = la*	fa·vors	*fvro*
fa·thers	*flrs*	fawn	*fn*
fa·tigue	*flg*	faze	*bz*
fa·tigu·ing	*flg_*	fear	*fr*
fats	*fls*	feared	*fr-*
fatu·ous	*fcus*	fear·ful	*frf*
fau·cet	*fsl*	fear·ing	*fr_*
fau·cets	*fslo*	fears	*frs*
fault	*fll*	fea·si·bil·ity	*bzBⁱ*
faulted	*fll-*	fea·si·ble	*bzB*
fault·ing	*fll_*	fea·si·bly	*bzB*
fault·less	*fllls*	feast	*fS*
faults	*flls*	feat	*fe*
faulty	*flle*	feather	*flr*
fauna	*fna*	feath·ers	*flrs*
faux pas	*fo pa*	feath·er·weight	*flr_a*
favor	*fvr*	fea·ture	*fCr*

fea·tured		feel·ing	
fea·tures		feel·ings	
fea·tur·ing		feels	
February		fees	
fed		feet	
fed·eral		fell	
fed·er·al·ist		fel·low	
fed·er·al·ize		fel·lows	
fed·er·ally		fel·low·ship	
fed·er·ate		fel·low·ships	
fed·er·ated		felo·nies	
fed·era·tion		fe·lo·ni·ous	
fee		felony	
fee·ble		felt	
feed		fe·male	
feed·back		fe·males	
feeder		femi·nine	
feed·ers		femi·nin·ity	
feed·ing		femo·ral	
feed·ings		femur	
feeds		fence	
feel		fenced	
feeler		fences	

fenc·ing	*fn̄*	fes·tive	*fsv*
fend	*fn̄*	fes·tiv·ities	*fsvls*
fender	*fnr*	fes·tiv·ity	*fsvl*
fer·ment	*frm*	fetal	*fll*
fer·men·ta·tion	*frmy*	fete	*fe*
fern	*frn*	fet·ish	*fls*
ferns	*frns*	fetus	*fls*
fe·ro·cious	*frss*	fe·tuses	*flss*
fe·roc·ity	*frsl*	fever	*fvr*
fer·ret	*frl*	fe·vers	*fvrs*
fer·ret·ing	*frl*	few	*fu*
fer·rous	*frs*	fewer	*fur*
fer·rule	*frl*	few·est	*fus*
fer·rules	*frls*	fi·ancé	*fensa*
ferry	*fre*	fi·ancée	*fensa*
fer·tile	*frll*	fi·asco	*fesco*
fer·til·ity	*frlll*	fib	*fb*
fer·til·iza·tion	*frllzy*	fiber	*fbr*
fer·til·ize	*frllz*	fi·ber·glass	*fbrgls*
fer·til·ized	*frllz-*	fi·bers	*fbrs*
fer·til·izer	*frllzr*	fib·ril·la·tion	*fbrly*
fer·vor	*frvr*	fic·tion	*fcy*
fes·ti·val	*fsvl*	fic·ti·tious	*fclss*

fid·dle	*fdl*	fig·ura·tive	*fgrv*
fi·del·ity	*fdl'*	fig·ure	*fgr*
fidget	*fjt*	fig·ured	*fgr-*
fi·du·ci·ary	*fdsere*	fig·ures	*fgrs*
field	*fld*	fig·ur·ing	*fgr_*
fielded	*fld-*	fila·ment	*flm*
field·ing	*fld_*	fila·ments	*flms*
fields	*flds*	file	*fl*
fiend	*fN*	filed	*fl-*
fierce	*frs*	fil·ers	*flrs*
fiercely	*frsl*	files	*fls*
fiery	*fre*	fili·bus·ter	*flbSr*
fif·teen	*15*	fil·ing	*fl_*
fifth	*5L*	fil·ings	*fl=*
fif·ti·eth	*50L*	fill	*fl*
fifty	*50*	filled	*fl-*
fig	*fg*	filler	*flr*
fight	*ft*	fil·let	*fla*
fighter	*ftr*	fil·lets	*flas*
fight·ers	*ftrs*	fill·ing	*fl_*
fight·ing	*ft_*	fill·ings	*fl=*
fig·ment	*fgm*	fills	*fls*
figs	*fgs*	film	*fl*

Word	Outline	Word	Outline
filmed		fi·nanced	
film·ing		fi·nances	
films		fi·nan·cial	
film·strip		fi·nan·cially	
film·strips		fin·an·cier	
fil·ter		fi·nanc·ing	
fil·tered		find	
fil·ter·ing		finder	
fil·ters		find·ing	
filth		find·ings	
filthy		finds	
fil·tra·tion		fine	
fin		fined	
final		finely	
fi·nal·ist		finer	
fi·nal·ists		fines	
fi·nal·ity		fin·est	
fi·nal·iza·tion		fin·ger	
fi·nal·ize		fin·ger·print	
fi·nal·ized		fin·ger·prints	
fi·nal·iz·ing		fin·gers	
fi·nally		fin·ger·tip	
fi·nance		fin·ger·tips	

fin·ish	_fns_	firm	_fr_
fin·ished	_fns-_	firmed	_fr-_
fin·ishes	_fnss_	firmer	_frr_
fin·ish·ing	_fns_	firm·est	_frs_
fi·nite	_fni_	firm·ing	_fr-_
fins	_fns_	firmly	_frl_
fir	_fr_	firm·ness	_fr'_
fire	_fr_	firms	_frs_
fire·arm	_frar_	first	_frs_
fire·arms	_frars_	first·hand	_frshn_
fire·cracker	_frcrcr_	firstly	_frsl_
fire·crack·ers	_frcrcrs_	fis·cal	_fscl_
fired	_fr-_	fish	_fs_
fire·man	_frn_	fish·er·ies	_fsres_
fire·men	_frm_	fish·er·man	_fsrn_
fire·place	_frpls_	fish·er·men	_fsrm_
fire·places	_frplss_	fish·ery	_fsre_
fire·proof	_frprf_	fishes	_fss_
fire·proof·ing	_frprf-_	fish·hook	_fshc_
fires	_frs_	fish·ing	_fs-_
fire·side	_frsd_	fis·sion	_fsn_
fire·works	_froo_	fis·sure	_fsr_
fir·ing	_fr-_	fist	_fs_

fists	*fss*	flags	*flgs*
fis·tula	*fsCla*	flair	*flr*
fit	*fl*	flake	*flc*
fit·ness	*fl'*	flakes	*flcs*
fits	*fls*	flam·boy·ant	*fl byN*
fit·ted	*fl-*	flame	*fl*
fit·ting	*fl̲*	flam·ing	*fl_*
fit·tings	*fl̲̲*	flam·ma·bil·ity	*fl Bl*
five	*5*	flam·ma·ble	*fl B*
five·fold	*5 fld*	flam·ma·bles	*fl Bs*
fix	*fx*	flange	*flng*
fixa·tion	*fxy*	flanges	*flngs*
fixed	*fx-*	flank	*flq*
fix·ers	*fxrs*	flan·nel	*flnl*
fixes	*fxs*	flap	*flp*
fix·ing	*fx_*	flare	*flr*
fix·ture	*fxCr*	flared	*flr-*
fix·tures	*fxCrs*	flash	*fls*
fiz·zle	*fzl*	flasher	*flsr*
flag	*flq*	flashes	*flss*
flag·ging	*flq_*	flash·ing	*fls*
fla·grant	*flgrN*	flash·ings	*fls̲*
fla·grantly	*flgrNl*	flash·light	*flsli*

flashy	*flse*	flex·ible	*flxB*
flat	*flt*	flier	*flir*
flat·ness	*flt'*	flies	*flis*
flat·ten	*fltn*	flight	*fli*
flat·tered	*fltr-*	flights	*flis*
flat·tery	*fltre*	flimsy	*flze*
flaunt	*fln*	fling	*flg*
fla·vor	*flvr*	flip	*flp*
fla·vored	*flvr-*	flirt	*flrt*
fla·vors	*flvrs*	float	*flo*
flaw	*fla*	floated	*flo-*
flaw·less	*flals*	float·ing	*flo̲*
flaws	*flas*	flock	*flc*
flea	*fle*	flocks	*flcs*
fledg·ling	*fljlg*	flood	*fld*
flee	*fle*	flooded	*fld-*
fleet	*fle*	flood·ing	*fld̲*
fleet·ing	*fle̲*	flood·light	*fldli*
fleets	*fles*	flood·lights	*fldlis*
flesh	*fls*	floods	*flds*
flew	*flu*	floor	*flr*
flex	*flx*	floored	*flr-*
flex·ibil·ity	*flxBˡ*	floor·ing	*flr̲*

floors	*flrs*	fluc·tu·ated	*flcCa-*
flop	*flp*	fluc·tu·ates	*flcCas*
flop·pi·ness	*flpe'*	fluc·tu·at·ing	*flcCa_*
floppy	*flpe*	fluc·tua·tion	*flcCuy*
flora	*flra*	fluc·tua·tions	*flcCuys*
flo·ral	*flrl*	flue	*flu*
flo·res·cent	*flrsN*	flu·ent	*fluN*
flo·rist	*flrS*	fluid	*flud*
floss	*fls*	flu·ids	*fluds*
flo·ta·tion	*fly*	fluke	*flc*
floun·der	*floNr*	flung	*flq*
flour	*flor*	flunk	*flq*
flour·ish	*flrs*	fluo·res·cence	*flrsN*
flout	*flot*	fluo·res·cent	*flrsN*
flow	*flo*	fluori·da·tion	*flrdy*
flow·chart	*floCrl*	flur·ries	*flres*
flower	*flor*	flurry	*flre*
flow·ers	*flors*	flush	*fls*
flow·ing	*flo_*	flushes	*flss*
flown	*fln*	flush·ing	*fls_*
flows	*flos*	flute	*flu*
flu	*flu*	flut·ter	*fllr*
fluc·tu·ate	*flcCa*	flux	*flx*

fly	*fli*	fold·ers	*fldrs*
flyer	*flir*	fold·ing	*fld*
fly·ers	*flirs*	fo·li·age	*fly*
fly·ing	*fli*	folio	*flo*
fly·leaf	*flilf*	folk	*fc*
fly·wheel	*flil*	folks	*fcs*
foam	*f*	fol·low	*flo*
foam·ing	*f*	fol·lowed	*flo-*
f.o.b.	*fob*	fol·low·ing	*flo*
focal	*fcl*	fol·lows	*flos*
focus	*fcs*	follow-up	*flo=p*
fo·cused	*fcs-*	folly	*fle*
fo·cuses	*fcss*	fond	*fn*
fo·cus·ing	*fcs*	fond·ness	*fn'*
foe	*fo*	font	*fn*
fog	*fg*	food	*fd*
foi·ble	*fyb*	foods	*fds*
foi·bles	*fybs*	fool	*fl*
foil	*fyl*	fool·ish	*fls*
foist	*fys*	foot	*fl*
fold	*fld*	foot·age	*fly*
folded	*fld-*	foot·ball	*flbl*
folder	*fldr*	foot·balls	*flbls*

footer	*flr*	ford	*fd*
foot·ing	*fl̲*	fore	*b*
foot·ings	*fl̲*	fore·arm	*far*
foot·light	*flli*	fore·bear·ance	*fbrn*
foot·lights	*fllis*	fore·cast	*fcs*
foot·note	*flnt*	fore·casted	*fcs-*
foot·notes	*flnts*	fore·cast·ing	*fcs̲*
foot·print	*flprn*	fore·casts	*fcss*
foot·wear	*flr*	fore·close	*fclz*
foot·work	*flo*	fore·closed	*fclz-*
for	*b*	fore·clo·sure	*fclzr*
for·age	*bf*	fore·clo·sures	*fclzrs*
for·bid	*fbd*	fore·front	*fbrn*
for·bid·den	*fbdn*	forego	*fq*
for·bid·ding	*fbd̲*	fore·go·ing	*fq-*
for·bids	*fbds*	fore·gone	*fgn*
force	*fs*	fore·head	*fhd*
forced	*fs-*	for·eign	*fn*
force·ful	*fsf*	for·eigner	*fnr*
for·ceps	*fsps*	fore·man	*fm*
forces	*fss*	fore·man·ship	*fms*
forc·ible	*fsB*	fore·men	*fm*
forc·ing	*fs̲*	fore·most	*fs*

fo·ren·sic		forge	
fore·see		forged	
fore·see·able		forg·ers	
fore·seen		for·gery	
fore·sight		for·get	
for·est		for·get·ful	
fore·stall		for·gets	
for·ester		for·get·ting	
for·estry		forg·ing	
for·ests		forg·ings	
fore·tell		for·give	
fore·tells		for·given	
fore·thought		for·give·ness	
fore·told		for·giv·ing	
for·ever		for·got	
fore·warn		for·got·ten	
fore·word		fork	
for·feit		fork·lift	
for·feited		form	
for·feit·ing		form·abil·ity	
for·feits		for·mal	
for·fei·ture		for·mal·ities	
for·fei·tures		for·mal·ity	

for·mal·ize		fort	
for·mal·ized		forth	
for·mally		forth·com·ing	
for·mat		forth·right	
for·ma·tion		forth·with	
for·ma·tive		for·ti·fi·ca·tion	
for·mats		for·tify	
for·mat·ting		for·ti·tude	
formed		for·tui·tous	
for·mer		for·tu·nate	
for·merly		for·tu·nately	
For·mica		for·tune	
for·mi·da·ble		forty	40
form·ing		forum	
forms		fo·rums	
for·mula		for·ward	
for·mu·las		for·warded	
for·mu·late		for·ward·ing	
for·mu·lated		for·wards	
for·mu·lat·ing		fos·sil	
for·mu·la·tion		fos·ter	
for·mu·la·tions		fos·tered	
for·sake		fos·ter·ing	

fos·ters	*ƒSrs*	frac·tions	*frcɣs*
fought	*ƒl*	frac·ture	*frcCr*
foul	*ƒol*	frac·tured	*frcCr-*
foul·ing	*ƒol̲*	frac·tures	*frcCrs*
found	*ƒon*	frac·tur·ing	*frcCr̲*
foun·da·tion	*ƒonɣ*	frag·ile	*ƒrɟl*
foun·da·tions	*ƒonɣs*	frag·ment	*frgm*
founded	*ƒon-*	frag·men·ta·tion	*frgmɣ*
foun·der	*ƒonr*	frag·mented	*frgm-*
foun·ders	*ƒonrs*	frag·ments	*frgms*
found·ing	*ƒon̲*	fra·grance	*frgrN*
foun·dries	*ƒoNres*	fra·grant	*frgrN*
foun·dry	*ƒoNre*	frail	*frl*
foun·tain	*ƒoNn*	frame	*fr⌐*
foun·tains	*ƒoNns*	framed	*fr⌐-*
four	*4*	frames	*fr⌐s*
four·some	*4s*	frame·work	*fr⌐o*
four·teen	*1 4*	fram·ing	*fr⌐̲*
fourth	*4l*	fran·chise	*frnCȝ*
fowl	*ƒol*	fran·chi·see	*frnCȝe*
fox	*ƒx*	fran·chi·sees	*frnCȝes*
foyer	*ƒyr*	fran·chises	*frnCȝs*
frac·tion	*frɣ*	fran·chis·ing	*frnCȝ-*

fran·chi·sor	*frnCzr*	free·ways	*fre as*
fran·chi·sors	*frnCzrs*	free·wheel·ing	*frel*
frank	*frq*	freeze	*frz*
frankly	*frql*	freezer	*frzr*
frank·ness	*frq'*	freez·ers	*frzrs*
fran·tic	*frNc*	freez·ing	*frz_*
fra·ter·nal	*frlrnl*	freight	*fra*
fra·ter·nity	*frlrnl'*	freighter	*frar*
fraud	*frd*	fre·quen·cies	*frqNes*
fraudu·lent	*frylN*	fre·quency	*frqNe*
fray	*fra*	fre·quent	*frqN*
frayed	*fra-*	fre·quently	*frqNl*
free	*fre*	fresh	*frs*
freed	*fre-*	freshly	*frsl*
free·dom	*fred*	fresh·man	*frs m*
free·hand	*frehN*	fresh·men	*frsm*
free·handed	*frehN-*	fresh·ness	*frs'*
free·ing	*fre_*	fret	*frl*
free·loader	*freldr*	fric·tion	*frcy*
free·load·ers	*freldrs*	Friday	*Fr*
freely	*frel*	friend	*frN*
free·stand·ing	*fresN_*	friend·li·ness	*frNl'*
free·way	*fre a*	friendly	*frNl*

Word	Shorthand	Word	Shorthand
friends	*frNs*	frost·ing	*frS_*
friend·ship	*frNs*	frost·less	*frSls*
friend·ships	*frNss*	frosty	*frSe*
fries	*fris*	frown	*fron*
fright	*fri*	frowned	*fron-*
frighten	*frin*	froze	*frz*
fright·ened	*frin-*	fro·zen	*frzn*
fright·en·ing	*frin_*	fruc·tose	*frcts*
fright·ful	*fruf*	fru·gal·ity	*frgl'*
frigid	*frjd*	fruit	*fru*
fringe	*frnj*	fruit·ful	*fruf*
fringes	*frnjs*	frui·tion	*fruj*
frisk	*frsc*	fruit·less	*fruls*
frivo·lous	*frvls*	fruits	*frus*
frog	*frg*	frus·trate	*frSra*
from	*f*	frus·trated	*frSra-*
front	*frN*	frus·trat·ing	*frSra_*
front·age	*frNj*	frus·tra·tion	*frSrj*
fron·tier	*frntr*	frus·tra·tions	*frSrjs*
front·ing	*frN_*	fry	*fri*
fronts	*frNs*	fuel	*ful*
frost	*frS*	fu·eled	*ful-*
frost·bite	*frSbi*	fu·el·ing	*ful_*

fuels	*fuels*	func·tions	*fqss*
fu·gi·tive	*bjv*	fund	*fn*
ful·fill	*bfl*	fun·da·men·tal	*fnml*
ful·filled	*bfl-*	fun·da·men·tals	*fnmls*
ful·fill·ing	*bfl̲*	funded	*fn-*
ful·fill·ment	*bflm*	funder	*fnr*
ful·fills	*bfls*	fund·ers	*fnrs*
full	*b*	fund·ing	*fn̲*
fuller	*br*	fund·ings	*fn̲̲*
full·est	*bs*	funds	*fns*
full·ness	*b'*	fu·neral	*fnrl*
fully	*bl*	fun·gus	*fgs*
fum·ble	*b ß*	fun·nel	*fnl*
fume	*b ⌢*	fun·neled	*fnl-*
fumes	*bs*	fun·nier	*fner*
fu·mi·gate	*b ga*	fun·ni·est	*fnes*
fun	*fn*	funny	*fne*
func·tion	*fql*	fur	*fr*
func·tional	*fqll*	fu·ri·ous	*fres*
func·tion·al·ity	*fqll'*	fur·nace	*frns*
func·tion·ally	*fqlll*	fur·naces	*frnss*
func·tioned	*fql-*	fur·nish	*frns*
func·tion·ing	*fql-*	fur·nished	*frns-*

fur·nishes	*frnss*	fuzzy	*fze*
fur·nish·ing	*frn_*		
fur·nish·ings	*frn=*	**G**	
fur·ni·ture	*frnCr*		
fur·ther	*frlr*	gable	*gB*
fur·ther·ance	*frlrN*	gadget	*gjl*
fur·ther·ing	*frlr_*	gag	*gg*
fur·ther·more	*frlr~*	gage	*gj*
fur·thest	*frlS*	gai·ety	*ga^l*
fury	*fre*	gain	*gn*
fuse	*fz*	gained	*gn-*
fused	*fz-*	gain·ful	*gnf*
fu·se·lage	*fslz*	gain·fully	*gnfl*
fuses	*fzs*	gain·ing	*gn_*
fus·ing	*fz-*	gains	*gns*
fu·sion	*fj*	gal	*gl*
fuss	*fs*	gala	*gla*
fussy	*fse*	gale	*gl*
fu·tile	*fll*	gall	*gl*
fu·til·ity	*fll^l*	gal·lant	*glN*
fu·ture	*fCr*	gall·blad·der	*glbldr*
fu·tures	*fCrs*	gal·ler·ies	*glres*
fu·tur·is·tic	*fCrSc*	gal·lery	*glre*

gal·ley	*gle*	garb	*grb*
gal·leys	*gles*	gar·bage	*grbz*
gal·lon	*gln*	gar·den	*grdn*
gal·lons	*glns*	gar·dener	*grdnr*
gal·lop	*glp*	gar·den·ing	*grdn̲*
gall·stone	*glSn*	gar·dens	*grdns*
ga·lore	*glr*	gar·lic	*grlc*
gals	*gls*	gar·ment	*grm*
gal·va·nize	*glvnz*	gar·ments	*grms*
gal·va·nized	*glvnz-*	gar·ner	*grnr*
gal·va·niz·ing	*glvnz_*	gar·nered	*grnr-*
gam·ble	*g B*	gar·nish	*grn+*
game	*g*	gar·ri·son	*grsn*
games	*g s*	gas	*gs*
gamma	*g a*	gase·ous	*gses*
gamut	*g l*	gases	*gss*
gang	*gg*	gash	*g+*
gan·try	*gnre*	gasi·fi·ca·tion	*gsfj*
gap	*gp*	gas·ket	*gscl*
gape	*gp*	gaso·line	*gsln*
gaps	*gps*	gaso·lines	*gslns*
ga·rage	*grz*	gas·tric	*gSrc*
ga·rages	*grzs*	gate	*ga*

gates	_gas_	gems	_ʃs_
gate·way	_ga a_	gen·der	_ʃnr_
gather	_glr_	gene	_ʃn_
gath·ered	_glr-_	gen·eral	_ʃn_
gath·er·ing	_glr_	gen·er·al·ist	_ʃnʃ_
gath·er·ings	_glr_	gen·er·al·ities	_ʃn ls_
gaudy	_gde_	gen·er·al·ity	_ʃn l_
gauge	_gʃ_	gen·er·al·iza·tion	_ʃnʒʃ_
gauged	_gʃ-_	gen·er·al·iza·tions	_ʃnʒʃs_
gauges	_gʃs_	gen·er·al·ize	_ʃnʒ_
gaug·ing	_gʃ-_	gen·er·al·ized	_ʃnʒ-_
gauze	_gʒ_	gen·er·al·izes	_ʃnʒs_
gave	_gv_	gen·er·al·iz·ing	_ʃnʒ-_
gaze	_gʒ_	gen·er·ally	_ʃnl_
gaz·ing	_gʒ-_	gen·er·als	_ʃns_
gear	_gr_	gen·er·ate	_ʃnra_
geared	_gr-_	gen·er·ated	_ʃnra-_
gear·ing	_gr_	gen·er·ates	_ʃnras_
gears	_grs_	gen·er·at·ing	_ʃnra_
geese	_gs_	gen·era·tion	_ʃnrʃ_
gel	_ʃl_	gen·era·tions	_ʃnrʃs_
gela·tin	_ʃlln_	gen·era·tor	_ʃnrar_
gelled	_ʃl-_	gen·era·tors	_ʃnrars_

ge·neric	*jnrc*	ge·ology	*jelje*
ge·ner·ics	*jnrcs*	geo·mag·netic	*je gnlc*
gen·er·os·ity	*jnrsl*	geo·met·ric	*je drc*
gen·er·ous	*jnrs*	ge·ome·try	*je dre*
gen·er·ously	*jnrsl*	geo·phys·ical	*jefzcl*
ge·netic	*jnlc*	geo·ther·mal	*jelrl*
ge·net·ics	*jnlcs*	geri·at·ric	*jrelrc*
geni·tal	*jnll*	germ	*jr*
gen·ius	*jnys*	German	*jrm*
gen·tle	*jNl*	ger·mane	*jrn*
gen·tle·man	*jNln*	ger·mi·nat·ing	*jrma*
gen·tle·men	*jNlm*	ges·ta·tion	*jSj*
gen·tly	*jNl*	ges·ture	*jsCr*
genu·ine	*jnun*	ges·tures	*jsCrs*
genu·inely	*jnunl*	ges·tur·ing	*jsCr*
genus	*jns*	get	*gl*
geo·graphic	*jegrfc*	gets	*gls*
geo·graph·ical	*jegrfcl*	get·ting	*gl*
geo·graph·ically	*jegrfcll*	gey·ser	*gzr*
ge·og·ra·phy	*jegrfe*	ghastly	*gSl*
geo·logic	*jeljc*	ghetto	*glo*
geo·log·ical	*jeljcl*	ghost	*gS*
ge·olo·gist	*jeljS*	giant	*jiN*

gibe	*jb*	give·away	*gva a*
giddy	*gde*	give·aways	*gva as*
gift	*gft*	given	*gvn*
gifted	*gft-*	giver	*gvr*
gifts	*gfts*	giv·ers	*gvrs*
gi·gan·tic	*jgNc*	gives	*gvs*
gig·gle	*ggl*	giv·ing	*gv̄*
gill	*gl*	gla·cier	*gls̄r*
gills	*gls*	glad	*gld*
gim·mick	*g—c*	gladly	*gldl*
gin	*jn*	glamor	*gl—r*
gin·ger	*jnjr*	glam·or·ous	*gl—rs*
gin·gerly	*jnjrl*	glance	*glN*
gi·raffe	*jrf*	gland	*glN*
girder	*grdr*	gland·less	*glNls*
gird·ers	*grdrs*	glands	*glNs*
gird·ing	*grd̄*	glan·du·lar	*glnjlr*
gir·dle	*grd̄l*	glare	*glr*
girl	*grl*	glar·ing	*glr̄*
girl·hood	*grlh*	glass	*gls*
girls	*grls*	glassed	*gls-*
gist	*js*	glasses	*glss*
give	*gv*	glassi·ness	*glse'*

glass·ware	*gls r*	gloomy	*gl e*
glassy	*glse*	glo·ri·ous	*glres*
glau·coma	*glc a*	glory	*glre*
glaze	*glz*	gloss	*gls*
glazed	*glz-*	glos·sary	*glsre*
glaz·ing	*glz-*	gloss·ies	*glses*
glaz·ings	*glz=*	glossy	*glse*
gleam	*gl*	glove	*glv*
glean	*gln*	gloved	*glv-*
gleaned	*gln-*	gloves	*glvs*
glee	*gle*	glow	*glo*
glib	*glb*	glu·cose	*glcs*
glide	*gld*	glue	*glu*
glider	*gldr*	glued	*glu-*
glimpse	*gl ps*	glum	*gl*
glimpses	*gl pss*	glut·ton	*glln*
glint	*glm*	gnat	*nl*
glis·ten	*glsn*	gnaw	*na*
glit·ter	*gllr*	GNP	*GNP*
gloat	*glo*	go	*g*
global	*glB*	goad	*gd*
globe	*glb*	goal	*gl*
globes	*glbs*	goals	*gls*

goat	*go*	good·ness	*g'*
goats	*gos*	goods	*gs*
gob	*gb*	good·will	*gl*
gob·ble	*gß*	goof	*gf*
god	*gd*	goofed	*gf-*
God	*gd*	goose	*gs*
gods	*gds*	goose·neck	*gsnc*
god·send	*gdsN*	gore	*gr*
goer	*gr*	gor·geous	*grys*
goers	*grs*	gory	*gre*
goes	*gs*	gos·pel	*gspl*
gog·gles	*ggls*	gos·sip	*gsp*
going	*g-*	got	*gl*
goi·ter	*gylr*	got·ten	*gln*
gold	*gld*	gouge	*goy*
golden	*gldn*	gour·met	*gr a*
golf	*glf*	gour·mets	*gr as*
golf·ing	*glf-*	gout	*gol*
gone	*gn*	gov·ern	*gvrn*
good	*g*	gov·ern·ance	*gvrnN*
good-bye	*g=b*	gov·erned	*gvrn-*
good·ies	*ges*	gov·ern·ing	*gvrn_*
goodly	*gl*	gov·ern·ment	*gvl*

gov·ern·mental	*gvll*	gradu·ate (v.)	*grya*
gov·ern·ment·ally	*gvlll*	gradu·ate (n.)	*gryul*
gov·ern·ments	*gvls*	gradu·ated	*grya-*
gov·er·nor	*gvrnr*	gradu·ates (v.)	*gryas*
gov·er·nors	*gvrnrs*	gradu·ates (n.)	*gryuls*
gov·erns	*gvrns*	gradu·at·ing	*grya_*
gown	*gon*	gradu·ation	*gryuy*
GPA	GPA	graf·fiti	*grfle*
grab	*grb*	graft	*grfl*
grace	*grs*	grain	*grn*
grace·ful	*grsf*	grained	*grn-*
grac·ing	*grs_*	gram	*g*
gra·cious	*grss*	gram·mar	*gr r*
gra·ciously	*grssl*	gram·mat·ical	*gr lcl*
grade	*grd*	grams	*gs*
graded	*grd-*	grand	*grN*
grader	*grdr*	grand·child	*grNCld*
grad·ers	*grdrs*	grand·chil·dren	*grNCldrn*
grades	*grds*	grand·daugh·ter	*grNdlr*
gra·di·ent	*grdeN*	grand·fa·ther	*grNflr*
grad·ing	*grd_*	grandma	*grN a*
gradual	*gryul*	grand·mother	*grN lr*
gradu·ally	*gryull*	grand·moth·ers	*grN lrs*

Word	Shorthand	Word	Shorthand
grand·par·ent	*grNprN*	graph·ics	*grfcs*
grand·par·ents	*grNprNs*	graph·ing	*grf-*
grand·son	*grNsn*	graph·ite	*grft*
grand·stand	*grNSN*	graphs	*grfs*
gran·ite	*grnt*	grasp	*grsp*
grant	*grN*	grasped	*grsp-*
granted	*grN-*	grass	*grs*
grantee	*grnte*	grassed	*grs-*
grant·ees	*grntes*	grasses	*grss*
grant·ing	*grN_*	grass·hop·per	*grshpr*
gran·tor	*grNr*	grass·roots	*grsrus*
gran·tors	*grNrs*	grate	*gr*
grants	*grNs*	grate·ful	*grf*
granu·late	*grnla*	grate·fully	*grfl*
granu·lated	*grnla-*	grates	*grs*
granu·la·tion	*grnlg*	grati·fi·ca·tion	*grlff*
gran·ule	*grnl*	grati·fied	*grlf-*
grape	*grp*	grati·fy·ing	*grlf_*
grape·vine	*grpvn*	grat·ing	*gr_*
graph	*grf*	gratis	*grts*
graphic	*grfc*	grati·tude	*grlld*
graph·ical	*grfcl*	gra·tu·ity	*grlut*
graph·ically	*grfcll*	grave	*grv*

gravel	*grvl*	green	*grn*
grav·eled	*grvl-*	green·house	*grnhoo*
gravely	*grvl*	green·ish	*grns*
grave·side	*grvsd*	greens	*grns*
gravi·tate	*grvla*	greet	*gre*
grav·ity	*grv^l*	greeted	*gre-*
gravy	*grve*	greet·ers	*grers*
gray	*gra*	greet·ing	*gre_*
gray·ish	*gras*	greet·ings	*gre=*
graze	*grz*	gre·gari·ous	*grgres*
graz·ing	*grz-*	grew	*gru*
grease	*grs*	grey·hound	*grahoN*
greasi·ness	*grse'*	grid	*grd*
greas·ing	*grs_*	grid·dle	*grdl*
greasy	*grse*	grids	*grds*
great	*gr*	grief	*grf*
greater	*grr*	griev·ance	*grvN*
great·est	*grs*	griev·ances	*grvNs*
greatly	*grl*	griev·ant	*grvN*
great·ness	*gr'*	grieve	*grv*
greed	*grd*	griever	*grvr*
greedily	*grdl*	griev·ously	*grvsl*
greedy	*grde*	grill	*grl*

grille	*grl*	groove	*grv*
grills	*grls*	gross	*grs*
grim	*gr*	grossly	*grsl*
grim·ace	*grs*	gro·tesque	*grlsc*
grimly	*grl*	grouch	*groc*
grind	*grM*	ground	*groN*
grinder	*grMr*	grounded	*groN-*
grind·ing	*grM_*	ground·ing	*groN_*
grip	*grp*	ground·less	*groNls*
gripe	*grp*	grounds	*groNs*
grips	*grps*	ground·wa·ter	*groN lr*
grit	*grl*	ground·work	*groN o*
grit·ting	*grl_*	group	*grp*
groan	*grn*	grouped	*grp-*
gro·cer	*grsr*	group·ing	*grp_*
gro·cer·ies	*grsres*	group·ings	*grp=*
gro·cers	*grsrs*	groups	*grps*
gro·cery	*grsre*	grouse	*groos*
groggy	*grge*	grout	*grol*
groin	*gryn*	grouted	*grol-*
groom	*gr*	grove	*grv*
groomed	*gr -*	grovel	*grvl*
groom·ing	*gr _*	groves	*grvs*

grow	*gro*	guarded	*grd-*
grower	*gror*	guardian	*grden*
grow·ers	*grors*	guardi·ans	*grdens*
grow·ing	*gro_*	guardi·an·ship	*grdens*
growl	*grol*	guard·ing	*grd_*
grown	*grn*	guards	*grds*
grows	*gros*	gu·ber·na·to·rial	*gbrntrel*
growth	*grt*	guer·rilla	*grla*
grub	*grb*	guess	*gs*
grudge	*gry*	guessed	*gs-*
gru·el·ing	*grul_*	guesses	*gss*
grue·some	*grs*	guess·ing	*gs_*
gruff	*grf*	guess·work	*gs o*
grum·ble	*gr B*	guest	*gS*
grumpy	*gr pe*	guests	*gSs*
guar·an·tee	*grnte*	guid·ance	*gdN*
guar·an·teed	*grnte-*	guide	*gd*
guar·an·tee·ing	*grnte_*	guided	*gd-*
guar·an·tees	*grntes*	guide·line	*gdln*
guar·an·tor	*grntr*	guide·lines	*gdlns*
guar·an·tors	*grntrs*	guides	*gds*
guar·anty	*grNe*	guide·way	*gd a*
guard	*grd*	guid·ing	*gd_*

guile	*gl*	guz·zle	*gzl*
guilt	*gll*	gym	*g*
guilty	*glle*	gym·na·sium	*g nze*
guise	*gz*	gym·na·si·ums	*g nze s*
gui·tar	*glr*	gym·nast	*g nS*
gulf	*glf*	gym·nas·tic	*g nSc*
gul·li·ble	*glB*	gym·nas·tics	*g nScs*
gulp	*glp*	gyms	*g s*
gum	*g*	gy·ne·cology	*gnclge*
gummed	*g -*	gyp	*gp*
gump·tion	*g ʔ*	gyp·sum	*gps*
gun	*gn*	gy·rate	*gra*
gunned	*gn-*	gy·rat·ing	*gra_*
gush	*gʃ*	gy·ra·tion	*grʃ*
gust	*gS*		
gusto	*gSo*		
gut	*gl*		

H

guts	*gls*	ha·bili·tate	*hblla*
gut·ter	*glr*	habit	*hbl*
gut·ters	*glrs*	hab·it·able	*hblB*
gut·ting	*gl_*	habi·tat	*hbll*
guy	*gı*	habi·tats	*hblls*
guys	*gıs*	hab·its	*hbls*

ha·bitual	*hbCul*	halls	*hls*
ha·bitu·ally	*hbCull*	hal·lu·ci·nate	*hlsna*
had	*h*	hal·lu·ci·na·tion	*hlsny*
hadn't	*hN*	hal·lu·cino·genic	*hlsnync*
hag·gard	*hgrd*	hall·way	*hla*
hag·gle	*hgl*	hall·ways	*hlas*
hail	*hl*	halo	*hlo*
hail·storm	*hlSr*	halt	*hll*
hair	*hr*	halted	*hll-*
hairdo	*hrdu*	halve	*hv*
hair·dos	*hrdus*	halves	*hvs*
hair·dresser	*hrdrsr*	ham	*h*
hairy	*hre*	ham·burger	*h brgr*
hale	*hl*	ham·burg·ers	*h brgrs*
half	*hf*	ham·mer	*h r*
half·back	*hfbc*	ham·mer·ing	*h r_*
half·tone	*hfln*	ham·mers	*h rs*
half·tones	*hflns*	ham·per	*h pr*
half·way	*hfa*	ham·pered	*h pr-*
hali·but	*hlbl*	ham·per·ing	*h pr_*
hall	*hl*	hams	*h s*
hall·mark	*hl rc*	ham·ster	*h Sr*
Halloween	*hl n*	ham·string	*h Srq*

hand	*hN*	hand·rails	*hNrls*
hand·ball	*hNbl*	hands	*hNs*
hand·bill	*hNbl*	hand·set	*hNsl*
hand·book	*hNbc*	hand·some	*hN⁓*
hand·books	*hNbcs*	hand·somely	*hN⁓l*
handed	*hN-*	hand·work	*hN⁓o*
hand·ful	*hNf*	hand·write	*hNru*
handi·cap	*hNcp*	hand·writ·ing	*hNru*
handi·capped	*hNcp-*	hand·writ·ten	*hNrtn*
handi·caps	*hNcps*	handy	*hNe*
handi·craft	*hNcrfl*	hang	*hq*
handi·work	*hN⁓o*	han·gar	*hgr*
hand·ker·chief	*hgrCf*	hanger	*hgr*
han·dle	*hNl*	hang·ers	*hgrs*
han·dled	*hNl-*	hang·ing	*hq_*
han·dler	*hNlr*	hangs	*hgs*
han·dlers	*hNlrs*	hang-up	*hq = p*
han·dles	*hNls*	hap·haz·ard	*hphzrd*
han·dling	*hNl_*	hap·pen	*hpn*
hand·made	*hN⁓d*	hap·pened	*hpn-*
hand·out	*hNol*	hap·pen·ing	*hpn_*
hand·outs	*hNols*	hap·pen·ings	*hpn=*
hand·rail	*hNrl*	hap·pens	*hpns*

hap·pier	*hper*	hare	*hr*
hap·pily	*hpl*	harm	*hr⌒*
hap·pi·ness	*hpe'*	harm·ful	*hr⌒f*
happy	*hpe*	harm·ing	*hr⌒*
ha·rangue	*hrq*	harm·less	*hr⌒ls*
ha·rass	*hrs*	har·monica	*hrmca*
ha·rassed	*hrs-*	har·mo·ni·ous	*hr⌒nes*
ha·rass·ing	*hrs_*	har·mo·nize	*hrmz*
ha·rass·ment	*hrsm*	har·mo·niz·ing	*hrmz_*
har·bin·ger	*hrbnjr*	har·mony	*hrme*
har·bor	*hrbr*	harms	*hr⌒s*
hard	*hrd*	har·ness	*hr'*
hard·back	*hrdbc*	harp	*hrp*
harden	*hrdn*	harsh	*hrs*
hard·en·ing	*hrdn_*	har·vest	*hrvS*
harder	*hrdr*	har·vested	*hrvS-*
hard·headed	*hrdhd-*	has	*hs*
hard·hearted	*hrdhrt-*	hash	*hs*
har·di·ness	*hrde'*	hasn't	*hsN*
hardly	*hrdl*	hasp	*hsp*
hard·ness	*hrd'*	hasps	*hsps*
hard·ship	*hrds*	has·sle	*hsl*
hard·ware	*hrd r*	haste	*hS*

has·ten	_hsn_	haz·ard·ous	_hzrds_
has·ten·ing	_hsn_	haz·ards	_hzrds_
hasty	_hSe_	haze	_hz_
hat	_hl_	hazy	_hze_
hatch	_hC_	he	_h_
hate	_ha_	head	_hd_
hate·ful	_haf_	head·ache	_hdac_
hates	_has_	head·aches	_hdacs_
hats	_hls_	headed	_hd-_
haughty	_hle_	header	_hdr_
haul	_hl_	head·ers	_hdrs_
haul·age	_hlg_	head·first	_hdfrS_
hauled	_hl-_	head·ing	_hd_
haul·ing	_hl_	head·ings	_hd_
haunt	_hN_	head·light	_hdli_
haunted	_hN-_	head·line	_hdln_
have	_v_	head·liner	_hdlnr_
haven't	_vN_	head·lin·ers	_hdlnrs_
hav·ing	_v_	head·lines	_hdlns_
havoc	_hvc_	head·long	_hdlg_
haw·ser	_hzr_	head·quar·ter	_hdqlr_
hay	_ha_	head·quar·tered	_hdqlr-_
haz·ard	_hzrd_	head·quar·ters	_hdqlrs_

head·room	*hdr*	heartily	*hrll*
heads	*hds*	hearts	*hrls*
head·strong	*hdsrq*	heart·warm·ing	*hrlr*
head·way	*hda*	hearty	*hrle*
heal	*hl*	heat	*he*
healed	*hl-*	heated	*he-*
heal·ing	*hl*	heater	*her*
health	*hēl*	heat·ers	*hers*
healthy	*hlle*	hea·then	*hln*
heap	*hp*	heather	*hlr*
hear	*hr*	heat·ing	*he*
heard	*hrd*	heats	*hes*
hear·ing	*hr*	heave	*hv*
hear·ings	*hr*	heaven	*hvn*
hear·say	*hrsa*	heavier	*hver*
hearse	*hrs*	heavily	*hvl*
heart	*hrl*	heav·ing	*hv*
heart·burn	*hrlbrn*	heavy	*hve*
hearten	*hrln*	heavy·set	*hvesl*
heart·ened	*hrln-*	heavy·weight	*hvea*
heart·en·ing	*hrln*	hec·tic	*hclc*
heart·felt	*hrlfll*	he'd	*h'd*
hearti·est	*hrles*	hedge	*hy*

heed	*hd*	helper	*hlpr*
heeded	*hd-*	help·ers	*hlprs*
heed·less	*hdls*	help·ful	*hlpf*
heel	*hl*	help·fully	*hlpfl*
heels	*hls*	help·ful·ness	*hlpf'*
heifer	*hfr*	help·ing	*hlp_*
heif·ers	*hfrs*	help·less	*hlpls*
height	*hu*	helps	*hlps*
heighten	*hun*	hem	*h*
heights	*hus*	hemi·sphere	*h sfr*
heir	*ar*	hemi·spheres	*h sfrs*
heirs	*ars*	hemmed	*h -*
heir·ship	*ars*	he·mo·glo·bin	*h glbn*
held	*hld*	he·mo·philiac	*h flec*
heli·cop·ter	*hlcplr*	hem·or·rhage	*h ry*
heli·cop·ters	*hlcplrs*	hem·or·rhag·ing	*h ry_*
hell	*hl*	hem·or·rhoid	*h ryd*
he'll	*h'l*	hem·or·rhoids	*h ryds*
hello	*hlo*	he·mo·stat	*h St*
helm	*hl*	he·mo·static	*h Stc*
hel·met	*hl d*	he·mo·stats	*h Sts*
help	*hlp*	hen	*hn*
helped	*hlp-*	hence	*hN*

hence·forth	*hnfl*	here·unto	*hrul*
hens	*hns*	here·with	*hr*
hepa·ti·tis	*hplls*	heri·tage	*hrly*
her	*hr*	her·mit	*hr—l*
herb	*hrb*	her·nia	*hrna*
her·bi·cide	*hrbsd*	her·nias	*hrnas*
her·bi·cides	*hrbsds*	her·ni·ated	*hrna—*
herd	*hrd*	hero	*hro*
herds	*hrds*	he·roes	*hros*
here	*hr*	he·roic	*hroc*
here·about	*hrab*	hers	*hrs*
here·af·ter	*hraf*	her·self	*hrsf*
hereby	*hrb*	he's	*h's*
he·redi·tary	*hrdlre*	hesi·tant	*hzlN*
he·red·ity	*hrd'*	hesi·tate	*hzla*
herein	*hrn*	hesi·tated	*hzla—*
here·in·af·ter	*hrnaf*	hesi·ta·tion	*hzly*
here·in·be·fore	*hrnbf*	het·ero·ge·ne·ous	*hlrynes*
hereof	*hrv*	hew	*hu*
hereon	*hro*	hex	*hx*
here's	*hrs*	hexa·gon	*hxgn*
hereto	*hrl*	hey	*ha*
here·to·fore	*hrlf*	hey·day	*had*

hi	*hi*	high·way	*hia*
hia·tus	*hils*	high·ways	*hi_as*
hi·ber·nate	*hbrna*	hi·jack	*hyc*
hickory	*hcre*	hike	*hc*
hid	*hd*	hikes	*hcs*
hid·den	*hdn*	hik·ing	*hc_*
hide	*hd*	hi·lari·ous	*hlres*
hide·ous	*hdes*	hill	*hl*
hid·ing	*hd_*	hills	*hls*
hi·er·ar·chy	*hirrce*	hilly	*hle*
high	*hi*	him	*h*
higher	*hir*	him·self	*hsf*
high·est	*hiS*	hind	*hN*
high·land	*hilN*	hin·der	*hNr*
high·lands	*hilNs*	hin·der·ing	*hNr_*
high·light	*hili*	hin·drance	*hNrN*
high·lighted	*hili-*	hind·sight	*hNsi*
high·lighter	*hilir*	hinge	*hny*
high·light·ing	*hili_*	hinges	*hnjs*
high·lights	*hilis*	hint	*hN*
highly	*hil*	hinted	*hN-*
highs	*his*	hints	*hNs*
high·tail	*hill*	hip	*hp*

hire	_hr_	hoarse·ness	_hrs'_
hired	_hr-_	hoax	_hx_
hires	_hrs_	hobby	_hbe_
hir·ing	_hr_	hobo	_hbo_
his	_)_	hockey	_hce_
Hispanic	_hspnc_	hodge·podge	_hypj_
Hispanics	_hspncs_	hoe	_ho_
his·ta·mine	_hs͜m_	hog	_hq_
his·to·rian	_hSren_	hoist	_hyS_
his·to·ri·ans	_hSrens_	hoists	_hySs_
his·toric	_hSrc_	hold	_hld_
his·tor·ical	_hSrcl_	holder	_hldr_
his·tor·ically	_hSrcll_	hold·ers	_hldrs_
his·to·ries	_hSres_	hold·ing	_hld_
his·tory	_hSre_	hold·ings	_hld̄_
hit	_hl_	hold·over	_hld̿O_
hitch	_hC_	holds	_hlds_
hitch·hike	_hChc_	holdup	_hldp_
hits	_hls_	hole	_hl_
hit·ting	_hl_	holes	_hls_
hives	_hvs_	holi·day	_hld_
hoard	_hrd_	holi·days	_hlds_
hoarse	_hrs_	ho·li·ness	_hl'_

Word	Shorthand	Word	Shorthand
hol·low		homo·nym	
holly		ho·mo·sexual	
holy		ho·mo·sexu·al·ity	
hom·age		ho·mo·sexu·als	
home		honed	
home·com·ing		hon·est	
home·less		hon·estly	
homely		hon·esty	
home·made		honey	
home·maker		hon·ey·moon	
home·mak·ers		honk	
home·mak·ing		honk·ing	
home·owner		honor	
home·own·ers		hon·or·able	
home·room		hon·or·ably	
home·rooms		hono·rarium	
homes		hon·or·ary	
home·sick		hon·ored	
home·spun		hon·oree	
home·stead		hon·or·ing	
home·work		hon·ors	
homi·cide		hood	
ho·mo·ge·ne·ous		hook	

hooked	*hc-*	horns	*hrns*
hook·ing	*hc̲*	horo·scope	*hrscp*
hooks	*hcs*	hor·ri·ble	*hrβ*
hookup	*hcp*	hor·ror	*hrr*
hoop	*hp*	horse	*hrs*
hoot	*hu*	horse·back	*hrsbc*
hop	*hp*	horse·play	*hrspla*
hope	*hp*	horse·power	*hrspor*
hoped	*hp-*	horse·shoe	*hrssu*
hope·ful	*hpf*	horse·shoes	*hrssus*
hope·fully	*hpfl*	hor·ti·cul·tural	*hrtclCrl*
hope·less	*hpls*	hor·ti·cul·ture	*hrtclCr*
hope·lessly	*hplsl*	hor·ti·cul·tur·ists	*hrtclCrss*
hope·less·ness	*hpls´*	hose	*hz*
hopes	*hps*	hoses	*hzs*
hop·ing	*hp̲*	hos·pice	*hsps*
hop·per	*hpr*	hos·pi·tal	*hsp*
hop·ping	*hp̲*	hos·pi·tal·ity	*hspllᶜ*
ho·ri·zon	*hrzn*	hos·pi·tal·iza·tion	*hspzj*
ho·ri·zons	*hrzns*	hos·pi·tal·ize	*hspz*
hori·zon·tal	*hrzNl*	hos·pi·tal·ized	*hspz-*
hor·mone	*hr⌐m*	hos·pi·tal·izes	*hspzs*
horn	*hrn*	hos·pi·tal·iz·ing	*hspz̲*

Word	Outline	Word	Outline
hos·pi·tals	*hsps*	house (n.)	*hos*
host	*hS*	house (v.)	*hoz*
hos·tage	*hSj*	house·coat	*hosco*
hos·tages	*hSjs*	housed	*hoz-*
hosted	*hS-*	house·hold	*hoshld*
host·ess	*hSs*	house·holds	*hoshlds*
host·esses	*hSss*	house·keep·ing	*hoscp_*
hos·tile	*hSl*	houses (n.)	*hoss*
hos·til·ity	*hSlˡ*	houses (v.)	*hozs*
host·ing	*hS_*	house·warm·ing	*hos⌣_*
hosts	*hS̄s*	house·wife	*hosf*
hot	*hl*	house·work	*hos‿o*
hotel	*hll*	hous·ing	*hoz_*
ho·tels	*hlls*	hous·ings	*hoz=*
hot·house	*hlhos*	hover	*hvɾ*
hot·line	*hlln*	hov·er·ing	*hvɾ_*
hot·lines	*hllns*	how	*ho*
hot·ter	*hlɾ*	how·ever	*hoE*
hound	*ho𝑁*	howl	*hol*
hour	*hɾ*	hub	*hb*
hour·glass	*hɾgls*	hubs	*hbs*
hourly	*hɾl*	hud·dle	*hdl*
hours	*hɾs*	huffy	*hfe*

hug		hu·mor·ous	
huge		hump	
hull		hunch	
hulls		hun·dred	
hum		hun·dreds	
human		hun·dredth	
hu·mane		hun·dred·weight	
hu·man·is·tic		hung	
hu·mani·tarian		hun·ger	
hu·man·ities		hun·gry	
hu·man·ity		hunk	
hu·manly		hunt	
hu·mans		hunter	
hum·ble		hunt·ers	
hum·bly		hunt·ing	
humid		hur·dle	
hu·midi·fier		hur·ri·cane	
hu·mid·ity		hur·ried	
hu·mili·ate		hurry	
hu·mili·ation		hurt	
hu·mil·ity		hurts	
hum·ming		hus·band	
humor		hus·bandry	

hus·bands	*hzbNs*	hymn	*h*
hush	*hƨ*	hy·per·ac·tive	*hpracv*
husk	*hsc*	hy·per·ac·tiv·ity	*hpracv'*
husky	*hsce*	hy·per·ki·netic	*hprcnlc*
hus·tle	*hsl*	hy·per·sen·si·tive	*hprsNv*
hut	*hl*	hy·per·ten·sion	*hprlny*
hy·brid	*hbrd*	hy·phen	*hfn*
hy·drant	*hdrN*	hy·phen·ated	*hfna-*
hy·drau·lic	*hdrlc*	hy·phena·tion	*hfny*
hy·dro·car·bon	*hdrcrbn*	hy·phens	*hfns*
hy·dro·car·bons	*hdrcrbns*	hyp·no·sis	*hpnss*
hy·dro·chlo·ride	*hdrclrd*	hyp·notic	*hpnlc*
hy·dro·elec·tric	*hdrelc*	hy·po·chon·driac	*hpkdrec*
hy·dro·gen	*hdrɟn*	hypo·crite	*hpcrl*
hy·dro·gen·ate	*hdrɟna*	hy·po·der·mic	*hpdr⌐c*
hy·dro·gen·ated	*hdrɟna-*	hy·pothe·ses	*hplsz*
hy·dro·gena·tion	*hdrɟny*	hy·pothe·sis	*hplss*
hy·dro·pho·bia	*hdrfba*	hy·po·thet·ical	*hpllcl*
hy·dro·static	*hdrƨlc*	hys·ter·ical	*hƨrcl*
hy·dro·sul·fide	*hdrslfd*		
hy·drox·ide	*hdrxd*		
hy·giene	*hɟn*		
hy·gien·ist	*hɟnƨ*		

I

I	*ι*

ice	ιs	iden·ti·fy·ing	$\iota dN_{\int}$
ice·box	ιsbx	iden·tity	ιdN^ι
iced	$\iota s-$	ide·ology	$\iota delse$
ici·cle	ιscl	idiom	ιde
icing	ιs_{-}	idi·osyn·crasy	$\iota desgrse$
icy	ιse	idi·otic	$\iota delc$
I'd	ιd	idle	ιdl
I.D.	ID	idle·ness	$\iota dl'$
idea	ιda	idol	ιdl
ideal	ιdel	idol·ize	ιdlz
ide·al·is·tic	$\iota delsc$	i.e.	ie
ide·ally	$\iota dell$	if	$\int$
ide·als	$\iota dels$	ig·ne·ous	$\iota gnes$
ideas	ιdas	ig·nite	$\iota gn\iota$
iden·ti·cal	$\iota dNcl$	ig·nited	$\iota gn\iota-$
iden·ti·cally	$\iota dNcll$	ig·ni·tion	ιgn_{γ}
iden·ti·fi·able	$\iota dN_{\int B}$	ig·ni·tions	$\iota gn_{\gamma}s$
iden·ti·fi·ca·tion	$\iota dN_{\int\gamma}$	ig·no·rance	$\iota gnrN$
iden·ti·fi·ca·tions	$\iota dN_{\int\gamma}s$	ig·no·rant	$\iota gnrN$
iden·ti·fied	$\iota dN_{\int}-$	ig·nore	ιgnr
iden·ti·fier	$\iota dN_{\int}r$	ig·nored	$\iota gnr-$
iden·ti·fies	$\iota dN_{\int}s$	ig·nor·ing	ιgnr_{-}
iden·tify	$\iota dN_{\int}$	ill	ιl

I'll		il·lus·tri·ous	
il·le·gal		I'm	
il·le·gally		image	
il·leg·ible		im·agery	
il·le·giti·mate		im·ages	
il·licit		imagi·na·ble	
il·lit·er·ate		imagi·nary	
ill·ness		imagi·na·tion	
ill·nesses		imagi·na·tively	
il·log·ical		imag·ine	
ills		imag·in·ing	
il·lu·mi·nate		im·bal·ance	
il·lu·mi·nated		im·bal·ances	
il·lu·mi·na·tion		imbed	
il·lu·sion		im·bed·ded	
il·lu·sions		imbue	
il·lus·trate		imi·tate	
il·lus·trated		imi·ta·tion	
il·lus·trates		imi·ta·tor	
il·lus·trat·ing		imi·ta·tors	
il·lus·tra·tion		im·macu·late	
il·lus·tra·tions		im·ma·te·rial	
il·lus·tra·tive		im·ma·ture	

im·ma·tur·ity	im·mu·ni·za·tions
im·meas·ur·able	im·mu·nize
im·me·di·ate	im·mu·nized
im·me·di·ately	im·pact
im·me·di·ate·ness	im·pacted
im·mense	im·pact·ing
im·mensely	im·pacts
im·merse	im·pair
im·mi·grant	im·paired
im·mi·grants	im·pair·ing
im·mi·grate	im·part
im·mi·gra·tion	im·parted
im·mi·nent	im·par·tial
im·mo·bile	im·par·ti·al·ity
im·mo·bi·lize	im·par·tially
im·mod·est	im·part·ing
im·moral	im·parts
im·mor·al·ity	im·passe
im·mor·tal	im·pas·sive
im·mor·tal·ity	im·pa·tient
im·mune	im·pec·ca·ble
im·mu·nity	im·pedi·ment
im·mu·ni·za·tion	im·pedi·ments

impel	*pl*	im·ple·ments	*plms*
im·pelled	*pl-*	im·pli·cate	*plca*
im·pend·ing	*pn*	im·pli·ca·tion	*plcy*
im·pene·tra·ble	*pntrB*	im·pli·ca·tions	*plcys*
im·pera·tive	*prv*	im·plicit	*plst*
im·pera·tives	*prvs*	im·plied	*pli-*
im·per·fect	*Pfc*	im·plies	*plis*
im·per·fec·tion	*Pfcy*	im·plore	*plr*
im·per·fec·tions	*Pfcys*	imply	*pli*
im·per·sonal	*Psnl*	im·po·lite	*pli*
im·per·son·ate	*Psna*	im·port	*pt*
im·per·ti·nent	*PlnN*	im·por·tance	*pt*
im·per·vi·ous	*Pves*	im·por·tant	*pt*
im·petu·ous	*pCus*	im·por·tantly	*ptl*
im·pe·tus	*pls*	im·por·ta·tion	*pty*
im·pinge	*pny*	im·ported	*pt-*
im·pinge·ment	*pnym*	im·porter	*ptr*
im·ping·ing	*pny-*	im·port·ers	*ptrs*
im·plant	*plN*	im·port·ing	*pt*
im·ple·ment	*plm*	im·ports	*pts*
im·ple·men·ta·tion	*plmy*	im·por·tun·ing	*prtn*
im·ple·mented	*plm-*	im·pose	*pz*
im·ple·ment·ing	*plm*	im·posed	*pz-*

im·poses		im·prison	
im·pos·ing		im·pris·oned	
im·po·si·tion		im·pris·on·ment	
im·pos·si·ble		im·prob·able	
im·po·tency		im·promptu	
im·po·tent		im·proper	
im·pound		im·prop·erly	
im·pounded		im·prove	
im·pov·er·ish		im·proved	
im·pov·er·ished		im·prove·ment	
im·prac·ti·cal		im·prove·ments	
im·pre·ci·sion		im·proves	
im·preg·nate		im·prov·ing	
im·press		im·pro·vi·sa·tion	
im·pressed		im·pro·vise	
im·presses		im·pru·dent	
im·press·ing		im·pu·dent	
im·pres·sion		im·pulse	
im·pres·sions		im·pulses	
im·pres·sive		im·pul·sive·ness	
im·print		im·pu·ri·ties	
im·printed		im·pu·rity	
im·print·ing		in	

in·abil·ity	_nßⁱ_	in·bound	_nbon_
in·ac·ces·si·ble	_nxsß_	in·bred	_nbrd_
in·ac·cu·rate	_nacrl_	in·can·des·cent	_ncdsn_
in·ac·tion	_nacy_	in·ca·pa·ble	_ncpß_
in·ac·tive	_nacv_	in·ca·paci·tate	_ncpsla_
in·ac·tiv·ity	_nacvⁱ_	in·ca·paci·tated	_ncpsla-_
in·ade·qua·cies	_nAqses_	in·car·cer·ate	_ncrsra_
in·ade·quacy	_nAqse_	in·car·cer·ated	_ncrsra-_
in·ade·quate	_nAql_	in·cen·tive	_nsnv_
in·ade·quately	_nAqll_	in·cen·tives	_nsnvo_
in·ad·mis·si·ble	_nA—sß_	in·cep·tion	_nspy_
in·ad·ver·tence	_nAvrln_	in·cest	_nsƌ_
in·ad·ver·tent	_nAvrln_	inch	_un_
in·ad·ver·tently	_nAvrlnl_	inched	_un-_
in·ad·vis·able	_nAvzß_	inches	_uns_
in·ap·pli·ca·ble	_naplcß_	inch·ing	_un_
in·ap·pro·pri·ate	_napo_	in·ci·dence	_ndn_
in·ap·pro·pri·ately	_napol_	in·ci·dences	_ndns_
in·as·much	_nz—C_	in·ci·dent	_ndn_
in·au·gu·rate	_nagra_	in·ci·den·tal	_ndnl_
in·au·gu·rated	_nagra-_	in·ci·den·tally	_ndnll_
in·au·gu·rates	_nagras_	in·ci·den·tals	_ndnls_
in·au·gu·ra·tion	_nagry_	in·ci·dently	_ndnl_

in·ci·dents	*NdNs*	in·com·mu·ni·ca·do	*nkncdo*
in·cin·era·tion	*nsnry*	in·com·pa·ra·ble	*nkprB*
in·cin·era·tor	*nsnrar*	in·com·pat·ible	*nkplB*
in·ci·sion	*nsy*	in·com·pe·tency	*nkplNe*
in·ci·sive	*nssv*	in·com·pe·tent	*nkplN*
in·cite	*nsi*	in·com·plete	*nkp*
in·clem·ent	*nclm*	in·com·pletes	*nkps*
in·cli·na·tion	*nclny*	in·con·sid·er·ate	*nksl*
in·cline	*ncln*	in·con·sis·ten·cies	*nksSNes*
in·clined	*ncln-*	in·con·sis·tency	*nksSNe*
in·clud·able	*IB*	in·con·sis·tent	*nksSN*
in·clude	*l*	in·con·spicu·ous	*nkspcus*
in·cluded	*l-*	in·con·ven·ience	*nkv*
in·cludes	*Is*	in·con·ven·ienced	*nkv-*
in·clud·ing	*l_*	in·con·ven·iences	*nkvs*
in·clu·sion	*Iy*	in·con·ven·ienc·ing	*nkv_*
in·clu·sions	*Iys*	in·con·ven·ient	*nkv*
in·clu·sive	*Isv*	in·cor·po·rate	*inc*
in·co·her·ent	*nchrN*	in·cor·po·rated	*inc*
in·come	*nk*	in·cor·po·rates	*incs*
in·comes	*nks*	in·cor·po·rat·ing	*inc_*
in·com·ing	*nk_*	in·cor·po·ra·tion	*incy*
in·com·mu·ni·ca·ble	*nkncB*	in·cor·po·ra·tions	*incys*

Word	Shorthand
in·cor·po·ra·tor	_incr_
in·cor·po·ra·tors	_incrs_
in·cor·rect	_ncrc_
in·cor·rect·ly	_ncrcl_
in·cor·ri·gi·ble	_ncrjß_
in·cor·rupt·ible	_ncrplß_
in·crease	_ncrs_
in·creased	_ncrs-_
in·creases	_ncrss_
in·creas·ing	_ncrs_
in·creas·ingly	_ncrsl_
in·cred·ible	_ncrdß_
in·cred·ibly	_ncrdß_
in·cre·ment	_ncrm_
in·cre·men·tal	_ncrml_
in·cre·men·tally	_ncrmll_
in·cre·ments	_ncrms_
in·crimi·nate	_ncrma_
in·cu·ba·tor	_ncbar_
in·cu·ba·tors	_ncbars_
in·cum·bency	_nkbNe_
in·cum·bent	_nkbN_
in·cum·bents	_nkbNs_

Word	Shorthand
incur	_ncr_
in·cur·able	_ncrß_
in·curred	_ncr-_
in·cur·ring	_ncr_
in·curs	_ncrs_
in·debted	_ndt-_
in·debt·ed·ness	_ndt-'_
in·de·cent	_ndsN_
in·de·ci·sion	_ndsj_
in·deed	_ndd_
in·de·fin·able	_ndfnß_
in·defi·nite	_ndfnt_
in·defi·nitely	_ndfntl_
in·dem·ni·fi·ca·tion	_nd_ _nfj_
in·dem·ni·fied	_nd_ _nfi-_
in·dem·nify	_nd_ _nfi_
in·dem·nity	_nd_ _nte_
in·dent	_ndN_
in·den·ta·tion	_ndNj_
in·den·ta·tions	_ndNjs_
in·dented	_ndN-_
in·den·ture	_ndnCr_
in·den·tures	_ndnCrs_

in·de·pend·ence	*npNN*	in·dict	*ndi*
in·de·pend·ent	*npNN*	in·dicted	*ndi —*
in·de·pend·ently	*npNNl*	in·dict·ment	*ndim*
in·de·pend·ents	*npNNs*	in·dict·ments	*ndims*
in-depth	*n = dpl*	in·dif·fer·ent	*ndfrN*
in·de·scrib·able	*nd SB*	in·dige·nous	*ndyns*
in·de·ter·mi·nate	*ndll*	in·di·gent	*NyN*
index	*Nx*	in·di·ges·tion	*Nysy*
in·dexed	*Nx —*	in·dig·nant	*ndgnN*
in·dexes	*Nxs*	in·dig·na·tion	*ndgny*
in·dex·ing	*Nx*	in·dig·ni·ties	*ndgnles*
Indian	*Nen*	in·dig·nity	*ndgnle*
Indians	*Nens*	in·di·rect	*ndr*
in·di·cate	*Nca*	in·di·rectly	*ndrl*
in·di·cated	*Nca —*	in·dis·creet	*nDcre*
in·di·cates	*Ncas*	in·dis·crimi·nate	*nDcrml*
in·di·cat·ing	*Nca*	in·dis·crimi·nately	*nDcrmll*
in·di·ca·tion	*Ncy*	in·dis·pen·sa·ble	*nDpNB*
in·di·ca·tions	*Ncys*	in·dis·posed	*nDpz —*
in·dica·tive	*ndcv*	in·dis·tinct	*nDlq*
in·di·ca·tor	*Ncar*	in·di·vidual	*Nv*
in·di·ca·tors	*Ncars*	in·di·vidu·al·ist	*NvS*
in·di·ces	*Nsz*	in·di·vidu·al·ity	*Nvl*

in·di·vid·u·al·ize	*Nvz*	in·dus·tri·al·ized	*Nlz-*
in·di·vid·u·al·ized	*Nvz-*	in·dus·tri·al·izes	*Nlzs*
in·di·vid·u·al·iz·ing	*Nvz-*	in·dus·tri·al·ly	*Nll*
in·di·vid·u·al·ly	*Nvl*	in·dus·tries	*Ns*
in·di·vid·u·als	*Nvs*	in·dus·tri·ous	*Ns*
in·di·vis·ible	*ndvzB*	in·dus·tri·ous·ly	*Nsl*
in·doc·tri·nate	*ndclrna*	in·dus·tri·ous·ness	*Ns'*
in·doc·tri·na·tion	*ndclrnj*	in·dus·try	*N*
in·door	*ndr*	in·ef·fec·tive	*nefcv*
in·doors	*ndrs*	in·ef·fec·tively	*nefcvl*
in·duce	*nds*	in·ef·fi·ciency	*nefsNe*
in·duced	*nds-*	in·ef·fi·cient	*nefsN*
in·duce·ment	*ndsm*	in·eli·gi·ble	*neljB*
in·duct	*ndc*	inept	*npl*
in·duc·tion	*ndcj*	in·equal·ity	*neql'*
in·dulge	*ndlj*	in·eq·ui·ta·ble	*neqlB*
in·dul·gence	*ndljN*	in·eq·ui·ties	*neqles*
in·dus·trial	*Nl*	in·eq·uity	*neqle*
in·dus·tri·al·ism	*Nlz*	inert	*nrl*
in·dus·tri·al·ist	*NlS*	in·er·tia	*nrsa*
in·dus·tri·al·ists	*NlSs*	in·es·cap·able	*nescpB*
in·dus·tri·al·iza·tion	*Nlzj*	in·es·ti·ma·ble	*neSB*
in·dus·tri·al·ize	*Nlz*	in·evi·ta·ble	*nevlB*

in·evi·ta·bly	*nevlB*	in·fes·ta·tions	*nfSjs*
in·ex·act	*nxc*	in·fested	*nfS-*
in·ex·cus·able	*nxczB*	in·fest·ing	*nfS_*
in·ex·pen·sive	*nxpNv*	in·fi·del·ity	*nfdl'*
in·ex·pe·ri·ence	*nxp*	in·field	*nfld*
in·ex·pe·ri·enced	*nxp-*	in·fil·trate	*nfltra*
in·ex·pli·ca·ble	*nxplcB*	in·fil·tra·tion	*nfltrj*
in·fal·li·ble	*nflB*	in·fi·nite	*nfnt*
in·fancy	*nfNe*	in·fi·nitely	*nfntl*
in·fant	*nfN*	in·fin·ity	*nfn'*
in·fants	*nfNs*	in·fir·mary	*nfrre*
in·fatu·ate	*nfCa*	in·fir·mi·ties	*nfr's*
in·fatu·ated	*nfCa-*	in·fir·mity	*nfr'*
in·fect	*nfc*	in·flam·ma·tion	*nfl_y*
in·fec·tion	*nfcj*	in·flate	*nfla*
in·fec·tions	*nfcjs*	in·flated	*nfla-*
infer	*nfr*	in·fla·tion	*nflj*
in·fer·ence	*nfrN*	in·fla·tion·ary	*nfljre*
in·fer·ences	*nfrNs*	in·fla·tions	*nfljs*
in·fe·rior	*nfrer*	in·flex·ible	*nflxB*
in·ferred	*nfr-*	in·flict	*nflc*
in·fest	*nfS*	in·flow	*nflo*
in·fes·ta·tion	*nfSj*	in·flu·ence	*nfluN*

in·flu·enced	*nfluN‑*	in·fringe·ment	*nfrnjm*
in·flu·ences	*nfluNs*	in·fu·ri·ate	*nfra*
in·flu·en·tial	*nfluNsl*	in·fu·sion	*nfj*
in·flu·enza	*nflunja*	in·gen·ious	*njnys*
in·flux	*nflx*	in·ge·nu·ity	*njnuˡ*
in·form	*nf*	in·ges·tion	*njsj*
in·for·mal	*nfl*	in·grained	*ngrn‑*
in·for·mal·ities	*nflˡs*	in·grati·tude	*ngrlld*
in·for·mal·ity	*nflˡ*	in·gre·di·ent	*ngrdeN*
in·for·mally	*nfll*	in·gre·di·ents	*ngrdeNs*
in·form·ant	*nfN*	in·gress	*ngrs*
in·for·ma·tion	*inf*	in·grown	*ngrn*
in·for·ma·tional	*infl*	in·habi·tant	*nhblN*
in·forma·tive	*nfⱽ*	in·habi·tants	*nhblNs*
in·formed	*nf‑*	in·ha·la·tion	*nhlj*
in·form·ing	*nf‑*	in·hale	*nhl*
in·forms	*nfs*	in·haler	*nhlr*
in·frac·tion	*nfrcj*	in·her·ent	*nhrN*
in·frac·tions	*nfrcjs*	in·her·ently	*nhrNl*
in·fra·struc·ture	*nfrSrcCr*	in·herit	*nhrl*
in·fre·quent	*nfrqN*	in·heri·tance	*nhrlN*
in·fre·quently	*nfrqNl*	in·her·ited	*nhrl‑*
in·fringe	*nfrnj*	in·hibit	*nhbl*

in·hib·it·ing	*nhbl*	in·jec·tion	*njcy*
in·hibi·tor	*nhbtr*	in·jec·tions	*njcys*
in·hibi·tors	*nhbtrs*	in·jects	*njcs*
in·hibi·tory	*nhbtre*	in·junc·tion	*njqy*
in·hib·its	*nhbts*	in·jured	*njr-*
in·hu·man	*nhm*	in·ju·ries	*njres*
ini·tial	*insl*	in·jury	*njre*
ini·tialed	*insl-*	in·jus·tice	*njss*
ini·tial·ing	*insl*	ink	*iq*
ini·tially	*insll*	inks	*iqs*
ini·tials	*insls*	in·laid	*nld*
ini·ti·ate	*insa*	in·land	*nln*
ini·ti·ated	*insa-*	inlet	*nll*
ini·ti·ates (v.)	*insas*	in·lets	*nlls*
ini·ti·ates (n.)	*insels*	in·mate	*n a*
ini·ti·at·ing	*insa_*	in·mates	*n as*
ini·tia·tion	*insej*	inn	*n*
ini·tia·tive	*insv*	in·nate	*na*
ini·tia·tives	*insvs*	inner	*nr*
ini·tia·tor	*insar*	inn·keeper	*ncpr*
in·ject	*njc*	in·no·cence	*nsn*
in·ject·able	*njcb*	in·no·cent	*nsn*
in·ject·ing	*njc_*	in·no·cently	*nsnl*

in·nocu·ous	*(shorthand)*
in·no·vate	*(shorthand)*
in·no·vat·ing	*(shorthand)*
in·no·va·tion	*(shorthand)*
in·no·va·tions	*(shorthand)*
in·no·va·tive	*(shorthand)*
in·no·va·tive·ness	*(shorthand)*
in·no·va·tor	*(shorthand)*
in·nu·endo	*(shorthand)*
in·nu·mer·able	*(shorthand)*
in·ocu·late	*(shorthand)*
in·ocu·la·tions	*(shorthand)*
in·op·er·able	*(shorthand)*
in·op·era·tive	*(shorthand)*
in·or·di·nate	*(shorthand)*
in·pa·tient	*(shorthand)*
input	*(shorthand)*
in·puts	*(shorthand)*
in·put·ting	*(shorthand)*
in·quest	*(shorthand)*
in·quire	*(shorthand)*
in·quired	*(shorthand)*
in·quir·ies	*(shorthand)*
in·quir·ing	*(shorthand)*
in·quiry	*(shorthand)*
in·qui·si·tion	*(shorthand)*
in·quisi·tive	*(shorthand)*
ins	*(shorthand)*
in·sane	*(shorthand)*
in·san·ity	*(shorthand)*
in·scribe	*(shorthand)*
in·scribed	*(shorthand)*
in·scrip·tion	*(shorthand)*
in·sect	*(shorthand)*
in·sec·ti·cide	*(shorthand)*
in·sects	*(shorthand)*
in·se·cure	*(shorthand)*
in·se·cu·rity	*(shorthand)*
in·sen·si·tive	*(shorthand)*
in·sepa·ra·ble	*(shorthand)*
in·sert	*(shorthand)*
in·serted	*(shorthand)*
in·sert·ing	*(shorthand)*
in·ser·tion	*(shorthand)*
in·ser·tions	*(shorthand)*
in·serts	*(shorthand)*

in-service	$n = Svo$	in-spected	$nspc-$
in-side	nsd	in-spect-ing	$nspc\underline{}$
in-sidi-ous	$nsdes$	in-spec-tion	$nspcy$
in-sight	nsi	in-spec-tions	$nspcys$
in-sight-ful	$nsif$	in-spec-tor	$nspcr$
in-sights	$nsis$	in-spec-tors	$nspcrs$
in-sig-nia	$nsgna$	in-spects	$nspcs$
in-sig-nifi-cant	$nsiq$	in-spi-ra-tion	$nspry$
in-sin-cere	$nsnsr$	in-spi-ra-tional	$nspryl$
in-sinu-ate	$nsna$	in-spire	$nspr$
in-sist	$ns8$	in-spired	$nspr-$
in-sisted	$ns8-$	in-spir-ing	$nspr\underline{}$
in-sis-tence	$ns8M$	in-sta-bil-ity	$n8B^{i}$
in-sist-ing	$ns\underline{8}$	in-stall	nSl
in-sists	$ns8s$	in-stal-la-tion	$nSly$
in-so-far	$nsofr$	in-stal-la-tions	$nSlys$
in-sole	nsl	in-stalled	$nSl-$
in-so-lence	NlM	in-staller	$nSlr$
in-solu-ble	$nslB$	in-stall-ers	$nSlrs$
in-sol-vency	$nslvNe$	in-stall-ing	$nS\underline{l}$
in-sol-vent	$nslvN$	in-stall-ment	$nSlm$
in-som-nia	$ns\frown na$	in-stall-ments	$nSlms$
in-spect	$nspc$	in-stance	nSM

in·stances	*nSNs*
in·stant	*nSN*
in·stan·ta·ne·ous	*nSntnes*
in·stan·ta·ne·ously	*nSntnesl*
in·stantly	*nSNl*
in·stead	*nSd*
in·step	*nSp*
in·sti·gate	*nSga*
in·still	*nSl*
in·stills	*nSls*
in·stinct	*nSq*
in·stinc·tive	*nSqv*
in·sti·tute	*nSlu*
in·sti·tuted	*nSlu-*
in·sti·tutes	*nSlus*
in·sti·tut·ing	*nSlu_*
in·sti·tu·tion	*nSly*
in·sti·tu·tional	*nSlyl*
in·sti·tu·tion·al·iza·tion	*nSlylzy*
in·sti·tu·tions	*nSlys*
in·struct	*nSrc*
in·structed	*nSrc-*
in·struct·ing	*nSrc_*

in·struc·tion	*nSrcy*
in·struc·tional	*nSrcyl*
in·struc·tions	*nSrcys*
in·struc·tive	*nSrcv*
in·struc·tor	*nSrcr*
in·struc·tors	*nSrcrs*
in·structs	*nSrcs*
in·stru·ment	*nSrm*
in·stru·men·tal	*nSrml*
in·stru·men·tal·ity	*nSrml^L*
in·stru·men·ta·tion	*nSrmy*
in·stru·ments	*nSrms*
in·sub·or·di·na·tion	*nsordny*
in·suf·fer·able	*nsfrB*
in·suf·fi·cient	*nsfsN*
in·suf·fi·ciently	*nsfsNl*
in·su·late	*Nla*
in·su·lated	*Nla-*
in·su·la·tion	*Nly*
in·su·la·tor	*Nlar*
in·su·la·tors	*Nlars*
in·su·lin	*Nln*
in·sult	*nsll*

in·sup·port·able	*nsplB*	in·te·grated	*Ngra-*
in·sur·abil·ity	*nArB^l*	in·te·grat·ing	*Ngra_*
in·sur·able	*nArB*	in·te·gra·tion	*Ngry*
in·sur·ance	*ins*	in·te·gra·tions	*Ngrys*
in·sur·ances	*inss*	in·te·gra·tive	*Ngrav*
in·sure	*nAr*	in·teg·rity	*ntgrte*
in·sured	*nAr-*	in·tel·lect	*Nlc*
in·surer	*nArr*	in·tel·lec·tual	*NlcCul*
in·sur·ers	*nArrs*	in·tel·lec·tu·ally	*NlcCull*
in·sures	*nArs*	in·tel·li·gence	*nllyN*
in·sur·ing	*nAr_*	in·tel·li·gent	*nllyN*
in·sur·mount·able	*nS—oNB*	in·tel·li·gently	*nllyNl*
in·sur·rec·tion	*nsrcy*	in·tel·li·gi·ble	*nllyB*
in·sur·rec·tions	*nsrcys*	in·tend	*nlN*
in·tact	*nlc*	in·tended	*nlN-*
in·take	*nlc*	in·tend·ing	*nlN_*
in·takes	*nlcs*	in·tends	*nlNs*
in·tan·gi·ble	*nlnjB*	in·tense	*nlN*
in·te·ger	*Nyr*	in·tensely	*nlNl*
in·te·gers	*Nyrs*	in·ten·si·fied	*nlNf-*
in·te·gral	*Ngrl*	in·ten·sify	*nlNf*
in·te·grally	*Ngrll*	in·ten·si·fy·ing	*nlNf_*
in·te·grate	*Ngra*	in·ten·sity	*nlN^l*

in·ten·sive	*nlNv*	in·ter·com·mu·ni·ca·tion	*Nknci*
in·tent	*nlN*	in·ter·com·pany	*Nco*
in·ten·tion	*nlny*	in·ter·con·nect	*Nkc*
in·ten·tional	*nlnyl*	in·ter·con·nected	*Nkc-*
in·ten·tion·ally	*nlnyll*	in·ter·con·nec·tion	*Nkci*
in·ten·tions	*nlnys*	in·ter·con·nec·tions	*Nkcys*
in·tents	*nlNs*	in·ter·course	*Ncrs*
inter	*nlr*	in·ter·de·part·men·tal	*Ndpll*
in·ter·act	*Nac*	in·ter·dict	*Ndc*
in·ter·ac·tion	*Naci*	in·ter·dis·ci·plin·ary	*NDplnre*
in·ter·ac·tions	*Nacys*	in·ter·di·vi·sional	*Ndvyl*
in·ter·ac·tive	*Nacv*	in·ter·est	*NS*
in·ter·cede	*Nsd*	in·ter·ested	*NS-*
in·ter·cept	*Nspl*	in·ter·est·ing	*NS_*
in·ter·cep·tor	*Nsplr*	in·ter·est·ingly	*NSl*
in·ter·cep·tors	*Nsplrs*	in·ter·ests	*NSs*
in·ter·ces·sion	*Nsi*	in·ter·face	*Nfs*
in·ter·change	*NCny*	in·ter·faces	*Nfss*
in·ter·change·abil·ity	*NCnyBL*	in·ter·fac·ing	*Nfs_*
in·ter·change·able	*NCnyB*	in·ter·fere	*Nfr*
in·ter·changed	*NCny-*	in·ter·fer·ence	*NfrN*
in·ter·col·le·giate	*Nclyl*	in·ter·feres	*Nfrs*
in·ter·com	*Nk*	in·ter·gov·ern·men·tal	*Ngvll*

in·terim	
in·te·rior	
in·ter·ject	
in·ter·li·brary	
in·ter·line	
in·ter·lock	
in·ter·loper	
in·ter·lude	
in·ter·marry	
in·ter·me·di·ate	
in·ter·me·di·ates	
in·ter·mi·na·ble	
in·ter·mis·sion	
in·ter·mit·tent	
in·ter·mit·tently	
in·ter·mix	
in·tern	
in·ter·nal	
in·ter·nal·ize	
in·ter·nally	
in·ter·na·tional	
in·ter·na·tion·al·iza·tion	
in·ter·na·tion·al·ize	
in·ter·na·tion·ally	
in·terned	
in·ter·nists	
in·terns	
in·tern·ship	
in·tern·ships	
in·ter·of·fice	
in·ter·per·sonal	
in·ter·plead	
in·ter·pleaded	
in·ter·pret	
in·ter·pre·ta·tion	
in·ter·pre·ta·tions	
in·ter·pre·ta·tive	
in·ter·preted	
in·ter·preter	
in·ter·pret·ers	
in·ter·pret·ing	
in·ter·pre·tive	
in·ter·prets	
in·ter·re·lated	
in·ter·re·la·tion·ship	
in·ter·ro·ga·tion	

in·ter·roga·tory	*Nglre*	in·ter·ven·tion·ist	*Nvnjs*
in·ter·rupt	*Npt*	in·ter·view	*Nvu*
in·ter·rupted	*Npt-*	in·ter·viewed	*Nvu-*
in·ter·rup·tion	*Npj*	in·ter·view·ees	*Nvues*
in·ter·rup·tions	*Npjs*	in·ter·viewer	*Nvur*
in·ter·rupts	*Npts*	in·ter·view·ing	*Nvu_*
in·ter·scho·las·tic	*Nsclsc*	in·ter·views	*Nvus*
in·ter·sect	*Nsc*	in·ter·wo·ven	*Nvn*
in·ter·sect·ing	*Nsc_*	in·tes·tines	*ntSns*
in·ter·sec·tion	*Nscj*	in·ti·mate (adj.)	*Nt*
in·ter·sec·tional	*Nscjl*	in·ti·mate (v.)	*Na*
in·ter·sec·tions	*Nscjs*	in·ti·mately	*Nll*
in·ter·sperse	*Nsprs*	in·timi·date	*nt da*
in·ter·state	*NSa*	in·timi·da·tion	*nt dj*
in·ter·twine	*Nln*	into	*nt*
in·ter·twined	*Nln-*	in·tol·er·able	*ntlrB*
in·ter·ur·ban	*Nurbn*	in·tol·er·ant	*ntlrN*
in·ter·val	*Nvl*	in·toxi·cant	*ntxcN*
in·ter·vals	*Nvls*	in·toxi·cants	*ntxcNs*
in·ter·vene	*Nvn*	in·toxi·cate	*ntxca*
in·ter·vened	*Nvn-*	in·toxi·cated	*ntxca-*
in·ter·ven·ing	*Nvn_*	in·toxi·ca·tion	*ntxcj*
in·ter·ven·tion	*Nvnj*	in·trac·ta·ble	*ntrcB*

in·tra·mu·ral	*Nr̃rl*	in·tui·tive	*nluv*
in·tra·state	*NrSa*	in·un·date	*nnda*
in·tra·ve·nous	*Nrvns*	in·un·dated	*nnda-*
in·tri·ca·cies	*Nrcses*	inure	*nr*
in·tri·cacy	*Nrcse*	in·ured	*nr-*
in·tri·cate	*Nrcl*	in·vade	*nvd*
in·trigue	*nlrg*	in·vaded	*nvd-*
in·trigued	*nlrg-*	in·va·lid (n.)	*nvld*
in·trigu·ing	*nlrg_*	in·valid (adj.)	*nvld*
in·trin·sic	*nlrÑc*	in·vali·date	*nvlda*
in·trin·si·cally	*nlrÑcl*	in·vali·dates	*nvldas*
in·tro·duce	*Nds*	in·vali·dat·ing	*nvlda_*
in·tro·duced	*Nds-*	in·vali·da·tion	*nvldj*
in·tro·duces	*Ndss*	in·vali·da·tions	*nvldjs*
in·tro·duc·ing	*Nds_*	in·va·lid·ity	*nvld¹*
in·tro·duc·tion	*Ndcj*	in·valu·able	*nvluß*
in·tro·duc·tions	*Ndcjs*	in·vari·ably	*nvreß*
in·tro·duc·tory	*Ndclre*	in·va·sion	*nvj*
in·tro·vert	*Nvrl*	in·va·sive	*nvsv*
in·trude	*nlrd*	in·ven·tion	*nvnj*
in·tru·sion	*nlrj*	in·ven·tor	*nvÑr*
in·tru·sive	*nlrsv*	in·ven·to·ried	*nvnlre-*
in·tui·tion	*nluj*	in·ven·to·ries	*nvnlres*

in·ven·tory	*nvnlre*	in·vi·ta·tions	*nvlys*
in·ven·to·ry·ing	*nvnlre̲*	in·vite	*nvi*
in·vert	*nvrl*	in·vited	*nvi-*
in·verted	*nvrl-*	in·vites	*nvis*
in·vest	*nvs*	in·vit·ing	*nvi̲*
in·vested	*nvs-*	in·vo·ca·tion	*nvcy*
in·ves·ti·gate	*nvsga*	in·voice	*inv*
in·ves·ti·gated	*nvsga-*	in·voiced	*inv-*
in·ves·ti·gat·ing	*nvsga̲*	in·voices	*invs*
in·ves·ti·ga·tion	*nvsgy*	in·voic·ing	*inv̲*
in·ves·ti·ga·tions	*nvsgys*	in·voke	*nvc*
in·ves·ti·ga·tive	*nvsgav*	in·voked	*nvc-*
in·ves·ti·ga·tor	*nvsgar*	in·vol·un·tarily	*nvlnlrl*
in·ves·ti·ga·tors	*nvsgars*	in·vol·un·tary	*nvlnlre*
in·vest·ing	*nvs̲*	in·volve	*nvlv*
in·vest·ment	*nvsm*	in·volved	*nvlv-*
in·vest·ments	*nvsms*	in·volve·ment	*nvlvm*
in·ves·tor	*nvsr*	in·volves	*nvlvs*
in·ves·tors	*nvsrs*	in·volv·ing	*nvlv̲*
in·vests	*nvss*	in·ward	*nw*
in·vis·ible	*nvzB*	iota	*ila*
in·vi·ta·tion	*nvly*	I.Q.	*IQ*
in·vi·ta·tional	*nvlyl*	irate	*ira*

Irish		ir·ri·tant	
irk		ir·ri·tate	
iron		ir·ri·tated	
iron·ical		ir·ri·ta·tion	
iron·ically		is	
irons		is·land	
ir·ra·dia·tion		is·lands	
ir·ra·tional		isn't	
ir·rec·on·cil·able		iso·late	
ir·re·cov·er·able		iso·lated	
ir·re·deem·able		iso·lat·ing	
ir·refu·ta·ble		iso·la·tion	
ir·regu·lar		is·su·ance	
ir·regu·lar·ities		is·su·ances	
ir·rele·vant		issue	
ir·re·place·able		is·sued	
ir·re·sis·ti·ble		is·suer	
ir·re·spec·tive		is·sues	
ir·re·spon·si·ble		is·su·ing	
ir·revo·ca·ble		it	
ir·ri·ga·tion		italic	
ir·ri·ta·bil·ity		ital·ics	
ir·ri·ta·ble		itch	

itch·ing		jade	
item		jag·ged	
item·iza·tion		jail	
item·ized		jails	
item·izes		jam	
items		jamb	
itin·er·ant		jam·bo·ree	
itin·er·ar·ies		jambs	
itin·er·ary		jammed	
its		jam·ming	
it's		jan·gle	
it·self		jani·tor	
I've		jani·to·rial	
ivory		jani·tors	
ivy		January	
		jar	
J		jar·gon	
		jars	
		jaun·dice	
jab		jaunt	
jack		jaunty	
jacket		jave·lin	
jack·ets		jaw	
jacks			

jay	*ja*	jilt	*jll*
jazz	*jz*	jin·gle	*jgl*
jeal·ous	*jls*	jin·gles	*jgls*
jeans	*jns*	jinx	*jgs*
jeep	*jp*	job	*jb*
jell	*jl*	job·ber	*jbr*
jelly	*jle*	job·bers	*jbrs*
jeop·ard·ize	*jprdz*	job·less	*jbls*
jeop·ard·iz·ing	*jprdz-*	job·less·ness	*jbls'*
jeop·ardy	*jprde*	jobs	*jbs*
jerk	*jrc*	jockey	*jce*
jerky	*jrce*	jocu·lar	*jclr*
jer·sey	*jrze*	jog	*jg*
jest	*js*	join	*jyn*
jet	*jl*	joined	*jyn-*
jetty	*jle*	join·ing	*jyn_*
jewel	*jul*	joins	*jyns*
jew·eler	*julr*	joint	*jyN*
jew·el·ers	*julrs*	jointly	*jyNl*
jew·elry	*julre*	joints	*jyNs*
jew·els	*juls*	joist	*jys*
jiffy	*jfe*	joists	*jyss*
jig	*jg*	joke	*jc*

joker	*jcr*	ju·di·cial	*jdsl*
jokes	*jcs*	ju·di·ci·ary	*jdsere*
jolly	*jle*	ju·di·cious	*jdss*
jolt	*jlt*	ju·di·ciously	*jdssl*
jos·tle	*jsl*	judo	*jdo*
jot	*jt*	jug	*jg*
jour·nal	*jrnl*	jug·gle	*jgl*
jour·nal·ism	*jrnlz*	jugs	*jgs*
jour·nal·ist	*jrnls*	jugu·lar	*jglr*
jour·nal·is·tic	*jrnlsc*	juice	*js*
jour·nals	*jrnls*	juices	*jss*
jour·ney	*jrne*	juicy	*jse*
jo·vial	*jvel*	July	*Jl*
joy	*jy*	jum·ble	*j ß*
joy·ful	*jyf*	jump	*j p*
joys	*jys*	jumped	*j p-*
ju·bi·lant	*jblm*	jump·ing	*j p_*
judge	*J*	junc·tion	*jgj*
judged	*J-*	junc·ture	*jgcr*
judges	*Js*	June	*Jn*
judg·ing	*J-*	jun·gle	*jgl*
judg·ment	*Jjm*	jun·ior	*jr*
judg·ments	*Jjms*	jun·iors	*jrs*

junk	*jq*	ju·ve·niles	*jvnls*
junk·ies	*jqes*	jux·ta·pose	*jxtpz*
junta	*jNa*		
ju·ries	*jres*	**K**	
ju·ris·dic·tion	*jrsdcj*		
ju·ris·dic·tional	*jrsdcjl*	ka·lei·do·scope	*cldscp*
ju·ris·dic·tions	*jrsdcjs*	kan·ga·roo	*cgru*
juror	*jrr*	ka·rate	*crte*
jury	*jre*	keen	*cn*
just	*jS*	keenly	*cnl*
jus·tice	*jSs*	keen·ness	*cn'*
jus·ti·fi·able	*jSfB*	keep	*cp*
jus·ti·fi·ably	*jSfB*	keeper	*cpr*
jus·ti·fi·ca·tion	*jSfj*	keep·ers	*cprs*
jus·ti·fi·ca·tions	*jSfjs*	keep·ing	*cp_*
jus·ti·fied	*jSf–*	keeps	*cps*
jus·ti·fi·ers	*jSfrs*	keep·sake	*cpsc*
jus·tify	*jSf*	keg	*cq*
jus·ti·fy·ing	*jSf*	kelp	*clp*
justly	*jSl*	ken·nel	*cnl*
just·ness	*jS'*	kept	*cpt*
jut	*jt*	ker·nel	*crnl*
ju·ve·nile	*jvnl*	kero·sene	*crsn*

ketchup	*Cp*	kid·napped	*cdnp-*
ket·tle	*Cll*	kid·nap·per	*cdnpr*
key	*ce*	kid·ney	*cdne*
key·board	*cebrd*	kid·neys	*cdnes*
key·board·ing	*cebrd*	kids	*cds*
keyed	*ce-*	kill	*cl*
key·ing	*ce*	killed	*cl-*
key·note	*cenl*	killer	*clr*
key·punch	*cepnC*	kill·ers	*clrs*
key·punched	*cepnC-*	kill·ing	*cl*
key·punch·ing	*cepnC*	kilo·gram	*kq*
keys	*ces*	kilo·me·ter	*km*
khaki	*cce*	kilo·watt	*kl*
kick	*cc*	kilo·watts	*kls*
kick·back	*ccbc*	ki·mono	*c mo*
kick·backs	*ccbcs*	kin	*cn*
kicked	*cc-*	kind	*M*
kicker	*ccr*	kin·der·gar·ten	*Mrgrln*
kick·ing	*cc*	kin·der·gart·ner	*Mrgrlnr*
kick·off	*ccof*	kin·der·gart·ners	*Mrgrlnrs*
kid	*cd*	kind·est	*MS*
kid·ding	*cd*	kind·hearted	*Mhrl-*
kid·nap	*cdnp*	kin·dle	*Ml*

kindly	*Ml*	knap·sack	*npsc*
kind·ness	*M'*	knead	*nd*
kind·nesses	*M"*	knee	*ne*
kin·dred	*Mrd*	kneel	*nl*
kinds	*Ms*	knees	*nes*
kin·es·thetic	*cnsllc*	knew	*nu*
ki·netic	*cnlc*	knick·knack	*ncnc*
king	*cg*	knick·knacks	*ncncs*
king·dom	*cgd*	knife	*nf*
kings	*cgs*	knight	*ni*
kink	*cg*	knights	*nis*
kiosk	*cesc*	knit	*nl*
kiss	*cs*	knits	*nls*
kiss·ing	*cs‾*	knit·ted	*nl‑*
kit	*cl*	knives	*nvz*
kitchen	*Cn*	knob	*nb*
kitch·ens	*Cns*	knobs	*nbs*
kite	*cl*	knock	*nc*
kits	*cls*	knocked	*nc‑*
kit·ten	*cln*	knocks	*ncs*
kit·tens	*clns*	knot	*nl*
klep·to·ma·niac	*clpl nec*	knots	*nls*
knack	*nc*	knotty	*nle*

know	*no*	la·bored	*lbr-*
know-how	*no = ho*	la·borer	*lbrr*
know·ing	*no_*	la·bor·ers	*lbrrs*
know·ingly	*nol*	la·bor·ing	*lbr_*
knowl·edge	*nlg*	la·bo·ri·ously	*lbresl*
knowl·edge·able	*nlgB*	la·bors	*lbrs*
known	*nn*	labs	*lbs*
knows	*nos*	lace	*ls*
knuckle	*ncl*	lac·era·tion	*lsry*
knuck·les	*ncls*	lac·era·tions	*lsrys*
ko·sher	*csr*	laces	*lss*
kudos	*cdos*	lack	*lc*
		lacka·dai·si·cal	*lcdzcl*
		lacked	*lc-*

L

		lack·ing	*lc_*
lab	*lb*	lacks	*lcs*
label	*lB*	lac·quer	*lcr*
la·beled	*lB-*	lac·quered	*lcr-*
la·bel·ing	*lB_*	lac·ta·tion	*lcy*
la·bels	*lBs*	lac·tic	*lctc*
labor	*lbr*	lac·tose	*lcts*
labo·ra·to·ries	*lbrtres*	lad	*ld*
labo·ra·tory	*lbrtre*	lad·der	*ldr*

lad·ders	*ldrs*	lami·na·tors	*lmars*
laden	*ldn*	lamp	*lp*
la·dies	*ldes*	lamps	*lps*
lad·ing	*ld_*	lance	*en*
lady	*lde*	land	*eN*
lag	*lg*	landed	*eN-*
lager	*lgr*	land·fill	*eNfl*
lag·gard	*lgrd*	land·fills	*eNfls*
lag·ging	*lg_*	land·ing	*eN*
la·goon	*lgn*	land·ings	*eN_*
lags	*lgs*	land·lady	*eNlde*
laid	*ld*	land·lord	*eNlrd*
lain	*ln*	land·mark	*eN rc*
laity	*la'*	land·marks	*eN rcs*
lake	*lc*	land·owner	*eNor*
lakes	*lcs*	land·own·ers	*eNors*
lake·shore	*lcsr*	lands	*eNs*
lamb	*l*	land·scape	*eNscp*
lame	*l*	land·scaped	*eNscp-*
la·men·ta·ble	*lmB*	land·scap·ing	*eNscp_*
lami·nate	*lma*	land·slide	*eNsld*
lami·nat·ing	*lma_*	land·slides	*eNslds*
lami·na·tor	*lmar*	lane	*ln*

lanes	*lns*	laser	*lzr*
lan·guage	*lg√*	la·sers	*lzrs*
lan·guages	*lg√s*	lash	*ls*
lan·guid	*lg∼d*	last	*ls*
lan·guish	*lg∼s*	lasted	*ls-*
lan·tern	*lNrn*	last·ing	*ls̱*
lap	*lp*	lastly	*lsl*
laps	*lps*	lasts	*lss*
lapse	*lps*	latch	*lC*
lapsed	*lps-*	latches	*lCs*
lapses	*lpss*	latch·ing	*lC̱*
lar·ceny	*lrsne*	late	*la*
lard	*lrd*	lately	*lal*
large	*lrj*	late·ness	*la'*
largely	*lrjl*	la·tent	*llN*
large·ness	*lrj'*	later	*lar*
larger	*lrjr*	lat·eral	*llrl*
larg·est	*lrjs*	lat·er·ally	*llrll*
lark	*lrc*	lat·est	*las*
larva	*lrva*	latex	*llx*
lar·vae	*lrve*	lathe	*ll*
lar·yn·gi·tis	*lrnjls*	lather	*llr*
lar·ynx	*lrqs*	lati·tude	*llld*

lati·tudes	
lat·ter	
laud	
laud·able	
laugh	
laugh·ing	
laugh·ter	
launch	
launched	
launches	
launch·ing	
launch·ings	
laun·dries	
laun·dry	
lava·tory	
lav·ish	
law	
law·ful	
law·fully	
law·less	
law·maker	
lawn	
lawns	
laws	
law·suit	
law·suits	
law·yer	
law·yers	
lax	
laxa·tive	
lax·ity	
lay	
layer	
lay·ers	
lay·ette	
lay·ing	
lay·man	
lay·men	
lay·off	
lay·offs	
lay·out	
lay·outs	
lay·over	
la·zi·ness	
lazy	
leach	

lead	*ld*	learned	*lrn-*
leaded	*ld-*	learner	*lrnr*
leader	*ldr*	learn·ers	*lrnrs*
lead·ers	*ldrs*	learn·ing	*lrn_*
lead·er·ship	*ldrs*	lease	*ls*
lead·ing	*ld_*	leased	*ls-*
leads	*lds*	lease·hold	*lshld*
leaf	*lf*	leases	*lss*
leaf·let	*lfl*	leash	*ls*
league	*lg*	leas·ing	*ls_*
leagues	*lgs*	least	*ls*
leak	*lc*	leather	*llr*
leak·age	*lcg*	leath·ers	*llrs*
leaked	*lc-*	leave	*lv*
leak·ing	*lc_*	leaves	*lvs*
leaks	*lcs*	leav·ing	*lv_*
leaky	*lce*	lech·er·ous	*lCrs*
lean	*ln*	lec·tern	*lctrn*
leaner	*lnr*	lec·ture	*lcCr*
lean·ing	*ln_*	lec·turer	*lcCrr*
leans	*lns*	lec·tur·ers	*lcCrrs*
leap	*lp*	lec·tures	*lcCrs*
learn	*lrn*	led	*ld*

ledge	*ℓ₁*	leg·ibly	*ℓᵧβ*
ledger	*ℓᵧʳ*	le·gion	*ℓᵧn*
ledg·ers	*ℓᵧʳs*	leg·is·late	*ℓᵧsla*
leer	*ℓʳ*	leg·is·lated	*ℓᵧsla-*
lee·way	*ℓe a*	leg·is·la·tion	*ℓᵧsly*
left	*ℓfℓ*	leg·is·la·tive	*ℓᵧslav*
left·ist	*ℓfℓ8*	leg·is·la·tor	*ℓᵧslar*
left·over	*ℓfℓO*	leg·is·la·tors	*ℓᵧslars*
leg	*ℓq*	leg·is·la·ture	*ℓᵧslℭr*
legacy	*ℓgse*	leg·is·la·tures	*ℓᵧslℭrs*
legal	*ℓgℓ*	le·giti·macy	*ℓᵧt—se*
le·gal·ities	*ℓgℓ ⁶ˢ*	le·giti·mate	*ℓᵧt—ℓ*
le·gal·ity	*ℓgℓ ᶦ*	legs	*ℓgs*
le·gal·iza·tion	*ℓgℓz₁*	leg·work	*ℓg—o*
le·gal·ize	*ℓgℓz*	lei·sure	*ℓzr*
le·gal·ized	*ℓgℓz-*	lei·surely	*ℓzrℓ*
le·gal·iz·ing	*ℓgℓz-*	lemon	*ℓm*
le·gally	*ℓgℓℓ*	lem·on·ade	*ℓmd*
leg·end	*ℓᵧN*	lend	*ℓN*
leg·en·dary	*ℓᵧNre*	lender	*ℓNr*
leg·ends	*ℓᵧNs*	lend·ers	*ℓNrs*
leg·ibil·ity	*ℓᵧβᶦ*	lend·ing	*ℓN*
leg·ible	*ℓᵧβ*	lends	*ℓN̄s*

length	*lgt*	less·en·ing	*lsn_*
lengthen	*lgtn*	lesser	*lsr*
length·ened	*lgtn-*	les·son	*lsn*
length·ens	*lgtns*	les·sons	*lsns*
lengths	*lgts*	les·sor	*lsr*
length·wise	*lgt₃*	les·sors	*lsrs*
lengthy	*lgte*	lest	*l8*
le·ni·ent	*lneN*	let	*ll*
lens	*lnz*	let·down	*lldon*
lenses	*lnzs*	le·thal	*lll*
lent	*eN*	le·thar·gic	*llryc*
len·til	*eNl*	lets	*lls*
leop·ard	*lprd*	let's	*ll's*
leo·tard	*lelrd*	let·ter	*L*
lep·re·chaun	*lprk*	let·tered	*L-*
lep·rosy	*lprse*	let·ter·head	*Lhd*
le·sion	*ly*	let·ter·heads	*Lhds*
le·sions	*lys*	let·ter·ing	*L_*
less	*ls*	let·ters	*Ls*
les·see	*lse*	let·ting	*ll*
les·sees	*lses*	let·tuce	*lls*
lessen	*lsn*	levee	*lve*
less·ened	*lsn-*	level	*lvl*

lev·el·ing	*lvl*	lib·er·al·iz·ing	*lbrlz*
lev·els	*lvls*	lib·er·ally	*lbrll*
lever	*lvr*	lib·er·als	*lbrls*
lev·er·age	*lvrj*	lib·er·ate	*lbra*
lev·ied	*lve-*	lib·era·tion	*lbrj*
lev·ies	*lves*	lib·erty	*lbrle*
lev·ity	*lvᴸ*	li·brarian	*lbrren*
levy	*lve*	li·brari·ans	*lbrrens*
levy·ing	*lve*	li·brar·ies	*lbrres*
lexi·cog·ra·pher	*lxcgrfr*	li·brary	*lbrre*
li·abil·ities	*liᏰᶫˢ*	lice	*ls*
li·abil·ity	*liᏰᴸ*	li·cense	*lsN*
li·able	*liᏰ*	li·censed	*lsN-*
li·ai·son	*lezn*	li·censee	*lsNe*
liar	*lir*	li·censes	*lsNs*
libel	*lᏰ*	li·cens·ing	*lsN*
li·bel·ous	*lᏰs*	li·cen·sor	*lsN̄r*
lib·eral	*lbrl*	lid	*ld*
lib·er·al·ism	*lbrlz*	lie	*li*
lib·er·al·ity	*lbrlᴸ*	lien	*ln*
lib·er·al·iza·tion	*lbrlzj*	liens	*lns*
lib·er·al·ize	*lbrlz*	lies	*lis*
lib·er·al·ized	*lbrlz-*	lieu	*lu*

lieu·ten·ant	*ltnN*	lighter	*lir*
life	*lf*	light·house	*lihos*
life·blood	*lfbld*	light·ing	*li*
life·guard	*lfgrd*	lightly	*lil*
life·less	*lfls*	light·ning	*ling*
life·like	*lflc*	lights	*lis*
life·long	*lflg*	light·weight	*li a*
life·saver	*lfsvr*	like	*lc*
life·sav·ing	*lfsv*	liked	*lc-*
life·style	*lfSl*	like·li·hood	*lclh*
life·styles	*lfSls*	likely	*lcl*
life·time	*lft*	like·ness	*lc'*
lift	*lft*	likes	*lcs*
lifted	*lft-*	like·wise	*lc з*
lift·ing	*lft*	lik·ing	*lc*
lifts	*lfts*	limb	*l*
liga·ment	*lgm*	lim·ber	*l br*
liga·ments	*lgms*	limbo	*l bo*
li·ga·tion	*lgj*	limbs	*l s*
light	*li*	lime	*l*
lighted	*li-*	lime·light	*l li*
lighten	*lin*	lim·er·ick	*l rc*
light·en·ing	*lin*	lime·stone	*l Sn*

limit	*ℓ ↲*	lin·ings	*ℓn̲*
limi·ta·tion	*ℓ ↲ɣ*	link	*ℓq*
limi·ta·tions	*ℓ ↲ɣs*	link·age	*ℓqƒ*
lim·ited	*ℓ ↲ -*	link·ages	*ℓqƒs*
lim·it·ing	*ℓ ↲*	linked	*ℓq -*
lim·its	*ℓ ↲s*	link·ing	*ℓq -*
lim·ou·sine	*ℓ ɀn*	links	*ℓqs*
limp	*ℓ p*	lint	*ℓN*
line	*ℓn*	lin·tel	*ℓNℓ*
line·age	*ℓneɣ*	lion	*ℓin*
lineal	*ℓneℓ*	lip	*ℓp*
linear	*ℓner*	lips	*ℓps*
lined	*ℓn -*	liq·ue·fied	*ℓqƒɪ -*
linen	*ℓnn*	liq·uefy	*ℓqƒɪ*
lin·ens	*ℓnns*	liq·uid	*ℓqd*
liner	*ℓnr*	liq·ui·date	*ℓqda*
lin·ers	*ℓnrs*	liq·ui·dated	*ℓqda -*
lines	*ℓns*	liq·ui·da·tion	*ℓqdɣ*
lineup	*ℓnp*	liq·ui·da·tor	*ℓqdar*
lin·ger	*ℓgr*	liq·ui·da·tors	*ℓqdars*
lin·ger·ing	*ℓgr̲*	li·quid·ity	*ℓqdᶥ*
lin·guist	*ℓg_S*	liq·uids	*ℓqds*
lin·ing	*ℓn̲*	liq·uor	*ℓcr*

Word	Outline	Word	Outline
list		li·thology	
listed		liti·gate	
lis·ten		liti·ga·tion	
lis·tened		lit·ter	
lis·tener		lit·tle	
lis·ten·ers		lit·urgy	
lis·ten·ing		live	
lis·tens		lived	
list·ing		live·li·hood	
list·ings		lively	
list·less		liven	
lists		liver	
lit		lives	
litany		live·stock	
liter		livid	
lit·eracy		liv·ing	
lit·eral		liz·ard	
lit·er·ally		load	
lit·er·ate		loaded	
lit·era·ture		loader	
li·ters		load·ing	
lithium		load·ings	
li·thog·ra·phy		loads	

loaf	*lf*	lo·cates	*lcas*
loan	*ln*	lo·cat·ing	*lca_*
loaned	*ln-*	lo·ca·tion	*lcq*
loan·ing	*ln_*	lo·ca·tions	*lcqs*
loans	*lns*	lo·ca·tor	*lcar*
loath·some	*lls*	lock	*lc*
loaves	*lvz*	locked	*lc-*
lob·bies	*lbes*	locker	*lcr*
lobby	*lbe*	lock·ers	*lcrs*
lob·by·ing	*lbe_*	lock·ing	*lc_*
lob·by·ist	*lbeS*	lock·out	*lcol*
lobe	*lb*	lock·outs	*lcols*
lob·ster	*lbSr*	locks	*lcs*
local	*lcl*	lock·smith	*lcs l*
lo·cale	*lcl*	lo·cust	*lcS*
lo·cal·ities	*lcl ls*	lodge	*lg*
lo·cal·ity	*lcl l*	lodges	*lgs*
lo·cal·iza·tion	*lclz1*	lodg·ing	*lg_*
lo·cal·ized	*lclz-*	loft	*lft*
lo·cally	*lcll*	lofty	*lfte*
lo·cals	*lcls*	log	*lg*
lo·cate	*lca*	logged	*lg-*
lo·cated	*lca-*	log·ger	*lgr*

Word	Shorthand	Word	Shorthand
log·gers	*lgrs*	lon·gi·tu·di·nal	*lnjtdnl*
log·ging	*lg_*	long-range	*lg = rnj*
logic	*ljc*	long-standing	*lg = SN_*
log·ical	*ljcl*	look	*lc*
log·ically	*ljcll*	looked	*lc-*
lo·gis·tic	*ljSc*	look·ing	*lc_*
lo·gis·ti·cal	*ljScl*	look·out	*lcol*
lo·gis·ti·cally	*ljScll*	looks	*lcs*
lo·gis·tics	*ljScs*	loom	*l*
logo	*lg*	looms	*l~s*
logos	*lgs*	loop	*lp*
logs	*lgs*	loop·hole	*lphl*
loll	*ll*	loops	*lps*
lone·li·ness	*lnl'*	loose	*ls*
lonely	*lnl*	loosely	*lsl*
lone·some	*lns*	loosen	*lsn*
long	*lg*	loos·en·ing	*lsn_*
longer	*lgr*	lord	*lrd*
long·est	*lgS*	lore	*lr*
lon·gev·ity	*lnjv'*	lose	*lz*
long·hand	*lghN*	loser	*lzr*
long·ing	*lg_*	los·ers	*lzrs*
lon·gi·tude	*lnjtd*	loses	*lzs*

Word	Shorthand
los·ing	*ez-*
loss	*es*
losses	*ess*
lost	*es*
lot	*el*
lo·tion	*ey*
lots	*els*
lot·tery	*eltre*
loud	*lod*
louder	*lodr*
loud·speaker	*lodspcr*
loud·speak·ers	*lodspcrs*
lounge	*lony*
lounges	*lonys*
louse	*los*
lou·ver	*lvr*
lou·vers	*lvrs*
love	*lv*
loved	*lv-*
love·li·ness	*lvl'*
lovely	*lvl*
lover	*lvr*
lov·ing	*lv_*

Word	Shorthand
low	*lo*
low-cost	*lo = cS*
lower	*lor*
lower-case	*lor = cs*
low·ered	*lor-*
low·er·ing	*lor_*
low·ers	*lors*
low·est	*loS*
lows	*los*
loyal	*lyl*
loy·alty	*lylle*
L.P.N.	*L P N*
lu·bri·cant	*lbrcN*
lu·bri·cants	*lbrcNs*
lu·bri·cate	*lbrca*
lu·bri·cated	*lbrca-*
lu·bri·cates	*lbrcas*
lu·bri·cat·ing	*lbrca_*
lu·bri·ca·tion	*lbrcj*
lucid	*lsd*
luck	*lc*
luckily	*lcl*
lucky	*lce*

lu·cra·tive	*lcrv*	lungs	*lgs*
lu·di·crous	*ldcrs*	lure	*lr*
lug	*lq*	lus·cious	*lss*
lug·gage	*lgj*	luxury	*lxre*
lug·ging	*lq̲*	lye	*li*
lull	*ll*	lying	*li̲*
lum·bago	*l � bq*	lymph	*l ⌒ f*
lum·bar	*l ⌒ br*	lyr·ical	*lrcl*
lum·ber	*l ⌒ br*		
lum·ber·ing	*l ⌒ br̲*		
lu·mi·nance	*lmN*	**M**	
lu·mi·nous	*lms*		
lump	*l ⌒ p*	mac·adam	*⌒cd*
lumped	*l ⌒ p-*	maca·roni	*⌒crne*
lumps	*l ⌒ ps*	mace	*⌒s*
lunar	*lnr*	mach	*⌒c*
lunch	*lnC*	ma·chine	*⌒An*
lunch·eon	*lnCn*	ma·chin·ery	*⌒Anre*
lunch·eons	*lnCns*	ma·chines	*⌒Ans*
lunches	*lnCs*	ma·chin·ist	*⌒AnS*
lunch·room	*lnCr*	ma·chin·ists	*⌒AnSs*
lung	*lq*	mac·ro·cosm	*⌒crcz*
lunge	*lnj*	mad	*⌒d*
		madam	*⌒d*

made	_d	maiden	_dn
maes·tro	_Sro	mail	_l
maga·zine	_gzn	mail·able	_lB
maga·zines	_gzns	mail·box	_lbx
magic	_jc	mail·boxes	_lbxs
mag·ical	_jcl	mailed	_l-
ma·gi·cian	_jj	mailer	_lr
mag·is·trate	_jSra	mail·ers	_lrs
mag·is·trates	_jSras	mail·ing	_l
mag·nani·mous	_gnn~s	mail·ings	_l
mag·ne·sium	_gnze	mail·man	_l~n
mag·net	_gnl	mail·out	_lol
mag·netic	_gnlc	mail·outs	_lols
mag·net·ics	_gnlcs	mail·room	_lr
mag·nets	_gnls	mails	_ls
mag·ni·fi·ca·tion	_gnfj	main	_n
mag·ni·fi·ca·tions	_gnfjs	main·frame	_nfr
mag·nifi·cent	_gnfsN	main·land	_nlN
mag·ni·fied	_gnfi-	mainly	_nl
mag·nify	_gnfi	mains	_ns
mag·ni·tude	_gnld	main·stream	_nSr
mag·ni·tudes	_gnlds	main·stream·ing	_nSr
maid	_d	main·tain	_nln

main·tained		males	
main·tain·ing		ma·levo·lent	
main·tains		mal·fea·sance	
main·te·nance		mal·func·tion	
ma·jes·tic		mal·func·tioned	
major		mal·func·tion·ing	
ma·jor·ing		mal·func·tions	
ma·jor·ity		ma·li·cious	
ma·jors		ma·lig·nancy	
make		ma·lig·nant	
maker		ma·lin·ger·ing	
mak·ers		mall	
makes		mal·le·able	
makeup		malls	
make·ups		mal·nu·tri·tion	
mak·ing		mal·prac·tice	
mak·ings		malt	
mal·ad·just·ment		mam·mal	
mal·ad·min·is·ter		mam·mals	
malady		mam·mo·gram	
mal·aise		mam·mog·ra·phy	
ma·laria		man	
male		man·age	

man·age·able		ma·niac	
man·aged		mani·cure	
man·age·ment		mani·fest	
man·age·ments		mani·fested	
man·ager		mani·fold	
mana·ge·rial		ma·nipu·late	
man·ag·ers		ma·nipu·la·tion	
man·ages		man·kind	
man·ag·ing		manly	
man·date		man·made	
man·dated		manned	
man·dates		man·ner	
man·dat·ing		man·nered	
man·da·tory		man·ner·ism	
ma·neu·ver·abil·ity		man·ner·isms	
ma·neu·ver·ing		man·ners	
man·ger		man·ning	
man·gle		man·power	
man·han·dle		man·sion	
man·hole		man·tel	
man·hood		man·tle	
man-hour		manual	
man-hours		manu·ally	

manu·als	*nuls*	march·ing	*rC*
manu·fac·ture	*f*	mar·ga·rine	*rjrn*
manu·fac·tured	*f-*	mar·gin	*rjn*
manu·fac·turer	*fr*	mar·ginal	*rjnl*
manu·fac·tur·ers	*frs*	mar·gin·ally	*rjnll*
manu·fac·tures	*fs*	mar·gins	*rjns*
manu·fac·tur·ing	*f-*	mari·juana	*r na*
manu·script	*nS*	ma·rina	*rna*
manu·scripts	*nSs*	mari·nade	*rnd*
many	*me*	ma·rine	*rn*
map	*p*	Marine	*rn*
maple	*pl*	mari·tal	*rll*
map·ping	*p-*	mari·time	*rl*
maps	*ps*	mark	*rc*
mar	*r*	mark·down	*rcdon*
mara·thon	*rln*	mark·downs	*rcdons*
mar·ble	*rB*	marked	*rc-*
mar·ble·ize	*rBz*	mark·edly	*rc-l*
mar·bles	*rBs*	marker	*rcr*
march	*rC*	mar·ket	*r*
March	*Mr*	mar·ket·abil·ity	*rB*
marched	*rC-*	mar·ket·able	*rB*
marches	*rCs*	mar·keted	*r-*

mar·ket·ing		marts	
mar·ket·ings		mar·tyr	
mar·ket·place		mar·vel·ous	
mar·kets		mas·cu·line	
mark·ing		mas·cu·lin·ity	
mark·ings		mash	
marks		mask	
markup		masked	
mark·ups		mask·ing	
mar·quee		masks	
marred		ma·son·ite	
mar·riage		ma·sonry	
mar·riage·able		mas·quer·ade	
mar·riages		mass	
mar·ried		mas·sa·cre	
mar·ries		mas·sage	
mar·ring		mas·saged	
mar·ry·ing		masses	
marsh		mas·sive	
mar·shal		mas·tec·tomy	
mar·shal·ing		mas·ter	
mart		mas·tered	
mar·tial		mas·ter·piece	

mas·ters		ma·trix	
mas·tery		mats	
mas·ti·cate		mat·ter	
mas·toid		mat·ters	
mat		mat·tress	
match		mat·tresses	
matched		matu·ra·tion	
matches		ma·ture	
match·ing		ma·tured	
match·less		ma·turely	
mate		ma·tures	
mated		ma·tur·ing	
ma·te·rial		ma·tur·ities	
ma·te·ri·al·ize		ma·tur·ity	
ma·te·ri·ally		maul	
ma·te·ri·als		maxim	
ma·ter·nal		maxi·mize	
ma·ter·nity		maxi·mized	
math		maxi·mizes	
mathe·mat·ical		maxi·miz·ing	
mathe·mat·ics		maxi·mum	
ma·tricu·late		may	
ma·tricu·la·tion		May	

maybe	*ab*	mea·sles	*zlz*
may·on·naise	*anz*	meas·ur·able	*zrʙ*
mayor	*ar*	meas·ure	*zr*
may·ors	*ars*	meas·ured	*zr-*
maze	*z*	meas·ure·ment	*zrm*
M.B.A.	*MBA*	meas·ure·ments	*zrms*
M.D.	*MD*	meas·ures	*zrs*
me	*e*	meas·ur·ing	*zr̠*
meadow	*do*	meat	*e*
mea·ger	*gr*	meats	*es*
meal	*l*	me·chanic	*cnc*
meals	*ls*	me·chan·ical	*cncl*
mean	*n*	me·chan·ically	*cncll*
me·an·der	*eNr*	me·chan·ics	*cncs*
me·an·der·ing	*eNr̠*	mecha·nism	*cnz*
mean·ing	*n̠*	mecha·nisms	*cnz s*
mean·ing·ful	*nf*	mecha·nize	*cnz*
mean·ing·fully	*nfl*	mecha·nized	*cnz-*
mean·ing·less	*nls*	medal	*dl*
means	*ns*	med·dle	*dl*
meant	*m*	media	*da*
mean·time	*ml*	me·dial	*del*
mean·while	*nl*	me·dian	*den*

me•dia•tion
me•dia•tor
me•dia•tors
med•ical
med•ically
medi•care
medi•cated
medi•ca•tion
medi•ca•tions
medi•cine
me•dio•cre
me•di•oc•rity
medi•ta•tion
me•dium
meek
meet
meet•ing
meet•ings
meets
mega•ton
mega•watt
mega•watts
mel•an•choly
mel•low
melody
melon
melt
melt•ing
melts
mem•ber
mem•bers
mem•ber•ship
mem•ber•ships
mem•brane
me•mento
memo
memo•ra•ble
memo•randa
memo•ran•dum
memo•ran•dums
me•mo•rial
memo•ries
memo•rize
memory
memos
men

men·ace	*ms*	mer·cury	*rcre*
mend	*m*	mercy	*rse*
me·nial	*nel*	mere	*r*
meno·pause	*mpz*	merely	*rl*
men·strual	*mSrul*	merge	*ry*
men·strua·tion	*mSruy*	merged	*ry-*
men·tal	*mll*	merger	*ryr*
men·tal·ity	*mll*	merg·ers	*ryrs*
men·tally	*mlll*	merges	*rys*
men·tion	*my*	merg·ing	*ry_*
men·tioned	*my-*	merit	*rl*
men·tion·ing	*my_*	meri·to·ri·ous	*rlres*
men·tions	*mys*	mer·its	*rls*
menu	*mu*	merry	*re*
menus	*mus*	mesh	*A*
mer·can·tile	*rcnll*	mess	*s*
mer·chan·dise	*dse*	mes·sage	*sy*
mer·chan·diser	*dser*	mes·sages	*sys*
mer·chan·dis·ers	*dsers*	mes·sen·ger	*snyr*
mer·chan·dises	*dses*	mess·ing	*s_*
mer·chan·dis·ing	*dse_*	messy	*se*
mer·chant	*rCN*	met	*l*
mer·chants	*rCNs*	meta·bolic	*llblc*

me·tabo·lism	_Ublz_
metal	_Ul_
me·tal·lic	_Ulc_
met·al·lur·gi·cal	_Ulrycl_
met·al·lur·gist	_Ulrys_
met·al·lurgy	_Ulye_
met·als	_Uls_
met·al·work·ing	_Ul o_
meta·phor	_Ufr_
mete	_e_
me·te·or·olo·gist	_Uerlys_
me·te·or·ology	_Uerlye_
meter	_m_
me·tered	_m-_
me·ter·ing	_m_
me·ters	_ms_
meth·ane	_Un_
method	_Ud_
meth·od·olo·gies	_Udlyes_
meth·od·ology	_Udlye_
meth·ods	_Uds_
me·ticu·lous	_Ucls_
me·ticu·lously	_Uclsl_

met·ric	_Urc_
metro	_Uro_
met·ro·poli·tan	_Urplln_
mez·za·nine	_znn_
mice	_s_
mi·crobe	_crb_
mi·crobes	_crbs_
mi·cro·bi·ology	_crblye_
mi·cro·cas·sette	_crcsl_
mi·cro·cod·ing	_crcd_
mi·cro·com·puter	_crkpur_
mi·cro·fiche	_crfs_
mi·cro·film	_crfl_
mi·cro·filmed	_crfl -_
mi·cro·film·ing	_crfl_
mi·cro·form	_crf_
mi·cro·forms	_crf s_
mi·cro·graph·ics	_crgrfcs_
mi·crome·ter	_cr lr_
mi·cron	_crn_
mi·crons	_crns_
mi·cro·phone	_crfn_
mi·cro·proc·ess·ing	_crfss_

mi·cro·proc·es·sor	*crpssr*	mi·grants	*grNs*
mi·cro·scope	*crscp*	mi·grate	*gra*
mi·cro·scopic	*crscpc*	mi·gra·tion	*gry*
mi·cro·wave	*crv*	mike	*c*
mid	*d*	mil	*l*
mid·day	*dd*	mild	*ld*
mid·dle	*dl*	mil·dew	*ldu*
midget	*jl*	mildly	*ldl*
mid·land	*dlN*	mile	*l*
mid·night	*dni*	mile·age	*ly*
mid·riff	*drf*	mile·ages	*lys*
midst	*dS*	miles	*ls*
mid·sum·mer	*ds r*	mile·stone	*lSn*
mid·term	*dlr*	mile·stones	*lSns*
mid·way	*d a*	mi·lieu	*lu*
mid·week	*d c*	mili·tant	*llN*
Midwest	*d W*	mili·tary	*llre*
mid·wife	*d f*	milk	*lc*
mid·year	*dyr*	milk·ing	*lc̲*
might	*i*	mill	*l*
mighty	*ie*	miller	*lr*
mi·graine	*grn*	mill·ers	*lrs*
mi·grant	*grN*	mil·li·gram	*mg*

mil·li·me·ter	*mm*	min·gle	*gl*
mil·lion	*M*	mini·ature	*mCr*
mil·lion·aire	*Mr*	mini·atur·ize	*mCrz*
mil·lions	*Ms*	mini·atur·ized	*mCrz-*
mil·lionth	*Ml*	mini·cas·sette	*mcst*
mil·li·sec·ond	*msec*	mini·com·puter	*mkpur*
mil·li·sec·onds	*msecs*	mini·com·put·ers	*mkpurs*
mills	*ls*	mini·mal	*m l*
mill·work	*lo*	mini·mally	*m ll*
mimic	*mc*	mini·mize	*m z*
mind	*m*	mini·mized	*m z-*
minded	*m-*	mini·mizes	*m zs*
mind·ful	*mf*	mini·miz·ing	*m z-*
mind·ing	*m_*	mini·mum	*mm*
mind·less	*mls*	mini·mums	*mms*
minds	*ms*	min·ing	*n_*
mine	*n*	min·is·ter	*mSr*
mined	*n-*	min·is·ters	*mSrs*
min·eral	*mrl*	min·is·tries	*mSres*
min·er·als	*mrls*	min·is·try	*mSre*
miner	*nr*	mink	*q*
min·ers	*nrs*	minor	*nr*
mines	*ns*	mi·nor·ities	*nrls*

mi·nor·ity	*ml*	mis·car·riage	*Mcy*
mi·nors	*nrs*	mis·car·riages	*Mcys*
mint	*m*	mis·cel·la·ne·ous	*Mlnes*
minus	*ns*	mis·chief	*Mcf*
mi·nuses	*nss*	mis·con·cep·tion	*Mkspf*
min·ute (n.)	*ml*	mis·con·cep·tions	*Mkspjs*
mi·nute (adj.)	*nu*	mis·con·duct	*Mkdc*
mi·nutely	*nul*	mis·con·strue	*MkSru*
min·utes	*mls*	mis·con·strued	*MkSru-*
mira·cle	*rcl*	mis·de·meanor	*Md nr*
mira·cles	*rcls*	mis·de·mean·ors	*Md nrs*
mir·ror	*rr*	mis·di·rect	*Mdr*
mir·rors	*rrs*	mis·di·rected	*Mdr-*
mis·align	*Maln*	miser	*zr*
mis·aligned	*Maln-*	mis·er·able	*zrB*
mis·align·ment	*Malnm*	mis·ery	*zre*
mis·ap·pli·ca·tion	*Maplcy*	mis·fire	*Mfr*
mis·ap·pre·hen·sion	*Maprhny*	mis·fit	*Mfl*
mis·ap·pro·pri·ate	*Mapo*	mis·guide	*Mgd*
mis·be·have	*Mbhv*	mis·guided	*Mgd-*
mis·be·haves	*Mbhvs*	mis·hap	*Mhp*
mis·be·hav·ior	*Mbhvr*	mis·in·for·ma·tion	*Minf*
mis·cal·cu·late	*Mclcla*	mis·in·form	*Mnf*

mis·in·formed	*Mnf —*	mis·rep·re·sen·ta·tion	*Mrep↑*
mis·in·ter·pre·ta·tion	*Mntrprly*	mis·rep·re·sent·ing	*Mrep_*
mis·in·ter·pret	*Mntrprt*	miss	*M*
mis·in·ter·preted	*Mntrprt—*	Miss	*M*
mis·judge	*Mj*	missed	*M—*
mis·judg·ing	*Mj_*	misses	*Ms*
mis·la·bel	*Mlß*	mis·sile	*Ml*
mis·la·bel·ing	*Mlß_*	mis·siles	*Mls*
mis·lay	*Mla*	miss·ing	*M_*
mis·lead	*Mld*	mis·sion	*↷↑*
mis·lead·ing	*Mld_*	mis·sion·ar·ies	*↷yres*
mis·led	*Mld*	mis·sion·ary	*↷yre*
mis·man·age	*M↷*	mis·sions	*↷ys*
mis·man·aged	*M↷—*	mis·spell	*Mpl*
mis·place	*Mpls*	mis·spell·ing	*Mpl_*
mis·placed	*Mpls—*	mis·state	*MSa*
mis·place·ment	*Mplsm*	mis·stated	*MSa—*
mis·plac·ing	*Mpls_*	mis·state·ment	*MSam*
mis·print	*MprN*	mis·state·ments	*MSams*
mis·quote	*Mqo*	mis·take	*Mlc*
mis·quoted	*Mqo—*	mis·taken	*Mlcn*
mis·read	*Mrd*	mis·takes	*Mlcs*
mis·re·port	*Mrpl*	mis·treat	*Mlre*

Word	Shorthand	Word	Shorthand
mis·trust		mo·bil·ity	
mis·un·der·stand		mo·bi·li·za·tion	
mis·un·der·stand·ing		mo·bi·lize	
mis·un·der·stands		mo·bi·lized	
mis·un·der·stood		mo·bi·liz·ing	
mis·use		mock	
miti·gate		mock·ery	
mitt		mockup	
mit·ten		mock·ups	
mit·tens		mod	
mix		mo·dal·ities	
mixed		mo·dal·ity	
mixer		mode	
mix·ers		model	
mixes		mod·eled	
mix·ing		mod·el·ing	
mix·ture		mod·els	
mix·tures		modem	
mix-up		mod·er·ate (adj. or n.)	
mne·monic		mod·er·ate (v.)	
moan		mod·er·ated	
mob		mod·er·ately	
mo·bile		mod·era·tion	

mod·era·tor	*drar*	mold	*ld*
mod·era·tors	*drars*	molded	*ld-*
mod·ern	*drn*	mold·ing	*ld*
mod·ern·iza·tion	*drnz*	molds	*lds*
modes	*ds*	mo·lecu·lar	*lclr*
mod·est	*ds*	mo·lest	*ls*
mod·estly	*dsl*	mo·ment	*m*
modi·fi·ca·tion	*df*	mo·men·tarily	*mrl*
modi·fi·ca·tions	*dfs*	mo·men·tary	*mre*
modi·fied	*df-*	mo·ments	*ms*
modi·fier	*dfr*	mo·men·tum	*m*
modify	*df*	Monday	*Mn*
modi·fy·ing	*df-*	mone·tary	*mtre*
modu·lar	*lr*	money	*me*
modu·lar·ize	*lrz*	mon·ey·mak·ing	*me c*
modu·lar·ized	*lrz-*	mon·eys	*mes*
modu·late	*la*	mon·ey·wise	*me z*
modu·la·tion	*l*	mon·ies	*mes*
mod·ule	*l*	moni·tor	*mtr*
mod·ules	*ls*	moni·tored	*mtr-*
moist	*ys*	moni·tor·ing	*mtr*
mois·ture	*ysCr*	moni·tors	*mtrs*
molar	*lr*	mo·nogamy	*ng e*

mono·gram	*mq*	mood	*‿d*
mono·graph	*mgrf*	moods	*‿ds*
mono·graphic	*mgrfc*	moody	*‿de*
mono·graphs	*mgrfs*	moon	*‿m*
mono·lithic	*mllc*	moon·light	*‿mli*
mono·logue	*mlq*	moor	*‿r*
mo·nopo·li·za·tion	*‿nplz*	moored	*‿r −*
mo·nopoly	*‿npl*	moor·ing	*‿r_*
mono·rail	*mrl*	moor·ings	*‿r=*
mono·syl·la·ble	*mslB*	moose	*‿s*
mono·tone	*mln*	moot	*‿u*
mo·noto·nous	*‿nlns*	mop	*‿p*
mon·ox·ide	*mxd*	mope	*‿p*
mon·soon	*msn*	moped	*‿p−*
mon·ster	*mSr*	mop·ing	*‿p_*
mon·stros·ity	*mSrsl*	mopped	*‿p−*
mon·strous	*mSrs*	mop·ping	*‿p_*
mon·tage	*mlz*	moral	*‿rl*
month	*‿o*	mo·rale	*‿rl*
monthly	*‿ol*	mo·ral·ity	*‿rll*
months	*‿os*	mor·ally	*‿rll*
monu·ment	*mm*	mor·als	*‿rls*
monu·men·tal	*mml*	mora·to·rium	*‿rlre‿*

mor·bid	*rbd*	motel	*ll*
mor·bid·ity	*rbd*	mo·tels	*lls*
more		moth	*l*
more·over		mother	*lr*
morgue	*rq*	moth·er·hood	*lrh*
morn·ing	*rn*	mother-in-law	*lr = n = la*
morn·ings	*rn*	moth·erly	*lrl*
mor·tal	*rll*	moth·ers	*lrs*
mor·tal·ities	*rll*	mo·tion	*y*
mor·tal·ity	*rll*	mo·tion·less	*yls*
mor·tar	*rlr*	mo·tions	*ys*
mort·gage	*rgj*	mo·ti·vate	*lva*
mort·gaged	*rgj-*	mo·ti·vated	*lva-*
mort·ga·gee	*rgje*	mo·ti·vat·ing	*lva*
mort·ga·gees	*rgjes*	mo·ti·va·tion	*lvy*
mort·gages	*rgjs*	mo·ti·va·tional	*lvyl*
mort·ga·gor	*rgjr*	mo·ti·va·tions	*lvys*
mort·ga·gors	*rgjrs*	mo·ti·va·tor	*lvar*
mor·ti·cian	*rly*	mo·tive	*v*
mos·quito	*sclo*	mo·tives	*vs*
moss	*s*	motor	*lr*
most	*S*	mo·tor·cy·cle	*lrscl*
mostly	*Sl*	mo·tor·cy·cles	*lrscls*

mo·tor·ist		move·ments	
mo·tors		mover	
motto		moves	
mound		movie	
mount		mov·ies	
moun·tain		mov·ing	
moun·tains		mowed	
mounted		mower	
mount·ing		mow·ers	
mount·ings		mown	
mounts		Mr.	
mourn·ful		Mrs.	
mourns		Ms.	
mouse		much	
mousey		muck	
mousy		mu·cous (adj.)	
mouth		mucus (n.)	
mouth·ful		mud	
mov·able		mud·dle	
move		muddy	
move·able		muf·fin	
moved		muf·fins	
move·ment		muf·fler	

mug	~q	mun·dane	mdn
mug·ger	gr	mu·nici·pal	nspl
mul·berry	lbre	mu·nici·pal·ities	nspl ls
mulch	lC	mu·nici·pal·ity	nspl l
mule	l	mural	rl
mull	l	mur·der	rdr
mul·ti·level	llvl	mur·mur	r r
mul·ti·me·dia	ll da	mus·cle	sl
mul·ti·mil·lion·aire	ll Mr	mus·cles	sls
mul·ti·na·tional	llnjl	mu·seum	ze
mul·ti·ple	llpl	mu·se·ums	ze s
mul·ti·ples	llpls	mush·room	sr
mul·ti·plex	llplx	mushy	se
mul·ti·pli·ca·tion	llplc	music	zc
mul·ti·plied	llpli-	mu·si·cal	zcl
mul·ti·plier	llplir	mu·si·cals	zcls
mul·ti·ply	llpli	mu·si·cian	zj
mul·ti·ply·ing	llpli_	mu·si·cians	zjs
mul·ti·stage	llsj	mus·lin	zln
mul·ti·tude	llld	must	S
mum·ble	mB	mus·tache	St
mum·bled	mB-	mus·tard	Srd
mumps	mps	mus·ter	Sr
munch·ing	mC	musty	Se

mu·ta·tion		nail	
mu·ta·tions		nails	
mute		naive	
mu·ti·late		na·iveté	
mu·ti·lated		naked	
mu·ti·la·tion		name	
mut·ter		named	
mu·tual		name·less	
mu·tu·ally		namely	
my		name·plate	
my·opic		name·plates	
myriad		names	
my·self		nam·ing	
mys·ter·ies		nap	
mys·te·ri·ous		nape	
mys·tery		nap·kin	
mys·ti·cal		nap·kins	
myth		napped	
		nar·cis·sis·tic	
		nar·cotic	
N		nar·cot·ics	
		nar·rate	
nab		nar·ra·tion	
nag		nar·ra·tive	
nagged			

nar·ra·tives	*nrvs*	natu·rally	*nCrll*
nar·ra·tor	*nrar*	na·ture	*nCr*
nar·row	*nro*	nau·ga·hyde	*nghd*
nar·rowed	*nro-*	naughty	*nle*
nar·rower	*nror*	nau·sea	*nza*
nar·rowly	*nrol*	nau·seous	*nss*
nasal	*nzl*	nau·ti·cal	*nlcl*
nas·ti·ness	*nSe'*	naval	*nvl*
nasty	*nSe*	navel	*nvl*
na·tion	*ny*	navi·ga·ble	*nvgB*
na·tional	*nyl*	navi·gate	*nvga*
na·tion·al·ity	*nyl'*	navi·ga·tion	*nvgy*
na·tion·al·ize	*nylz*	navy	*nve*
na·tion·al·ized	*nylz-*	Navy	*nve*
na·tion·ally	*nyll*	nay	*na*
na·tion·als	*nyls*	nays	*nas*
na·tions	*nys*	near	*nr*
na·tion·wide	*nyd*	nearby	*nrb*
na·tive	*nv*	neared	*nr-*
na·tives	*nvs*	nearer	*nrr*
na·tiv·ity	*nvl*	near·est	*nrS*
natu·ral	*nCrl*	near·ing	*nr_*
natu·ral·iza·tion	*nCrlzy*	nearly	*nrl*

near·ness	*nr'*	ne·gated	*nga-*
nears	*nrs*	ne·gates	*ngas*
near·sighted	*nrsi-*	ne·gat·ing	*nga_*
neat	*ne*	nega·tive	*ngv*
nec·es·sarily	*nesl*	nega·tively	*ngvl*
nec·es·sary	*nes*	nega·tives	*ngvs*
ne·ces·si·tate	*nssta*	ne·glect	*nglc*
ne·ces·si·tated	*nssta-*	ne·glected	*nglc-*
ne·ces·si·tates	*nsstas*	ne·glect·ing	*nglc_*
ne·ces·si·ties	*nss ts*	neg·li·gence	*nglyN*
ne·ces·sity	*nss'*	neg·li·gent	*nglyN*
neck	*nc*	neg·li·gently	*nglyNl*
neck·lace	*ncls*	neg·li·gi·ble	*nglyB*
necks	*ncs*	ne·go·tia·ble	*ngsB*
need	*nd*	ne·go·ti·ate	*ngsa*
needed	*nd-*	ne·go·ti·ated	*ngsa-*
need·ing	*nd_*	ne·go·ti·ates	*ngsas*
nee·dle	*ndl*	ne·go·ti·at·ing	*ngsa_*
need·less	*ndls*	ne·go·tia·tion	*ngsej*
need·lessly	*ndlsl*	ne·go·tia·tions	*ngsejs*
needs	*nds*	ne·go·tia·tor	*ngsar*
needy	*nde*	ne·go·tia·tors	*ngsars*
ne·gate	*nga*	neigh·bor	*nbr*

neigh·bor·hood	*nbrh*	neu·ral·gia	*nrlja*
neigh·bor·ing	*nbr*	neu·ri·tis	*nrls*
neigh·borly	*nbrl*	neu·ro·log·ical	*nrljcl*
neigh·bors	*nbrs*	neu·rolo·gist	*nrljs*
nei·ther	*nlr*	neu·rology	*nrlje*
neon	*nen*	neu·ro·sur·geon	*nrSjn*
nephew	*nfu*	neu·ro·sur·gery	*nrSjre*
ne·phri·tis	*nfrls*	neu·rotic	*nrlc*
nepo·tism	*nplz*	neu·tral	*nlrl*
nerve	*nrv*	neu·tron	*nlrn*
nerves	*nrvs*	never	*nvr*
nerv·ous	*nrvs*	nev·er·the·less	*nvrls*
nerv·ous·ness	*nrvs'*	new	*nu*
nest	*nS*	new·born	*nubrn*
nes·tle	*nsl*	new·comer	*nukr*
nes·tled	*nsl-*	newer	*nur*
net	*nl*	new·est	*nuS*
nets	*nls*	newly	*nul*
net·ted	*nl-*	new·ness	*nu'*
net·work	*nlo*	news	*nz*
net·work·ing	*nlo*	news·cast	*nzcS*
net·works	*nloo*	news·caster	*nzcSr*
neu·ral	*nrl*	news·let·ter	*nzL*

news·let·ters	*nzLs*	night·time	*nlt*
news·pa·per	*nzppr*	nil	*nl*
news·pa·pers	*nzpprs*	nim·ble	*n B*
news·print	*nzprN*	nine	*9*
news·room	*nzr*	ninety	*90*
news·stand	*nzSN*	ninth	*9L*
news·wor·thy	*nzrle*	nip	*np*
next	*nx*	nip·ping	*np_*
nib·ble	*nB*	nip·ple	*npl*
nice	*ns*	nip·ples	*npls*
nicely	*nsl*	nit·pick	*nlpc*
nic·est	*nsS*	ni·trate	*nlra*
ni·ce·ties	*ns ls*	ni·trated	*nlra-*
ni·cety	*nsl*	ni·trates	*nlras*
niche	*nC*	ni·trite	*nlri*
nick	*nc*	ni·tro·gen	*nlrjn*
nickel	*ncl*	nit·wit	*nlt*
nick·name	*ncn*	no	*no*
nico·tine	*ncln*	noble	*nB*
niece	*ns*	nobly	*nB*
night	*nl*	no·body	*nobde*
night·mare	*nl r*	nod	*nd*
nights	*nls*	nod·ule	*njl*

noise	*nyz*	non·con·trac·tual	*nnkcul*
nois·ily	*nyzl*	non·credit	*nncr*
noisy	*nyze*	non·de·duct·ible	*nnddcB*
nomad	*n——d*	non·de·script	*nndS*
no·men·cla·ture	*nmclCr*	non·dis·clo·sure	*nnDclzr*
nomi·nal	*nml*	non·dis·crimi·na·tion	*nnDcrmj*
nomi·nally	*nmll*	non·du·ra·ble	*nndrB*
nomi·nate	*nma*	none	*nn*
nomi·nated	*nma-*	non·es·sen·tial	*nnesnSl*
nomi·nat·ing	*nma_*	none·the·less	*nnls*
nomi·na·tion	*nmj*	non·ex·ist·ence	*nnxSN*
nomi·na·tions	*nmjs*	non·ex·ist·ent	*nnxSN*
nomi·nee	*nme*	non·fea·sance	*nnfzN*
nomi·nees	*nmes*	non·fic·tion	*nnfcj*
non·aca·demic	*nnacd——c*	non·par·ti·san	*nnplzn*
non·bank·ing	*nnbq*	non·pay·ment	*nnpam*
non·bind·ing	*nnbN*	non·profit	*nnoft*
non·busi·ness	*nnbs*	non·re·fund·able	*nnrfNB*
non·com·mis·sioned	*nnkj-*	non·re·newal	*nnrnul*
non·com·mit·tal	*nnkll*	non·re·turn·able	*nnrelB*
non·com·peti·tive	*nnkplv*	non·sense	*nnsN*
non·com·pli·ance	*nnkpliN*	non·smoker	*nns——cr*
non·con·form·ist	*nnkf——S*	non·smok·ing	*nns——c*

non·stop		north·erly	
non·sup·port		north·ern	
non·tax·able		north·erner	
non·tech·ni·cal		north·ern·ers	
non·un·ion		north·ern·most	
non·ver·bal		north·ward	
non·vio·lent		north·west	
non·work·ing		north·west·ern	
noon		nose	
noon·day		nos·tal·gic	
noon·time		not	
nor		no·ta·ble	
norm		no·ta·bly	
nor·mal		no·ta·rize	
nor·mal·ity		no·ta·rized	
nor·mal·ize		no·tary	
nor·mal·iz·ing		no·tated	
nor·mally		no·ta·tion	
nor·ma·tive		no·ta·tions	
north		notch	
north·east		notch·ing	
north·east·erly		note	
north·east·ern		note·book	

Word	Shorthand	Word	Shorthand
note·books	*nlbcs*	nov·elty	*nvlle*
noted	*nl-*	November	*Nv*
notes	*nls*	nov·ice	*nvs*
note·wor·thy	*nlrle*	nov·ices	*nvss*
noth·ing	*nlg*	now	*no*
no·tice	*nls*	nowa·days	*nods*
no·tice·able	*nlsB*	no·where	*nor*
no·tice·ably	*nlsB*	nox·ious	*ncss*
no·ticed	*nls-*	noz·zle	*nzl*
no·tices	*nlss*	noz·zles	*nzls*
no·ti·fi·ca·tion	*nlff*	nu·clear	*ncler*
no·ti·fi·ca·tions	*nlffs*	nu·cleus	*ncles*
no·ti·fied	*nlf-*	nude	*nd*
no·ti·fies	*nlfs*	nudge	*ny*
no·tify	*nlf*	nui·sance	*nsN*
no·ti·fy·ing	*nlf-*	null	*nl*
not·ing	*nl_*	nul·lify	*nlf*
no·tion	*ny*	numb	*n*
not·with·stand·ing	*n SN*	num·ber	*No*
noun	*non*	num·bered	*No-*
nour·ish	*nrs*	num·ber·ing	*No_*
novel	*nvl*	num·ber·less	*Nols*
nov·el·ist	*nvlS*	num·bers	*Nos*

nu·meral	*n—rl*	oasis	*oss*
nu·meric	*n—rc*	oath	*ol*
nu·mer·ical	*n—rcl*	oaths	*ols*
nu·mer·ically	*n—rcll*	oat·meal	*ol—l*
nu·mer·ous	*n—rs*	obe·di·ence	*obdeN*
nurse	*nrs*	obese	*obs*
nurs·er·ies	*nrsres*	obe·sity	*obs'*
nurs·ery	*nrsre*	obey	*oba*
nurses	*nrss*	obeyed	*oba-*
nurs·ing	*nrs_*	obitu·ary	*obCure*
nut	*nl*	ob·ject	*objc*
nu·tri·tion	*nlry*	ob·jected	*objc-*
nu·tri·tional	*nlryl*	ob·ject·ing	*objc_*
nu·tri·tious	*nlrss*	ob·jec·tion	*objcy*
nuts	*nls*	ob·jec·tion·able	*objcyß*
nut·shell	*nlsl*	ob·jec·tions	*objcys*
nylon	*nln*	ob·jec·tive	*objcv*
		ob·jec·tively	*objcvl*
	O	ob·jec·tives	*objcvs*
		ob·jec·tiv·ity	*objcv'*
		ob·jects	*objcs*
oak	*oc*	ob·li·gate	*oblga*
oaks	*ocs*	ob·li·gated	*oblga-*
oar	*or*		

ob·li·gat·ing	*oblga*	ob·serve	*obzrv*
ob·li·ga·tion	*oblgj*	ob·served	*obzrv-*
ob·li·ga·tions	*oblgjs*	ob·server	*obzrvr*
oblige	*oblj*	ob·serv·ers	*obzrvrs*
obliged	*oblj-*	ob·serves	*obzrvs*
ob·li·gee	*oblje*	ob·serv·ing	*obzrv-*
oblig·ing	*oblj-*	ob·so·les·cence	*obslsN*
ob·li·gor	*oblgr*	ob·so·les·cent	*obslsN*
oblit·er·ate	*obltra*	ob·so·lete	*obsle*
oblit·er·ated	*obltra-*	ob·sta·cle	*obScl*
oblivi·ous	*oblves*	ob·sta·cles	*obScls*
ob·long	*oblg*	ob·stet·ric	*obStrc*
ob·nox·ious	*obncss*	ob·stet·ri·cal	*obStrcl*
ob·scene	*obsn*	ob·ste·tri·cian	*obStry*
ob·scen·ity	*obsnl*	ob·stet·rics	*obStrcs*
ob·scure	*obscr*	ob·sti·nate	*obSnl*
ob·scu·rity	*obscrl*	ob·struct	*obSrc*
ob·serv·able	*obzrvB*	ob·struct·ing	*obSrc_*
ob·ser·vance	*obzrvN*	ob·struc·tion	*obSrcy*
ob·ser·vant	*obzrvN*	ob·struc·tions	*obSrcys*
ob·ser·va·tion	*obzrvy*	ob·struc·tive	*obSrcv*
ob·ser·va·tional	*obzrvyl*	ob·tain	*obln*
ob·ser·va·tions	*obzrvys*	ob·tain·able	*oblnB*

ob·tained	*obtn-*	oc·cu·pa·tions	*ocpjs*
ob·tain·ing	*obtn*	oc·cu·pied	*ocpi-*
ob·tains	*obtns*	oc·cu·pies	*ocpis*
ob·tru·sive	*obtrsv*	oc·cupy	*ocpi*
ob·tuse	*obts*	oc·cu·py·ing	*ocpi*
ob·vi·ate	*obva*	occur	*ocr*
ob·vi·ous	*obves*	oc·curred	*ocr-*
ob·vi·ously	*obvesl*	oc·cur·rence	*ocrN*
oc·ca·sion	*ocy*	oc·cur·rences	*ocrNs*
oc·ca·sional	*ocyl*	oc·cur·ring	*ocr_*
oc·ca·sion·ally	*ocyll*	oc·curs	*ocrs*
oc·ca·sioned	*ocy-*	ocean	*oy*
oc·ca·sions	*ocys*	ocean·front	*oyfrN*
oc·clude	*ocld*	oceans	*oys*
oc·cluded	*ocld-*	o'clock	*°*
oc·clu·sion	*ocly*	oc·ta·gon	*oclgn*
oc·cult	*ocll*	oc·tane	*ocln*
oc·cu·pancy	*ocpNe*	October	*Oc*
oc·cu·pant	*ocpN*	ocu·lar	*oclr*
oc·cu·pants	*ocpNs*	ocu·list	*ocls*
oc·cu·pa·tion	*ocpj*	odd	*od*
oc·cu·pa·tional	*ocpjl*	odd·ities	*od ᴸˢ*
oc·cu·pa·tion·ally	*ocpjll*	odd·ity	*od ᴸ*

oddly	*odl*	off·hand	*ofhN*
odds	*ods*	of·fice	*ofs*
ode	*od*	of·fi·cer	*ofsr*
odi·ous	*odes*	of·fi·cers	*ofsrs*
odome·ter	*od ∽lr*	of·fices	*ofss*
odor	*odr*	of·fi·cial	*ofsl*
odor·less	*odrls*	of·fi·cially	*ofsll*
of	*v*	of·fi·cials	*ofsls*
off	*of*	of·fi·ci·ate	*ofsa*
off·cast	*ofcs*	of·fi·ci·at·ing	*ofsa̱*
of·fend	*ofN*	off·set	*ofsl*
of·fender	*ofNr*	off·sets	*ofsls*
of·fend·ers	*ofNrs*	off·shoot	*ofsu*
of·fend·ing	*ofN̄*	off·shoots	*ofsus*
of·fense	*ofN̄*	off·shore	*ofsr*
of·fenses	*ofNs*	off·spring	*ofsprq*
of·fen·sive	*ofNv*	often	*ofn*
offer	*ofr*	of·ten·times	*ofnt ∽s*
of·fered	*ofr -*	ogle	*ogl*
of·ferer	*ofrr*	oil	*yl*
of·fer·ing	*ofr̠*	oiler	*ylr*
of·fer·ings	*ofr̠=*	oils	*yls*
of·fers	*ofrs*	oily	*yle*

oint·ment	*ynm*	one·self	*1 sf*
O.K.	*OK*	on·go·ing	*og_*
okay	*ok*	onion	*uyn*
okayed	*ok-*	on-line	*o=ln*
old	*old*	on·looker	*olcr*
older	*oldr*	on·look·ing	*olc_*
old·est	*olds*	only	*ol*
olive	*olv*	on·rush	*ors*
ome·let	*oll*	onset	*ost*
omen	*om*	on·slaught	*osll*
omi·nous	*oms*	onto	*ot*
omis·sion	*oy*	on·ward	*ow*
omis·sions	*oys*	on·wards	*ows*
omit	*ot*	opac·ity	*opsl*
omit·ted	*ot-*	opal	*opl*
om·ni·bus	*ombs*	opaque	*opc*
om·nipo·tent	*omptn*	open	*opn*
om·nis·cient	*omsn*	opened	*opn-*
on	*o*	opener	*opnr*
once	*on*	open·ers	*opnrs*
on·com·ing	*ok_*	open·ing	*opn_*
one	*1*	open·ings	*opn_*
ones	*1s*	openly	*opnl*

open·ness	*opn´*	op·por·tu·nity	*opt*
opens	*opns*	op·pose	*opz*
opera	*opra*	op·posed	*opz-*
op·er·abil·ity	*opßl*	op·poses	*opzs*
op·er·able	*opß*	op·pos·ing	*opz-*
op·er·ate	*op*	op·po·site	*opzt*
op·er·ated	*op-*	op·po·si·tion	*opzl*
op·er·ates	*ops*	op·pres·sive	*oprsv*
op·er·at·ing	*op_*	opted	*opt-*
op·era·tion	*opl*	optic	*optc*
op·era·tional	*opjl*	op·ti·cal	*optcl*
op·era·tion·ally	*opjll*	op·ti·cian	*oply*
op·era·tions	*opjs*	op·tics	*optcs*
op·era·tive	*opv*	op·ti·mal	*optl*
op·era·tor	*opr*	op·ti·mism	*opt z*
op·era·tors	*oprs*	op·ti·mist	*opt s*
opin·ion	*opn*	op·ti·mis·tic	*opt sc*
opin·ion·ated	*opna-*	op·ti·mize	*opt z*
opin·ions	*opns*	op·ti·mum	*optm*
opium	*ope*	opt·ing	*opt_*
op·po·nent	*opnN*	op·tion	*opl*
op·por·tune	*oprtn*	op·tional	*opjl*
op·por·tu·ni·ties	*opts*	op·tion·ally	*opjll*

op·tions	*opjs*	or·derly	*odl*
op·tome·trist	*opt lrs*	or·ders	*ods*
opu·lent	*oplN*	or·di·nance	*ordnN*
or	*or*	or·di·nances	*ordnNs*
oral	*orl*	or·di·narily	*ordl*
orally	*orll*	or·di·nary	*ord*
or·ange	*orny*	or·di·na·tion	*ordny*
ora·tion	*ory*	ore	*or*
orbit	*orbl*	organ	*orgn*
or·bit·ing	*orbl*	or·ganic	*orgnc*
or·bits	*orbls*	or·gan·ism	*orgnz*
or·chard	*orCrd*	or·gan·isms	*orgnz s*
or·chards	*orCrds*	or·gan·ist	*orgnS*
or·ches·tra	*orcSra*	or·gan·iza·tion	*ogj*
or·ches·trate	*orcSra*	or·gan·iza·tional	*ogjl*
or·chid	*orcd*	or·gan·iza·tion·ally	*ogjll*
or·dain	*ordn*	or·gan·iza·tions	*ogjs*
or·deal	*ordl*	or·gan·ize	*og*
order	*od*	or·gan·ized	*og-*
or·dered	*od-*	or·gan·izer	*ogr*
or·der·ing	*od*	or·gan·iz·ers	*ogrs*
or·der·lies	*odls*	or·gan·iz·ing	*og-*
or·der·li·ness	*odl'*	or·gans	*orgns*

ori·ent	*oreN*	or·nate	*orna*
Orient	*oreN*	or·phan	*orfn*
ori·en·ta·tion	*oreŇ*	or·phan·age	*orfny*
ori·en·ta·tions	*oreŇs*	or·tho·don·tic	*orldNc*
ori·ented	*oreN-*	or·tho·dox	*orldx*
ori·ent·ing	*oreN̲*	or·thog·ra·phy	*orlgrfe*
ori·fice	*orfs*	or·tho·pe·dic	*orlpdc*
ori·gin	*oryn*	or·tho·pe·dics	*orlpdcs*
origi·nal	*orynl*	os·cil·late	*osla*
origi·nal·ity	*orynlʹ*	os·cil·lat·ing	*osla̲*
origi·nally	*orynll*	os·cil·la·tions	*oslys*
origi·nals	*orynls*	os·sify	*osf*
origi·nate	*oryna*	os·ten·si·ble	*oSNB*
origi·nated	*oryna-*	os·ten·ta·tious	*oSnlss*
origi·nates	*orynas*	os·tra·cize	*oSrsz*
origi·nat·ing	*oryna̲*	os·trich	*oSrC*
origi·na·tion	*oryny*	other	*ol*
origi·na·tions	*orynys*	oth·ers	*ols*
origi·na·tor	*orynar*	oth·er·wise	*olȝ*
origi·na·tors	*orynars*	otter	*olr*
ori·gins	*oryns*	ought	*ol*
or·na·ment	*ornm*	ounce	*oȝ*
or·na·men·tal	*ornml*	ounces	*ozs*

our	$\mathcal{r}$	out·field	olfld
ours	$\mathcal{rs}$	out·fit	olfl
our·selves	$\mathcal{rsvs}$	out·fit·ted	olfl-
out	ol	out·go·ing	olg-
out·age	oly	out·grow	olgro
out·ages	olys	out·grown	olgrn
out·bid	olbd	out·ing	ol
out·board	olbrd	out·ings	ol
out·bound	olboN	out·land·ish	olLNs
out·break	olbrc	out·last	olLS
out·breaks	olbrcs	out·law	olla
out·burst	olbrS	out·lay	olla
out·bursts	olbrSs	out·lays	ollas
out·cast	olcS	out·let	olll
out·come	olk	out·lets	olls
out·comes	olks	out·line	olln
out·cry	olcri	out·lined	olln-
out·date	olda	out·lines	ollns
out·dated	olda-	out·lin·ing	olln
outdo	oldu	out·live	ollv
out·door	oldr	out·look	ollc
out·doors	oldrs	out·ly·ing	olli
outer	olr	out·pa·tient	olpsN

out·pa·tients	*olpsNs*	ovary	*ovre*
out·per·form	*olpf*	ova·tion	*ovy*
out·per·formed	*olpf-*	oven	*ovn*
out·pour	*olpr*	ovens	*ovns*
out·pour·ing	*olpr̠*	over	*O*
out·put	*olpt*	over·abun·dance	*OabNN*
out·rage	*olrj*	over·age (n.)	*Oj*
out·ra·geous	*olrjs*	over·age (adj.)	*Oaj*
out·reach	*olrC*	over·all	*Oa*
out·right	*olri*	over·bear·ing	*Obr̠*
outs	*ols*	over·board	*Obrd*
out·sell	*olsl*	over·bur·den	*Obrdn*
out·set	*olsl*	over·cast	*OcS*
out·side	*olsd*	over·charge	*OG*
out·sider	*olsdr*	over·charged	*OG-*
out·sid·ers	*olsdrs*	over·coat	*Oco*
out·spo·ken	*olspcn*	over·come	*Ok*
out·stand·ing	*olSN̠*	over·com·ing	*Ok̠*
out·ward	*olw*	overdo	*Odu*
out·wards	*olws*	over·dose	*Ods*
out·weigh	*ola*	over·draft	*Odrfl*
out·worn	*ol rn*	over·drafts	*Odrfls*
oval	*ovl*	over·drawn	*Odrn*

over·due	_Odu_	over·loads	_Olds_
over·em·pha·size	_O fsz_	over·look	_Olc_
over·em·pha·sized	_O fsz-_	over·looked	_Olc-_
over·es·ti·mate (v.)	_Oes a_	over·look·ing	_Olc_
over·es·ti·mate (n.)	_Oes l_	overly	_Ol_
over·ex·pen·di·ture	_OxpNCr_	over·night	_Oni_
over·flow	_Oflo_	over·paid	_Opd_
over·flow·ing	_Oflo_	over·pass	_Ops_
over·hang	_Ohg_	over·pay·ment	_Opam_
over·hang·ing	_Ohg_	over·pay·ments	_Opams_
over·haul	_Ohl_	over·price	_Oprs_
over·haul·ing	_Ohl_	over·priced	_Oprs-_
over·head	_Ohd_	over·print	_OprN_
over·heads	_Ohds_	over·printed	_OprN-_
over·joy	_Ojy_	over·print·ing	_OprN_
over·joyed	_Ojy-_	over·ride	_Ord_
over·laid	_Old_	over·rid·ing	_Ord_
over·lap	_Olp_	over·rule	_Orl_
over·lap·ping	_Olp_	over·ruled	_Orl-_
over·lay	_Ola_	over·run	_Orn_
over·lays	_Olas_	over·runs	_Orns_
over·load	_Old_	over·seas	_Oses_
over·loaded	_Old-_	over·see	_Ose_

over·see·ing	*Ose_*	over·tures	*OCrs*
over·seen	*Osn*	over·turn	*Olrn*
over·seer	*Oser*	over·turned	*Olrn-*
over·sight	*Osι*	over·val·ued	*Ovlu-*
over·sights	*Osιs*	over·view	*Ovu*
over·size	*Osʒ*	over·views	*Ovus*
over·sized	*Osʒ-*	over·weight	*Oa*
over·sleep	*Oslp*	over·whelm	*Ol*
over·sleep·ing	*Oslp_*	over·whelmed	*Ol-*
over·spend	*OspN*	over·whelm·ing	*Ol_*
over·spend·ing	*OspN_*	over·whelm·ingly	*Oll*
over·spent	*OspN̄*	over·work	*Oo*
over·stay	*OSa*	over·worked	*Oo-*
over·stayed	*OSa-*	owe	*O*
over·stock	*OSc*	owed	*O-*
over·stocked	*OSc-*	owes	*os*
overt	*ovrl*	owing	*O_*
over·take	*Olc*	owl	*ol*
over·takes	*Olcs*	own	*O*
over·throw	*Olro*	owned	*O-*
over·thrown	*Olrn*	owner	*or*
over·time	*Ol*	own·ers	*ors*
over·ture	*OCr*	own·er·ship	*orℐ*

own·er·ships	*orts*	pac·ing	*ps̲*
own·ing	*o̲*	pack	*pc*
owns	*oo*	pack·age	*pcy*
ox	*ox*	pack·aged	*pcy-*
oxi·dize	*vdz*	pack·ages	*pcys*
oxi·dized	*vdz-*	pack·ag·ing	*pcy_*
oxi·diz·ing	*vdz_*	packed	*pc-*
oxy·gen	*ym*	packer	*pcr*
oys·ter	*ysr*	pack·ers	*pcrs*
oys·ters	*ysrs*	packet	*pct*
ozone	*ozn*	pack·ets	*pcts*
		pack·ing	*pc̲*

<h1 style="text-align:center">P</h1>

		packs	*pcs*
		pact	*pc*
pace	*ps*	pad	*pd*
paced	*ps-*	pad·ding	*pd̲*
pacer	*psr*	pad·dle	*pdl*
pac·ers	*psrs*	pad·lock	*pdlc*
paces	*pss*	pads	*pds*
pa·cific	*psfc*	page	*pj*
Pacific	*psfc̲*	pages	*pjs*
paci·fist	*psfs*	pagi·na·tion	*pjny*
pacify	*psf*	pag·ing	*pj-*

word	shorthand	word	shorthand
paid	*pd*	pall·bearer	*plbrr*
pail	*pl*	pal·let	*pll*
pails	*pls*	pal·lets	*plls*
pain	*pn*	palm	*p*
pain·ful	*pnf*	pal·pa·ble	*plpB*
pain·fully	*pnfl*	pal·pi·tate	*plpta*
pain·less	*pnls*	pal·pi·ta·tion	*plpt*
pains	*pns*	pal·pi·ta·tions	*plpts*
paint	*pN*	palsy	*plze*
painted	*pN-*	pal·try	*pltre*
painter	*pNr*	pam·per	*p pr*
paint·ers	*pNrs*	pam·phlet	*p fll*
paint·ing	*pN̄*	pam·phlets	*p flls*
paint·ings	*pN̄̄*	pan	*pn*
paints	*pN̄s*	pana·cea	*pnsa*
pair	*pr*	pan·cake	*pncc*
pair·ing	*pr̠*	pan·creas	*pncres*
pairs	*prs*	pan·der	*pNr*
pa·ja·mas	*pj as*	pane	*pn*
pal·at·able	*pllB*	panel	*pnl*
pal·ate	*pll*	pan·eled	*pnl-*
pale	*pl*	pan·el·ing	*pnl̠*
pall	*pl*	pan·el·ist	*pnls*

pan·el·ists	*pnlss*	pa·rade	*prd*
pan·els	*pnls*	para·dise	*prds*
panes	*pns*	para·dox	*prdx*
pang	*pq*	para·gon	*prgn*
panic	*pnc*	para·graph	*prgrf*
pano·ramic	*pnr c*	para·graphs	*prgrfs*
pans	*pns*	para·le·gal	*prlgl*
pan·to·mine	*pN n*	par·al·lel	*prll*
pan·try	*pNre*	par·al·lel·ism	*prllz*
pants	*pNs*	par·al·lels	*prlls*
pant·suit	*pNsu*	pa·raly·sis	*prlss*
pant·suits	*pNsus*	para·lyz·ing	*prlz*
paper	*ppr*	para·medic	*pr dc*
pa·per·back	*pprbc*	pa·rame·ter	*pr tr*
pa·per·flow	*pprflo*	pa·rame·ters	*pr trs*
pa·per·mill	*ppr l*	para·mount	*pr oN*
pa·pers	*pprs*	para·noid	*prnyd*
pa·per·weight	*ppr a*	para·pher·na·lia	*prfrnla*
pa·per·work	*ppr o*	para·phrase	*prfrz*
par	*pr*	para·phrased	*prfrz-*
par·able	*prB*	para·site	*prsi*
para·bolic	*prblc*	par·cel	*prsl*
para·chute	*prsu*	par·cels	*prsls*

parch·ment	_prCm_	par·lor	_prlr_
par·don	_prdn_	pa·ro·chial	_prcel_
pare	_pr_	pa·role	_prl_
pared	_pr-_	pa·roled	_prl-_
par·ent	_prN_	pa·rolee	_prle_
pa·ren·tal	_prNl_	pa·rol·ees	_prles_
pa·ren·the·ses	_prnlsz_	parry	_pre_
pa·ren·the·sis	_prnlss_	par·son	_prsn_
par·en·thet·ical	_prnllcl_	part	_pl_
par·ent·hood	_prNh_	par·take	_prlc_
par·ents	_prNs_	parted	_pl-_
par·ish	_prs_	par·tial	_prsl_
par·ishes	_prss_	par·tially	_prsll_
pa·rish·ioner	_prsnr_	par·tici·pant	_ppN_
pa·rish·ion·ers	_prsnrs_	par·tici·pants	_ppNs_
par·ity	_prl_	par·tici·pate	_pp_
park	_prc_	par·tici·pated	_pp-_
parked	_prc-_	par·tici·pates	_pps_
park·ing	_prc_	par·tici·pat·ing	_pp_
parks	_prcs_	par·tici·pa·tion	_ppj_
park·way	_prc a_	par·ti·cle	_plcl_
par·lia·men·tarian	_prlmren_	par·ti·cles	_plcls_
par·lia·men·tary	_prlmre_	par·ticu·lar	_plc_

par·ticu·larly	*ptcl*	pas·sen·ger	*psnjr*
par·ticu·lars	*ptcs*	pas·sen·gers	*psnjrs*
par·ties	*ples*	passes	*pss*
part·ing	*pt*	pass·ing	*ps*
par·ti·san	*ptzn*	pas·sion	*pj*
par·ti·tion	*plj*	pas·sion·ate	*pjt*
par·ti·tions	*pljs*	pas·sive	*psv*
partly	*ptl*	pass·key	*psce*
part·ner	*ptnr*	Passover	*pso*
part·ners	*ptnrs*	pass·port	*pspt*
part·ner·ship	*ptnrs*	pass·word	*psrd*
part·ner·ships	*ptnrss*	past	*ps*
parts	*pts*	paste	*ps*
party	*pte*	pas·tel	*pstl*
par·ty·ing	*pte*	pas·teur·ize	*psCrz*
pass	*ps*	pas·teur·ized	*psCrz-*
pas·sage	*psj*	pas·time	*pst*
pas·sages	*psjs*	pas·tor	*pSr*
pas·sage·way	*psj_a*	pas·toral	*pSrl*
pass·book	*psbc*	pas·tor·ate	*pSrt*
pass·books	*psbcs*	pas·tor·ates	*pSrts*
passé	*psa*	pas·tors	*pSrs*
passed	*ps-*	pas·tries	*pSres*

pas·try	*psre*	path·way	*pla*
pas·ture	*pscr*	path·ways	*plas*
pat	*pl*	pa·tience	*psn*
patch	*pc*	pa·tient	*psn*
patched	*pc-*	pa·tiently	*psnl*
patches	*pcs*	pa·tients	*psns*
patch·ing	*pc‿*	patio	*plo*
patch·work	*pco*	pa·tri·arch	*plrerc*
pate	*pa*	pa·tri·otic	*plrelc*
paté	*pla*	pa·tri·ot·ism	*plrelz*
pat·ent	*pln*	pa·trol	*plrl*
pat·ent·able	*plnß*	pa·trol·man	*plrl‿n*
pat·ented	*pln-*	pa·tron	*plrn*
pat·ents	*plns*	pa·tron·age	*plrny*
pa·ter·nal	*plrnl*	pa·tron·ize	*plrnz*
pa·ter·nity	*plrnˡ*	pa·trons	*plrns*
path	*pl*	pats	*pls*
pa·thetic	*pllc*	pat·ter	*plr*
patho·log·ical	*pllycl*	pat·tern	*plrn*
pa·tholo·gist	*pllys*	pat·terned	*plrn-*
pa·tholo·gists	*pllyss*	pat·terns	*plrns*
pa·thology	*pllye*	pau·per	*ppr*
paths	*pls*	pause	*pz*

pauses	*pzs*	pay·out	*paol*
pave	*pv*	pay·roll	*parl*
paved	*pv-*	pay·rolls	*parls*
pave·ment	*pvm*	pays	*pas*
paves	*pvs*	PBX	*PBX*
pa·vil·ion	*pvlyn*	P.E.	*PE*
pa·vil·ions	*pvlyns*	pea	*pe*
pav·ing	*pv̲*	peace	*ps*
pawn	*pn*	peace·ful	*psf*
pawn·shop	*pnʌp*	peach	*pC*
pay	*pa*	peak	*pc*
pay·able	*paß*	peaked	*pc-*
pay·ables	*paßs*	peak·ing	*pc̲*
pay·check	*paCc*	peaks	*pcs*
pay·checks	*paCcs*	peal	*pl*
pay·day	*pad*	pea·nut	*pnl*
payee	*pae*	pea·nuts	*pnls*
payer	*par*	pearl	*prl*
pay·ers	*pars*	pears	*prs*
pay·ing	*pa̲*	peas	*pes*
pay·ment	*pam*	peas·ant	*pzN*
pay·ments	*pams*	peat	*pe*
pay·off	*paof*	peb·ble	*pß*

word	shorthand	word	shorthand
pecan	*pcn*	peer	*pr*
peck	*pc*	peers	*prs*
pe·cu·liar	*pclr*	pee·vish	*pvs*
pe·cu·li·ar·ities	*pcler ʰ*	peg	*pg*
pe·cu·li·ar·ity	*pcler ʰ*	pegged	*pg-*
pe·cu·ni·ary	*pcnere*	pel·let	*pll*
peda·gogy	*pdgje*	pel·lets	*plls*
pedal	*pdl*	pelt·ing	*pll_*
pe·dan·tic	*pdNc*	pel·vis	*plvs*
ped·dle	*pdl*	pen	*pn*
ped·dler	*pdlr*	penal	*pnl*
ped·dlers	*pdlrs*	pe·nal·ize	*pnlz*
ped·es·tal	*pdSl*	pe·nal·ized	*pnlz-*
ped·es·tals	*pdSls*	pe·nal·iz·ing	*pnlz_*
pe·des·trian	*pdSren*	pen·al·ties	*pnltes*
pe·di·at·ric	*pdetrc*	pen·alty	*pnlte*
pe·dia·tri·cian	*pdetry*	pen·chant	*pnCN*
pe·dia·tri·cians	*pdetrys*	pen·cil	*pNl*
pe·di·at·rics	*pdetrcs*	pen·ciled	*pNl-*
pedi·gree	*pdgre*	pen·cils	*pNls*
peek	*pc*	pen·dant	*pNN*
peel	*pl*	pend·ing	*pN_*
peel·ing	*pl_*	pen·du·lum	*pnjl*

pene·trate	*pntra*	pep·tic	*pptc*
pene·trated	*pntra-*	per	*p*
pene·trat·ing	*pntra*	per annum	*pa*
pene·tra·tion	*pntry*	per·cale	*pcl*
pene·tra·tions	*pntrys*	per capita	*pcpla*
peni·cil·lin	*pnsln*	per·ceive	*psv*
pen·in·sula	*pnNla*	per·ceived	*psv-*
peni·tent	*pnlN*	per·ceives	*psvs*
pen·man·ship	*pnms*	per cent	*%*
pen·nant	*pnN*	per·cent	*%*
penned	*pn-*	per·cent·age	*%y*
pen·ni·less	*pnels*	per·cent·ages	*%ys*
penny	*pne*	per·cen·tile	*%l*
pens	*pns*	per·cen·tiles	*%ls*
pen·sion	*pny*	per·cents	*%s*
pen·sive	*pNv*	per·cep·ti·ble	*PsplB*
pen·ta·gon	*pNgn*	per·cep·tion	*Pspy*
pent·house	*pNhos*	per·cep·tions	*Pspys*
peony	*pene*	per·cep·tive	*Pspv*
peo·ple	*ppl*	per·cep·tual	*PspCul*
peo·ples	*ppls*	perch	*PC*
pep	*pp*	per·co·late	*Pcla*
pep·per	*ppr*	per·co·lat·ing	*Pcla*

per·co·la·tor	*Pclar*	per·forms	*Pfs*
per·cus·sion	*Pcq*	per·fume	*Pf*
per diem	*P de*	per·func·tory	*Pfqlre*
per·en·nial	*prnel*	per·haps	*Ph*
per·fect	*Pfc*	peril	*prl*
per·fected	*Pfc-*	per·il·ous	*prls*
per·fect·ible	*PfcB*	per·ils	*prls*
per·fect·ing	*Pfc_*	pe·rime·ter	*pr lr*
per·fec·tion	*Pfcq*	peri·na·tal	*prnll*
per·fec·tion·ist	*Pfcqs*	pe·riod	*pred*
per·fectly	*Pfcl*	pe·ri·odic	*predc*
per·fo·rate	*Pfra*	pe·ri·od·ical	*predcl*
per·fo·rated	*Pfra-*	pe·ri·od·ically	*predcll*
per·fo·rat·ing	*Pfra_*	pe·ri·od·icals	*predcls*
per·fo·ra·tion	*Pfrq*	pe·ri·ods	*preds*
per·fo·ra·tions	*Pfrqs*	pe·riph·eral	*prfrl*
per·form	*Pf*	pe·riph·er·ally	*prfrll*
per·form·ance	*Pf M*	pe·riph·ery	*prfre*
per·form·ances	*Pf Ms*	per·ish	*prs*
per·formed	*Pf -*	per·ish·able	*prsB*
per·former	*Pf r*	per·ish·ables	*prsBs*
per·form·ers	*Pf rs*	peri·win·kle	*pr ql*
per·form·ing	*Pf _*	per·jure	*Pjr*

per·jury	*Pjre*	per·petu·at·ing	*PpCa*
perks	*Pcs*	per·pe·tu·ity	*Pplu*
perky	*Pce*	per·plex	*Pplx*
per·ma·nence	*PmN*	per·plexed	*Pplx-*
per·ma·nency	*PmNe*	per·qui·site	*Pqzt*
per·ma·nent	*PmN*	per·qui·sites	*Pqzts*
per·ma·nently	*PmNl*	per se	*P sa*
per·me·ate	*P a*	per·se·cute	*Pscu*
per·mis·si·ble	*P sB*	per·se·cu·tion	*Pscy*
per·mis·sion	*P y*	per·se·ver·ance	*PsvrN*
per·mis·sions	*P ys*	per·se·vere	*Psvr*
per·mis·sive	*P sv*	per·sist	*Ps8*
per·mit	*P l*	per·sisted	*Ps8-*
per·mits	*P ls*	per·sist·ence	*PsSN*
per·mit·ted	*P l-*	per·sist·ency	*PsSNe*
per·mit·ting	*P l*	per·sist·ent	*PsSN*
per·ox·ide	*prxd*	per·sist·ently	*PsSNl*
per·ox·ides	*prxds*	per·snick·ety	*Psnc*
per·pen·dicu·lar	*Ppndclr*	per·son	*Psn*
per·pe·trate	*Pplra*	per·son·able	*PsnB*
per·pe·trated	*Pplra-*	per·sonal	*Psnl*
per·pe·tra·tor	*Pplrar*	per·son·al·ities	*Psnls*
per·petual	*PpCul*	per·son·al·ity	*Psnl*

per·son·al·ize	*Psnlz*	per·ti·nent	*Plnn*
per·son·al·ized	*Psnlz-*	per·turb	*Plrb*
per·son·ally	*Psnll*	pe·rusal	*przl*
per·son·hood	*Psnh*	pe·ruse	*prz*
per·soni·fi·ca·tion	*Psnfj*	pe·rus·ing	*prz-*
per·soni·fied	*Psnf-*	per·vade	*Pvd*
per·sonify	*Psnf*	per·vad·ing	*Pvd_*
per·son·nel	*Psnl*	per·va·sive	*Pvsv*
per·sons	*Psns*	per·verse	*Pvrs*
per·spec·tive	*Pspcv*	per·ver·sion	*Pvrj*
per·spec·tives	*Pspcvs*	per·vert	*Pvrt*
per·spi·cac·ity	*Pspcsl*	per·verted	*Pvrt-*
per·spi·ra·tion	*Pspry*	pes·si·mist	*ps___S*
per·spire	*Pspr*	pes·si·mis·tic	*ps___Sc*
per·suade	*Psd*	pest	*pS*
per·suad·ing	*Psd_*	pes·ter	*pSr*
per·sua·sion	*Psj*	pes·ti·cide	*pSsd*
per·sua·sive	*Pssv*	pes·ti·lence	*pSln*
per·tain	*Pln*	pet	*pt*
per·tained	*Pln-*	petal	*ptl*
per·tain·ing	*Pln_*	pet·als	*ptls*
per·tains	*Plns*	pe·tite	*ple*
per·ti·nence	*Plnn*	pe·ti·tion	*ply*

pe·ti·tioned	*ply-*	phe·nome·non	*fnmn*
pe·ti·tioner	*plyr*	phil·an·thropic	*flntrpc*
pe·ti·tions	*plys*	phi·lan·thropy	*flntrpe*
pet·rify	*ptrft*	phi·loso·pher	*flsfr*
pet·ro·chem·ical	*ptrcml*	philo·soph·ical	*flsfcl*
pe·tro·leum	*ptrle*	philo·soph·ically	*flsfcll*
pets	*pts*	phi·loso·phy	*flsfe*
petty	*pte*	phlegm	*fl*
petu·lant	*pcln*	pho·bia	*fba*
pew	*pu*	phone	*fn*
pew·ter	*ptr*	phoned	*fn-*
phan·tom	*fn*	phones	*fns*
phar·ma·ceu·ti·cal	*frmstcl*	pho·netic	*fntc*
phar·ma·cist	*frmss*	pho·net·ics	*fntcs*
phar·ma·cology	*frmclge*	phon·ics	*fncs*
phar·macy	*frmse*	phon·ing	*fn_*
phase	*fz*	phony	*fne*
phased	*fz-*	phos·phate	*fsfa*
phases	*fzs*	photo	*flo*
phas·ing	*fz-*	pho·to·com·po·si·tion	*flokpzl*
pheas·ant	*fzn*	pho·to·cop·ied	*flocpe-*
phe·nomena	*fnma*	pho·to·cop·ies	*flocpes*
phe·nome·nal	*fnml*	pho·to·copy	*flocpe*

pho·to·copy·ing	*flocpe*	phy·sique	*fzc*
pho·to·genic	*flync*	pi·an·ist	*pens*
pho·to·graph	*flogrf*	piano	*peno*
pho·tog·ra·pher	*flgrfr*	pica	*pca*
pho·tog·ra·phers	*flgrfrs*	pic·colo	*pclo*
pho·to·graphic	*flogrfc*	pick	*pc*
pho·to·graphs	*flogrfs*	picked	*pc-*
pho·tog·ra·phy	*flgrfe*	picker	*pcr*
pho·tos	*floos*	pick·ers	*pcrs*
pho·to·stat	*flSt*	picket	*pcl*
pho·to·static	*flStc*	pick·ets	*pcls*
pho·to·type·set·ter	*flolpstr*	pick·ing	*pc_*
pho·to·type·set·ting	*flolpst*	pickle	*pcl*
phrase	*frz*	pick·les	*pcls*
phrases	*frzs*	picks	*pcs*
phys·ical	*fzcl*	pickup	*pcp*
phys·ically	*fzcll*	pick·ups	*pcps*
phy·si·cian	*fz1*	pic·nic	*pcnc*
phy·si·cians	*fzjs*	pic·nics	*pcncs*
physi·cist	*fzsS*	pic·to·rial	*pctrel*
phys·ics	*fzcs*	pic·ture	*pctr*
physi·olog·ical	*fzelycl*	pic·tures	*pctrs*
physi·ology	*fzelye*	pic·tur·esque	*pctrsc*

pid·dle	*pdl*
pie	*pi*
piece	*ps*
piece·meal	*psl*
pieces	*pss*
piece·work	*ps o*
pie·crust	*picrs*
pier	*pr*
pierced	*prs -*
piers	*prs*
pies	*pis*
piety	*pi*
pig	*pg*
pi·geon	*pjn*
pi·geon·hole	*pjnhl*
pig·gy·back	*pgebc*
pig·ment	*pgm*
pig·men·ta·tion	*pgmy*
pig·ments	*pgms*
pigs	*pgs*
pig·skin	*pgscn*
pike	*pc*
pile	*pl*

piled	*pl-*
piles	*pls*
pil·fer	*plfr*
pil·fer·age	*plfry*
pil·grim	*plgr*
Pilgrim	*plgr*
pil·grim·age	*plgry*
pill	*pl*
pil·lar	*plr*
pil·low	*plo*
pil·low·case	*plocs*
pil·lows	*ploo*
pills	*pls*
pilot	*pll*
pi·lot·ing	*pll_*
pi·lots	*plls*
pim·ple	*p pl*
pim·ples	*p pls*
pin	*pn*
pinch	*pnc*
pinch·ing	*pnc_*
pine	*pn*
pine·ap·ple	*pnapl*

ping	*pq*	pi·quant	*pcm*
pin·head	*pnhd*	pique	*pc*
pin·ion	*pnyn*	pi·rate	*prt*
pink	*pq*	pi·rat·ing	*prt*
pin·na·cle	*pncl*	pis·tol	*pstl*
pin·ning	*pn*	pis·ton	*pstn*
pin·point	*pnpy*	pit	*pt*
pin·pointed	*pnpy-*	pitch	*pc*
pin·points	*pnpys*	pitched	*pc-*
pins	*pns*	pitcher	*pcr*
pint	*pn*	pitches	*pcs*
pints	*pns*	pit·fall	*ptfl*
pinup	*pnp*	pit·falls	*ptfls*
pio·neer	*pinr*	pithy	*pte*
pio·neered	*pinr-*	piti·able	*pteß*
pio·neers	*pinrs*	piti·ful	*ptef*
pious	*pis*	pits	*pts*
pipe	*pp*	pi·tui·tary	*ptutre*
piped	*pp-*	pity	*pte*
pipe·line	*ppln*	piv·otal	*pvtl*
pipe·lines	*pplns*	pizza	*ptza*
pipes	*pps*	piz·zas	*ptzas*
pip·ing	*pp*	pla·cate	*plca*

place	*pls*	plane·tarium	*plntre*
placed	*pls-*	plank	*plq*
place·ment	*plsm*	planned	*pln-*
place·ments	*plsms*	plan·ner	*plnr*
pla·centa	*plsNa*	plan·ners	*plnrs*
places	*plss*	plan·ning	*pln_*
placid	*plsd*	plans	*plns*
plac·ing	*pls_*	plant	*plN*
pla·gia·rism	*pljrz*	plan·ta·tion	*plNy*
plague	*plq*	plan·ta·tions	*plNjs*
plagued	*plq-*	planted	*plN-*
plagu·ing	*plq_*	planter	*plNr*
plaid	*pld*	plant·ing	*plN_*
plain	*pln*	plant·ings	*plN_*
plainly	*plnl*	plants	*plNs*
plains	*plns*	plant·wide	*plN d*
plain·tiff	*plNy*	plaque	*plc*
plain·tiffs	*plNjs*	plaques	*plcs*
plain·tive	*plNv*	plasma	*plz a*
plan	*pln*	plas·ter	*plSr*
plane	*pln*	plas·tered	*plSr-*
planes	*plns*	plas·ter·ing	*plSr_*
planet	*plnl*	plas·tic	*plSc*

plas·ti·cally	*plscl*	play·ers	*plars*
plas·tics	*plscs*	play·ful	*plaf*
plat	*plt*	play·ground	*plagroN*
plate	*pla*	play·house	*plahos*
pla·teau	*pllo*	play·ing	*pla_*
plated	*pla-*	play·mate	*pla—a*
platen	*plln*	play·mates	*pla—as*
plates	*plas*	play·room	*plar—*
plat·form	*pllf*	plays	*plas*
plat·forms	*pllf—s*	play·wright	*plari*
plat·ing	*pla_*	plaza	*plza*
plati·num	*plln—*	pla·zas	*plzas*
plati·tude	*pllld*	plea	*ple*
pla·tonic	*pllnc*	plead·ing	*pld_*
plats	*plls*	plead·ings	*pld=*
plat·ted	*pll-*	pleas	*ples*
plat·ter	*pllr*	pleas·ant	*plzN*
plau·dit	*pldl*	pleas·antly	*plzNl*
plau·si·ble	*plzß*	please	*p*
play	*pla*	pleased	*p-*
play·back	*plabc*	pleases	*ps*
played	*pla-*	pleas·ing	*p_*
player	*plar*	pleas·ingly	*pl*

pleas·ur·able	*plzrß*	plugged	*plg-*
pleas·ure	*plzr*	plug·ging	*plg_*
pleas·ures	*plzrs*	plugs	*plgs*
pledge	*plj*	plum	*pl⌒*
pledged	*plj-*	plumb	*pl⌒*
pledges	*pljs*	plumber	*pl⌒r*
pledg·ing	*plj_*	plumb·ers	*pl⌒rs*
ple·nary	*plnre*	plumb·ing	*pl⌒_*
plen·ti·ful	*plNef*	plume	*pl⌒*
plenty	*plNe*	plum·met	*pl⌒l*
plethora	*pltra*	plump	*pl⌒p*
pleu·risy	*plrse*	plums	*pl⌒s*
pli·able	*pliß*	plun·der	*plNr*
pli·ers	*plirs*	plunge	*plnj*
plight	*pli*	plunged	*plnj-*
plod	*pld*	plunger	*plnjr*
plot	*pll*	plunk	*plq*
plots	*plls*	plu·ral	*plrl*
plot·ter	*pllr*	plu·ral·ism	*plrlz*
plot·ting	*pll_*	plu·ral·is·tic	*plrlSc*
plow	*plo*	plu·rals	*plrls*
pluck	*plc*	plus	*pls*
plug	*plg*	pluses	*plss*

plush	*pls*	point·ing	*py_*
ply	*pli*	point·less	*pyls*
ply·wood	*plid*	points	*pys*
p.m.	*p*	poise	*pyz*
pneu·matic	*n lc*	poi·son	*pyzn*
pneu·mo·nia	*n na*	poi·soned	*pyzn-*
poach	*pc*	poi·son·ing	*pyzn_*
pocket	*pcl*	poi·sons	*pyzns*
pock·et·book	*pclbc*	poke	*pc*
pock·et·books	*pclbcs*	polar	*plr*
pock·ets	*pcls*	po·lar·ity	*plr'*
pod	*pd*	po·lar·iza·tion	*plrzj*
po·dia·trist	*pdilrs*	po·lar·ize	*plrz*
po·dium	*pde*	pole	*pl*
poem	*po*	poles	*pls*
poet	*pol*	po·lice	*pls*
po·etic	*polc*	po·lice·man	*pls m*
po·et·ical	*polcl*	po·lices	*plss*
po·etry	*polre*	poli·cies	*plses*
poin·set·tia	*pynsla*	po·lic·ing	*pls_*
point	*py*	policy	*plse*
pointed	*py-*	poli·cy·holder	*plsehldr*
pointer	*pyr*	poli·cy·hold·ers	*plsehldrs*

polio	*plo*	po·lygamy	*plg e*
pol·ish	*pls*	poly·gon	*plgn*
Polish	*pls*	poly·graph	*plgrf*
pol·ished	*pls-*	poly·syl·la·ble	*plslß*
po·lite	*pli*	poly·tech·nic	*pltcnc*
po·litely	*plil*	poly·un·satu·rated	*plusCra-*
po·lit·ical	*pltcl*	poly·ure·thane	*plurtn*
po·lit·ically	*pltcll*	pom·pous	*p ps*
poli·ti·cian	*plly*	pond	*pN*
poli·ti·cians	*pllys*	pon·der	*pNr*
poli·tics	*pltcs*	ponds	*pNs*
poll	*pl*	pony	*pne*
polled	*pl-*	poo·dle	*pdl*
pol·len	*pln*	pool	*pl*
poll·ing	*pl̲*	pooled	*pl-*
polls	*pls*	pool·ing	*pl̲*
poll·ster	*plSr*	pools	*pls*
pol·lut·ant	*pluN*	poor	*pr*
pol·lut·ants	*pluNs*	poorer	*prr*
pol·lute	*plu*	poorly	*prl*
pol·lu·tion	*ply*	pop	*pp*
polo	*plo*	pop·corn	*ppcrn*
poly·es·ter	*plesr*	pop·per	*ppr*

poppy	*ppe*	por·tion	*pry*
popu·lar	*pplr*	por·tions	*prys*
popu·lar·ity	*pplr*	portly	*ptl*
popu·larly	*pplrl*	por·trait	*prtrt*
popu·la·tion	*pply*	por·tray	*prtra*
popu·la·tions	*pplys*	por·trayed	*prtra-*
por·ce·lain	*prsln*	por·trays	*prtras*
porch	*prC*	ports	*pts*
pore	*pr*	pose	*pz*
pork	*prc*	posed	*pz-*
por·no·graphic	*prngrfc*	poses	*pzs*
por·nog·ra·phy	*prngrfe*	pos·ing	*pz-*
po·ros·ity	*prs*	po·si·tion	*pzy*
po·rous	*prs*	po·si·tioned	*pzy-*
port	*pt*	po·si·tion·ing	*pzy-*
port·able	*ptB*	po·si·tions	*pzys*
port·age	*pty*	posi·tive	*pzv*
por·tal	*ptl*	posi·tively	*pzvl*
por·tend	*prtN*	pos·sess	*pzs*
por·ter	*ptr*	pos·sessed	*pzs-*
port·fo·lio	*ptflo*	pos·sesses	*pzss*
port·fo·lios	*ptflos*	pos·ses·sion	*pzy*
port·hole	*pthl*	pos·ses·sions	*pzys*

pos·si·bil·ities	*psβ⁶*	post·poned	*pSpn-*
pos·si·bil·ity	*psβ'*	post·pone·ment	*pSpnm*
pos·si·ble	*psβ*	post·pon·ing	*pSpn̲*
pos·si·bly	*psβ*	posts	*pSs*
post	*pS*	post·script	*pSS*
post·age	*pSj*	pos·tu·late	*psCla*
postal	*pSl*	pos·ture	*psCr*
post·card	*pScrd*	post·war	*pSr*
post·date	*pSda*	pot	*pt*
posted	*pS-*	po·tas·sium	*ptse*
poster	*pSr*	po·tato	*ptto*
pos·te·rior	*pSrer*	po·tent	*ptN*
pos·ter·ity	*pSr'*	po·ten·tial	*ptnsl*
post·ers	*pSrs*	po·ten·tially	*ptnsll*
post·gradu·ate	*pSgryul*	po·ten·tials	*ptnsls*
post·hu·mous	*psC—s*	pot·hole	*pthl*
post·ing	*pS̲*	pot·holes	*pthls*
post·man	*pS—m*	pot·pourri	*ppre*
post·mark	*pS—rc*	pots	*pts*
post·marked	*pS—rc-*	pot·tery	*ptre*
post·na·tal	*pSnll*	pouch	*poC*
post·paid	*pSpd*	pouches	*poCs*
post·pone	*pSpn*	poul·try	*pltre*

pounce	*pon*	prac·ti·cal	*prctcl*
pound (n.)	*lb*	prac·ti·cal·ity	*prctcl*
pound (v.)	*pon*	prac·ti·cally	*prctcll*
pound·age	*lbj*	prac·tice	*prcls*
pound·ing	*pon*	prac·ticed	*prcls-*
pounds (n.)	*lbs*	prac·tices	*prclss*
pounds (v.)	*pons*	prac·tic·ing	*prcls*
pour	*pr*	prac·ti·cum	*prclk*
poured	*pr-*	prac·ti·cums	*prclks*
pour·ing	*pr*	prac·ti·tioner	*prclyr*
pout	*pot*	prac·ti·tion·ers	*prclyrs*
pov·erty	*pvrte*	prag·matic	*prg tc*
POW	*POW*	prag·mat·ical	*prg tcl*
pow·der	*podr*	prag·mat·ically	*prg tcll*
pow·dered	*podr-*	prai·rie	*prre*
pow·ders	*podrs*	praise	*prz*
power	*por*	praise·wor·thy	*prz rle*
pow·ered	*por-*	prance	*prn*
pow·er·ful	*porf*	prank	*prg*
pow·er·less	*porls*	prat·tle	*prtl*
pow·ers	*pors*	praxis	*prxs*
prac·ti·ca·bil·ity	*prclcßl*	pray	*pra*
prac·ti·ca·ble	*prclcß*	prayer	*prr*

prayer·ful	*prrf*	pre·ced·ing	*Psd_*
prayer·fully	*prrfl*	pre·cept	*Pspt*
prayers	*prrs*	pre·cinct	*Psq*
pray·ing	*pra_*	pre·cious	*prss*
prays	*pras*	pre·cipi·tate	*Pspla*
preach	*PC*	pre·cipi·tated	*Pspla-*
preacher	*PCr*	pre·cipi·tat·ing	*Pspla_*
preach·ing	*PC_*	pre·cipi·ta·tion	*Psply*
pre·ad·mis·sion	*PA~y*	pre·cipi·ta·tor	*Psplar*
pre·am·ble	*P_B*	pre·cipi·ta·tors	*Psplars*
pre·ap·proved	*Papv-*	pré·cis	*prse*
pre·ar·ranged	*Par-*	pre·cise	*Pss*
pre·as·signed	*Pasn-*	pre·cisely	*Pssl*
pre·cari·ous	*Pcres*	pre·ci·sion	*Psy*
pre·cari·ously	*Pcresl*	pre·clude	*Pcld*
pre·cau·tion	*Pcy*	pre·cluded	*Pcld-*
pre·cau·tion·ary	*Pcyre*	pre·cludes	*Pclds*
pre·cau·tions	*Pcys*	pre·clu·sion	*Pcly*
pre·cede	*Psd*	pre·co·cious	*Pcss*
pre·ceded	*Psd-*	pre·con·ceive	*Pksv*
prece·dence	*prsdN*	pre·con·ceived	*Pksv-*
prece·dent	*prsdN*	pre·con·cep·tion	*Pkspy*
prece·dents	*prsdNs*	pre·cur·sor	*Pcrsr*

pre·cur·sory	Pcrsre
pre·cut	Pct
preda·tor	prdlr
preda·tors	prdlrs
preda·tory	prdlre
pre·de·ceased	Pdss-
prede·ces·sor	prdssr
pre·des·tined	PdSn-
pre·de·ter·mined	Pdl-
pre·dica·ment	Pdcm
predi·cated	prdca-
pre·dict	Pdc
pre·dict·able	PdcB
pre·dict·ably	PdcB
pre·dicted	Pdc-
pre·dict·ing	Pdc_
pre·dic·tion	Pdcq
pre·dic·tions	Pdcqs
pre·dic·tor	Pdcr
pre·dicts	Pdcs
pre·dis·posed	PDpz-
pre·domi·nant	PdmN
pre·domi·nantly	PdmNl
pre·domi·nated	Pdma-
pre·domi·nately	Pdmll
pre·em·ploy·ment	P_pm
pre·empt	P_l
pre·empted	P_l-
pre·empt·ing	P_l
pre·ex·ist·ing	P_S_
pre·fab	Pfb
pre·fab·ri·cated	Pfbrca-
pref·ace	prfs
pre·fer	Pfr
pref·er·able	prfrB
pref·er·ably	prfrB
pref·er·ence	prfrN
pref·er·ences	prfrNs
pref·er·en·tial	prfrnsl
pre·ferred	Pfr-
pre·fer·ring	Pfr_
pre·fers	Pfrs
pre·fix	Pfx
preg·nancy	prgnNe
preg·nant	prgnN
pre·heat	Phe

pre·heat·ing	*Phe*
pre·his·toric	*PhSrc*
preju·dice	*pryds*
preju·diced	*pryds-*
preju·dices	*prydss*
pre·law	*Pla*
pre·limi·nar·ies	*Plmres*
pre·limi·narily	*Plmrl*
pre·limi·nary	*Plmre*
prel·ude	*prld*
pre·ma·ture	*P⌐lr*
pre·ma·turely	*P⌐lrl*
pre·med	*P⌐d*
pre·medi·tated	*P⌐dla-*
pre·mier	*P⌐r*
pre·miere	*P⌐r*
prem·ise	*prs*
prem·ises	*prss*
pre·mium	*P⌐e*
pre·mi·ums	*P⌐es*
pre·mo·ni·tion	*Pmy*
pre·na·tal	*Pnll*
pre·num·bered	*PNo-*

pre·oc·cu·pa·tion	*Pocpy*
prep	*prp*
pre·paid	*Ppd*
prepa·ra·tion	*prpry*
prepa·ra·tions	*prprys*
pre·para·tory	*Pprlre*
pre·pare	*Ppr*
pre·pared	*Ppr-*
pre·par·ed·ness	*Ppr-'*
pre·pares	*Pprs*
pre·par·ing	*Ppr*
pre·pay	*Ppa*
pre·pay·ment	*Ppam*
pre·plan·ning	*Ppln*
pre·pon·der·ance	*PpNrN*
prepo·si·tion	*prpzy*
prepo·si·tions	*prpzys*
pre·pos·ter·ous	*PpSro*
pre·print	*PprN*
pre·printed	*PprN-*
pre·proc·es·sor	*PPssr*
pre·proc·es·sors	*PPssrs*
pre·pub·li·ca·tion	*Ppby*

pre·re·corded	*Prec-*	pre·sent·ers	*Prs*
pre·reg·is·ter	*PryŚr*	pre·sent·ing	*P*
pre·reg·is·tered	*PryŚr-*	pres·ently	*Pl*
pre·reg·is·tra·tion	*PryŚry*	pres·ents (n.)	*Ps*
pre·req·ui·site	*Prqzl*	pre·sents (v.)	*Ps*
pre·req·ui·sites	*Prqzls*	pres·er·va·tion	*przrv*
pre·roga·tive	*Prgv*	pre·ser·va·tive	*Pzrv*
pre·school	*Pscl*	pre·serve	*Pzrv*
pre·schooler	*Psclr*	pre·served	*Pzrv-*
pre·school·ers	*Psclrs*	pre·serves	*Pzrvs*
pre·scribe	*PS*	pre·serv·ing	*Pzrv_*
pre·scribed	*PS-*	pre·set	*Psl*
pre·scribes	*PSs*	pre·shrunk	*Psrq*
pre·scrip·tion	*PSy*	pre·side	*Pzd*
pre·scrip·tions	*PSys*	pre·sided	*Pzd-*
pres·ence	*przM*	presi·dency	*Pse*
pres·ent (n. or adj.)	*P*	presi·dent	*P*
pre·sent (v.)	*P*	president-elect	*P=elc*
pre·sent·able	*PB*	presi·den·tial	*Psl*
pres·en·ta·tion	*Py*	presi·dents	*Ps*
pres·en·ta·tions	*Pys*	pre·sid·ing	*Pzd_*
pre·sented	*P-*	pre·split	*Pspll*
pre·senter	*Pr*	press	*prs*

pressed		pre·tests	
presser		pre·trial	
presses		pretty	
press·ing		pret·zel	
press·room		pret·zels	
pres·sure		pre·vail	
pres·sures		pre·vailed	
pres·sur·ized		pre·vail·ing	
pres·tige		pre·vails	
pres·ti·gious		preva·lence	
pre·sum·ably		preva·lent	
pre·sume		pre·vari·cate	
pre·sumed		pre·vent	
pre·sumes		pre·vent·able	
pre·sum·ing		pre·ven·ta·tive	
pre·sump·tion		pre·vented	
pre·sump·tu·ous		pre·vent·ing	
pre·tax		pre·ven·tion	
pre·tend		pre·ven·tive	
pre·tense		pre·vents	
pre·test		pre·view	
pre·tested		pre·viewed	
pre·test·ing		pre·vi·ous	

pre•vi•ously	Pvesl
pre•war	P⌣r
price	prs
priced	prs-
price•less	prsls
prices	prss
pric•ing	prs_
prickly	prcl
pride	prd
pride•ful	prdf
priest	PS
prim	pr⌢
pri•marily	pr⌢rl
pri•mary	pr⌢re
prime	pr⌢
primer	pr⌢r
prim•ers	pr⌢rs
primi•tive	pr⌢v
prin•ci•pal	prNpl
prin•ci•pally	prNpll
prin•ci•pals	prNpls
prin•ci•pal•ship	prNpl+
prin•ci•ple	prNpl
prin•ci•ples	prNpls
print	prN
print•able	prNB
printed	prN-
printer	prNr
print•ers	prNrs
print•ing	prN_
print•out	prNol
print•outs	prNols
prints	prNs
prior	prir
pri•or•ities	prir^{ls}
pri•or•ity	prir^{l}
prism	prz⌢
pris•matic	prz⌢tc
prison	przn
pris•oner	prznr
pris•on•ers	prznrs
pris•ons	przns
pri•vacy	prvse
pri•vate	prvt
pri•vately	prvtl
privi•lege	prvlj

privi·leged	*prvlg-*	pro·ceeded	*Psd-*
privi·leges	*prvlgs*	pro·ceed·ing	*Psd_*
prize	*prz*	pro·ceed·ings	*Psd̠*
prizes	*przs*	pro·ceeds	*Psds*
pro	*p*	proc·ess (n. or v.)	*Pss*
prob·abil·ities	*Pbßls*	pro·cess (v.)	*Pss*
prob·abil·ity	*Pbßl*	proc·essed	*Pss-*
prob·able	*Pbß*	proc·esses	*Psss*
prob·ably	*Pbß*	proc·ess·ing	*Pss_*
pro·bate	*Pba*	pro·ces·sion	*Psg*
pro·bated	*Pba-*	pro·ces·sional	*Psgl*
pro·ba·tion	*Pbg*	pro·ces·sor	*Pssr*
pro·ba·tional	*Pbgl*	pro·ces·sors	*Pssrs*
pro·ba·tion·ary	*Pbgre*	pro·claim	*Pcl*
probe	*Pb*	pro·claimed	*Pcl-*
prob·ing	*Pb_*	pro·claim·ing	*Pcl_*
prob·lem	*Pbl*	proc·la·ma·tion	*Pclg*
prob·lem·atic	*Pbllc*	pro·cliv·ity	*Pclvl*
prob·lems	*Pbls*	pro·cras·ti·nate	*Pcrßna*
pro·ce·dural	*Psgrl*	pro·cre·ate	*Pcra*
pro·ce·dure	*Psgr*	pro·cure	*Pcr*
pro·ce·dures	*Psgrs*	pro·cured	*Pcr-*
pro·ceed	*Psd*	pro·cure·ment	*Pcrm*

pro·cure·ments	*Pcrms*	pro·fes·sion	*Pfz*
pro·cur·ing	*Pcr*	pro·fes·sional	*Pfzl*
prod	*Pd*	pro·fes·sion·al·ism	*Pfzlz*
prod·ding	*Pd*	pro·fes·sion·ally	*Pfzll*
prodi·gal	*Pdgl*	pro·fes·sion·als	*Pfzls*
prodigy	*Pdje*	pro·fes·sions	*Pfzs*
pro·duce	*Pds*	pro·fes·sor	*Pfsr*
pro·duced	*Pds-*	pro·fes·sors	*Pfsrs*
pro·ducer	*Pdsr*	pro·fes·sor·ship	*Pfsrs*
pro·duc·ers	*Pdsrs*	prof·fer	*Pfr*
pro·duces	*Pdss*	pro·fi·ciency	*Pfsne*
pro·duc·ible	*PdsB*	pro·fi·cient	*Pfsn*
pro·duc·ing	*Pds*	pro·file	*Pfl*
prod·uct	*Pdc*	pro·files	*Pfls*
pro·duc·tion	*Pdcq*	profit	*Pfl*
pro·duc·tions	*Pdcqs*	prof·it·abil·ity	*PflBl*
pro·duc·tive	*Pdcv*	prof·it·able	*PflB*
pro·duc·tively	*Pdcvl*	prof·it·ably	*PflB*
pro·duc·tiv·ity	*Pdcv l*	prof·ited	*Pfl-*
prod·ucts	*Pdcs*	prof·its	*Pfls*
pro·fane	*Pfn*	pro forma	*Pf a*
pro·fan·ity	*Pfn l*	pro·found	*Pfon*
pro·fess	*Pfs*	pro·fuse	*Pfs*

pro·fu·sion	*Pfy*	pro·hi·bi·tion	*Pby*
progeny	*Pjne*	pro·hi·bi·tions	*Pbys*
prog·no·sis	*Pgnss*	pro·hibi·tive	*Phbv*
pro·gram	*Pg*	pro·hib·its	*Phbts*
pro·gram·ma·ble	*PgB*	proj·ect (n.)	*Pjc*
pro·gram·matic	*Pglc*	pro·ject (v.)	*Pjc*
pro·grammed	*Pg-*	pro·jected	*Pjc-*
pro·gram·mer	*Pgr*	pro·ject·ing	*Pjc_*
pro·gram·mers	*Pgrs*	pro·jec·tion	*Pjcy*
pro·gram·ming	*Pg_*	pro·jec·tions	*Pjcys*
pro·grams	*Pgs*	pro·jec·tor	*Pjcr*
prog·ress (n.)	*Pgrs*	pro·jec·tors	*Pjcrs*
pro·gress (v.)	*Pgrs*	proj·ects (n.)	*Pjcs*
pro·gressed	*Pgrs-*	pro·jects (v.)	*Pjcs*
pro·gresses	*Pgrss*	pro·life	*Plf*
pro·gress·ing	*Pgrs_*	pro·lif·era·tion	*Plfy*
pro·gres·sion	*Pgry*	pro·lific	*Plfc*
pro·gres·sions	*Pgrys*	pro·logue	*Plg*
pro·gres·sive	*Pgrsv*	pro·long	*Plg*
pro·gres·sively	*Pgrsvl*	pro·longed	*Plg-*
pro·hibit	*Phbl*	prom	*P⌣*
pro·hib·ited	*Phbl-*	promi·nence	*PmN*
pro·hib·it·ing	*Phbl_*	promi·nent	*PmN*

promi·nently	*PmNl*	prom·ul·gated	*P—lga-*
pro·mis·cu·ous	*P—scus*	prom·ul·gat·ing	*P—lga_*
prom·ise	*P—s*	prom·ul·ga·tion	*P—lg1*
prom·ised	*P—s-*	prone	*Pm*
prom·ises	*P—ss*	prong	*prq*
prom·is·ing	*P—s_*	pronged	*prq-*
prom·is·sory	*P—sre*	pro·noun	*Pnon*
promo	*P—o*	pro·nounce	*PnoN*
pro·mote	*P—o*	pro·nounced	*PnoN-*
pro·moted	*P—o-*	pro·nounce·ment	*PnoNm*
pro·moter	*P—or*	pro·nounce·ments	*PnoNms*
pro·motes	*P—os*	pro·nun·cia·tion	*PnNe1*
pro·mot·ing	*P—o_*	proof	*prf*
pro·mo·tion	*P—1*	proof·ing	*prf-*
pro·mo·tional	*P—yl*	proof·read	*prfrd*
pro·mo·tions	*P—ys*	proof·reader	*prfrdr*
prompt	*P—l*	proof·read·ers	*prfrdrs*
prompted	*P—l-*	proof·read·ing	*prfrd_*
prompter	*P—lr*	proofs	*prfs*
promptly	*P—ll*	prop	*Pp*
prompt·ness	*P—l'*	propa·ganda	*PpgNa*
prompts	*P—ls*	propa·ga·tion	*Ppg1*
prom·ul·gate	*P—lga*	pro·pane	*Ppn*

pro·pel	*Ppl*	pro·pos·ers	*Ppzrs*
pro·pel·ler	*Pplr*	pro·poses	*Ppzs*
pro·pel·ling	*Ppl‾*	pro·pos·ing	*Ppz‾*
pro·pen·sity	*Ppml*	propo·si·tion	*Ppzj*
proper	*Ppr*	pro·pound	*PpoN*
prop·erly	*Pprl*	pro·pounded	*PpoN‾*
prop·er·ties	*prps*	propped	*Pp‾*
prop·erty	*prp*	pro·prie·tary	*Pprlre*
prophecy	*Pfse*	pro·prie·tor	*Pprlr*
prophesy	*Pfsi*	pro·prie·tor·ship	*Pprlrs*
pro·phetic	*Pflc*	pro·pri·ety	*Pprl*
pro·po·nent	*PpnN*	pro·pul·sion	*Pplj*
pro·por·tion	*Pprj*	pro rata	*Prla*
pro·por·tional	*Pprjl*	pro·rate	*Pra*
pro·por·tion·ally	*Pprjll*	pro·rated	*Pra‾*
pro·por·tion·ate	*Pprjl*	pro·ra·tion	*Prj*
pro·por·tioned	*Pprj‾*	pro·ra·tions	*Prjs*
pro·por·tions	*Pprjs*	pros	*Ps*
pro·posal	*Ppzl*	prose	*Pz*
pro·pos·als	*Ppzls*	prose·cute	*Pscu*
pro·pose	*Ppz*	prose·cuted	*Pscu‾*
pro·posed	*Ppz‾*	prose·cut·ing	*Pscu‾*
pro·poser	*Ppzr*	prose·cu·tion	*Pscj*

Word	Shorthand	Word	Shorthand	Shorthand
prose·cu·tor	Pscur	pro·tects		Plcs
prose·cu·tors	Pscurs	pro·tegé		Plza
pros·pect	Pspc	pro·te·gée		Plza
pros·pect·ing	Pspc_	pro·tein		Pln
pro·spec·tive	Pspcv	pro tem		P L
pros·pects	Pspcs	pro·test		PLS
pro·spec·tus	Pspcs	Protestant		PLSN
pros·per	Pspr	pro·tested		PLS-
pros·per·ity	Psprʟ	pro·tester		PLSr
pros·per·ous	Psprs	pro·test·ers		PLSrs
pros·tate	PSa	pro·test·ing		PLS_
pros·the·sis	Pslss	pro·to·col		Plcl
pros·ti·tute	PSlu	pro·ton		Pln
pros·trate	PSra	pro·to·type		PUp
pros·tra·tion	PSry	pro·to·types		PUps
pro·tect	Plc	pro·tracted		Plrc-
pro·tected	Plc-	pro·trac·tor		Plrcr
pro·tect·ing	Plc_	pro·trude		Plrd
pro·tec·tion	Plcy	pro·tru·sion		Plry
pro·tec·tions	Plcys	proud		prod
pro·tec·tive	Plcv	prove		pv
pro·tec·tor	Plcr	proved		pv-
pro·tec·tors	Plcrs	proven		pvn

prov·erb	*Pvrb*	pro·voked	*Pvc-*
pro·ver·bial	*Pvrbel*	pro·vok·ing	*Pvc,*
proves	*pvo*	pro·vost	*Pvs*
pro·vide	*Pvd*	prow·ess	*proo*
pro·vided	*Pvd-*	prowl	*prol*
provi·dence	*PvdM*	prox·ies	*Pves*
provi·dent	*PvdM*	proxi·mal	*Pvl*
pro·vider	*Pvdr*	proxi·mate	*Pvl*
pro·vid·ers	*Pvdrs*	prox·im·ity	*Pvl*
pro·vides	*Pvds*	proxy	*Pve*
pro·vid·ing	*Pvd*	prude	*prd*
prov·ince	*PvM*	pru·dent	*prdM*
prov·inces	*PvMs*	pru·dently	*prdMl*
pro·vin·cial	*PvnMl*	prune	*prn*
prov·ing	*pv*	pry	*pru*
pro·vi·sion	*Pvy*	psalm	*s*
pro·vi·sional	*Pvyl*	pseu·do·nym	*sdn*
pro·vi·sion·ally	*Pvyll*	psy·che	*sce*
pro·vi·sions	*Pvys*	psy·chi·at·ric	*scelrc*
pro·viso	*Pvzo*	psy·chia·trist	*scilrs*
provo·ca·tion	*Pvcy*	psy·chia·try	*scilre*
pro·voca·tive	*Pvcv*	psy·chic	*scc*
pro·voke	*Pvc*	psy·cho·analy·sis	*scanlss*

psy·cho·dy·nam·ics	*scdnrcs*	pub·lisher	*pblsr*
psy·cho·log·ical	*sclycl*	pub·lish·ers	*pblsrs*
psy·cholo·gist	*sclys*	pub·lishes	*pblss*
psy·cholo·gists	*sclyss*	pub·lish·ing	*pbls̲*
psy·chology	*sclye*	pucker	*pcr*
psy·cho·neu·rotic	*scnrtc*	pud·ding	*pd̲*
psy·cho·path	*scpl*	pud·dle	*pdl*
psy·cho·pathic	*scplc*	pudgy	*pje*
psy·cho·sis	*scss*	puff	*pf*
psy·cho·so·matic	*scstc*	pug	*pg*
psy·cho·therapy	*sclrpe*	pu·gi·list	*pgls*
psy·chotic	*sclc*	pug·nac·ity	*pgns'*
pu·berty	*pbrle*	pull	*pl*
pub·lic	*pb*	pulled	*pl-*
pub·li·ca·tion	*pby*	pul·let	*pll*
pub·li·ca·tions	*pbys*	pul·ley	*ple*
pub·lic·ity	*pbls'*	pul·leys	*ples*
pub·li·cize	*pblsz*	pull·ing	*pl̲*
pub·li·cized	*pblsz-*	pull·over	*plO*
pub·li·ciz·ing	*pblsz_*	pull·overs	*plOs*
pub·licly	*pbl*	pulls	*pls*
pub·lish	*pbls*	pul·mo·nary	*plmre*
pub·lished	*pbls-*	pulp	*plp*

pul·pit	*plpt*	punc·tured	*pqCr-*
pul·pits	*plpts*	pun·gent	*pnjM*
pul·sa·tion	*plsj*	pun·ish	*pnA*
pul·sa·tions	*plsjs*	pun·ish·able	*pnAB*
pulse	*pls*	pun·ished	*pnA-*
pulses	*plss*	pun·ish·ment	*pnAm*
pul·ver·ize	*plvrz*	pu·ni·tive	*pnv*
pump	*p~p*	punt	*pM*
pumped	*p~p-*	puny	*pne*
pumper	*p~pr*	pup	*pp*
pump·ing	*p~p_*	pupil	*ppl*
pump·kin	*p~cn*	pu·pils	*ppls*
pump·kins	*p~cns*	pup·pet	*ppt*
pumps	*p~ps*	pup·pets	*ppts*
pun	*pn*	pup·pies	*ppes*
punch	*pnC*	puppy	*ppe*
punched	*pnC-*	pur·chas·able	*PCsB*
punch·ing	*pnC_*	pur·chase	*PCs*
punc·tual	*pqCul*	pur·chased	*PCs-*
punc·tu·al·ity	*pqCul^L*	pur·chaser	*PCsr*
punc·tu·ate	*pqCa*	pur·chas·ers	*PCsrs*
punc·tua·tion	*pqCuj*	pur·chases	*PCss*
punc·ture	*pqCr*	pur·chas·ing	*PCs_*

pure	*pr*	pur·suit	*Psu*
purely	*prl*	pur·suits	*Psus*
purge	*P₁*	pur·view	*Pvu*
purged	*P₁-*	push	*pʃ*
pu·ri·fi·ca·tion	*prfy*	pushed	*pʃ-*
pu·rify	*prf*	pushes	*pʃs*
pu·ri·tan	*prtn*	push·ing	*pʃ_*
Puritan	*prtn*	put	*pt*
pu·rity	*prⁱ*	pu·tre·fac·tion	*ptrfcy*
pur·ple	*prpl*	puts	*pts*
pur·port	*Ppt*	putt	*pt*
pur·ported	*Ppt-*	put·ter	*ptr*
pur·port·edly	*Pptl*	put·ting	*pt_*
pur·port·ing	*Ppt_*	putty	*pte*
pur·pose	*Pps*	puz·zle	*pzl*
pur·posely	*Ppsl*	puz·zles	*pzls*
pur·poses	*Ppss*	py·or·rhea	*pira*
purse	*Ps*	pyra·mid	*pr⌐d*
purses	*Pss*	py·ro·ma·niac	*pr⌐nec*
pur·su·ant	*PsuN*		
pur·sue	*Psu*	**Q**	
pur·sued	*Psu-*		
pur·sues	*Psus*	quack	*qc*
pur·su·ing	*Psu_*	quad·ran·gle	*qdrgl*

quad·rant		qualm	
quad·ren·nial		quan·dary	
quad·ri·lat·eral		quan·tify	
quad·ru·ple		quan·ti·fy·ing	
quad·ru·plet		quan·ti·ta·tive	
quad·ru·pli·cate (adj. or n.)		quan·ti·ta·tively	
quad·ru·pli·cate (v.)		quan·ti·ties	
quad·ru·pling		quan·tity	
quag·mire		quar·an·tine	
quail		quar·rel	
quaint		quarry	
quake		quart	
quakes		quar·ter	
quak·ing		quar·ter·back	
quali·fi·ca·tion		quar·tered	
quali·fi·ca·tions		quar·ter·ing	
quali·fied		quar·ter·lies	
quali·fies		quar·terly	
qualify		quar·ters	
quali·fy·ing		quarts	
quali·ta·tive		quartz	
qual·ities		quat·rain	
qual·ity		qua·ver	
		queen	

queer	*qr*	qui·es·cent	*qisN*
quell	*ql*	quiet	*qit*
quench	*qnC*	quietly	*qitl*
quench·ing	*qnC_*	quie·tus	*qits*
que·ries	*qres*	quilt	*qlt*
query	*qre*	quilted	*qlt-*
quest	*qS*	quilt·ing	*qlt_*
ques·tion	*q*	quin·quen·nial	*qnqnel*
ques·tion·able	*qB*	quin·tet	*qntt*
ques·tioned	*q-*	quin·tu·plet	*qntplt*
ques·tion·ing	*q_*	quip	*qp*
ques·tion·naire	*qr*	quire	*q*
ques·tion·naires	*qrs*	quirk	*qrc*
ques·tions	*qs*	quit	*qt*
queue	*cu*	quite	*qt*
quib·ble	*qB*	quits	*qts*
quick	*qc*	quit·ting	*qt_*
quicken	*qcn*	quiver	*qvr*
quicker	*qcr*	quix·otic	*qxtc*
quick·est	*qcS*	quiz	*q3*
quickly	*qcl*	quiz·zes	*qzs*
quick·ness	*qc'*	quiz·zi·cal	*qzcl*
quick·sand	*qcsN*	quo·rum	*qr*

quota	*qla*	ra·cially	*rʌll*
quot·able	*qoƀ*	rac·ing	*rs_*
quo·tas	*qlas*	rack	*rc*
quo·ta·tion	*qly*	racket	*rcl*
quo·ta·tions	*qlys*	racks	*rcs*
quote	*qo*	rac·quet·ball	*rclbl*
quoted	*qo-*	radar	*rdr*
quotes	*qos*	ra·dial	*rdel*
quo·tient	*qʌn*	ra·di·ant	*rdeʌn*
quot·ing	*qo_*	ra·di·antly	*rdeʌnl*
		ra·di·ate	*rda*

R

		ra·di·ated	*rda-*
		ra·di·at·ing	*rda_*
		ra·dia·tion	*rdej*
rabbi	*rbr*	ra·dia·tor	*rdar*
rab·bit	*rbl*	ra·dia·tors	*rdars*
rab·bits	*rbls*	rad·ical	*rdcl*
rab·ble	*rƀ*	rad·ically	*rdcll*
rabid	*rbd*	radio	*rdo*
ra·bies	*rbʒ*	ra·dio·ac·tive	*rdoacv*
race	*rs*	ra·dio·gram	*rdoq*
racer	*rsr*	ra·di·olo·gist	*rdeljs*
races	*rss*	ra·di·ology	*rdelje*
ra·cial	*rʌl*		

ra·dios	*rdoo*	rain·bow	*rnbo*
rad·ish	*rd∱*	rain·coat	*rnco*
ra·dium	*rde*	rain·fall	*rnfl*
ra·dius	*rdes*	rains	*rns*
raf·fle	*rfl*	rainy	*rne*
raft	*rft*	raise	*rz*
rafter	*rftr*	raised	*rz-*
raft·ers	*rftrs*	raiser	*rzr*
rag	*rq*	raises	*rzs*
rage	*r*	rai·sin	*rzn*
rag·ged	*rq-*	rais·ing	*rz-*
ra·gout	*rgu*	rai·sins	*rzns*
rags	*rgs*	rake	*rc*
raid	*rd*	raked	*rc-*
rail	*rl*	rak·ing	*rc̄*
rail·ing	*rl̄*	rally	*rle*
rail·ings	*rl̄*	ram	*r*
rail·road	*rlrd*	ram·ble	*r B*
rail·roads	*rlrds*	rami·fi·ca·tion	*r fj*
rails	*rls*	rami·fi·ca·tions	*r fjs*
rail·way	*rla*	rammed	*r -*
rail·ways	*rlas*	ram·ming	*r -*
rain	*rn*	ramp	*r p*

ram·page	*r p⌐*	ranks	*rqs*
ramps	*r ps*	ran·sack	*rnsc*
rams	*r s*	ran·som	*rN*
ran	*rn*	rant	*rN*
ranch	*rnC*	rap	*rp*
rancher	*rnCr*	rape	*rp*
ranch·ers	*rnCrs*	rapid	*rpd*
ranches	*rnCs*	ra·pid·ity	*rpdˡ*
ran·cid	*rNd*	rap·idly	*rpdl*
ran·dom	*rN*	rap·ids	*rpds*
ran·domly	*rNl*	rap·ping	*rp‗*
rang	*rq*	rap·port	*rpr*
range	*rnj*	rap·ture	*rpCr*
ranged	*rnj‑*	rare	*rr*
ranger	*rnjr*	rarely	*rrl*
rang·ers	*rnjrs*	rarer	*rrr*
ranges	*rnjs*	rar·ity	*rrˡ*
rang·ing	*rnj‗*	ras·cal	*rscl*
rank	*rq*	rash	*rↄ*
ranked	*rq‑*	rasp·berry	*rzbre*
rank·ing	*rq‑*	rat	*rl*
rank·ings	*rq=*	rat·able	*raß*
ran·kle	*rql*	rate	*ra*

rated	*ra-*	raved	*rv-*
rates	*ras*	ra·vine	*rvn*
rather	*rlr*	rav·ing	*rv_*
rati·fi·ca·tion	*rlff*	raw	*ra*
rati·fi·ca·tions	*rlfjs*	ray	*ra*
rati·fied	*rlf-*	rayon	*ran*
ratify	*rlf*	rays	*ras*
rat·ing	*ra_*	raze	*rz*
rat·ings	*ra=*	razed	*rz-*
ratio	*rAo*	razor	*rzr*
ra·tion	*ry*	reach	*rC*
ra·tional	*ryl*	reached	*rC-*
ra·tion·ale	*ryl*	reaches	*rCs*
ra·tion·al·iza·tion	*rylz1*	reach·ing	*rC_*
ra·tion·al·ize	*rylz*	react	*rac*
ra·tion·al·iz·ing	*rylz-*	re·acted	*rac-*
ra·tion·ing	*ry_*	re·act·ing	*rac_*
ra·tios	*rAos*	re·ac·tion	*racy*
rats	*rls*	re·ac·tion·ary	*racre*
rat·tle	*rll*	re·ac·tions	*racys*
rav·age	*rvy*	re·ac·ti·vate	*racva*
rav·aged	*rvy-*	re·ac·ti·vated	*racva-*
rave	*rv*	re·ac·ti·va·tion	*racvy*

re·ac·tor	*racr*	re·af·firmed	*rafr-*
re·acts	*racs*	re·af·firm·ing	*rafr*
read	*rd*	re·af·firms	*rafrs*
read·abil·ity	*rdßl*	real	*rl*
read·able	*rdß*	re·align	*raln*
reader	*rdr*	re·aligned	*raln-*
read·ers	*rdrs*	re·align·ment	*ralnm*
read·er·ship	*rdr*ᴀ	re·aligns	*ralns*
read·ied	*rde-*	re·al·is·tic	*relsc*
readily	*rdl*	re·al·is·ti·cally	*relscl*
readi·ness	*rde´*	re·al·ities	*rel*ᴸˢ
read·ing	*rd̄*	re·al·ity	*rel*ˡ
read·ings	*rd̲*	re·al·iz·able	*relzß*
re·ad·just	*rajß*	re·al·iza·tion	*relzy*
re·ad·justed	*rajß-*	re·al·ize	*relz*
re·ad·mis·sion	*ra*	re·al·ized	*relz-*
re·ad·mit	*ra*	re·al·izes	*relzs*
re·ad·mit·ted	*ra-*	re·al·iz·ing	*relz-*
read·out	*rdot*	re·al·lo·cate	*rAca*
reads	*rds*	re·al·lo·cated	*rAca-*
ready	*rde*	re·al·lo·ca·tion	*rAcy*
re·af·firm	*rafr*	really	*rll*
re·af·fir·ma·tion	*rafry*	realm	*rl*

real·tor	*rllr*	re·as·sess·ments	*rassms*
real·tors	*rllrs*	re·as·sign	*rasn*
realty	*rlle*	re·as·signed	*rasn-*
ream	*r*	re·as·sign·ing	*rasn_*
re·ana·lyze	*ralz*	re·as·sign·ment	*rasnm*
reap	*rp*	re·as·sign·ments	*rasnms*
re·ap·plied	*rapli-*	re·as·sume	*ras⌒*
re·ap·ply	*rapli*	re·as·sumes	*ras⌒s*
re·ap·point	*rapy*	re·as·sump·tion	*ras⌒y*
re·ap·pointed	*rapy-*	re·as·sur·ance	*rasrN*
re·ap·point·ment	*rapym*	re·as·sure	*rasr*
re·ap·praisal	*raprzl*	re·as·sured	*rasr-*
rear	*rr*	re·as·sur·ing	*rasr_*
rea·son	*rzn*	re·bate	*rba*
rea·son·able	*rznB*	re·bates	*rbas*
rea·son·able·ness	*rznB'*	rebel (v.)	*rbl*
rea·son·ably	*rznB*	rebel (n.)	*rB*
rea·soned	*rzn-*	re·belled	*rbl-*
rea·son·ing	*rzn_*	re·bel·ling	*rbl_*
rea·sons	*rzns*	re·bel·lion	*rblyn*
re·as·sess	*rass*	rebid	*rbd*
re·as·sessed	*rass-*	re·bill	*rbl*
re·as·sess·ment	*rassm*	re·bill·ing	*rbl_*

re·birth	*rbrt*	re·cede	*rsd*
re·bound	*rbon*	re·ceipt	*rse*
re·bounded	*rbon-*	re·ceipts	*rses*
re·broad·cast	*rbrdc8*	re·ceiv·able	*rsvB*
re·build	*rbld*	re·ceiv·ables	*rsvBs*
re·builder	*rbldr*	re·ceive	*rsv*
re·build·ers	*rbldrs*	re·ceived	*rsv-*
re·build·ing	*rbld*	re·ceiver	*rsvr*
re·builds	*rblds*	re·ceiv·ers	*rsvrs*
re·built	*rblt*	re·ceives	*rsvs*
re·buke	*rbc*	re·ceiv·ing	*rsv*
rebut	*rbt*	re·cent	*rsN*
re·but·tal	*rbtl*	re·cently	*rsNl*
re·cal·cu·late	*rclcla*	re·cep·ta·cle	*rsptcl*
re·cal·cu·lated	*rclcla-*	re·cep·ta·cles	*rsptcls*
re·call	*rcl*	re·cep·tion	*rspj*
re·called	*rcl-*	re·cep·tion·ist	*rspj8*
re·call·ing	*rcl*	re·cep·tion·ists	*rspj8s*
recap	*rcp*	re·cep·tions	*rspjs*
re·ca·pitu·late	*rcpCla*	re·cep·tive	*rspv*
re·ca·pitu·la·tion	*rcpCl*	re·cess	*rss*
re·cap·ture	*rcpCr*	re·cessed	*rss-*
re·cap·tured	*rcpCr-*	re·ces·sion	*rsj*

re·ces·sion·ary	*rsjre*	reck·oned	*rcn-*
re·ces·sions	*rsjs*	re·claim	*rcl*
re·charge	*rCj*	re·claimed	*rcl-*
re·check·ing	*rCc*	re·claimer	*rcl-r*
recipe	*rspe*	re·claim·ing	*rcl_*
reci·pes	*rspes*	rec·la·ma·tion	*rclj*
re·cipi·ent	*rspeN*	re·clas·si·fi·ca·tion	*rclsfj*
re·cipi·ents	*rspeNs*	re·clas·si·fied	*rclsf-*
re·cip·ro·cal	*rsprcl*	re·clas·sify	*rclsf*
re·cip·ro·cate	*rsprca*	re·clean·ing	*rcln_*
re·cip·ro·cated	*rsprca-*	re·cline	*rcln*
re·cip·ro·cat·ing	*rsprca_*	re·clin·ing	*rcln_*
reci·proc·ity	*rsprs^l*	rec·og·ni·tion	*rcgnj*
re·cir·cu·late	*rScla*	rec·og·niz·able	*rcgnzß*
re·cir·cu·lated	*rScla-*	rec·og·nize	*rcgnz*
re·cir·cu·la·tion	*rSclj*	rec·og·nized	*rcgnz-*
re·cital	*rsil*	rec·og·nizes	*rcgnzs*
reci·ta·tion	*rsly*	rec·og·niz·ing	*rcgnz_*
re·cite	*rsi*	rec·ol·lect	*rclc*
re·cites	*rsis*	rec·ol·lec·tion	*rclcj*
re·cit·ing	*rsi_*	rec·ol·lec·tions	*rclcjs*
reck	*rc*	rec·om·mend	*rcm*
reck·less	*rcls*	rec·om·men·da·tion	*rcmj*

rec·om·men·da·tions	*rcmjs*	re·con·sid·ered	*rks-*
rec·om·mended	*rcm-*	re·con·sign	*rksn*
rec·om·mend·ing	*rcm_*	re·con·struct	*rkSrc*
rec·om·mends	*rcms*	re·con·struct·ing	*rkSrc_*
re·com·mits	*rkls*	re·con·struc·tion	*rkSrcj*
re·com·pute	*rkpu*	re·con·tacted	*rklc-*
rec·on·cile	*rksl*	re·con·vene	*rkvn*
rec·on·ciled	*rksl-*	re·cord (v.)	*rec*
rec·on·cile·ment	*rkslm*	rec·ord (n.)	*rec*
rec·on·cile·ments	*rkslms*	re·corded	*rec-*
rec·on·cili·ation	*rkslej*	re·corder	*recr*
rec·on·cil·ing	*rksl_*	re·cord·ers	*recrs*
re·con·di·tion	*rkdj*	re·cord·ing	*rec_*
re·con·di·tioned	*rkdj-*	re·cord·ings	*rec_*
re·con·firm	*rkfr*	re·cords (v.)	*recs*
re·con·firmed	*rkfr-*	rec·ords (n.)	*recs*
re·con·firm·ing	*rkfr_*	re·coup	*rcp*
re·con·nais·sance	*rksN*	re·couped	*rcp-*
re·con·nect	*rkc*	re·coup·ing	*rcp_*
re·con·nected	*rkc-*	re·coup·ment	*rcpm*
re·con·nec·tion	*rkcj*	re·course	*rcrs*
re·con·sider	*rks*	re·cover	*rcvr*
re·con·sid·era·tion	*rksj*	re·cov·er·able	*rcvrB*

re·cov·ered	*rcvr-*	re·cu·per·ate	*rcpra*
re·cov·er·ies	*rcvres*	re·cu·pera·tion	*rcpry*
re·cov·er·ing	*rcvr?*	recur	*rcr*
re·cov·ers	*rcvrs*	re·cur·rence	*rcrN*
re·cov·ery	*rcvre*	re·cur·rent	*rcrN*
re-create	*rcra*	re·cur·ring	*rcr_*
rec·rea·tion	*rcrej*	re·cy·cle	*rscl*
rec·rea·tional	*rcrejl*	re·cy·cled	*rscl-*
rec·rea·tions	*rcrejs*	re·cy·cling	*rscl_*
re·crimi·na·tion	*rcrmy*	red	*rd*
re·cruit	*rcru*	re·deem	*rd*
re·cruited	*rcru-*	re·deem·able	*rd B*
re·cruiter	*rcrur*	re·deemed	*rd -*
re·cruit·ers	*rcrurs*	re·deem·ing	*rd _*
re·cruit·ing	*rcru_*	re·de·fine	*rdfn*
re·cruit·ment	*rcrum*	re·defi·ni·tion	*rdfny*
rec·tan·gu·lar	*rclglr*	re·demp·tion	*rd y*
rec·ti·fi·ca·tion	*rclfj*	re·de·sign	*rdzn*
rec·ti·fied	*rclf-*	re·des·ig·nate	*rdzgna*
rec·tify	*rclf*	re·des·ig·nated	*rdzgna-*
rec·ti·fy·ing	*rclf_*	re·de·signed	*rdzn-*
rec·tor	*rclr*	re·de·sign·ing	*rdzn_*
rec·tum	*rcl*	re·de·vel·op·ment	*rdvm*

red·head	*rdhd*	reel	*rl*
re·di·rect	*rdr*	re·elect	*relc*
re·di·rect·ing	*rdr*	re·elected	*relc-*
re·di·rec·tion	*rdry*	re·elec·tion	*relcy*
re·dis·cover	*rDcvr*	reels	*rls*
re·dis·cov·er·ing	*rDcvr*	re·em·pha·size	*r fsz*
re·dis·trib·ute	*rD*	re·em·pha·sized	*r fsz-*
re·dis·tri·bu·tion	*rDy*	re·em·ploy	*r p*
redo	*rdu*	re·em·ploy·ment	*r pm*
re·do·ing	*rdu*	re·en·force	*rnfs*
re·done	*rdn*	re·en·forced	*rnfs-*
re·dress	*rdrs*	re·en·list	*rnlS*
re·duce	*rds*	re·en·listed	*rnlS-*
re·duced	*rds-*	re·en·list·ment	*rnlSm*
re·duces	*rdss*	re·en·ter	*rN*
re·duc·ing	*rds*	re·en·tered	*rN-*
re·duc·tion	*rdcy*	re·en·ter·ing	*rN*
re·duc·tions	*rdcys*	re·en·try	*rNre*
re·dun·dant	*rdNN*	re·es·tab·lish	*resl*
red·wood	*rdd*	re·es·tab·lished	*resl-*
reed	*rd*	re·es·tab·lish·ment	*reslm*
reef	*rf*	re·evalu·ate	*revla*
reek	*rc*	re·evalu·ated	*revla-*

re·evalu·ation	*revluy*	re·fi·nanc·ing	*rfnN_*
re·ex·ami·na·tion	*rxmy*	re·fine	*rfn*
re·ex·am·ine	*rxm*	re·fined	*rfn-*
refer	*rf*	re·fine·ment	*rfnm*
refe·ree	*rfe*	re·fine·ments	*rfnms*
refe·rees	*rfes*	re·fin·er·ies	*rfnres*
ref·er·ence	*rfN*	re·fin·ery	*rfnre*
ref·er·enced	*rfN-*	re·fin·ing	*rfn_*
ref·er·ences	*rfNs*	re·fin·ish	*rfns*
ref·er·enc·ing	*rfN_*	re·fin·ished	*rfns-*
ref·er·en·dum	*rfN_*	re·fin·ish·ing	*rfns_*
re·fer·ral	*rfl*	re·flect	*rflc*
re·fer·rals	*rfls*	re·flected	*rflc-*
re·ferred	*rf-*	re·flect·ing	*rflc_*
re·fer·ring	*rf_*	re·flec·tion	*rflcy*
re·fers	*rfs*	re·flec·tions	*rflcys*
re·fig·ured	*rfgr-*	re·flec·tive	*rflcv*
re·file	*rfl*	re·flec·tor	*rflcr*
re·fil·ing	*rfl_*	re·flec·tors	*rflcrs*
re·fill	*rfl_*	re·flects	*rflcs*
re·fills	*rfls*	re·flex	*rflx*
re·fi·nance	*rfnN*	re·flexes	*rflxs*
re·fi·nanced	*rfnN-*	re·form	*rf*

re·for·mat	*rfl*	re·fund·ing	*rfN*	
re·for·mat·ted	*rfl-*	re·funds	*rfNs*	
re·for·mat·ting	*rfl*	re·fur·bish	*rfrbs*	
re·formed	*rf -*	re·fur·bish·ing	*rfrbs*	
re·form·ing	*rf _*	re·fur·nish	*rfrns*	
re·forms	*rfs*	re·fur·nish·ing	*rfrns*	
re·fract	*rfrc*	re·fusal	*rfzl*	
re·frac·tion	*rfrcy*	re·fus·als	*rfzls*	
re·frac·tory	*rfrcre*	re·fuse (v.)	*rfz*	
re·frain	*rfrn*	ref·use (n.)	*rfs*	
re·fresh	*rfr4*	re·fused	*rfz-*	
re·fresher	*rfr4r*	re·fuses	*rfzs*	
re·fresh·ing	*rfr4*	re·fus·ing	*rfz_*	
re·fresh·ment	*rfr4m*	re·fut·able	*rfuB*	
re·fresh·ments	*rfr4ms*	re·fute	*rfu*	
re·frig·er·ant	*rfryrN*	re·gain	*rgn*	
re·frig·era·tion	*rfryry*	re·gain·ing	*rgn_*	
re·frig·era·tor	*rfryrar*	re·gard	*re*	
ref·uge	*rfy*	re·garded	*re-*	
refu·gee	*rfye*	re·gard·ing	*re_*	
re·fund	*rfN*	re·gard·less	*rels*	
re·fund·able	*rfNB*	re·gards	*res*	
re·funded	*rfN-*	re·gen·er·ate	*rynra*	

re·gen·er·at·ing	*rynra*	re·gret·fully	*rgrlfl*
re·gents	*ryNs*	re·grets	*rgrls*
regi·men	*rym*	re·gret·ta·ble	*rgrlB*
regi·ment	*rym*	re·gret·ta·bly	*rgrlB*
regi·men·ta·tion	*rymy*	regu·lar	*rglr*
re·gion	*ryn*	regu·lar·ity	*rglr'*
re·gional	*rynl*	regu·larly	*rglrl*
re·gions	*ryns*	regu·late	*rgla*
reg·is·ter	*rySr*	regu·lated	*rgla-*
reg·is·tered	*rySr-*	regu·lat·ing	*rgla_*
reg·is·ter·ing	*rySr_*	regu·la·tion	*rgly*
reg·is·ters	*rySrs*	regu·la·tions	*rglys*
reg·is·trant	*rySrN*	regu·la·tor	*rglar*
reg·is·trants	*rySrNs*	regu·la·tors	*rglars*
reg·is·trar	*rySrr*	regu·la·tory	*rgllre*
reg·is·tra·tion	*rySry*	re·ha·bili·tate	*rhblla*
reg·is·tra·tions	*rySrys*	re·ha·bili·tated	*rhblla-*
reg·is·try	*rySre*	re·ha·bili·ta·tion	*rhblly*
re·gress	*rgrs*	re·ha·bili·ta·tive	*rhbllav*
re·gressed	*rgrs-*	re·hearsal	*rhrsl*
re·gres·sion	*rgry*	re·hears·als	*rhrsls*
re·gres·sions	*rgrys*	re·hearse	*rhrs*
re·gret	*rgrl*	re·hearsed	*rhrs-*

re·hire	*rhr*	re·in·stated	*rnSa-*
re·hired	*rhr-*	re·in·state·ment	*rnSam*
re·hir·ing	*rhr_*	re·in·stat·ing	*rnSa_*
reign	*rn*	re·in·sti·tuted	*rnSlu-*
re·im·burs·able	*r brsB*	re·in·struct	*rnSrc*
re·im·burse	*r brs*	re·in·sur·ance	*rns*
re·im·bursed	*r brs-*	re·in·sure	*rnsr*
re·im·burse·ment	*r brsm*	re·in·vest	*rnvS*
re·im·burse·ments	*r brsms*	re·in·vested	*rnvS-*
re·im·burses	*r brss*	re·in·vest·ment	*rnvSm*
re·im·burs·ing	*r brs_*	re·is·su·ance	*risuN*
re·in·dus·tri·al·iza·tion	*rNlzy*	re·is·sue	*risu*
re·in·force	*rnfs*	re·is·sued	*risu-*
re·in·forced	*rnfs-*	re·is·su·ing	*risu_*
re·in·force·ment	*rnfsm*	re·it·er·ate	*rilra*
re·in·force·ments	*rnfsms*	re·it·er·ated	*rilra-*
re·in·forces	*rnfss*	re·it·er·at·ing	*rilra_*
re·in·forc·ing	*rnfs_*	re·ject	*ryc*
reins	*rns*	re·jected	*ryc-*
re·in·sert	*rnsrl*	re·ject·ing	*ryc_*
re·in·serted	*rnsrl-*	re·jec·tion	*rycy*
re·in·spec·tion	*rnspcy*	re·jects	*rycs*
re·in·state	*rnSa*	re·joice	*ryys*

re·joiced	*ryys-*	re·leased	*rls-*
re·join	*ryyn*	re·leases	*rlss*
re·lapse	*rlps*	re·leas·ing	*rls*
re·late	*rla*	rele·gate	*rlga*
re·lated	*rla-*	rele·gated	*rlga-*
re·lates	*rlas*	re·lent	*rlN*
re·lat·ing	*rla*	re·lented	*rlN-*
re·la·tion	*rly*	rele·vance	*rlvN*
re·la·tions	*rlys*	rele·vant	*rlvN*
re·la·tion·ship	*rlys*	re·li·abil·ity	*rliB¹*
re·la·tion·ships	*rlyss*	re·li·able	*rliB*
rela·tive	*rlv*	re·li·ably	*rliB*
rela·tively	*rlvl*	re·li·ance	*rliN*
rela·tives	*rlvs*	re·lied	*rli-*
relax	*rlx*	re·lief	*rlf*
re·laxa·tion	*rlxy*	re·lies	*rlis*
re·laxed	*rlx-*	re·lieve	*rlv*
re·lax·ing	*rlx*	re·lieved	*rlv-*
relay	*rla*	re·liever	*rlvr*
re·layed	*rla-*	re·lieves	*rlvs*
re·lay·ing	*rla*	re·liev·ing	*rlv*
re·lays	*rlas*	re·light·ing	*rli*
re·lease	*rls*	re·lig·ion	*rlyn*

re·lig·ious	*rljs*	re·mark	*r ~rc*
re·lin·quish	*rlq ɔ*	re·mark·able	*r ~rcB*
re·lin·quished	*rlq ɔ-*	re·mark·ably	*r ~rcB*
rel·ish	*rlɔ*	re·marked	*r ~rc-*
re·lo·cate	*rlca*	re·mar·ket	*r ~r*
re·lo·cated	*rlca-*	re·marks	*r ~rcs*
re·lo·cat·ing	*rlca_*	re·mar·ried	*r ~re-*
re·lo·ca·tion	*rlcq*	re·marry	*r ~re*
re·luc·tance	*rlclN*	re·me·dial	*r ~del*
re·luc·tant	*rlclN*	reme·died	*r ~de-*
rely	*rli*	reme·dies	*r ~des*
re·ly·ing	*rli_*	remedy	*r ~de*
re·made	*r ~d*	re·mem·ber	*rmbr*
re·main	*r ~m*	re·mem·bered	*rmbr-*
re·main·der	*r ~Mr*	re·mem·ber·ing	*rmbr_*
re·mained	*r ~m-*	re·mem·bers	*rmbrs*
re·main·ing	*r ~m_*	re·mem·brance	*rmbrN*
re·mains	*r ~ms*	re·mind	*rm*
re·make	*r ~c*	re·minded	*rm-*
re·manded	*rm -*	re·minder	*rmr*
re·mand·ing	*rm_*	re·mind·ers	*rmrs*
re·manu·fac·ture	*r ~f*	re·mind·ing	*rm_*
re·manu·fac·tured	*r ~f-*	re·minds	*rms*

remi·nisce	*rms*	re·mov·ing	
remi·nis·cent	*rmsN*	re·mu·nera·tion	
re·miss	*rM*	Renaissance	*rnsN*
re·mis·sion		renal	*rnl*
remit		re·name	*rn*
re·mits		ren·der	*rNr*
re·mit·tance		ren·dered	*rNr-*
re·mit·tances		ren·der·ing	*rNr*
re·mit·ted		ren·dez·vous	*rNvu*
re·mit·ting		rene·gade	*rngd*
re·model		re·ne·go·ti·ate	*rngsa*
re·mod·eled		re·ne·go·ti·ated	*rngsa-*
re·mod·el·ing		re·ne·go·tia·tion	*rngsej*
re·morse		renew	*rnu*
re·mote		re·new·able	*rnuB*
re·motely		re·newal	*rnul*
re·mount		re·new·als	*rnuls*
re·mov·able		re·newed	*rnu-*
re·moval		re·new·ing	*rnu_*
re·move		re·no·ti·fied	*rnlf-*
re·moved		re·nounce	*rnoN*
re·mover		re·nounced	*rnoN-*
re·moves		reno·vate	*rnva*

reno·vated	*rnva—*	re·or·gan·izes	*rogs*
reno·va·tion	*rnvy*	re·or·gan·iz·ing	*roq_*
reno·va·tions	*rnvys*	rep	*rp*
rent	*rN*	re·pack·ing	*rpc_*
rent·able	*rNB*	re·pagi·na·tion	*rpjny*
rental	*rNl*	re·paid	*rpd*
rent·als	*rNls*	re·painted	*rpN—*
rented	*rN—*	re·pair	*rpr*
renter	*rNr*	re·paired	*rpr—*
rent·ers	*rNrs*	re·pair·ing	*rpr_*
rent·ing	*rN*	re·pair·man	*rpr⁓n*
rents	*rNs*	re·pair·men	*rprm*
re·num·ber	*rNo*	re·pairs	*rprs*
re·num·bered	*rNo—*	re·pa·tri·ated	*rplra—*
re·open	*ropn*	re·pav·ing	*rpv_*
re·opened	*ropn—*	repay	*rpa*
re·open·ing	*ropn_*	re·pay·able	*rpaB*
re·or·der	*rod*	re·pay·ing	*rpa_*
re·or·dered	*rod—*	re·pay·ment	*rpam*
re·or·der·ing	*rod_*	re·peal	*rpl*
re·or·gan·iza·tion	*rogy*	re·pealed	*rpl—*
re·or·gan·ize	*roq*	re·peal·ing	*rpl_*
re·or·gan·ized	*roq—*	re·peals	*rpls*

Word	Outline	Word	Outline
re·peat	rpe	re·plant·ing	rplN‾
re·peated	rpe-	re·play	rpla
re·peat·edly	rpe-l	re·plen·ish	rplns
re·peater	rper	re·plen·ish·ment	rplnsm
re·peat·ers	rpers	rep·lica	rplca
re·peat·ing	rpe_	rep·li·cate	rplca
re·peats	rpes	re·plied	rpli-
repel	rpl	re·plies	rplis
re·pel·lent	rplN	reply	rpli
re·pent	rpN	re·ply·ing	rpli_
rep·er·toire	rprlr	re·port	rpt
rep·er·tory	rprtre	re·port·able	rplB
repe·ti·tion	rply	re·ported	rpt-
repe·ti·tious	rplss	re·port·edly	rpt-l
re·peti·tive	rplv	re·porter	rptr
re·place	rpls	re·port·ers	rptrs
re·place·able	rplsB	re·port·ing	rpt_
re·placed	rpls-	re·ports	rpts
re·place·ment	rplsm	re·pose	rpz
re·place·ments	rplsms	re·po·si·tion	rpzj
re·places	rplss	re·posi·tory	rpztre
re·plac·ing	rpls_	re·pos·sess	rpzs
re·planted	rplN-	re·pos·sessed	rpzs-

re·pos·ses·sion	*rpzſ*	re·pro·duced	*rᴾds-*
rep·re·sent	*rep*	re·pro·duc·ible	*rᴾdsB*
rep·re·sen·ta·tion	*repſ*	re·pro·duc·ing	*rᴾds_*
rep·re·sen·ta·tions	*repſs*	re·pro·duc·tion	*rᴾdcſ*
rep·re·sen·ta·tive	*rep*	re·pro·duc·tions	*rᴾdcſs*
rep·re·sen·ta·tives	*reps*	re·pro·duc·tive	*rᴾdcv*
rep·re·sented	*rep-*	re·pro·gram	*rᴾg*
rep·re·sent·ing	*rep_*	re·pro·grammed	*rᴾg-*
rep·re·sents	*reps*	re·pro·graph·ics	*rprgrfcs*
re·press	*rprs*	re·prove	*rpv*
re·pressed	*rprs-*	re·proved	*rpv-*
re·pres·sion	*rprſ*	re·proves	*rpvs*
re·prieve	*rprv*	re·prov·ing	*rpv_*
rep·ri·mand	*rprm*	reps	*rps*
rep·ri·manded	*rprm-*	rep·tile	*rpll*
re·print	*rprN*	rep·tiles	*rplls*
re·printed	*rprN-*	re·pub·lic	*rpb*
re·print·ing	*rprN_*	Republican	*rpbn*
re·prints	*rprNs*	re·pub·li·ca·tion	*rpbſ*
re·proach	*rprC*	re·pul·sive	*rplsv*
re·proc·ess	*rᴾss*	re·pur·chase	*rᴾCs*
re·proc·essed	*rᴾss-*	repu·ta·ble	*rplB*
re·pro·duce	*rᴾds*	repu·ta·tion	*rplſ*

repu·ta·tions	*rplys*	res·cue	*rscu*
re·quest	*rqs*	re·seal·ing	*rsl*
re·quested	*rqs-*	re·search	*rSC*
re·quest·ing	*rqs*	re·searched	*rSC-*
re·quests	*rqss*	re·searcher	*rSCr*
re·quire	*rq*	re·search·ers	*rSCrs*
re·quired	*rq-*	re·search·ing	*rSC*
re·quire·ment	*rqm*	re·sec·tion	*rscy*
re·quire·ments	*rqms*	re·sell	*rsl*
re·quires	*rqs*	re·seller	*rslr*
re·quir·ing	*rq_*	re·sem·blance	*rz BN*
req·ui·site	*rqzl*	re·sem·ble	*rz B*
req·ui·si·tion	*rqzl*	re·sem·bled	*rz B-*
req·ui·si·tioned	*rqzl-*	re·sem·bles	*rz Bs*
req·ui·si·tion·ing	*rqzl-*	re·sem·bling	*rz B_*
req·ui·si·tions	*rqzjs*	re·sent	*rzN*
re·read	*rrd*	re·sent·ful	*rzNf*
rerun	*rrn*	re·sent·ment	*rzNm*
re·sale	*rsl*	res·er·va·tion	*rzrvy*
re·sched·ule	*rscjl*	res·er·va·tions	*rzrvys*
re·sched·uled	*rscjl-*	re·serve	*rzrv*
re·sched·ul·ing	*rscjl_*	re·served	*rzrv-*
re·scind	*rsN*	re·serves	*rzrvs*

re·serv·ing	*rzrv̲*
res·er·voir	*rzrv̲r*
res·er·voirs	*rzrv̲rs*
reset	*rsl*
re·sets	*rsls*
re·set·ting	*rsl̲*
re·ship	*rʃ*
re·ship·ment	*rʃm*
re·side	*rzd*
re·sided	*rzd-*
resi·dence	*rzdN*
resi·dences	*rzdNs*
resi·dency	*rzdNe*
resi·dent	*rzdN*
resi·den·tial	*rzdnʃl*
resi·dents	*rzdNs*
re·sides	*rzds*
re·sid·ing	*rzd̲*
re·sidual	*rzʄul*
re·sidu·als	*rzʄuls*
resi·due	*rzdu*
re·sign	*rzn*
res·ig·na·tion	*rzgny*

res·ig·na·tions	*rzgnys*
re·signed	*rzn-*
re·sign·ing	*rzn̲*
re·signs	*rzns*
re·sil·iency	*rzlyNe*
re·sil·ient	*rzlyN*
resin	*rzn*
res·ins	*rzns*
re·sist	*rzʃ*
re·sis·tance	*rzʃN*
re·sis·tant	*rzʃN*
re·sisted	*rzʃ-*
re·sist·ing	*rzʃ̲*
re·sists	*rzʃs*
reso·lu·tion	*rzlʄ*
reso·lu·tions	*rzlʄs*
re·solve	*rzlv*
re·solved	*rzlv -*
re·solv·ing	*rzlv̲*
reso·nant	*rznN*
re·sort	*rzrl*
re·sorts	*rzrls*
re·sound·ing	*rzoN̲*

re·source	*rsrs*	re·sponses	*rsps*
re·source·ful	*rsrsf*	re·spon·si·bil·ities	*rspℬ ls*
re·sources	*rsrss*	re·spon·si·bil·ity	*rspℬ l*
re·spect	*rspc*	re·spon·si·ble	*rspℬ*
re·spect·abil·ity	*rspcℬ l*	re·spon·si·bly	*rspℬ*
re·spect·able	*rspcℬ*	re·spon·sive	*rspv*
re·spected	*rspc-*	rest	*rↄ*
re·spect·ful	*rspcf*	re·start	*rↄrt*
re·spect·fully	*rspcfl*	re·start·ing	*rↄrt̲*
re·spect·ing	*rspc̲*	re·state	*rↄa*
re·spec·tive	*rspcv*	re·state·ment	*rↄam*
re·spec·tively	*rspcvl*	re·states	*rↄas*
re·spects	*rspcs*	re·stat·ing	*rↄa̲*
res·pi·ra·tor	*rsprar*	res·tau·rant	*rↄrn*
res·pi·ra·tory	*rsprtre*	res·tau·rants	*rↄrns*
res·pite	*rspt*	rested	*rↄ-*
re·spond	*rsp*	rest·ing	*rↄ̲*
re·sponded	*rsp-*	res·ti·tu·tion	*r̄ↄ ly*
re·spon·dent	*rspN*	re·stock	*rↄc*
re·spon·dents	*rspNs*	re·stock·ing	*rↄc̲*
re·spond·ing	*rsp̲*	res·to·ra·tion	*rↄry*
re·sponds	*rsps*	re·store	*rↄr*
re·sponse	*rsp*	re·stored	*rↄr-*

re·strain	*rSrn*	re·sul·tant	*rzllN*
re·strained	*rSrn-*	re·sulted	*rzll-*
re·strain·ing	*rSrn*	re·sult·ing	*rzll*
re·straint	*rSrN*	re·sults	*rzlls*
re·straints	*rSrNs*	re·sume	*rz*
re·strict	*rSrc*	resumé	*rz a*
re·stricted	*rSrc-*	re·sumed	*rz -*
re·strict·ing	*rSrc*	re·sumes	*rz s*
re·stric·tion	*rSrcy*	resu·més	*rz as*
re·stric·tions	*rSrcys*	re·sum·ing	*rz -*
re·stric·tive	*rSrcv*	re·sump·tion	*rz y*
re·stricts	*rSrcs*	re·sur·face	*rSfs*
rest·room	*rSr*	re·sur·fac·ing	*rSfs*
rest·rooms	*rSr s*	res·ur·rect	*rzrc*
re·struc·ture	*rSrcCr*	res·ur·rected	*rzrc-*
re·struc·tured	*rSrcCr-*	re·sus·ci·tate	*rssla*
re·struc·tur·ing	*rSrcCr*	re·sus·ci·ta·tion	*rssly*
rests	*rSs*	re·tail	*rll*
re·stud·ied	*rSde -*	re·tailed	*rll-*
re·sub·mis·sion	*rs y*	re·tailer	*rllr*
re·sub·mit	*rs l*	re·tail·ers	*rllrs*
re·sub·mit·ting	*rs l*	re·tails	*rlls*
re·sult	*rzll*	re·tain	*rln*

re·tained	*rtn-*	re·tir·ing	*rtṟ*
re·tainer	*rtnr*	re·tort	*rtrt*
re·tain·ers	*rtnrs*	re·touch	*rtC*
re·tain·ing	*rtṉ*	re·tract	*rtrc*
re·tain·ment	*rtnm*	re·tract·able	*rtrcB*
re·tains	*rtns*	re·train	*rtrn*
re·take	*rtc*	re·trained	*rtrn-*
re·tali·ate	*rtla*	re·train·ing	*rtrṉ*
re·tard	*rtrd*	re·treat	*rtre*
re·tar·da·tion	*rtrdy*	re·treats	*rtres*
re·tarded	*rtrd-*	re·trench	*rtrnC*
re·tard·ing	*rtrḏ*	re·trench·ment	*rtrnCm*
re·ten·tion	*rtny*	re·triev·able	*rtrvB*
re·test	*rtS*	re·trieval	*rtrvl*
re·think	*rtq*	re·trieve	*rtrv*
retina	*rtna*	re·trieved	*rtrv-*
re·tire	*rtr*	re·triever	*rtrvr*
re·tired	*rtr-*	re·trieves	*rtrvs*
re·tiree	*rtre*	re·triev·ing	*rtrv̱*
re·tir·ees	*rtres*	ret·ro·ac·tive	*rtracv*
re·tire·ment	*rtrm*	ret·ro·ac·tively	*rtracvl*
re·tire·ments	*rtrms*	ret·ro·ces·sion	*rtrsy*
re·tires	*rtrs*	ret·ro·fit	*rtrft*

Word	Shorthand
ret·ro·fits	
ret·ro·gres·sion	
ret·ro·spect	
ret·ro·spec·tive	
re·turn	
re·turn·able	
re·turned	
re·turn·ing	
re·turns	
re·type	
re·typed	
re·typ·ing	
re·un·ion	
re·us·able	
reuse (v.)	
reuse (n.)	
re·used	
re·valu·ation	
re·vamp	
re·veal	
re·vealed	
re·veal·ing	
re·veals	

Word	Shorthand
reve·la·tion	
re·venge	
reve·nue	
reve·nues	
re·ver·bera·tion	
rev·er·ence	
rev·er·end	
rev·erie	
re·ver·sal	
re·verse	
re·versed	
re·verses	
re·vers·ible	
re·vers·ing	
re·vert	
re·verted	
re·view	
re·viewed	
re·viewer	
re·view·ers	
re·view·ing	
re·views	
re·vise	

re·vised	*rvz-*	re·volve	*rvlv*
re·vises	*rvzo*	re·volver	*rvlvr*
re·vis·ing	*rvz-*	re·volv·ers	*rvlvrs*
re·vi·sion	*rvj*	re·volves	*rvlvo*
re·vi·sions	*rvjo*	re·volv·ing	*rvlv-*
re·visit	*rvzl*	revue	*rvu*
re·vi·tal·iza·tion	*rvllzj*	re·vues	*rvus*
re·vi·tal·ize	*rvllz*	re·vul·sion	*rvlj*
re·vi·tal·iz·ing	*rvllz-*	re·ward	*rw*
re·vival	*rvvl*	re·ward·ing	*rw-*
re·viv·als	*rvvls*	re·wards	*rws*
re·vive	*rvv*	re·wired	*r r-*
revo·ca·ble	*rvcB*	re·word	*r rd*
revo·ca·tion	*rvcy*	re·work	*r o*
re·vok·able	*rvcB*	re·worked	*r o-*
re·voke	*rvc*	re·work·ing	*r o_*
re·voked	*rvc-*	re·wove	*r v*
re·vok·ing	*rvc_*	re·write	*rru*
re·volt	*rvll*	re·writ·ing	*rru-*
revo·lu·tion	*rvlj*	re·writ·ten	*rrln*
revo·lu·tion·ary	*rvljre*	re·zone	*rzn*
revo·lu·tion·ize	*rvljz*	re·zon·ing	*rzn-*
revo·lu·tions	*rvljo*	rhe·tor·ical	*rlrcl*

rheu·ma·tism	*r ⁀ tz*	ri·dicu·lous	*rdcls*
rhyme	*r*	rid·ing	*rd‾*
rhythm	*rt*	rifle	*rfl*
rib	*rb*	ri·fled	*rfl-*
rib·bon	*rbn*	rift	*rft*
rib·bons	*rbns*	rig	*rg*
ribs	*rbs*	rigged	*rg-*
rice	*rs*	rig·ger	*rgr*
rich	*rC*	rig·gers	*rgrs*
richer	*rCr*	rig·ging	*rg‾*
rich·est	*rCS*	right	*ri*
richly	*rCl*	right·eous	*rCs*
rico·chet	*rcSa*	right·ful	*rif*
rid	*rd*	right·fully	*rifl*
rid·den	*rdn*	rights	*ris*
rid·ding	*rd‾*	rigid	*rjd*
rid·dle	*rdl‾*	ri·gid·ity	*rjdᶫ*
ride	*rd*	rigor	*rgr*
rider	*rdr*	rig·or·ous	*rgrs*
rid·ers	*rdrs*	rig·or·ously	*rgrsl*
rides	*rds*	rigs	*rgs*
ridge	*rj*	rile	*rl*
ridi·cule	*rdcl*	rim	*r*

rimmed	$r\smile-$	rises	*rzs*
rims	$r\smile s$	ris·ing	*rz_*
rind	*rM*	risk	*rsc*
ring	*rq*	risk·ing	*rsc_*
ring·ing	*rq_*	risks	*rscs*
rings	*rgs*	risky	*rsce*
ring·side	*rgsd*	rite	*ru*
rink	*rq*	ritual	*rCul*
rinks	*rqs*	rival	*rvl*
rinse	*rM*	river	*rvr*
rinses	*rMs*	riv·ers	*rvrs*
rins·ing	*rM*	rivet	*rvl*
riot	*rul*	riv·eter	*rvlr*
riots	*ruls*	riv·et·ers	*rvlrs*
rip	*rp*	riv·et·ing	*rvl_*
ripe	*rp*	riv·ets	*rvls*
ripen	*rpn*	R.N.	*RN*
rip·ping	*rp_*	roach	*rC*
rip·ple	*rpl*	road	*rd*
rise	*rz*	road·bed	*rdbd*
risen	*rzn*	road·block	*rdblc*
riser	*rzr*	road·blocks	*rdblcs*
ris·ers	*rzrs*	road·run·ner	*rdrnr*

roads	*rds*	rode	*rd*
road·side	*rdsd*	ro·dent	*rdN*
road·way	*rd_a*	ro·dents	*rdNs*
roam	*r*	rodeo	*rdo*
roam·ing	*r*	rods	*rds*
roar	*rr*	role	*rl*
roast	*rS*	roles	*rls*
roast·ing	*rS*	roll	*rl*
rob	*rb*	rolled	*rl-*
robbed	*rb-*	roller	*rlr*
rob·ber	*rbr*	roll·ers	*rlrs*
rob·bery	*rbre*	roll·ing	*rl*
robe	*rb*	rolls	*rls*
robin	*rbn*	ro·mance	*r_M*
robot	*rbl*	ro·man·tic	*r_Mc*
ro·bust	*rbS*	romp	*r_p*
rock	*rc*	roof	*rf*
rocked	*rc-*	roofed	*rf-*
rocket	*rcl*	roof·ing	*rf-*
rock·ets	*rcls*	roofs	*rfs*
rock·ing	*rc*	room	*r*
rocky	*rce*	room·mate	*r_a*
rod	*rd*	room·mates	*r_as*

rooms	*r͜s*	rot·ten	*rtn*
roost	*rS*	rough	*rf*
rooster	*rSr*	rougher	*rfr*
root	*ru*	roughly	*rfl*
rooted	*ru-*	rough·ness	*rf'*
roots	*rus*	round	*roN*
rope	*rp*	rounded	*roN-*
roped	*rp-*	round·ness	*roN'*
rose	*rz*	rounds	*roNs*
roses	*rzs*	rout	*rol*
ros·ter	*rSr*	route	*ru*
ros·ters	*rSrs*	routed	*ru-*
ros·trum	*rSr͜*	router	*rur*
rot	*rt*	routes	*rus*
ro·tary	*rtre*	rou·tine	*rtn*
ro·tate	*rta*	rou·tinely	*rtnl*
ro·tated	*rta-*	rout·ing	*ru_*
ro·tat·ing	*rta_*	rove	*rv*
ro·ta·tion	*rty*	rov·ing	*rv_*
ro·ta·tional	*rtyl*	row	*ro*
rote	*ro*	rowdy	*rode*
rotor	*rtr*	rows	*ros*
ro·tors	*rtrs*	royal	*ryl*

roy·al·ties	*rylles*	rum·ble	*r B*
roy·alty	*rylle*	rumor	*r r*
r.p.m.	*rpm*	ru·mors	*r rs*
rub	*rb*	run	*rn*
rub·ber	*rbr*	run·around	*rnaroN*
rub·bish	*rb+*	run·away	*rna a*
rub·ble	*rB*	run·aways	*rna as*
ru·bella	*rbla*	rung	*rq*
ruby	*rbe*	rungs	*rqs*
ru·di·ment	*rdm*	run·ner	*rnr*
ru·di·men·tary	*rdmre*	run·ning	*rn_*
rue	*ru*	runs	*rns*
ruf·fle	*rfl*	runt	*rN*
rug	*rq*	run·way	*rn a*
rugs	*rqs*	rup·ture	*rpCr*
ruin	*run*	rup·tured	*rpCr-*
ru·ined	*run-*	rup·tures	*rpCrs*
rule	*rl*	rup·tur·ing	*rpCr_*
ruled	*rl-*	rural	*rrl*
rules	*rls*	ruse	*rz*
rul·ing	*rl_*	rush	*rA*
rul·ings	*rl=*	rushed	*rA-*
rum	*r*	rust	*rS*

Word	Shorthand
rus·tic	*rSc*
rusty	*rSe*
rut	*rt*
ruth·less	*rtls*
rut·ted	*rt-*
rye	*ri*

S

Word	Shorthand
sab·bat·ical	*sblcl*
sabo·tage	*sbtz*
sa·chet	*sAa*
sack	*sc*
sack·ing	*sc_*
sacks	*scs*
sac·ra·ment	*scrm*
sa·cred	*scrd*
sac·ri·fice	*scrfs*
sac·ri·ficed	*scrfs-*
sac·ri·fic·ing	*scrfs_*
sac·ro·sanct	*scrsq*
sa·crum	*scr*
sad	*sd*

Word	Shorthand
sad·den	*sdn*
sad·dened	*sdn-*
sad·dle	*sdl*
sadly	*sdl*
sad·ness	*sd'*
sa·fari	*sfre*
safe	*sf*
safe·guard	*sfgrd*
safe·guard·ing	*sfgrd_*
safe·guards	*sfgrds*
safe·keep·ing	*sfcp_*
safely	*sfl*
safer	*sfr*
saf·est	*sfs*
safety	*sfle*
sag	*sg*
saga	*sga*
sage	*sj*
sag·ging	*sg_*
said	*sd*
sail	*sl*
sail·boat	*slbo*
sail·cloth	*slcll*

sail·ing	*sl̄*	sali·cylic	*slslc*
sailor	*slr*	sa·li·ent	*sleN*
saint	*sN*	sa·lin·ity	*sln^l*
saintly	*sNl*	sa·liva	*slva*
sake	*sc*	sal·low	*slo*
sal·abil·ity	*slB^l*	salmon	*sm*
sal·able	*slB*	salon	*sln*
salad	*sld*	salt	*sll*
sal·ads	*slds*	salts	*slts*
sala·ried	*slre-*	sa·lu·bri·ous	*slbres*
sala·ries	*slres*	salu·ta·tion	*slq*
salary	*slre*	sa·lute	*slu*
sale	*sl*	sal·vage	*slvq*
sale·able	*slB*	sal·vaged	*slvq-*
sales	*sls*	sal·vag·ing	*slvq_*
sales·man	*sls~n*	sal·va·tion	*slvq*
sales·man·ship	*slsms*	same	*s*
sales·men	*slsm*	sam·ple	*sa⌐*
sales·peo·ple	*slsppl*	sam·pled	*sa⌐-*
sales·per·son	*sls'sn*	sam·pler	*sa⌐r*
sales·room	*slsr~*	sam·ples	*sa⌐s*
sales·woman	*sls~n*	sam·pling	*sa⌐_*
sales·women	*sls~m*	sam·plings	*sa⌐=*

sanc·tion	*sq1*	sar·donic	*srdnc*
sanc·tions	*sqjs*	sash	*sA*
sanc·tu·ary	*sqCure*	sat	*st*
sand	*sN*	sa·tanic	*stnc*
san·dal	*sNl*	satchel	*sCl*
san·dals	*sNls*	sat·el·lite	*stli*
sanded	*sN-*	sat·el·lites	*stlis*
sand·ing	*sN̄*	satin	*stn*
sand·pa·per	*sN̄ppr*	sa·tir·ical	*strcl*
sands	*sNs*	sati·rize	*strz*
sand·stone	*sNSn*	sati·rized	*strz-*
sand·wich	*sNC*	sat·is·fac·tion	*saly*
sand·wiches	*sNCs*	sat·is·fac·to·rily	*sall*
sane	*sn*	sat·is·fac·tory	*sal*
sang	*sq*	sat·is·fied	*sal-*
sani·tary	*sntre*	sat·is·fies	*sals*
sani·ta·tion	*snly*	sat·isfy	*sal*
san·ity	*snl*	sat·is·fy·ing	*sal̲*
sank	*sq*	satu·rate	*sCra*
sap	*sp*	satu·rated	*sCra-*
sap·phire	*sfr*	satu·rates	*sCras*
sar·cas·tic	*srcSc*	satu·ra·tion	*sCry*
sar·dine	*srdn*	Saturday	*St*

sauce	*ss*	say	*sa*
sau·cer	*ssr*	say·ing	*sa_*
sau·cers	*ssrs*	say·ings	*sa=*
sauna	*sna*	says	*sz*
sau·sage	*ssj*	scab	*scb*
sauté	*sta*	scabs	*scbs*
sav·age	*svj*	scaf·fold	*scfld*
save	*sv*	scaf·fold·ing	*scfld_*
saved	*sv-*	scale	*scl*
saver	*svr*	scaled	*scl-*
sav·ers	*svrs*	scales	*scls*
saves	*svs*	scal·lop	*sclp*
sav·ing	*sv_*	scalp	*sclp*
sav·ings	*sv=*	scal·pel	*sclpl*
savor	*svr*	scalp·ing	*sclp_*
sa·vory	*svre*	scaly	*scle*
saw	*sa*	scam·per	*sc pr*
saw·dust	*sads*	scan	*scn*
sawed	*sa-*	scan·dal	*scNl*
saw·horse	*sahrs*	scan·ner	*scnr*
saw·mill	*sal*	scan·ning	*scn_*
saws	*sas*	scans	*scns*
saxo·phone	*sxfn*	scant	*scN*

scanty	*scNe*	sche·matic	*sc tc*
scar	*scr*	scheme	*sc*
scarce	*scrs*	schemes	*sc s*
scar·city	*scrs'*	schizo·phrenic	*sclsfrnc*
scare	*scr*	scholar	*sclr*
scared	*scr-*	schol·arly	*sclrl*
scarf	*scrf*	schol·ars	*sclrs*
scarred	*scr-*	schol·ar·ship	*sclrs*
scars	*scrs*	schol·ar·ships	*sclrss*
scat·ter	*sclr*	scho·las·tic	*sclsc*
scat·tered	*sclr-*	school	*scl*
scav·en·ger	*scvnjr*	school·ing	*scl*
sce·nario	*snro*	schools	*scls*
scene	*sn*	school·work	*scl o*
scen·ery	*snre*	sci·atic	*silc*
scenes	*sns*	sci·atica	*silca*
sce·nic	*snc*	sci·ence	*siN*
scent	*sN*	sci·ences	*siNs*
scent·ing	*sN*	sci·en·tific	*sinlfc*
sched·ule	*scjl*	sci·en·tif·ically	*sinlfcl*
sched·uled	*scjl-*	sci·en·tist	*sinlS*
sched·ules	*scjls*	sci·en·tists	*sinlSs*
sched·ul·ing	*scjl*	scin·til·la·tion	*sNlq*

scis·sors	*szrs*	scouts	*scols*
scoff	*scf*	scram·ble	*scr—β*
scold	*scld*	scrap	*scrp*
scoop	*scp*	scrap·book	*scrpbc*
scooter	*scur*	scraped	*scrp-*
scope	*scp*	scraper	*scrpr*
scopes	*scps*	scrap·ers	*scrprs*
scorch	*scrC*	scrapped	*scrp-*
scorch·ing	*scrC̲*	scraps	*scrps*
score	*scr*	scratch	*scrC*
scored	*scr-*	scratched	*scrC-*
score·keeper	*scrcpr*	scratches	*scrCs*
scorer	*scrr*	scrawl	*scrl*
scores	*scrs*	scrawny	*scrne*
scor·ing	*scr̲*	scream	*scr—*
scorn	*scrn*	screen	*scrn*
scorn·ful	*scrnf*	screened	*scrn-*
scotch	*scC*	screen·ing	*scrn̲*
Scotch	*scC*	screens	*scr̄ns*
scoun·drel	*scoNrl*	screw	*scru*
scour	*scor*	screw·ing	*scru̲*
scout	*scol*	screws	*scrus*
scout·ing	*scol̲*	scrib·ble	*scrβ*

scrim·mage		scum	
script		scut·tle	
scripts		sea	
scrip·tural		sea·bed	
Scripture		sea·board	
Scriptures		sea·coast	
scroll		sea·food	
scroll·ing		sea·go·ing	
scrub		seal	
scrub·ber		seal·ant	
scrub·bers		seal·ants	
scrub·bing		sealed	
scru·pu·lous		sealer	
scru·ti·nize		seal·ing	
scru·ti·nized		seals	
scru·tiny		seam	
scuba		sea·man	
scuff		seam·less	
scuff·ing		seams	
scuf·fle		seam·stress	
sculpt		sea·port	
sculpted		sea·ports	
sculp·ture		sear	

search	*SC*	sea·wor·thy	*se rle*
searched	*SC -*	se·cede	*ssd*
searcher	*SCr*	se·ces·sion	*ssy*
search·ers	*SCrs*	se·clude	*scld*
searches	*SCs*	se·cluded	*scld-*
search·ing	*SC_*	se·clu·sion	*scly*
seas	*ses*	sec·ond	*sec*
sea·shore	*sehr*	sec·ond·arily	*secrl*
sea·sick	*sesc*	sec·ond·ary	*secre*
sea·side	*sesd*	sec·onded	*sec-*
sea·son	*szn*	sec·ond·hand	*sechN*
sea·son·able	*sznB*	sec·ond·ing	*sec_*
sea·sonal	*sznl*	sec·ondly	*secl*
sea·son·ally	*sznll*	sec·onds	*secs*
sea·soned	*szn-*	se·crecy	*scrse*
sea·sons	*szns*	se·cret	*scrl*
seat	*se*	sec·re·tarial	*secl*
seated	*se-*	sec·re·tariat	*secl*
seat·ing	*se_*	sec·re·tar·ies	*secs*
seats	*ses*	sec·re·tary	*sec*
sea·ward	*sew*	se·crete	*scre*
sea·wa·ter	*se lr*	se·creted	*scre-*
sea·weed	*se d*	se·cre·tion	*scry*

se·cre·tive	*scrv*	se·duc·tive	*sdcv*
se·cre·tive	*screv*	see	*se*
sect	*sc*	seed	*sd*
sec·tarian	*scren*	seeded	*sd-*
sec·tion	*scq*	seed·ing	*sd_*
sec·tional	*scql*	seeds	*sds*
sec·tioned	*scq-*	see·ing	*se_*
sec·tions	*scqs*	seek	*sc*
sec·tor	*scr*	seeker	*scr*
sec·tors	*scrs*	seek·ers	*scrs*
secu·lar	*sclr*	seek·ing	*sc_*
se·cure	*scr*	seeks	*scs*
se·cured	*scr-*	seem	*s⌒*
se·cure·ly	*scrl*	seemed	*s⌒-*
se·cur·ing	*scr_*	seem·ing	*s⌒_*
se·cu·ri·ties	*scr_ls*	seem·ingly	*s⌒l*
se·cu·rity	*scr^l*	seems	*s⌒s*
sedan	*sdn*	seen	*sn*
seda·tive	*sdv*	seep	*sp*
sed·en·tary	*sdnlre*	seep·age	*spq*
sedi·ment	*sdm*	seep·ing	*sp_*
sedi·men·ta·tion	*sdmq*	sees	*ses*
se·duc·tion	*sdcq*	seethe	*sl*

seg·ment	*sgm*	self	*sf*
seg·ment·ing	*sgm_*	self-addressed	*sfadrs-*
seg·ments	*sgms*	self-adhering	*sfAhr_*
seg·re·gate	*sgrga*	self-assurance	*sfasrN*
seg·re·gated	*sgrga-*	self-centered	*sfsNr-*
seg·re·ga·tion	*sgrgs*	self-cleaning	*sfcln_*
seis·mic	*sz c*	self-closing	*sfclz_*
seis·mo·graph	*sz grf*	self-confidence	*sfkfdN*
seiz·able	*szb*	self-conscious	*sfkss*
seize	*sz*	self-contained	*sfkln-*
seized	*sz-*	self-control	*sfkl*
sei·zure	*szr*	self-defense	*sfdfN*
sei·zures	*szrs*	self-described	*sfdS-*
sel·dom	*sld*	self-determination	*sfdly*
se·lect	*slc*	self-development	*sfdvm*
se·lected	*slc-*	self-discipline	*sfDpln*
se·lect·ing	*slc_*	self-educated	*sfeyca-*
se·lec·tion	*slcy*	self-employed	*sf p-*
se·lec·tions	*slcys*	self-esteem	*sfes*
se·lec·tive	*slcv*	self-evaluation	*sfevluy*
se·lec·tively	*slcvl*	self-evident	*sfevdN*
se·lec·tiv·ity	*slcvl*	self-explanatory	*sfxplnlre*
se·lects	*slcs*	self-expression	*sfxpry*

self-government	*sfgvt*	self-respect	*sfrspc*
self-help	*sfhlp*	self-satisfaction	*sfsaly*
self-image	*sf᷑*	self-service	*sfSvs*
self-imposed	*sf᷑pz-*	self-study	*sfSde*
self-improvement	*sf᷑pvm*	self-sufficient	*sfsfAN*
self-indulgence	*sfndlgN*	self-supporting	*sfspt_*
self-inflicted	*sfnflc-*	self-sustaining	*sfsSn_*
self-insurance	*sfins*	self-taught	*sfll*
self-insured	*sfnsr-*	self-understanding	*sfUSN_*
self-interest	*sfNS*	self-worth	*sfrl*
self·ish	*sfs*	sell	*sl*
self·ish·ness	*sfs'*	seller	*slr*
self·less	*sfls*	sell·ers	*slrs*
self-loading	*sfld_*	sell·ing	*sl_*
self-locking	*sflc_*	sell·out	*slol*
self-made	*sf᷑d*	sells	*sls*
self-management	*sf᷑ym*	se·man·tics	*sNcs*
self-motivated	*sf᷑lva-*	sem·blance	*sBN*
self-organized	*sfoq-*	se·mes·ter	*sSr*
self-paced	*sfps-*	se·mes·ters	*sSrs*
self-pity	*sfple*	semi·an·nual	*saul*
self-protection	*sflcy*	semi·an·nu·ally	*saull*
self-reliance	*sfrliN*	semi·au·to·mated	*sal᷑a-*

semi·au·to·matic	*s̄ al̄ tc*	se·nil·ity	*snl̄ᶥ*
semi·co·lon	*s̄ cln*	sen·ior	*sr*
semi·con·duc·tor	*s̄ kdcr*	sen·ior·ity	*srᶥ*
semi·de·tached	*s̄ dlC-*	sen·iors	*srs*
semi·fi·nal	*s̄ fnl*	sen·sa·tion	*sNj*
semi·fi·nal·ist	*s̄ fnls*	sen·sa·tional	*sNjl*
semi·monthly	*s̄ ol*	sen·sa·tions	*sNjs*
semi·nar	*smr*	sense	*sN*
semi·nars	*smrs*	sensed	*sN-*
semi·nary	*smre*	sense·less	*sNls*
semi·pri·vate	*s̄ prvl*	senses	*sNs*
semi·skilled	*s̄ scl-*	sen·si·ble	*sNB*
semi·solid	*s̄ sld*	sens·ing	*sN̄*
semi·trailer	*s̄ lrlr*	sen·si·tive	*sN̄v*
semi·trail·ers	*s̄ lrlrs*	sen·si·tiv·ities	*sN̄v ls*
sen·ate	*snl*	sen·si·tiv·ity	*sN̄vᶥ*
sena·tor	*snlr*	sen·si·tize	*sNlz*
sena·tors	*snlrs*	sen·si·tized	*sNlz-*
send	*sN*	sen·sor	*sNr*
sender	*sNr*	sen·sors	*sNrs*
send·ing	*sN̄*	sen·sory	*sNre*
sends	*sN̄s*	sen·sual	*snsul*
se·nile	*snl*	sen·su·ous	*snsus*

sent	*sN*	se·quence	*sqN*
sen·tence	*sNN*	se·quences	*sqNs*
sen·tenced	*sNN-*	se·quenc·ing	*sqN_*
sen·tences	*sNNs*	se·quen·tial	*sqnsl*
sen·tenc·ing	*sNN_*	se·quen·tially	*sqnsll*
sen·ti·ment	*sNm*	se·ques·ter	*sqsr*
sen·ti·men·tal	*sNml*	se·quin	*sqn*
sen·ti·ments	*sNms*	sere·nade	*srnd*
sen·try	*sNre*	se·rene	*srn*
sepa·ra·ble	*sprB*	se·ren·ity	*srn*
sepa·rate (v.)	*spra*	ser·geant	*sryN*
sepa·rate (adj. or n.)	*sprl*	se·rial	*srel*
sepa·rated	*spra-*	se·ri·al·ize	*srelz*
sepa·rately	*sprll*	se·ri·als	*srels*
sepa·rat·ing	*spra_*	se·ries	*srz*
sepa·ra·tion	*spry*	se·ri·ous	*sres*
sepa·ra·tions	*sprys*	se·ri·ously	*sresl*
sepa·ra·tor	*sprar*	se·ri·ous·ness	*sres'*
sepa·ra·tors	*sprars*	ser·mon	*Sm*
sep·sis	*spss*	ser·pent	*SpN*
September	*Sp*	serum	*sr*
sep·tic	*splc*	ser·vant	*SvN*
se·quel	*sql*	ser·vants	*SvNs*

serve	Sv	set·tings	stl
served	$Sv-$	set·tle	stl
server	Svr	set·tled	$stl-$
serves	Svs	set·tle·ment	$stlm$
serv·ice	Svs	set·tle·ments	$stlms$
serv·ice·able	$SvsB$	set·tler	$stlr$
serv·iced	$Svs-$	set·tlers	$stlrs$
serv·ice·man	$Svs\,m$	set·tles	$stls$
serv·ice·men	$Svsm$	set·tling	stl
serv·ices	$Svss$	setup	stp
serv·ice·woman	$Svs\,m$	seven	7
serv·ice·women	$Svs\,m$	sev·en·teen	17
serv·ic·ing	Svs	sev·enth	$7l$
serv·ing	Sv	sev·enty	70
ses·sion	sj	sever	svr
ses·sions	sjs	sev·er·abil·ity	$svrBl$
set	st	sev·er·able	$svrB$
set·back	$stbc$	sev·eral	sv
set·backs	$stbcs$	sev·er·ally	svl
sets	sts	sev·er·ance	$svrN$
set·ter	str	se·vere	svr
set·ters	$strs$	sev·ered	$svr-$
set·ting	st	se·verely	$svrl$

Word	Shorthand	Word	Shorthand
se·ver·ity	*svrl*	shaggy	*Age*
sew	*so*	shaken	*Acn*
sew·age	*suy*	shakes	*Acs*
sewer	*sur*	shak·ing	*Ac_*
sewer	*sor*	shaky	*Ace*
sew·er·age	*sury*	shale	*Al*
sew·ers	*surs*	shall	*Al*
sew·ers	*sors*	shal·low	*Alo*
sew·ing	*so_*	shame	*A*
sewn	*sn*	shame·ful	*Af*
sex	*sx*	shame·less	*Als*
sexual	*sxul*	sham·poo	*A pu*
sexu·al·ity	*sxull*	sham·pooed	*A pu-*
shab·bi·ness	*Abe'*	sham·poo·ing	*A pu_*
shabby	*Abe*	shape	*Ap*
shack	*Ac*	shaped	*Ap-*
shade	*Ad*	shapes	*Aps*
shades	*Ads*	shap·ing	*Ap_*
shad·ing	*Ad_*	share	*Ar*
shadow	*Ado*	shared	*Ar-*
shad·owy	*Adoe*	share·holder	*Arhldr*
shaft	*Afl*	share·hold·ers	*Arhldrs*
shafts	*Afls*	shares	*Ars*

shar·ing	*Ar*	shel·tered	*Sltr-*
sharp	*Arp*	shel·ter·ing	*Sltr*
sharpen	*Arpn*	shel·ters	*Sltrs*
sharp·ened	*Arpn-*	shelve	*Slv*
sharp·ener	*Arpnr*	shelved	*Slv-*
sharp·en·ing	*Arpn*	shelves	*Slvs*
sharply	*Arpl*	shelv·ing	*Slv*
shat·ter	*Str*	sher·bet	*Srbt*
shaver	*Svr*	sher·iff	*Srf*
shav·ers	*Svrs*	sher·iffs	*Srfs*
she	*Se*	shield	*Sld*
shear	*Ar*	shielded	*Sld-*
shed	*Sd*	shields	*Slds*
sheds	*Sds*	shift	*Sft*
sheep	*Sp*	shifted	*Sft-*
sheer	*Ar*	shift·ing	*Sft*
sheet	*Se*	shifts	*Sfts*
sheet·ing	*Se*	shin	*An*
sheet·rock	*Serc*	shine	*An-*
sheets	*Ses*	shin·gle	*Agl*
shelf	*Slf*	shin·gles	*Agls*
shell	*Sl*	ship	*S*
shel·ter	*Sltr*	ship·build·ing	*Sbld*

ship·ment	*Am*	shoot·ing	*Au_*
ship·ments	*Ams*	shoot·ings	*Au=*
shipped	*A-*	shop	*Ap*
ship·per	*Ar*	shop·lift	*Aplfl*
ship·pers	*Ars*	shop·lifter	*Aplflr*
ship·ping	*A_*	shop·lift·ers	*Aplflrs*
ships	*As*	shop·lift·ing	*Aplfl_*
ship·shape	*AAp*	shop·lifts	*Aplfls*
ship·wreck	*Arc*	shop·per	*Apr*
ship·yard	*Ayd*	shop·ping	*Ap_*
ship·yards	*Ayds*	shops	*Aps*
shirk	*Arc*	shore	*Ar*
shirt	*Arl*	shore·line	*Arln*
shirts	*Arls*	shores	*Ars*
shiver	*Avr*	shor·ing	*Ar_*
shock	*Ac*	short	*Arl*
shocked	*Ac-*	short·age	*Arly*
shoddy	*Ade*	short·ages	*Arlys*
shoe	*Au*	short·com·ing	*Arlk_*
shoe·box	*Aubx*	short·com·ings	*Arlk=*
shoes	*Aus*	shorted	*Arl-*
shook	*Ac*	shorten	*Arln*
shoot	*Au*	short·ened	*Arln-*

Word	Shorthand	Word	Shorthand
short·en·ing		show	
shorter		show·case	
short·est		show·down	
short·fall		showed	
short·hand		shower	
short·ing		show·ers	
shortly		show·ing	
short·ness		show·ings	
shorts		show·man·ship	
shot		shown	
shot·gun		show·room	
shots		show·rooms	
should		shows	
shoul·der		showy	
shoul·der·ing		shred	
shoul·ders		shred·ded	
shouldn't		shred·der	
shout		shred·ders	
shout·ing		shred·ding	
shove		shrewd	
shovel		shriek	
shov·els		shrill	
shov·ing		shrimp	

shrine	*Arn*	sicken	*scn*
shrink	*Arq*	sickle	*scl*
shrink·age	*Arqj*	sick·ness	*sc'*
shrink·ing	*Arq*	sick·room	*scr*
shrivel	*Arvl*	side	*sd*
shrub·bery	*Arbre*	sided	*sd-*
shrubs	*Arbs*	side·light	*sdli*
shrug	*Arq*	side·lights	*sdlis*
shud·der	*Adr*	sides	*sds*
shuf·fle	*Afl*	side·track	*sdlrc*
shuf·fle·board	*Aflbrd*	side·walk	*sd c*
shuf·fled	*Afl-*	side·walks	*sd cs*
shut	*Al*	side·ways	*sd as*
shut·down	*Aldon*	sid·ing	*sd*
shut·downs	*Aldons*	siege	*sj*
shuts	*Als*	sift	*sfl*
shut·ter	*Alr*	sift·ing	*sfl*
shut·ters	*Alrs*	sigh	*si*
shut·ting	*Al*	sight	*si*
shut·tle	*Atl*	sighted	*si-*
shut·tles	*Atls*	sight·less	*sils*
shy	*Ai*	sights	*sis*
sick	*sc*	sight·see·ing	*sise*

sign	*sn*	sili·cone	*slcn*
sig·nal	*sgnl*	silk	*slc*
sig·naled	*sgnl-*	sills	*sls*
sig·nal·ing	*sgnl̲*	silly	*sle*
sig·nals	*sgnl̄s*	silos	*slos*
sig·na·tory	*sgntre*	silt	*slt*
sig·na·ture	*sig*	sil·ver	*slvr*
sig·na·tures	*sigs*	sil·ver·ware	*slvr r*
signed	*sn-*	simi·lar	*s lr*
signer	*snr*	simi·lar·ities	*s lr ls*
sign·ers	*snrs*	simi·lar·ity	*s lr l*
sig·nifi·cance	*sig*	simi·larly	*s lrl*
sig·nifi·cant	*sig*	sim·mer	*s r*
sig·nifi·cantly	*sigl*	sim·ple	*s pl*
sig·ni·fies	*sgnfis*	sim·pler	*s plr*
sig·nify	*sgnfi*	sim·plest	*s pls*
sign·ing	*sn̲*	sim·plic·ity	*s pls l*
signs	*sns*	sim·pli·fi·ca·tion	*s plff*
si·lence	*slN*	sim·pli·fi·ca·tions	*s plfjs*
si·lent	*slN*	sim·pli·fied	*s plfi-*
si·lently	*slNl*	sim·plify	*s plfi*
silica	*slca*	sim·pli·fy·ing	*s plfi*
sili·con	*slk*	sim·plis·tic	*s plsc*

Word	Shorthand	Word	Shorthand
sim·ply	*s~pl*	sin·is·ter	*snSr*
simu·late	*s~la*	sink	*sq*
simu·lated	*s~la-*	sinker	*sqr*
simu·la·tion	*s~ly*	sink·ing	*sq_*
simu·la·tor	*s~lar*	sinks	*sqs*
si·mul·ta·ne·ous	*s~llnes*	sins	*sns*
si·mul·ta·ne·ously	*s~llnesl*	sinus	*sns*
sin	*sn*	si·nuses	*snss*
since	*sN*	sip	*sp*
sin·cere	*snsr*	si·phon	*sfn*
sin·cerely	*snsrl*	sir	*S*
sin·cer·est	*snsrS*	sired	*sr-*
sin·cer·ity	*snsrˡ*	sir·loin	*Slyn*
sing	*sq*	sis·ter	*sSr*
singe	*sny*	sister-in-law	*sSr=n=la*
singe·ing	*sny_*	sis·ters	*sSrs*
singer	*sgr*	sit	*sl*
sing·ing	*sq_*	site	*sı*
sin·gle	*sgl*	sites	*sıs*
sin·gled	*sgl-*	sits	*sls*
sin·gles	*sgls*	sit·ter	*slr*
sin·gu·lar	*sglr*	sit·ting	*sl̄*
sin·gu·larly	*sglrl*	sit·tings	*sl̲̄*

situ·ate	*sil*	sketches	*scCs*
situ·ated	*sil-*	sketch·ing	*scC̄*
situ·ates	*sils*	sketchy	*scC̄e*
situ·at·ing	*sil̄*	ski	*sce*
situ·ation	*sily*	skid	*scd*
situ·ations	*silys*	skids	*scds*
six	6	ski·ing	*sce̲*
six·teen	16	skill	*scl*
sixth	61	skilled	*scl-*
sixty	60	skill·ful	*sclf*
siz·able	*szβ*	skill·fully	*sclfl*
size	*sz*	skills	*scls*
size·able	*szβ*	skim	*sc⁓*
sized	*sz-*	skimp	*sc⁓p*
sizes	*szs*	skin	*scn*
siz·ing	*sz̲*	skin·less	*scnls*
siz·zle	*szl*	skin·ning	*scn̲*
skate	*sca*	skinny	*scne*
skat·ing	*sca̲*	skip	*scp*
skele·tal	*scltl*	skipped	*scp-*
skele·ton	*sclln*	skip·ping	*scp̲*
skep·ti·cal	*scptcl*	skirt	*scrl*
sketch	*scC*	skirts	*scrls*

Word	Outline	Word	Outline	Outline
skit	*scl*	slate	*sla*	*sla*
skull	*scl*	slated	*sla-*	*sla-*
skunk	*scq*	slaugh·ter	*sltr*	*sltr*
sky	*sci*	slave	*slv*	*slv*
sky·dive	*scidv*	slay	*sla*	*sla*
sky·light	*scili*	sled	*sld*	*sld*
sky·line	*sciln*	sleep	*slp*	*slp*
sky·rocket	*scircl*	sleep·ing	*slp_*	*slp_*
sky·scraper	*sciscrpr*	sleep·less	*slpls*	*slpls*
sky·way	*scia*	sleep·wear	*slpr*	*slpr*
slab	*slb*	sleet	*sle*	*sle*
slabs	*slbs*	sleeve	*slv*	*slv*
slack	*slc*	sleeves	*slvs*	*slvs*
slacken	*slcn*	sleight	*sli*	*sli*
slacks	*slcs*	slen·der	*slNr*	*slNr*
slag	*slg*	slept	*slpt*	*slpt*
slam	*sl*	slice	*sls*	*sls*
slan·der	*slNr*	sliced	*sls-*	*sls-*
slant	*slN*	slices	*slss*	*slss*
slap	*slp*	slick	*slc*	*slc*
slapped	*slp-*	slicks	*slcs*	*slcs*
slap·ping	*slp_*	slide	*sld*	*sld*
slash	*slt*	slides	*slds*	*slds*

slid·ing	*sld*	slots	*slls*
slight	*sli*	slot·ted	*sll-*
slightly	*slil*	slough	*slf*
slim	*sl*	slow	*slo*
slime	*sl*	slow·down	*slodon*
sling	*slg*	slowed	*slo-*
sling·shot	*slgsl*	slower	*slor*
slink	*slg*	slow·ing	*slo*
slip	*slp*	slowly	*slol*
slip·page	*slpy*	slow·ness	*slo'*
slipped	*slp-*	slows	*sloo*
slip·per	*slpr*	sludge	*sly*
slip·pery	*slpre*	slug	*slg*
slip·ping	*slp*	slum	*sl*
slips	*slps*	slum·ber	*sl br*
slit	*sll*	slump	*sl p*
sliver	*slvr*	slung	*slg*
slo·gan	*slgn*	slur	*slr*
slop	*slp*	sly	*sli*
slope	*slp*	smack	*s c*
slopes	*slps*	small	*s l*
sloppy	*slpe*	smaller	*s lr*
slot	*sll*	small·est	*s ls*

smart		smother	
smash		smudge	
smear		smug	
smell		smut	
smell·ing		snack	
smells		snacks	
smile		snag	
smiled		snag·ging	
smil·ing		snail	
smock		snake	
smocks		snap	
smog		snappy	
smoke		snare	
smoked		snatch	
smoke·house		sneak	
smoker		sneer	
smok·ers		sneeze	
smok·ing		snicker	
smooth		snide	
smoother		sniff	
smooth·est		snif·ter	
smoothly		snif·ters	
smooth·ness		snob	

snob·bish	*snbs*	so·cially	*ssll*
snoop	*snp*	so·cials	*ssls*
snore	*snr*	so·cie·tal	*ssll*
snow	*sno*	so·ci·ety	*ssi^l*
snow·fall	*snofl*	so·cio·eco·nomic	*sseeco*
snow·mo·bile	*sno B*	so·cio·log·ical	*sselcl*
snow·mo·biles	*sno Bs*	so·ci·olo·gist	*sselcs*
snub	*snb*	so·ci·ology	*sselc*
snug	*snq*	sock	*sc*
so	*so*	socket	*scl*
soak	*sc*	sod	*sd*
soaked	*sc-*	soda	*sda*
soap	*sp*	sodas	*sdas*
soar	*sr*	sod·ded	*sd-*
soar·ing	*sr̄*	so·dium	*sde*
sob	*sb̄*	sofa	*sfa*
sober	*sbr*	soft	*sfl*
soc·cer	*scr*	soft·ball	*sflbl*
so·cial	*ssl*	soft·balls	*sflbls*
so·cial·ism	*sslz*	soften	*sfn*
so·cial·is·tic	*sslsc*	soft·ener	*sfnr*
so·cial·ize	*sslz*	soft·en·ing	*sfn̄*
so·cial·iz·ing	*sslz-*	softly	*sfll*

soft·ness	*sft'*	so·lici·tors	*slstrs*
soft·ware	*sftr*	solid	*sld*
soggy	*sge*	soli·dar·ity	*sldr'*
soil	*syl*	so·lidi·fied	*sldf-*
soiled	*syl-*	so·lidify	*sldf*
soils	*syls*	so·lidi·fy·ing	*sldf_*
solar	*slr*	so·lid·ity	*sld'-*
so·larium	*slre*	sol·idly	*sldl*
sold	*sld*	sol·ids	*slds*
sol·der·ing	*sdr*	so·lilo·quy	*sllqe*
sol·dier	*sljr*	soli·tary	*sltre*
sole	*sl*	soli·tude	*slld*
solely	*sll*	solo	*slo*
sol·emn	*sl*	so·lo·ist	*slos*
sol·em·nize	*sl-mz*	solu·bil·ity	*slBl*
so·le·noid	*slnyd*	solu·ble	*slB*
soles	*sls*	so·lu·tion	*sly*
so·licit	*slsl*	so·lu·tions	*slys*
so·lici·ta·tion	*slsly*	solv·able	*slvB*
so·lici·ta·tions	*slslys*	solve	*slv*
so·lic·ited	*slsl-*	solved	*slv-*
so·lic·it·ing	*slsl_*	sol·vency	*slvNe*
so·lici·tor	*slslr*	sol·vent	*slvN*

sol·vents	*slvⁿs*	soon	*sn*
solves	*slvs*	sooner	*snr*
solv·ing	*slv̱*	soon·est	*sn8*
som·ber	*s͡br*	soot	*st*
some	*s*	soothe	*st*
some·body	*s͡bde*	sooth·ing	*sṯ*
some·day	*s͡d*	so·phis·ti·cated	*sfŝca-*
some·how	*s͡ho*	so·phis·ti·ca·tion	*sfŝcy*
some·one	*s͡ı*	sopho·more	*sf*
some·place	*s͡pls*	sopho·mores	*sf͡s*
some·thing	*s͡ı̱*	so·prano	*sprno*
some·time	*s͡t*	sor·did	*srdd*
some·times	*s͡ts*	sore	*sr*
some·what	*s͡l*	sore·ness	*sr'*
some·where	*s͡r*	so·ror·ity	*srrᴸ*
son	*sn*	sor·row	*sro*
sonar	*snr*	sorry	*sre*
song	*sq*	sort	*srt*
songs	*sqs*	sorted	*srt-*
sonic	*snc*	sorter	*srtr*
son-in-law	*sn = n = la*	sor·tie	*srte*
son·net	*snt*	sort·ing	*srṯ*
sons	*sns*	sorts	*srts*

sot	*sl*	sou·ve·nir	*svnr*
sought	*sl*	sow	*so*
soul	*sl*	soy	*sy*
souls	*sls*	soy·bean	*sybn*
sound	*soN*	soy·beans	*sybns*
sounded	*soN-*	space	*sps*
sound·ing	*soN*	spaced	*sps-*
soundly	*soNl*	spaces	*spss*
sound·ness	*soN'*	space·ship	*spss*
sounds	*soNs*	spac·ing	*sps_*
soup	*sp*	spa·cious	*spss*
sour	*sor*	spade	*spd*
source	*srs*	spa·ghetti	*spgle*
sources	*srss*	span	*spn*
south	*S*	Spanish	*spns*
south·east	*SE*	spank	*spq*
south·east·erly	*SErl*	spans	*spns*
south·east·ern	*SErn*	spar	*spr*
south·erly	*Srl*	spare	*spr*
south·ern	*Srn*	spares	*sprs*
south·ward	*Sw*	spark	*sprc*
south·west	*SW*	spar·kle	*sprcl*
south·west·ern	*SWrn*	spar·kling	*sprcl_*

sparks	*sprcs*	spe·cial·iza·tion	*spslzn*
spar·row	*spro*	spe·cial·ize	*spslz*
sparse	*sprs*	spe·cial·ized	*spslz-*
sparsely	*sprsl*	spe·cial·izes	*spslzs*
spas·modic	*spz—dc*	spe·cial·iz·ing	*spslz_*
spas·tic	*spsc*	spe·cially	*spsll*
spat	*spl*	spe·cials	*spsls*
spate	*spa*	spe·cial·ties	*spslles*
spa·tial	*spsl*	spe·cialty	*spslle*
spat·ter	*splr*	spe·cie	*spse*
spawn·ing	*spn_*	spe·cies	*spses*
speak	*spc*	spe·cific	*sp*
speaker	*spcr*	spe·cif·ically	*spl*
speak·ers	*spcrs*	speci·fi·ca·tion	*spj*
speak·ing	*spc_*	speci·fi·ca·tions	*spjs*
speaks	*spcs*	spe·cif·ics	*sps*
spear	*spr*	speci·fied	*sp-*
spear·head	*sprhd*	speci·fies	*sps*
spe·cial	*spsl*	specify	*sp*
spe·cial·ist	*spsl8*	speci·fy·ing	*sp_*
spe·cial·ists	*spsl8s*	speci·men	*spsm*
spe·ci·al·ities	*spslel'ls*	speci·mens	*spsms*
spe·ci·al·ity	*spslel'*	speck	*spc*

specs	*spcs*	spells	*spls*
spec·ta·cle	*spclcl*	spend	*spM*
spec·tacu·lar	*spclclr*	spend·ing	*spM̄*
spec·ta·tor	*spclar*	spends	*spMs*
spec·trum	*spcdr*	spent	*spM*
specu·late	*spcla*	sperm	*spr*
specu·la·tion	*spclj*	sphere	*sfr*
speech	*spC*	spheres	*sfrs*
speeches	*spCs*	spher·ical	*sfrcl*
speech·less	*spCls*	spice	*sps*
speed	*spd*	spicy	*spse*
speedily	*spdl*	spi·der	*spdr*
speed·ing	*spd̄*	spike	*spc*
speed·ome·ter	*spd̄lr*	spill	*spl*
speeds	*spds*	spill·age	*splj*
speedy	*spde*	spilled	*spl-*
spell	*spl*	spill·ing	*spl̄*
spell·bind·ing	*splbM̄*	spills	*spl̄s*
spell·bound	*splbōM*	spill·way	*spla*
spelled	*spl-*	spill·ways	*splas*
speller	*splr*	spilt	*spll*
spell·ing	*spl̠*	spin	*spn*
spell·ings	*spl̲*	spin·ach	*spnC*

spi·nal	
spin·dle	
spin·dles	
spin·dling	
spine	
spine·less	
spin·ner	
spin·ners	
spin·ning	
spi·ral	
spirit	
spir·ited	
spir·its	
spiri·tual	
spiri·tu·al·ity	
spiri·tu·ally	
spit	
spite	
spite·ful	
splash	
splat·ter	
spleen	
splen·did	

splen·dor	
splice	
splicer	
splic·ers	
splic·ing	
splint	
splin·ter	
splin·tered	
splint·ing	
split	
splits	
split·ting	
splurge	
spoil	
spoil·ing	
spoke	
spo·ken	
spokes·man	
spokes·woman	
sponge	
spon·sor	
spon·sored	
spon·sor·ing	

spon·sors	*spNrs*	spouse	*spos*
spon·sor·ship	*spNrs*	spouses	*sposs*
spon·ta·ne·ous	*spnlnes*	spout	*spol*
spon·ta·ne·ously	*spnlnesl*	spout·ing	*spol‾*
spool	*spl*	sprain	*sprn*
spool·ing	*spl‾*	sprains	*sprns*
spools	*spls*	spray	*spra*
spoon	*spn*	sprayed	*spra-*
spo·radic	*sprdc*	sprayer	*sprar*
sport	*spl*	spray·ers	*sprars*
sport·ing	*spl‾*	spray·ing	*spra‾*
sports	*spls*	sprays	*spras*
sports·man·ship	*splsms*	spread	*sprd*
sports·wear	*spls r*	spreader	*sprdr*
spot	*spl*	spread·ing	*sprd‾*
spot·less	*splls*	spree	*spre*
spot·light	*splli*	spring	*sprg*
spot·lighted	*splli-*	spring·board	*sprgbrd*
spot·lights	*spllis*	springs	*sprgs*
spots	*spls*	sprin·kler	*sprglr*
spot·ted	*spl-*	sprint	*sprN*
spot·ting	*spl‾*	sprocket	*sprcl*
spotty	*sple‾*	sprock·ets	*sprcls*

spruce	*sprs*	squeeze	*sqz*
spry	*spru*	squeezed	*sqz-*
spud	*spd*	squeez·ing	*sqz_*
spud·ded	*spd-*	squid	*sqd*
spun	*spn*	squint	*sqN*
spunk	*spq*	squirm	*sqr*
spur	*spr*	squir·rel	*sqrl*
spur·ring	*spr_*	squirt	*sqrl*
spy	*spu*	stab	*Sb*
squab·ble	*sqB*	sta·bil·ity	*SBl*
squad	*sqd*	sta·bi·li·za·tion	*SBzj*
squad·ron	*sqdrn*	sta·bi·lize	*SBz*
squads	*sqds*	sta·bi·lized	*SBz-*
squan·der	*sqNr*	sta·ble	*SB*
square	*sq*	stack	*Sc*
squared	*sq-*	stacked	*Sc-*
squares	*sqs*	stacker	*Scr*
squar·est	*sqs*	stack·ing	*Sc_*
squar·ing	*sq_*	stacks	*Scs*
squash	*sqsh*	sta·dium	*Sde*
squeak	*sqc*	staff	*Sf*
squeal	*sql*	staffed	*Sf-*
squeam·ish	*sqsh*	staffer	*Sfr*

staff·ing	*Sf-*	stake·out	*Scol*
staffs	*Sfs*	stakes	*Scs*
stage	*Sj*	stak·ing	*Sc-*
staged	*Sj-*	stale	*Sl*
stages	*Sjs*	stale·mate	*Sl—a*
stag·ger	*Sgr*	stall	*Sl*
stag·gered	*Sgr-*	stalled	*Sl-*
stag·ger·ing	*Sgr-*	stal·wart	*Sl rl*
stag·ing	*Sj-*	stamina	*Sma*
stag·nant	*SgnN*	stam·mer	*S r*
stain	*Sn*	stamp	*S p*
stained	*Sn-*	stamped	*S p-*
stain·ing	*Sn-*	stam·pede	*S pd*
stain·less	*Snls*	stamper	*S pr*
stains	*Sns*	stamp·ing	*S p-*
stair	*Sr*	stamp·ings	*S p=*
stair·case	*Srcs*	stamps	*S ps*
stairs	*Srs*	stance	*SN*
stair·way	*Sr a*	stand	*SN*
stair·ways	*Sr as*	stan·dard	*Sd*
stair·well	*Sr l*	stan·dard·iza·tion	*Sdz*
stake	*Sc*	stan·dard·ize	*Sdz*
staked	*Sc-*	stan·dard·ized	*Sdz-*

stan·dard·izes	*Sdzs*		star·tle	*Srll*
stan·dard·iz·ing	*Sdz_*		star·tling	*Srll_*
stan·dards	*Sds*		starts	*Srls*
standby	*SNb*		star·va·tion	*Srvy*
stand·ing	*SN_*		starve	*Srv*
stand·ings	*SN̄*		state	*Sa*
stand·point	*SNpy*		stated	*Sa-*
stands	*SNs*		stately	*Sal*
stand·still	*SNSl*		state·ment	*Sam*
sta·ple	*Spl*		state·ments	*Sams*
sta·ples	*Spls*		states	*Sas*
star	*Sr*		state·wide	*Sad*
star·board	*Srbrd*		static	*Slc*
starch	*SrC*		stat·ing	*Sa_*
stare	*Sr*		sta·tion	*Sy*
star·ing	*Sr_*		sta·tion·ary	*Syre*
star·ring	*Sr_*		sta·tioned	*Sy-*
stars	*Srs*		sta·tioner	*Syr*
start	*Srl*		sta·tion·ery	*Syre*
started	*Srl-*		sta·tions	*Sys*
starter	*Srlr*		sta·tis·tic	*SlSc*
start·ers	*Srlrs*		sta·tis·ti·cal	*SlScl*
start·ing	*Srl_*		sta·tis·ti·cally	*SlScll*

sta·tis·tics		steam·ship	
statue		steel	
stat·ues		steels	
stat·ure		steel·worker	
status		steel·work·ers	
sta·tus quo		steep	
stat·ute		steeply	
stat·utes		steer·ing	
statu·tory		stem	
stay		stemmed	
stayed		stem·ming	
stay·ing		stems	
stays		stench	
stead·fast		sten·cil	
stead·fast·ness		sten·cil·ing	
steadily		sten·cils	
steady		ste·nog·ra·pher	
steak		ste·nog·ra·phers	
steal		steno·graphic	
steal·ing		step	
stealth		stepped	
steam		step·ping	
steam·ing		steps	

step·wise	*Sp₃*	stigma	*Sg a*
stereo	*Sro*	stile	*Sl*
stere·otype	*Srelp*	sti·letto	*Sllo*
stere·otyped	*Srelp-*	still	*Sl*
stere·otypes	*Srelps*	stills	*Sls*
ster·ile	*Srl*	stilted	*Sll-*
ste·ril·ity	*Srlᴸ*	stimu·lant	*S lM*
ster·il·ize	*Srlz*	stimu·late	*S la*
ster·ling	*Srlq*	stimu·lated	*S la-*
stern	*Srn*	stimu·lates	*S las*
stet	*Sl*	stimu·lat·ing	*S la*
stew·ard	*Sw*	stimu·la·tion	*S lj*
stew·ard·ess	*Sws*	stimu·la·tive	*S lav*
stew·ard·ship	*Sw⁴*	stimu·lus	*S ls*
stick	*Sc*	sting	*Sq*
sticker	*Scr*	stings	*Sgs*
stick·ers	*Scrs*	stingy	*Snje*
stick·ing	*Sc*	stink	*Sq*
stick·ler	*Sclr*	stint	*SM*
sticks	*Scs*	sti·pend	*SpM*
sticky	*Sce*	stipu·late	*Spla*
stiff	*Sf*	stipu·lated	*Spla-*
sti·fle	*Sfl*	stipu·lates	*Splas*

stipu·la·tion	*Sply*	sto·len	*Sln*
stipu·la·tions	*Splys*	stom·ach	*S—c*
stir	*Sr*	stomp	*S—p*
stirred	*Sr–*	stomps	*S—ps*
stitch	*SC*	stone	*Sn*
stitched	*SC–*	stones	*Sns*
stitches	*SCs*	stood	*Sd*
stitch·ing	*SC_*	stool	*Sl*
stock	*Sc*	stools	*Sls*
stock·bro·ker	*Scbrcr*	stoop	*Sp*
stocked	*Sc–*	stooped	*Sp–*
stock·holder	*Schldr*	stop	*Sp*
stock·hold·ers	*Schldrs*	stop·gap	*Spgp*
stock·ing	*Sc_*	stop·over	*SpO*
stock·pile	*Scpl*	stop·page	*Spy*
stock·piles	*Scpls*	stop·pages	*Spys*
stock·pil·ing	*Scpl_*	stopped	*Sp–*
stock·room	*Scr*	stop·per	*Spr*
stocks	*Scs*	stop·ping	*Sp_*
stock·yard	*Scyd*	stops	*Sps*
stock·yards	*Scyds*	stor·abil·ity	*SrBl*
stokes	*Scs*	stor·age	*Sry*
stole	*Sl*	store	*Sr*

stored	*Sr-*	straight·ened	*Sran-*
store·front	*Srfrn*	straight·en·ing	*Sran_*
store·house	*Srhos*	straight·for·ward	*Srafw*
store·keeper	*Srcpr*	strain	*Srn*
store·room	*Srr*	strained	*Srn-*
store·rooms	*Srrs*	strainer	*Srnr*
stores	*Srs*	strain·ers	*Srnrs*
sto·ries	*Sres*	strain·ing	*Srn_*
stor·ing	*Sr_*	strains	*Srns*
storm	*Sr*	strait	*Sra*
storms	*Srs*	straits	*Sras*
stormy	*Sre*	strand	*Srn*
story	*Sre*	strands	*Srns*
sto·ry·board	*Srebrd*	strange	*Srnj*
sto·ry·board·ing	*Srebrd_*	strangely	*Srnjl*
sto·ry·boards	*Srebrds*	stranger	*Srnjr*
stout	*Sol*	strang·ers	*Srnjrs*
stove	*Sv*	stran·gle	*Srgl*
stoves	*Svs*	strap	*Srp*
stowed	*So-*	strapped	*Srp-*
strad·dle	*Srdl*	straps	*Srps*
straight	*Sra*	strata	*Srla*
straighten	*Sran*	stra·te·gic	*Srljc*

stra·te·gi·cal	*Srlycl*	stressed	*Srs-*
stra·te·gi·cally	*Srlycll*	stresses	*Srss*
strate·gies	*Srlyes*	stress·ful	*Srsf*
strategy	*Srlye*	stress·ing	*Srs_*
stra·tum	*Srl*	stretch	*SrC*
straw	*Sra*	stretched	*SrC-*
stray	*Sra*	stretcher	*SrCr*
streak·ing	*Src_*	stretch·ing	*SrC_*
streaks	*Srcs*	stricken	*Srcn*
stream	*Sr*	strict	*Src*
stream·line	*Sr In*	stricter	*Srcr*
stream·lin·ing	*Sr In_*	strict·est	*Srcß*
streams	*Sr s*	strictly	*Srcl*
street	*S*	stride	*Srd*
street·car	*Scr*	strides	*Srds*
streets	*Ss*	strife	*Srf*
strength	*Srql*	strike	*Src*
strengthen	*Srqln*	striker	*Srcr*
strength·ened	*Srqln-*	strik·ers	*Srcrs*
strength·en·ing	*Srqln_*	strikes	*Srcs*
strengths	*Srqls*	strik·ing	*Src_*
strenu·ous	*Srnus*	string	*Srq*
stress	*Srs*	strin·gent	*SrnyN*

stringer	*Srgr*	struck	*Src*
string·ers	*Srgrs*	struc·tural	*SrcCrl*
string·ing	*Srq_*	struc·tur·ally	*SrcCrll*
strings	*Srgs*	struc·ture	*SrcCr*
strip	*Srp*	struc·tured	*SrcCr-*
stripe	*Srp*	struc·tures	*SrcCrs*
striped	*Srp-*	struc·tur·ing	*SrcCr_*
stripes	*Srps*	strug·gle	*Srgl*
stripped	*Srp-*	strug·gled	*Srgl-*
strip·per	*Srpr*	strug·gles	*Srgls*
strip·ping	*Srp_*	strug·gling	*Srgl_*
strips	*Srps*	strung	*Srq*
strive	*Srv*	strut	*Srl*
strives	*Srvs*	stub	*Sb*
striv·ing	*Srv_*	stub·born	*Sbrn*
strobe	*Srb*	stub·born·ness	*Sbrn'*
stroke	*Src*	stubs	*Sbs*
strokes	*Srcs*	stuck	*Sc*
stroll	*Srl*	stud	*Sd*
strong	*Srq*	stu·dent	*SdN*
stronger	*Srgr*	stu·dents	*SdNs*
strong·est	*Srgs*	stud·ied	*Sde-*
strongly	*Srgl*	stud·ies	*Sdes*

stu·dio	*Sdo*	styled	*Sl-*
stu·dios	*Sdos*	styles	*Sls*
stu·di·ous	*Sdes*	styl·ing	*Sl-*
studs	*Sds*	styl·ish	*Sls*
study	*Sde*	sty·lis·tic	*SlSc*
study·ing	*Sde*	suave	*sv*
stuff	*Sf*	sub	*s*
stuffed	*Sf-*	sub·class	*scls*
stuf·fer	*Sfr*	sub·classes	*sclss*
stuf·fers	*Sfrs*	sub·com·mit·tee	*sk*
stum·ble	*S B*	sub·com·mit·tees	*sks*
stum·bled	*S B-*	sub·con·scious	*skss*
stump	*S p*	sub·con·tract	*skc*
stumps	*S ps*	sub·con·tract·ing	*skc*
stun	*Sn*	sub·con·trac·tor	*skcr*
stun·ning	*Sn*	sub·con·trac·tors	*skcrs*
stunt	*SN*	sub·con·tracts	*skcs*
stu·pefy	*Spf*	sub·di·vide	*sdvd*
stu·pen·dous	*SpNs*	sub·di·vided	*sdvd-*
stu·pid	*Spd*	sub·di·vider	*sdvdr*
sturdy	*Srde*	sub·di·vid·ing	*sdvd*
stut·ter	*Slr*	sub·di·vi·sion	*sdvj*
style	*Sl*	sub·di·vi·sions	*sdvjs*

sub·due	*sdu*	sub·mit·tal	
sub·grade	*sgrd*	sub·mit·ted	
sub·group	*sgrp*	sub·mit·ting	
sub·head·ings	*shd*	sub·or·di·nate (adj. or n.)	*sordnl*
sub·ject	*sjc*	sub·or·di·nate (v.)	*sordna*
sub·jected	*sjc-*	sub·or·di·nates (n.)	*sordnls*
sub·jec·tive	*sjcv*	sub·or·di·nates (v.)	*sordnas*
sub·jects	*sjcs*	sub·or·di·na·tion	*sordny*
sub·ju·gate	*sjga*	sub·poena	*spna*
sub·lease	*sls*	sub·poe·nas	*spnas*
sub·leases	*slss*	sub·ro·ga·tion	*srgy*
sub·let	*sll*	sub·rou·tine	*srln*
sub·limi·nal	*slml*	sub·scribe	*sS*
sub·ma·rine		sub·scribed	*sS-*
sub·merge		sub·scriber	*sSr*
sub·merged		sub·scrib·ers	*sSrs*
sub·merse		sub·scribes	*sSs*
sub·mer·sion		sub·scrib·ing	*sS*
sub·mis·sion		sub·scrip·tion	*sSy*
sub·mis·sions		sub·scrip·tions	*sSys*
sub·mis·sive		sub·scripts	*sSs*
sub·mit		sub·sec·tion	*sscy*
sub·mits			

sub·sec·tions	*sscjs*	sub·stan·tive	*sSnv*
sub·se·quent	*ssqN*	sub·stan·tively	*sSnvl*
sub·se·quently	*ssqNl*	sub·sta·tion	*sSy*
sub·side	*ssd*	sub·sta·tions	*sSys*
sub·si·dence	*ssdN*	sub·sti·tute	*sStu*
sub·sidi·ar·ies	*ssderes*	sub·sti·tuted	*sStu-*
sub·sidi·ary	*ssdere*	sub·sti·tutes	*sStus*
sub·si·dies	*ssdes*	sub·sti·tut·ing	*sStu_*
sub·si·dize	*ssdz*	sub·sti·tu·tion	*sSty*
sub·si·dized	*ssdz-*	sub·sti·tu·tions	*sStys*
sub·si·diz·ing	*ssdz_*	sub·struc·ture	*sSrcCr*
sub·sidy	*ssde*	sub·sur·face	*sSfs*
sub·sis·tence	*ssSN*	sub·sys·tem	*ssS*
sub·stance	*sSN*	sub·sys·tems	*ssS_s*
sub·stances	*sSNs*	sub·ter·fuge	*strfj*
sub·stan·dard	*sSd*	sub·ter·ra·nean	*strnen*
sub·stan·tial	*sSnsl*	sub·ti·tle	*sltl*
sub·stan·tially	*sSnsll*	sub·tle	*stl*
sub·stan·ti·ate	*sSnsa*	sub·topic	*slpc*
sub·stan·ti·ated	*sSnsa-*	sub·top·ics	*slpcs*
sub·stan·ti·ates	*sSnsas*	sub·to·tal	*slol*
sub·stan·ti·at·ing	*sSnsa_*	sub·to·tals	*slols*
sub·stan·tia·tion	*sSnsej*	sub·tract	*strc*

sub·tracted	*strc-*	suc·cinct	*scsq*
sub·tract·ing	*strc̲*	suc·cinctly	*scsql*
sub·trac·tion	*strcq*	such	*sC*
sub·trop·ical	*strpcl*	sucker	*scr*
sub·urb	*srb*	suc·tion	*scq*
sub·ur·ban	*srbn*	sud·den	*sdn*
sub·urbs	*srbo*	sud·denly	*sdnl*
sub·ver·sion	*svrq*	sue	*su*
sub·vert	*svrl*	sued	*su-*
sub·way	*s a*	suede	*s d*
suc·ceed	*scsd*	suf·fer	*sfr*
suc·ceeded	*scsd-*	suf·fered	*sfr-*
suc·ceed·ing	*scsd̲*	suf·fer·ing	*sfr̲*
suc·ceeds	*scsds*	suf·fers	*sfrs*
suc·cess	*suc*	suf·fice	*sfs*
suc·cesses	*sucs*	suf·fi·ciency	*sfsNe*
suc·cess·ful	*sucf*	suf·fi·cient	*sfsN*
suc·cess·fully	*sucfl*	suf·fi·ciently	*sfsNl*
suc·ces·sion	*sucq*	suf·fix	*sfx*
suc·ces·sive	*sucv*	suf·fixes	*sfxs*
suc·ces·sively	*sucvl*	suf·fo·cate	*sfca*
suc·ces·sor	*sucr*	sugar	*Agr*
suc·ces·sors	*sucrs*	sug·gest	*suq*

sug·gested	*sug-*	sum·ma·rize	*s ~rz*
sug·gest·ing	*sug_*	sum·ma·rized	*s ~rz-*
sug·ges·tion	*sugʃ*	sum·ma·rizes	*s ~rzs*
sug·ges·tions	*sugʃs*	sum·ma·riz·ing	*s ~rz_*
sug·ges·tive	*sugv*	sum·mary	*s ~re*
sug·gests	*sugs*	sum·ma·tion	*s ~y*
sui·cide	*susd*	summed	*s ~-*
suit	*su*	sum·mer	*s ~r*
suit·abil·ity	*suℬˡ*	sum·mers	*s ~rs*
suit·able	*suℬ*	sum·ming	*s ~_*
suit·ably	*suℬ*	sum·mit	*s ~l*
suit·case	*sucs*	sum·mons	*sms*
suite	*s e*	sums	*s ~s*
suited	*su-*	sun	*sn*
suites	*s es*	sun·beam	*snb*
suitor	*sur*	sun·burn	*snbrn*
suits	*sus*	sun·burst	*snbr8*
sul·fate	*slfa*	Sunday	*Sn*
sul·fur	*slfr*	sun·dry	*sNre*
sulk	*slc*	sun·flower	*snflor*
sul·len	*sln*	sun·flow·ers	*snflors*
sum	*s ~*	sun·glasses	*snglss*
sum·ma·ries	*s ~res*	sun·light	*snlu*

sun·ning	*sn_*	su·per·sede	*Ssd*
sunny	*sne*	su·per·seded	*Ssd-*
sun·rise	*snrz*	su·per·sedes	*Ssds*
sun·set	*snsl*	su·per·sed·ing	*Ssd_*
sun·sets	*snsls*	su·per·sonic	*S snc*
sun·shine	*snʌn*	su·per·sti·tion	*SSi*
sun·tan	*snln*	su·per·sti·tious	*SSss*
super	*S*	su·per·vise	*Svz*
su·perb	*sprb*	su·per·vised	*Svz-*
su·per·cili·ous	*Ssles*	su·per·vises	*Svzs*
su·per·fi·cial	*Sfsl*	su·per·vis·ing	*Svz-*
su·per·fi·cially	*Sfsll*	su·per·vi·sion	*Svy*
su·per·im·pose	*S⁻pz*	su·per·vi·sor	*Svzr*
su·per·im·posed	*S⁻pz-*	su·per·vi·sors	*Svzrs*
su·per·in·ten·dent	*S*	su·per·vi·sory	*Svzre*
su·per·in·ten·dents	*Ss*	sup·per	*spr*
su·pe·rior	*sprer*	sup·plant	*splʼn*
su·pe·ri·or·ity	*sprerʼ*	sup·plant·ing	*splʼn_*
su·per·man	*S⁻m*	sup·ple·ment	*splm*
su·per·mar·ket	*S⁻r*	sup·ple·men·tal	*splml*
su·per·mar·kets	*S⁻rs*	sup·ple·men·tary	*splmre*
su·per·script	*SS*	sup·ple·mented	*splm-*
su·per·scripts	*SSs*	sup·ple·ment·ing	*splm_*

sup·ple·ments	*splms*	sure	*Ar*
sup·pli·ca·tion	*splcy*	surely	*Arl*
sup·plied	*spli-*	sur·eties	*Arls*
sup·plier	*splir*	sur·ety	*Arl*
sup·pli·ers	*splirs*	surf	*Sf*
sup·plies	*splis*	sur·face	*Sfs*
sup·ply	*spli*	sur·faced	*Sfs-*
sup·ply·ing	*spli_*	sur·faces	*Sfss*
sup·port	*spt*	sur·fac·ing	*Sfs_*
sup·ported	*spt-*	surge	*Sj*
sup·porter	*sptr*	sur·geon	*Sjn*
sup·port·ers	*sptrs*	sur·geons	*Sjns*
sup·port·ing	*spt_*	sur·gery	*Sjre*
sup·por·tive	*sptv*	sur·gi·cal	*Sjcl*
sup·ports	*spts*	surly	*Sl*
sup·pose	*spz*	sur·mise	*Smz*
sup·posed	*spz-*	sur·mount	*Smot*
sup·pos·edly	*spz-l*	sur·name	*Sm*
sup·po·si·tion	*spzj*	sur·pass	*Sps*
sup·press	*sprs*	sur·passed	*Sps-*
sup·pres·sion	*spry*	sur·plus	*Spls*
su·preme	*spr*	sur·pluses	*Splss*
sur·charge	*SG*	sur·prise	*Sprz*

sur·prised	*Sprz-*	sur·viv·able	*Svvß*
sur·prises	*Sprzs*	sur·vival	*Svvl*
sur·pris·ing	*Sprz-*	sur·vive	*Svv*
sur·pris·ingly	*Sprzl*	sur·viv·ing	*Svv-*
sur·ren·der	*SNr*	sur·vi·vor	*Svvr*
sur·ren·dered	*SNr-*	sur·vi·vors	*Svvrs*
sur·ren·der·ing	*SNr-*	sur·vi·vor·ship	*Svvrs*
sur·ren·ders	*SNrs*	sus·cep·ti·ble	*ssplß*
sur·ro·gate (n. or adj.)	*Sgl*	sus·pect	*sspc*
sur·ro·gate (v.)	*Sga*	sus·pected	*sspc-*
sur·round	*SoN*	sus·pects	*sspcs*
sur·rounded	*SoN-*	sus·pend	*sspN*
sur·round·ing	*SoN-*	sus·pended	*sspN-*
sur·round·ings	*SoN=*	sus·pend·ing	*sspN-*
sur·tax	*Slx*	sus·pense	*sspN*
sur·veil·lance	*SvlN*	sus·pen·sion	*sspnj*
sur·vey	*Sva*	sus·pen·sions	*sspnjs*
sur·veyed	*Sva-*	sus·pi·cion	*sspj*
sur·vey·ing	*Sva-*	sus·pi·cious	*sspss*
sur·veyor	*Svar*	sus·tain	*sSn*
sur·vey·ors	*Svars*	sus·tained	*sSn-*
sur·veys	*Svas*	sus·tainer	*sSnr*
sur·viv·abil·ity	*Svvßl*	sus·tain·ers	*sSnrs*

word	shorthand	word	shorthand
sus·tain·ing		sweep·ing	
sus·te·nance		sweep·stakes	
su·ture		sweet	
su·tures		sweet·ener	
swab		swell·ing	
swabbed		swept	
swab·bing		swerve	
swag·ger		swift	
swal·low		swim	
swal·lowed		swim·mer	
swamp		swim·ming	
swan		swim·suit	
swanky		swin·dle	
swap		swin·dler	
swap·ping		swine	
swarm		swing	
sway		swing·ing	
swear		swirl	
sweat		swish	
sweater		switch	
sweep		switch·board	
sweeper		switched	
sweep·ers		switches	

switch·ing		symp·to·matic	
swivel		symp·toms	
swol·len		syn·chro·nize	
swoop		syn·chro·nized	
sword		syn·chro·nous	
sworn		syn·di·cate (n.)	
swung		syn·di·cate (v.)	
syl·labic		syn·di·cated	
syl·labi·cate		syn·di·ca·tion	
syl·la·ble		syn·di·ca·tions	
syl·la·bus		syn·drome	
sym·bol		syn·er·getic	
sym·bolic		syn·er·gis·tic	
sym·bol·ize		syno·nym	
sym·bols		syn·ony·mous	
sym·met·ri·cal		syno·nyms	
sym·pa·thetic		syn·op·sis	
sym·pa·thize		syn·the·sis	
sym·pa·thy		syn·the·size	
sym·phonic		syn·the·siz·ing	
sym·phony		syn·thetic	
sym·po·sium		sy·phon	
symp·tom		sy·ringe	

sy·ringes	*Snjs*
syrup	*Sp*
sys·tem	*ss*
sys·tem·atic	*ss tc*
sys·tem·at·ical	*ss tcl*
sys·tem·at·ically	*ss tcll*
sys·tema·tize	*ss tz*
sys·tems	*ss s*

T

tab	*Ub*
table	*lB*
tab·leau	*Ublo*
ta·ble·cloth	*lBcll*
ta·bled	*lB-*
ta·bles	*lBs*
ta·ble·spoon	*lBspn*
tab·let	*Ublt*
tab·lets	*Ublts*
ta·ble·ware	*lB r*
tab·loid	*Ublyd*
taboo	*Ubu*

tabs	*Ubs*
tabu·lar	*Ublr*
tabu·late	*Ubla*
tabu·lated	*Ubla-*
tabu·lat·ing	*Ubla_*
tabu·la·tion	*Ublj*
tabu·la·tions	*Ubljs*
tabu·la·tor	*Ublar*
ta·chome·ter	*Uklr*
tacit	*lsl*
taci·turn	*lslrn*
tack	*lc*
tacked	*lc-*
tack·ing	*lc_*
tackle	*lcl*
tack·ling	*lcl_*
tact	*lc*
tact·ful	*lcf*
tac·tic	*lcc*
tac·ti·cal	*lccl*
tac·tics	*lccs*
tac·tile	*lcl*
tact·less	*lcls*

tag	*Lq*	tal·cum	*Ulk*
tagged	*Lq-*	tale	*Ul*
tag·ging	*Lq_*	tal·ent	*Uln*
tags	*Lqs*	tal·ented	*Uln-*
tail	*Ul*	tal·ents	*Ulns*
tail·gate	*Ulga*	talk	*Lc*
tail·ing	*Ul*	talka·tive	*Lcv*
tail·ings	*Ul*	talked	*Lc-*
tail·light	*Ulli*	talk·ing	*Lc*
tai·lor	*Ulr*	talks	*Lcs*
tai·lored	*Ulr-*	tall	*Ul*
tai·lors	*Ulrs*	taller	*Ulr*
take	*Lc*	tal·lied	*Ule-*
take·down	*Lcdon*	tally	*Ule*
taken	*Lcn*	tal·ly·ing	*Ule*
take·off	*Lcof*	talon	*Uln*
take·out	*Lcol*	ta·male	*Lml*
take·over	*LcO*	ta·ma·les	*Lmls*
taker	*Lcr*	tame	*Lm*
tak·ers	*Lcrs*	tam·per	*Lmpr*
takes	*Lcs*	tam·pered	*Lmpr-*
tak·ing	*Lc*	tam·pon	*Lmpn*
talc	*Ulc*	tan	*Ln*

Word	Shorthand	Word	Shorthand	Word	Shorthand
tan·dem	*Ⱳ*	tap·ing	*Ⱡⱷ*		
tang	*Ⱡⱬ*	tapped	*Ⱡⱷ-*		
tan·gent	*ⰾⱬⰾ*	tap·ping	*Ⱡⱷ₌*		
tan·gi·ble	*ⰾⱬⰵ*	tap·pings	*Ⱡⱷ₌*		
tan·gle	*Ⱡⱬⰾ*	taps	*Ⱡⱷₛ*		
tan·gled	*Ⱡⱬⰾ-*	tar	*Ⱡⱬ*		
tank	*Ⱡⱬ*	tar·dies	*ⰾⱬⰴⰾ*		
tank·age	*Ⱡⱬⱡ*	tar·di·ness	*ⰾⱬⰴⰵ'*		
tanker	*Ⱡⱬⱬ*	tardy	*ⰾⱬⰴⰵ*		
tanks	*Ⱡⱬₛ*	tar·get	*ⰾⱬⱡⰾ*		
tan·ning	*Ⱡⱬ*	tar·geted	*ⰾⱬⱡⰾ-*		
tan·ta·lize	*Ⱳⱬ*	tar·get·ing	*ⰾⱬⱡⰾ₋*		
tan·ta·mount	*ⱲₒⱲ*	tar·gets	*ⰾⱬⱡⰾₛ*		
tan·trum	*Ⱳⱬ*	tar·iff	*ⰾⱬⱡ*		
tan·trums	*Ⱳⱬₛ*	tar·iffs	*ⰾⱬⱡₛ*		
tap	*Ⱡⱷ*	tar·nish	*ⰾⱬⱬₛ*		
tape	*Ⱡⱷ*	tar·pau·lin	*ⰾⱬⱷⱬ*		
taped	*Ⱡⱷ-*	tarry	*ⰾⱬⰵ*		
taper	*Ⱡⱷⱬ*	tart	*ⰾⱬⰾ*		
ta·pered	*Ⱡⱷⱬ-*	task	*ⰾₛⱶ*		
ta·per·ing	*Ⱡⱷⱬ₋*	tasks	*ⰾₛⱶₛ*		
tapes	*Ⱡⱷₛ*	taste	*Ⱡ8*		
tap·es·try	*ⱠⱷⱾⱡ*	tasted	*Ⱡ8-*		

taste·fully	*ᒪᓯᒎᒪ*	teacher	*ᑌᑕᖇ*
taste·less	*ᒪᓯᒪᔆ*	teach·ers	*ᑌᑕᖇᔆ*
tastes	*ᒪᓯᔆ*	teaches	*ᑌᑕᔆ*
tast·ing	*ᒪᓯ*	teach·ing	*ᑌᑕ*
tasty	*ᒪᓯᐁ*	teach·ings	*ᑌᑕ*
tat·tle	*ᑌᒪ*	team	*ᒪ*
tat·tling	*ᑌᒪ*	teamed	*ᒪ*
tat·too	*ᑌᑌ*	team·mate	*ᒪᗩ*
taught	*ᑌ*	teams	*ᒪᔆ*
taut	*ᑌ*	team·ster	*ᒪᔕᖇ*
tav·ern	*ᒪᐁᖇᑎ*	team·sters	*ᒪᔕᖇᔆ*
tax	*ᒪᕽ*	team·work	*ᒪ*
tax·able	*ᒪᕽᗷ*	tea·pot	*ᒉᑭᒪ*
taxa·tion	*ᒪᕽᓱ*	tear	*ᒪᖇ*
taxed	*ᒪᕽ-*	tear·ing	*ᒪᖇ*
taxes	*ᒪᕽᔆ*	tears	*ᒪᖇᔆ*
taxi	*ᒪᕽᐁ*	tease	*ᒪᕾ*
tax·ing	*ᒪᕽ*	teased	*ᒪᕾ-*
tax·payer	*ᒪᕽᑭᗩᖇ*	tea·spoon	*ᒉᔆᑭᑎ*
tax·pay·ers	*ᒪᕽᑭᗩᖇᔆ*	tech·ni·cal	*ᒪᑕᑎᑕᒪ*
tax·pay·ing	*ᒪᕽᑭᗩ*	tech·ni·cal·ity	*ᒪᑕᑎᑕᒪᒪ*
tea	*ᒉ*	tech·ni·cally	*ᒪᑕᑎᑕᒪᒪ*
teach	*ᑌᑕ*	tech·ni·cian	*ᒪᑕᑎᕽ*

tech·ni·cians	*Lcnjs*	te·leg·ra·phy	*Llgrfe*
tech·nique	*Lcnc*	tele·lec·ture	*LllcCr*
tech·niques	*Lcncs*	te·leme·try	*Ll_lre*
tech·no·log·ical	*Lcnljcl*	te·lepa·thy	*Llple*
tech·nolo·gies	*Lcnljes*	tele·phone	*Llfn*
tech·nolo·gist	*LcnljS*	tele·phoned	*Llfn-*
tech·nolo·gists	*LcnljSs*	tele·phones	*Llfns*
tech·nology	*Lcnlje*	tele·phon·ing	*Llfn_*
te·di·ous	*Ldes*	tele·photo	*Lllflo*
te·di·ously	*Ldesl*	tele·printer	*LlprNr*
tee	*Le*	tele·promp·ter	*Lll_lr*
teen	*Ln*	tele·scope	*Llscp*
teen·age	*Lnaj*	tele·scoped	*Llscp-*
teen·ager	*Lnajr*	tele·scop·ing	*Llscp_*
teen·ag·ers	*Lnajrs*	tele·thon	*Llln*
teeth	*Ll*	tele·type	*Lllp*
Teflon	*Yfln*	tele·type·writer	*Lllprur*
tele·cast	*LllcS*	tele·type·writ·ers	*Lllprurs*
tele·com·mu·ni·ca·tion	*Lllkncy*	tele·vise	*Llvz*
tele·con·fer·ence	*LllkfrN*	tele·vised	*Llvz-*
tele·con·fer·enc·ing	*LllkfrN_*	tele·vi·sion	*Llvj*
tele·gram	*Llg*	tele·vi·sions	*Llvjs*
tele·graph	*Llgrf*	telex	*Llx*

tell		te·na·ciously	
teller		te·nac·ity	
tell·ers		ten·an·cies	
tell·ing		ten·ancy	
tells		ten·ant	
te·mer·ity		ten·ants	
tem·per		tend	
tem·pera·ment		tended	
tem·pera·ture		ten·den·cies	
tem·pera·tures		ten·dency	
tem·pered		ten·der	
tem·pers		ten·dered	
tem·plate		ten·der·ing	
tem·ple		ten·der·ness	
tempo		tend·ing	
tem·po·rar·ies		ten·don	
tem·po·rarily		tends	
tem·po·rary		tene·ment	
temp·ta·tion		tenet	
temp·ta·tions		ten·nis	
ten		tenor	
ten·able		tens	
te·na·cious		tense	

ten·sile	ter·race
ten·sion	ter·rain
tent	ter·res·trial
ten·ta·tive	ter·ri·ble
ten·ta·tively	ter·ri·bly
tenth	ter·ri·fic
tenu·ous	ter·rify
ten·ure	ter·ri·to·rial
ten·ured	ter·ri·to·ries
tepid	ter·ri·tory
term	ter·ror
termed	ter·ror·ism
ter·mi·nal	ter·ror·ist
ter·mi·nals	ter·ror·ize
ter·mi·nate	terse
ter·mi·nated	ter·ti·ary
ter·mi·nates	test
ter·mi·nat·ing	tes·ta·ment
ter·mi·na·tion	tested
ter·mi·na·tions	tester
ter·mi·nology	test·ers
ter·mite	tes·ti·fied
terms	tes·tify

tes·ti·fy·ing		thanks·giv·ing	
tes·ti·mo·nial		Thanksgiving	
tes·ti·mo·nies		that	
tes·ti·mony		that's	
test·ing		thaw	
tests		thaw·ing	
teta·nus		the	
text		thea·ter	
text·book		thea·ters	
text·books		theft	
tex·tile		thefts	
tex·tiles		their	
texts		theirs	
tex·ture		them	
tex·tured		theme	
than		themes	
thank		them·selves	
thanked		then	
thank·ful		thence	
thank·fully		thence·forth	
thank·ing		theo·lo·gian	
thank·less		theo·lo·gians	
thanks		theo·log·ical	

the·ology	*lelje*	there·with	*lr*
theo·rem	*ler*	ther·mal	*lrl*
theo·ret·ical	*lerlcl*	ther·mally	*lrll*
theo·ret·ically	*lerlcll*	ther·mo·dy·nam·ics	*lrdncs*
theo·ries	*leres*	ther·mome·ter	*lrlr*
theo·rize	*lerz*	ther·mo·nu·clear	*lrncler*
theory	*lere*	ther·mo·stat	*lrSl*
thera·peu·tic	*lrplc*	ther·mo·stats	*lrSls*
thera·pist	*lrpS*	these	*lz*
thera·pists	*lrpSs*	the·ses	*lsz*
therapy	*lrpe*	the·sis	*lss*
there	*lr*	they	*ly*
there·af·ter	*lraf*	they'll	*ly'l*
thereby	*lrb*	they're	*ly'r*
there·fore	*lrf*	they've	*ly'v*
there·from	*lrf*	thick	*lc*
therein	*lrn*	thick·en·ing	*lcn_*
thereof	*lrv*	thicker	*lcr*
thereon	*lro*	thick·ness	*lc'*
thereto	*lrl*	thief	*lf*
there·to·fore	*lrlf*	thieves	*lvs*
there·un·der	*lrU*	thigh	*li*
there·upon	*lrpo*	thim·ble	*lB*

thin		though	
thing		thought	
things		thought·ful	
think		thought·fully	
thinker		thought·ful·ness	
think·ing		thoughts	
thinks		thou·sand	
thin·ner		thou·sands	
thin·ness		thou·sandth	
thin·ning		thrash	
third		thread	
thirsty		thread·bare	
thir·teen		threaded	
thirty		threads	
this		threat	
this·tle		threaten	
tho·racic		threat·ened	
thorn		threat·en·ing	
thor·ough		threats	
thor·ough·fare		three	
thor·oughly		thresh·old	
thor·ough·ness		threw	
those		thrift	

thrifts	*Lrfls*	thus	*Ls*
thrill	*Lrl*	thusly	*Lsl*
thrilled	*Lrl-*	thwart	*Lrt*
thrill·ing	*Lrl_*	thy·roid	*Lryd*
thrive	*Lrv*	tic	*Lc*
throat	*Lro*	tick	*Lc*
throb	*Lrb*	ticker	*Lcr*
throng	*Lrq*	ticket	*Lcl*
throt·tle	*Lrll*	tick·eted	*Lcl-*
throt·tling	*Lrll_*	tick·et·ing	*Lcl_*
through	*Lru*	tick·ets	*Lcls*
through·out	*Lruol*	tickle	*Lcl*
throw	*Lro*	tick·ler	*Lclr*
throw·ing	*Lro_*	tick·lers	*Lclrs*
thrown	*Lrn*	tick·lish	*Lcl4*
thrust	*LrS*	tidal	*Ldl*
thrust·ing	*LrS_*	tid·bit	*Ldbl*
thud	*Ld*	tide	*Ld*
thug	*Lq*	tidy	*Lde*
thumb	*L*	tie	*Li*
thump	*Lp*	tied	*Li-*
thun·der	*Lnr*	tier	*Lr*
Thursday	*Th*	ties	*Lis*

tiff		time·less	
tiger		time·li·ness	
ti·gers		timely	
tight		timer	
tighten		tim·ers	
tight·en·ing		times	
tight·ens		time·saver	
tighter		time·sav·ing	
tightly		time·ta·ble	
tight·ness		time·ta·bles	
tile		time·wise	
tiled		timid	
til·ing		ti·mid·ity	
till		tim·idly	
till·age		tim·ing	
tilt		tin	
tilt·ing		tinge	
tim·ber		tin·gle	
tim·bered		tinker	
tim·bers		tin·sel	
tim·bre		tinted	
time		tiny	
time·keeper		tip	

tip·ping	*Lp̄*	today	*Ld*
tip·ple	*Lpl*	tod·dler	*Ldlr*
tips	*Lps*	toes	*Los*
tip·toe	*Lplo*	to·gether	*Lglr*
tip·top	*Lplp*	to·geth·er·ness	*Lglr'*
ti·rade	*Lrd*	tog·gle	*Lgl*
tire	*Lr*	toil	*Lyl*
tired	*Lr-*	toi·let	*Lyll*
tired·ness	*Lr-'*	toi·lets	*Lylls*
tires	*Lrs*	token	*Lcn*
tire·some	*Lrs⌒*	to·kens	*Lcns*
tis·sue	*Lɟu*	told	*Lld*
tis·sues	*Lɟus*	tol·er·able	*LlrB*
title	*Ul*	tol·er·ance	*LlrN*
ti·tled	*Ul-*	tol·er·ances	*LlrNs*
ti·tles	*Uls*	tol·er·ant	*LlrN*
to	*L*	tol·er·ate	*Llra*
toad	*Ld*	tol·er·ated	*Llra-*
toast	*LS*	tol·er·at·ing	*Llra_*
toasted	*LS-*	toll	*Ll*
toaster	*LSr*	to·mato	*Llo*
toast·ing	*LS̄*	to·ma·toes	*Lloo*
to·bacco	*Ubco*	tomb	*L*

tome	⎾	tooth·brush	Ubrs
to·mor·row	⎾ro	tooth·paste	Ups
ton	⎿n	tooth·pick	Upc
tonal	⎿nl	top	Lp
tone	⎿n	topaz	Lpz
tones	⎿ns	top·coat	Lpco
tongs	⎿gs	top·flight	Lpflı
tongue	⎿g	topic	Lpc
tonic	⎿nc	top·ical	Lpcl
to·night	⎿nı	top·ics	Lpcs
ton·nage	⎿ny	topo·graphic	Lpgrfc
tons	⎿ns	to·pog·ra·phy	Lpgrfe
ton·sil·li·tis	Mels	topped	Lp-
ton·sils	Mls	top·ple	Lpl
too	l	tops	Lps
took	lc	top·soil	Lpsyl
tool	Ll	torch	lrC
tool·ing	Ll	tore	lr
tool·ma·ker	Lē̄cr	tor·ment	lrm
tools	lls	torn	lrn
toot	lu	tor·nado	lrndo
tooth	Ll	tor·pedo	lrpdo
tooth·ache	Llac	torque	lrc

Word	Shorthand	Word	Shorthand
tor·rent	*LrN*	tough·ness	*Uf'*
tor·ren·tial	*Lrnsl*	tour	*Lr*
tor·sion	*Lry*	toured	*Lr-*
torso	*Lrso*	tour·ing	*Lr_*
tort	*Lrl*	tour·ism	*Lrz*
tor·toise	*Lrlo*	tour·ist	*LrS*
tor·tu·ous	*LrCus*	tour·ists	*LrSs*
tor·ture	*LrCr*	tour·na·ment	*Lrnm*
toss	*Lo*	tour·na·ments	*Lrnms*
tossed	*Lo-*	tour·ney	*Lrne*
tosses	*Lss*	tour·ni·quet	*Lrncl*
tot	*U*	tours	*Lrs*
total	*Lol*	tou·sle	*Lozl*
to·taled	*Lol-*	tout	*Lol*
to·tal·ing	*Lol_*	touted	*Lol-*
to·tally	*Loll*	tow	*Lo*
to·tals	*Lols*	to·ward	*Lw*
touch	*UC*	to·wards	*Lws*
touched	*UC-*	towed	*Lo-*
touches	*UCs*	towel	*Lol*
touch·ing	*UC_*	tow·els	*Lols*
tough	*Uf*	tower	*Lor*
tougher	*Ufr*	tow·ers	*Lors*

Word	Shorthand	Word	Shorthand
tow·ing	_Lo_	track·ing	_lrc_
town	_Lon_	tracks	_lrcs_
town·house	_Lonhoo_	tract	_lrc_
towns	_Lons_	trac·ta·ble	_lrcB_
town·ship	_Lons_	trac·tion	_lrcq_
town·ships	_Lonss_	trac·tor	_lrcr_
tows	_Loo_	trac·tors	_lrcrs_
toxe·mia	_Lx a_	tracts	_lrcs_
toxic	_Lxc_	trade	_lrd_
tox·ic·ities	_Lxs ls_	traded	_lrd-_
tox·ic·ity	_Lxs l_	trade·mark	_lrd rc_
toxi·cology	_Lxclje_	trade·marks	_lrd rcs_
toxin	_Lxn_	trader	_lrdr_
toy	_Ly_	trad·ers	_lrdrs_
toys	_Lys_	trades	_lrds_
trace	_lrs_	trad·ing	_lrd_
trace·abil·ity	_lrsBl_	tra·di·tion	_lrdq_
trace·able	_lrsB_	tra·di·tional	_lrdjl_
traced	_lrs-_	tra·di·tion·ally	_lrdjll_
tracer	_lrsr_	tra·di·tions	_lrdjs_
tra·chea	_lrca_	traf·fic	_lrfc_
trac·ing	_lrs_	trage·dies	_lrjdes_
track	_lrc_	tragedy	_lrjde_

tragic	*lryc*	tramp·ing	*lr—p*
trail	*lrl*	tram·ple	*lr—pl*
trailed	*lrl-*	trance	*lrN*
trailer	*lrlr*	tran·quil	*Tql*
trail·ers	*lrlrs*	tran·quil·ity	*Tql'*
trail·ing	*lrl_*	tran·quil·ize	*Tqlz*
trails	*lrls*	tran·quil·izer	*Tqlzr*
train	*lrn*	trans·act	*Tac*
train·able	*lrnB*	trans·acted	*Tac-*
trained	*lrn-*	trans·act·ing	*Tac_*
trainee	*lrne*	trans·ac·tion	*Tacy*
train·ees	*lrnes*	trans·ac·tions	*Tacys*
trainer	*lrnr*	trans·at·lan·tic	*TatlNc*
train·ers	*lrnrs*	tran·scend	*TN*
train·ing	*lrn_*	tran·scribe	*TS*
trains	*lrns*	tran·scribed	*TS-*
traipse	*lrps*	tran·scriber	*TSr*
trait	*lra*	tran·scribes	*TSs*
traits	*lras*	tran·scrib·ing	*TS_*
tra·jec·to·ries	*lrycres*	tran·script	*TS_*
tra·jec·tory	*lrycre*	tran·scrip·tion	*TSy*
tram	*lr—*	tran·scrip·tion·ist	*TSys*
tramp	*lr—p*	tran·scripts	*TSs*

trans·fer	
trans·fer·able	
trans·ferred	
trans·fer·ring	
trans·fers	
trans·form	
trans·for·ma·tion	
trans·formed	
trans·former	
trans·form·ers	
trans·fu·sion	
trans·gress	
trans·gres·sion	
tran·sient	
tran·sis·tor	
tran·sis·tors	
tran·sit	
tran·si·tion	
tran·si·tional	
tran·si·tions	
tran·si·tory	
trans·late	
trans·lated	

trans·lat·ing	
trans·la·tion	
trans·la·tor	
trans·la·tors	
trans·lu·cent	
trans·mis·sion	
trans·mis·sions	
trans·mit	
trans·mits	
trans·mit·tal	
trans·mit·tals	
trans·mit·ted	
trans·mit·ter	
trans·mit·ters	
trans·mit·ting	
trans·par·en·cies	
trans·par·ency	
trans·par·ent	
tran·spire	
tran·spired	
trans·plant	
trans·plants	
trans·port	

trans·port·abil·ity	$Tpl\beta^l$	trav·el·ers	lrvlrs
trans·port·able	$Tpl\beta$	trav·el·ing	lrvl
trans·por·ta·tion	Tpl	trav·els	lrvls
trans·ported	Tpl-	trav·esty	lrvSe
trans·porter	Tplr	tray	lra
trans·port·ing	Tpl	trays	lras
trans·ports	Tpls	treach·er·ous	lrCrs
trans·pose	Tpz	treach·ery	lrCre
trans·posed	Tpz-	tread	lrd
trans·po·si·tion	Tpz	treads	lrds
trans·verse	Tvrs	trea·son	lrzn
trap	lrp	treas·ure	lrzr
trap·per	lrpr	treas·ured	lrzr-
trap·pers	lrprs	treas·urer	lrzrr
trap·ping	lrp	treas·ur·ers	lrzrrs
traps	lrps	treas·ury	lrzre
trash	lr4	treat	lre
trauma	lr a	treated	lre-
trau·matic	lr lc	trea·ties	lrees
tra·vail	lrvl	treat·ing	lre
travel	lrvl	trea·tise	lres
trav·eled	lrvl-	treat·ment	lrem
trav·eler	lrvlr	treat·ments	lrems

treats	*lres*	tribal	*lrß*
treaty	*lree*	tribe	*lrb*
tree	*lre*	tribes	*lrbs*
trees	*lres*	tribu·la·tion	*lrblg*
trek	*lrc*	tri·bu·nal	*lrbnl*
trem·ble	*lr—ß*	tri·bu·nals	*lrbnls*
trem·bling	*lr—ß*	trib·une	*lrbn*
tre·men·dous	*lrmds*	tribu·tar·ies	*lrbtres*
tre·men·dously	*lrmdsl*	tribu·tary	*lrbtre*
tremor	*lr—r*	trib·ute	*lrbu*
trench	*lrnC*	trick	*lrc*
trench·ant	*lrnCM*	trickle	*lrcl*
trencher	*lrnCr*	tri·color	*lrclr*
trench·ers	*lrnCrs*	tri·cy·cle	*lrscl*
trend	*lrM*	tried	*lri-*
trends	*lrMs*	tries	*lris*
tres·pass	*lrsps*	tri·fle	*lrfl*
tres·pass·ing	*lrsps_*	tri·fled	*lrfl-*
tres·tle	*lrsl*	trig·ger	*lrgr*
triad	*lrid*	trig·gered	*lrgr-*
trial	*lril*	trim	*lr—*
tri·als	*lrils*	trimmed	*lr—-*
tri·an·gle	*lragl*	trim·mer	*lr—r*

Word	Shorthand	Word	Shorthand
trim·mers		tro·phies	
trim·ming		tro·phy	
trim·mings		trop·ical	
trims		trot·ter	
trin·ity		trot·ters	
trin·ket		trou·ble	
trip		trou·bled	
tri·par·tite		trou·ble·ma·ker	
tri·ple		trou·bles	
tri·pled		trou·ble·some	
trip·let		trou·bling	
trip·li·cate (adj. or n.)		trough	
trip·li·cate (v.)		troupe	
tri·pling		trou·sers	
tripped		trous·seau	
trip·ping		trout	
trips		trowel	
trite		trow·els	
tri·umph		tru·ancy	
trivia		tru·ant	
trivial		truce	
trom·bone		truck	
troop		trucker	

truck·ers	*Lrcrs*	trust·wor·thy	*LrSrle*
truck·ing	*Lrc_*	trusty	*LrSe*
truck·load	*Lrcld*	truth	*Lrl*
truck·loads	*Lrclds*	truth·ful	*Lrlf*
trucks	*Lrcs*	truth·fully	*Lrlfl*
trucu·lent	*LrclN*	truths	*Lrls*
trudge	*Lry*	try	*Lru*
true	*Lru*	try·ing	*Lru_*
truly	*Lrul*	tub	*Ub*
trump	*Lr~p*	tube	*Ub*
trumped	*Lr~p-*	tu·ber·cu·lin	*Ubrcln*
trum·pet	*Lr~pl*	tu·ber·cu·lo·sis	*Ubrclss*
trun·cate	*Lrqa*	tubes	*Ubs*
trunk	*Lrq*	tub·ing	*Ub_*
truss	*Lrs*	tu·bu·lar	*Ublr*
trusses	*Lrss*	tucked	*lc-*
trust	*LrS*	Tuesday	*Ju*
trus·tee	*LrSe*	tug	*Lq*
trus·tees	*LrSes*	tugs	*Lgs*
trus·tee·ship	*LrSet*	tui·tion	*Luy*
trust·ful	*LrSf*	tulip	*Ulp*
trust·ing	*LrS_*	tu·lips	*Ulps*
trusts	*LrSs*	tum·ble	*LB*

tum·bled	⌐B-	turn·ing	ʅrn_
tum·bler	⌐Br	turn·key	ʅrnce
tum·bling	⌐B_	turn·off	ʅrnof
tumor	⌐r	turn·out	ʅrnot
tu·mult	⌐ll	turn·over	ʅrnO
tune	ʅn	turn·pike	ʅrnpc
tuner	ʅnr	turns	ʅrns
tunic	ʅnc	turn·ta·ble	ʅrnlB
tun·ing	ʅn_	tur·quoise	ʅrqyʒ
tun·nel	ʅnl	tur·tle	ʅrll
tun·nels	ʅnls	tus·sle	ʅsl
tur·bine	ʅrbn	tutor	Ʉr
tur·bines	ʅrbns	tu·tored	Ʉr-
tur·bo·charged	ʅrbCⱼ-	tu·tor·ing	Ʉr_
tur·bo·jet	ʅrbʒl	tu·tors	Ʉrs
tur·bu·lence	ʅrblN	tuxedo	ʅxdo
tur·bu·lent	ʅrblN	TV	TV
tur·key	ʅrce	twang	⌐q
Turkey	ʅrce,	tweed	⌐d
tur·moil	ʅryl	tweeds	⌐ds
turn	ʅrn	tweez·ers	⌐zrs
turn·around	ʅrnaroN	twelve	12
turned	ʅrn-	twenty	20

twice		type·writer	
twi·light		type·writ·ers	
twin		type·writ·ing	
twine		type·writ·ten	
twinge		ty·phoon	
twin·kle		typ·ical	
twirl		typ·ically	
twist		typify	
twisted		typ·ing	
twist·ing		typ·ist	
twitch		typ·ists	
two		typo	
two·fold		typo·graph·ical	
ty·coon		typos	
tying		ty·rant	
type			
type·cast			
typed			
type·face			
types			
type·script			
type·set·ter			
type·set·ting			

U

ubiq·ui·tous	
ug·li·ness	
ugly	
ulcer	
ul·cers	

ul·te·rior	*ultrer*	un·af·fected	*uafc-*
ul·ti·mate	*ultↄ*	un·afraid	*uafrd*
ul·ti·mately	*ultↄl*	un·aided	*uad-*
ul·ti·ma·tum	*ultↄ*	un-American	*uA*
ultra	*ultra*	unani·mous	*unn⌒s*
ul·tra·high	*ultrhi*	unani·mously	*unn⌒sl*
ul·tra·sonic	*ultrsnc*	un·an·nounced	*uanoN-*
ul·tra·son·ically	*ultrsncl*	un·an·swered	*uasr-*
ul·tra·sound	*ultrsoN*	un·an·tici·pated	*uatspa-*
ul·tra·vio·let	*ultrvlt*	un·ap·pre·ci·ated	*uap-*
um·bil·ical	*u⌒blcl*	un·ap·pro·pri·ated	*uapo-*
um·brage	*u⌒brↄ*	un·ap·proved	*uapv-*
um·brella	*u⌒brla*	un·as·serted	*uasrt-*
um·brel·las	*u⌒brlas*	un·as·signed	*uasn-*
um·pire	*u⌒pr*	un·as·sisted	*uass-*
un·abashed	*uabↄ-*	un·as·sum·ing	*uas⌒*
un·able	*uB*	un·at·tached	*uatC-*
un·abridged	*uabrↄ-*	un·at·tain·able	*uatnB*
un·ac·cept·able	*uacB*	un·at·tended	*uatN-*
un·ac·com·pa·nied	*uaco-*	un·at·trac·tive·ness	*uatrcv´*
un·ac·count·able	*uakB*	un·au·dited	*uadt-*
un·ac·counted	*uak-*	un·au·thor·ized	*uatrz-*
un·ac·cus·tomed	*uacↄ⌒-*	un·avail·abil·ity	*uavlBᴸ*

un·avail·able	*uavlB*	un·claimed	*ucl─*
un·avoid·able	*uavydB*	un·clas·si·fi·able	*uclsfB*
un·avoid·ably	*uavydB*	un·clas·si·fied	*uclsf─*
un·aware	*uar*	uncle	*uql*
un·bal·anced	*ublN─*	un·clean	*ucln*
un·bear·able	*ubrB*	un·clear	*uclr*
un·be·com·ing	*ubk─*	un·clogged	*uclq─*
un·be·liev·able	*ublvB*	un·col·lected	*uclc─*
un·bi·ased	*ubrs─*	un·col·lect·ible	*uclcB*
un·bid·den	*ubdn*	un·col·ored	*uclr─*
un·billed	*ubl─*	un·com·fort·able	*ukflB*
un·blocked	*ublc─*	un·com·mit·ted	*ukl─*
un·bolted	*ubll─*	un·com·mon	*ukn*
un·born	*ubrn*	un·com·pleted	*ukp─*
un·branded	*ubrN─*	un·com·pli·cated	*ukplca─*
un·busi·ness·like	*ubslc*	un·con·di·tional	*ukdjl*
un·canny	*uce*	un·con·di·tion·ally	*ukdjll*
un·cashed	*ucA─*	un·con·firmed	*ukfr─*
un·cer·tain	*uSln*	un·con·scious	*ukso*
un·cer·tain·ties	*uSlnles*	un·con·soli·dated	*ukslda─*
un·cer·tainty	*uSlnle*	un·con·trol·la·ble	*uklB*
un·changed	*uCnj─*	un·con·trolled	*ukl─*
un·civi·lized	*usvlz─*	un·con·vinced	*ukvN─*

Word	Outline	Word	Outline
un·co·op·era·tive	*ucopv*	un·der·gradu·ate	*Ugryul*
un·co·or·di·nated	*ucordna-*	un·der·gradu·ates	*Ugryuls*
un·cor·rected	*ucrc-*	un·der·ground	*UgroN*
un·cover	*ucvr*	un·der·handed	*UhN-*
un·cov·ered	*ucvr-*	un·der·lie	*Uli*
uncut	*ucl*	un·der·line	*Uln*
un·dated	*uda-*	un·der·lined	*Uln-*
un·de·cided	*udsd-*	un·der·lines	*Ulns*
un·de·clared	*udclr-*	un·der·lin·ing	*Uln_*
un·de·fined	*udfn-*	un·der·ly·ing	*Uli_*
un·de·liv·er·able	*udlB*	un·der·mine	*U⌢n*
un·de·ni·able	*udniB*	un·der·mined	*U⌢n-*
un·de·pend·able	*udpNB*	un·der·neath	*Unl*
under	*U*	un·der·paid	*Upd*
un·der·bid	*Ubd*	un·der·pay·ment	*Upam*
un·der·clothes	*Uclls*	un·der·pin·ning	*Upn_*
un·der·cover	*Ucvr*	un·der·priced	*Uprs-*
un·der·cur·rent	*UcrN*	un·der·rate	*Ura*
un·der·de·vel·oped	*Udv-*	un·der·score	*Uscr*
un·dergo	*Uq*	un·der·scored	*Uscr-*
un·der·goes	*Ugs*	un·der·scores	*Uscrs*
un·der·go·ing	*Uq_*	un·der·scor·ing	*Uscr_*
un·der·gone	*Ugn*	un·der·sea	*Use*

un·der·sell·ing		un·der·took	
un·der·shirt		un·der·used	
un·der·side		un·der·valu·ation	
un·der·signed		un·der·wa·ter	
un·der·size		un·der·way	
un·der·spend·ing		un·der·wear	
un·der·staffed		un·der·weight	
un·der·stand		un·der·went	
un·der·stand·able		un·der·world	
un·der·stand·ably		un·der·write	
un·der·stand·ing		un·der·writer	
un·der·stand·ings		un·der·writ·ers	
un·der·stands		un·der·writ·ing	
un·der·stated		un·der·writ·ten	
un·der·state·ment		un·de·sir·able	
un·der·stood		un·de·ter·mined	
un·der·study		un·de·vel·oped	
un·der·take		un·di·ag·nosed	
un·der·taken		un·dig·ni·fied	
un·der·taker		un·dis·closed	
un·der·takes		un·dis·puted	
un·der·tak·ing		un·dis·trib·uted	
un·der·tone		un·dis·turbed	

un·di·vided	*udvd-*	un·err·ing	*uer_*
undo	*udu*	un·eth·ical	*uetcl*
un·docu·mented	*udcm-*	un·even	*uevn*
un·doubt·edly	*udot-l*	un·ex·cused	*uxcz-*
undue	*udu*	un·ex·er·cised	*uxrsz-*
un·duly	*udul*	un·ex·pected	*uxpc-*
un·earned	*uern-*	un·ex·pect·edly	*uxpc-l*
un·easy	*ueze*	un·ex·pended	*uxpN-*
un·eco·nom·ical	*uecol*	un·ex·plained	*uxpln-*
un·em·ploy·able	*u~pß*	un·fair	*ufr*
un·em·ployed	*u~p-*	un·fairly	*ufrl*
un·em·ploy·ment	*u~pm*	un·fa·mil·iar	*uf~lr*
un·en·cum·bered	*unkbr-*	un·fa·vor·able	*ufvrß*
un·end·ing	*uN_*	un·fa·vor·ably	*ufvrß*
un·en·dorsed	*undrs-*	un·fea·si·ble	*ufzß*
un·en·force·able	*unfsß*	un·filled	*ufl-*
un·en·forced	*unfs-*	un·fin·ished	*ufn4-*
un·en·tered	*uN-*	unfit	*ufl*
un·equal	*ueql*	un·fold	*ufld*
un·equaled	*ueql-*	un·fore·seen	*ufsn*
un·equipped	*ueqp-*	un·for·tu·nate	*ufCnt*
un·equivo·cal	*ueqvcl*	un·for·tu·nately	*ufCnll*
un·equivo·cally	*ueqvcll*	un·freez·ing	*ufrz_*

un·glam·or·ous	_ugl̸rs_	un·in·sured	_unAr-_
un·grate·ful	_ugrf_	un·in·ten·tional	_unlnyl_
un·guarded	_ugrd-_	un·in·ter·ested	_unꙅ-_
un·happy	_uhpe_	un·in·ter·est·ing	_unꙅ_
un·healthy	_uhlle_	un·in·ter·rupted	_unpt-_
un·heard	_uhrd_	union	_unyn_
un·hur·ried	_uhre-_	un·ions	_unyns_
un·iden·ti·fied	_uιdNf-_	unique	_unc_
uni·fi·ca·tion	_unfj_	uniquely	_uncl_
uni·fied	_unf-_	unique·ness	_unc'_
uni·fies	_unfs_	un·is·sued	_uιAu-_
uni·form	_unf_	unit	_unl_
uni·formed	_unf-_	uni·tary	_unlre_
uni·for·mity	_unf ι_	unite	_unι_
uni·formly	_unf l_	united	_unι-_
uni·forms	_unf s_	unit·ing	_unι_
uni·lat·eral	_unllrl_	units	_unls_
uni·lat·er·ally	_unllrll_	unity	_un ι_
un·im·por·tant	_u pt_	uni·ver·sal	_unvrsl_
un·im·proved	_u pv-_	uni·verse	_unvrs_
un·in·cor·po·rated	_uιnc_	uni·ver·si·ties	_Us_
un·in·formed	_unf-_	uni·ver·sity	_U_
un·in·sur·able	_unArβ_	un·jus·ti·fi·able	_yꙅfβ_

un·known	*unn*	un·ma·tured	
un·law·ful	*ulaf*	un·named	
un·law·fully	*ulafl*	un·natu·ral	
un·leaded	*uld-*	un·nec·es·sarily	
un·less	*uls*	un·nec·es·sary	
un·like	*ulc*	un·needed	
un·likely	*ulcl*	un·no·ticed	
un·lim·ited	*ul—l-*	un·num·bered	
un·lined	*uln-*	un·oc·cu·pied	
un·listed	*ulS-*	un·of·fi·cial	
un·load	*uld*	un·opened	
un·loaded	*uld-*	un·or·gan·ized	
un·load·ing	*uld—*	un·pack·ing	
un·loads	*ulds*	un·paid	
un·lock	*ulc*	un·par·al·leled	
un·locked	*ulc-*	un·paved	
un·locks	*ulcs*	un·planned	
un·lucky	*ulce*	un·plugged	
un·mail·able	*u—lB*	un·pre·dict·able	
un·manned	*u—m-*	un·pre·pared	
un·mar·ket·able	*u—rB*	un·pre·ten·tious	
un·mar·ried	*u—re-*	un·pro·duc·tive	
un·matched	*u—C-*	un·prof·it·able	

un·pro·tected	uPlc-	un·ri·valed	urvl-
un·proven	upvn	un·roll	url
un·pub·lished	upbls-	un·ruly	url
un·quali·fied	uqlf-	un·safe	usf
un·ques·tion·able	uqß	un·sani·tary	usntre
un·ques·tion·ably	uqß	un·sat·is·fac·to·rily	usall
un·read	urd	un·sat·is·fac·tory	usal
un·read·able	urdß	un·sat·is·fied	usal-
un·real	url	un·sealed	usl-
un·rea·son·able	urznß	un·sea·son·ably	usznß
un·rea·son·ably	urznß	un·se·cured	uscr-
un·re·corded	urec-	un·self·ishly	usfsl
un·re·lated	urla-	un·set·tled	ustl-
un·re·leased	urls-	un·sight·li·ness	usil'
un·re·li·abil·ity	urlißl	un·sightly	usil
un·re·li·able	urliß	un·signed	usn-
un·re·ported	urpl-	un·skilled	uscl-
un·re·quested	urqs-	un·sold	usld
un·re·served	urzrv-	un·so·lic·ited	uslsl-
un·re·solved	urzlv-	un·solved	uslv-
un·re·spon·sive	urspv-	un·sound	usoN
un·rest	urs	un·speak·able	uspcß
un·re·stricted	urSrc-	un·spe·cific	usp

un·speci·fied	*usp-*	un·used	*uuz-*
un·spo·ken	*uspcn*	un·usual	*uuz*
un·sta·ble	*uSB*	un·usu·ally	*uuzl*
un·struc·tured	*uSrcCr-*	un·veil·ing	*uvl*
un·suc·cess·ful	*usucf*	un·waived	*u v-*
un·suc·cess·fully	*usucfl*	un·wanted	*u M-*
un·suit·able	*usuB*	un·war·ranted	*u rM-*
un·sup·ported	*uspl-*	un·wel·come	*ulk*
un·sure	*uAr*	un·will·ing	*ul*
un·sur·passed	*uSps-*	un·will·ingly	*ulf*
un·sus·tain·able	*usSnB*	un·will·ing·ness	*ul'*
un·tapped	*ulp-*	un·wind	*u M*
un·tax·able	*ulxB*	un·wise	*u z*
un·ten·able	*ulnB*	un·wit·tingly	*u ll*
untie	*uli*	un·work·able	*u oB*
until	*ull*	un·wor·thy	*u rle*
un·timely	*ul l*	un·writ·ten	*urln*
unto	*ul*	up	*p*
un·told	*ulld*	up·beat	*pbe*
un·touched	*ulC-*	up·bring·ing	*pbrq*
un·trimmed	*ulr-*	up·com·ing	*pk*
un·truth·ful	*ulrlf*	up·date	*pda*
un·us·able	*uuzB*	up·dated	*pda-*

up·dates	*pdas*	up·stream	*psr*
up·dat·ing	*pda_*	up·take	*ptc*
up·grade	*pgrd*	up·tight	*pti*
up·graded	*pgrd-*	up-to-date	*pda*
up·grades	*pgrds*	up·turn	*ptrn*
up·grad·ing	*pgrd*	up·turns	*ptrns*
up·heav·als	*phvls*	up·ward	*pw*
up·held	*phld*	up·wards	*pws*
up·hold	*phld*	ura·nium	*urne*
up·hold·ing	*phld*	urban	*urbn*
up·hol·stery	*phlṢre*	ur·ban·ized	*urbnz-*
up·keep	*pcp*	urge	*urj*
up·lift·ing	*plft_*	urged	*urj-*
upon	*po*	ur·gency	*urjNe*
upper	*pr*	ur·gent	*urjN*
upper-case	*pr = cs*	ur·gently	*urjNe*
up·right	*pru*	urges	*urjs*
up·root	*pru*	urg·ing	*urj_*
ups	*ps*	urn	*urn*
upset	*pst*	urolo·gist	*urljS*
up·set·ting	*pst_*	urology	*urlje*
up·stairs	*pSrs*	us	*s*
up·state	*pSa*	U.S.	*US*

us·able	*uzß*	util·iza·tion	*ullzʃ*
usage	*usʃ*	util·ize	*ullz*
use (v.)	*uz*	util·ized	*ullz-*
use (n.)	*us*	util·izes	*ullzs*
use·able	*uzß*	util·iz·ing	*ullz-*
used	*uz-*	ut·most	*ut—s*
use·ful	*usf*	uto·pia	*ulpa*
use·ful·ness	*usf'*	utter	*ulr*
use·less	*usls*	ut·ter·ance	*ulrɲ*
user	*uzr*	ut·terly	*ulrl*
users	*uzrs*		
uses (v.)	*uzs*		
uses (n.)	*uss*		
usher	*uʌr*	**V**	
using	*uz-*	va·can·cies	*vcɲes*
usual	*uz*	va·cancy	*vcɲe*
usu·ally	*uzl*	va·cant	*vcɲ*
usurp	*usrp*	va·cate	*vca*
usury	*uzre*	va·cated	*vca-*
uten·sil	*ulɲl*	va·cates	*vcas*
uterus	*ulrs*	va·cat·ing	*vca_*
util·ities	*ull ᵗˢ*	va·ca·tion	*vcʃ*
util·ity	*ull ᵗ*	va·ca·tion·ing	*vcʃ-*
		va·ca·tions	*vcʃs*

vac·ci·na·tion	*vcsny*	valor	*vlr*
vac·ci·na·tions	*vcsnys*	valu·able	*vluß*
vac·cine	*vcsn*	valu·ables	*vlußs*
vac·il·late	*vsla*	valu·ation	*vluy*
vacu·ous	*vcus*	valu·ations	*vluys*
vacuum	*vcy*	value	*vlu*
vacuumed	*vcy-*	val·ued	*vlu-*
vaga·bond	*vgbN*	val·ues	*vlus*
va·grancy	*vgrNe*	valu·ing	*vlu_*
va·grant	*vgrN*	valve	*vlv*
vague	*vq*	valves	*vlvs*
vain	*vn*	van	*vn*
vale·dic·to·rian	*vldclren*	van·dal	*vNl*
val·en·tine	*vlnln*	van·dal·ism	*vNlz*
valet	*vla*	van·dal·ized	*vNlz-*
val·iant	*vlyN*	van·dals	*vNls*
valid	*vld*	vane	*vn*
vali·date	*vlda*	va·nilla	*vnla*
vali·dated	*vlda-*	van·ish	*vn4*
vali·da·tion	*vldy*	van·ishes	*vn4s*
va·lid·ity	*vld^l*	van·ish·ing	*vn4*
val·ley	*vle*	van·ity	*vn^l*
val·leys	*vles*	van·quish	*vnq4*

vans	_vns_	vary·ing	_vre_
van·tage	_vny_	vas·cu·lar	_vsclr_
vapor	_vpr_	vase	_vs_
va·por·iza·tion	_vprzj_	vast	_vs_
va·por·ize	_vprz_	vastly	_vsl_
va·por·iz·ing	_vprz-_	vault	_vlt_
va·pors	_vprs_	veer	_vr_
vari·abil·ity	_vreßl_	veered	_vr-_
vari·able	_vreß_	vege·ta·ble	_vglß_
vari·ables	_vreßs_	vege·ta·bles	_vglßs_
vari·ance	_vreN_	vege·ta·tion	_vglj_
vari·ances	_vreNs_	ve·he·ment	_vem_
vari·ation	_vrej_	ve·hi·cle	_vhcl_
vari·ations	_vrejs_	ve·hi·cles	_vhcls_
vari·cose	_vrcs_	ve·hicu·lar	_vhclr_
var·ied	_vre-_	veil	_vl_
var·ies	_vres_	vein	_vn_
va·ri·eties	_vrils_	veins	_vns_
va·ri·ety	_vril_	ve·loc·ity	_vlsl_
vari·ous	_vres_	ve·lour	_vlr_
var·nish	_vrn4_	vel·vet	_vlvt_
var·sity	_vrsl_	vel·vety	_vlvte_
vary	_vre_	venal	_vnl_

vend		venue	
vendee		verb	
vend·ing		ver·bal	
ven·dor		ver·bal·ize	
ven·dors		ver·bal·ized	
ve·neer		ver·bally	
ven·er·able		ver·ba·tim	
ven·er·ate		ver·bi·age	
ven·geance		verbs	
venge·ful		ver·dict	
venom		ver·dicts	
vent		verge	
vented		veri·fi·ca·tion	
ven·ti·late		veri·fi·ca·tions	
ven·ti·lat·ing		veri·fied	
ven·ti·la·tion		veri·fier	
ven·ti·la·tor		veri·fies	
ven·ti·la·tors		verify	
vent·ing		veri·fy·ing	
ven·tri·cle		veri·ta·ble	
vents		ver·ity	
ven·ture		ver·min	
ven·tures		ver·nacu·lar	

ver·sa·tile	*vrstl*	vest·ing	*vS͟*
ver·sa·til·ity	*vrstlˡ*	vest·ment	*vSm*
verse	*vrs*	ves·try	*vSre*
versed	*vrs-*	vet	*vt*
verses	*vrss*	vet·eran	*vtrn*
ver·sion	*vrj*	vet·er·ans	*vtrns*
ver·sions	*vrjs*	vet·eri·narian	*vtrnren*
ver·sus	*vrss*	vet·eri·nary	*vtrnre*
ver·te·bra	*vrtbra*	veto	*vto*
ver·te·brae	*vrtbre*	ve·toed	*vto-*
ver·te·brates	*vrtbrts*	ve·toes	*vtos*
ver·ti·cal	*vrtcl*	vex	*vx*
ver·ti·cally	*vrtcll*	vexa·tion	*vxj*
ver·ti·cals	*vrtcls*	via	*va*
ver·tigo	*vrtg*	vi·abil·ity	*viβˡ*
verve	*vrv*	vi·able	*viβ*
very	*v*	vial	*vil*
ves·sel	*vsl*	vi·brant	*vbrN*
ves·sels	*vsls*	vi·brate	*vbra*
vest	*vS*	vi·brat·ing	*vbra-*
vested	*vS-*	vi·bra·tion	*vbrj*
ves·ti·bule	*vSbl*	vi·bra·tor	*vbrar*
ves·tige	*vSj*	vi·cari·ous	*vcres*

vice	$\vee\!\!\!\!\backslash$	view·ing	$\vee u\_$
vice presi·dent	VP	view·point	$\vee upy$
vice-presidential	$V\!=\!P\!\!\!\!\backslash l$	view·points	$\vee upys$
vice presi·dents	$VP\!\!\backslash$	views	$\vee us$
vices	$\vee\!\!\backslash s$	vigil	$\vee yl$
vice versa	$\vee\!\!\backslash \quad \vee rsa$	vigi·lant	$\vee yln$
vi·cin·ity	$\vee sn^l$	vigor	$\vee gr$
vi·cious	$\vee\!\!\!\backslash s$	vig·or·ous	$\vee grs$
vic·tim	$\vee cl$	vig·or·ously	$\vee grsl$
vic·tim·ize	$\vee cl_3$	vile	$\vee l$
vic·tim·ized	$\vee cl_3-$	vil·ify	$\vee lf$
vic·tims	$\vee cl\!\!\backslash s$	villa	$\vee la$
vic·tory	$\vee clre$	vil·lage	$\vee lg$
video	$\vee do$	vil·lain	$\vee ln$
video·tape	$\vee dolp$	vin·di·cate	$\vee nca$
video·taped	$\vee dolp-$	vin·di·ca·tion	$\vee ncy$
video·tapes	$\vee dolps$	vine	$\vee n$
vie	$\vee l$	vine·gar	$\vee ngr$
view	$\vee u$	vin·tage	$\vee ny$
view·able	$\vee u\beta$	vinyl	$\vee nl$
viewed	$\vee u-$	vio·late	$\vee la$
viewer	$\vee ur$	vio·lated	$\vee la-$
view·ers	$\vee urs$	vio·lates	$\vee las$

vio·lat·ing	_vrla_	vis·ible	_vȝϴ_
vio·la·tion	_vrlϳ_	vi·sion	_vȝ_
vio·la·tions	_vrlϳs_	vi·sion·ary	_vȝre_
vio·la·tor	_vrlar_	vi·sions	_vȝs_
vio·la·tors	_vrlars_	visit	_vȝt_
vio·lence	_vrlN_	visi·ta·tion	_vȝtϳ_
vio·lent	_vrlN_	visi·ta·tions	_vȝtϳs_
vio·lently	_vrlNl_	vis·ited	_vȝt-_
vio·let	_vrll_	vis·it·ing	_vȝt_
vio·lin	_vrln_	visi·tor	_vȝtr_
VIP	_VIP_	visi·tors	_vȝtrs_
viper	_vpr_	vis·its	_vȝts_
vir·gin	_vryn_	visor	_vȝr_
vir·ile	_vrl_	vista	_vSa_
vir·tu·ally	_vrCull_	visual	_vȝul_
vir·tue	_vrCu_	visu·al·iza·tion	_vȝulȝϳ_
vir·tues	_vrCus_	visu·al·iza·tions	_vȝulȝϳs_
vir·tu·ous	_vrCus_	visu·al·ize	_vȝulȝ_
virus	_vrs_	visu·ally	_vȝull_
visa	_vȝa_	vital	_vtl_
vis·cos·ity	_vscsl_	vi·tal·ity	_vtll_
vise	_vs_	vi·tally	_vtll_
vis·ibil·ity	_vȝϴl_	vi·ta·min	_vtm_

vi·ta·mins	*vlms*	vol·cano	*vlcno*
vit·re·ous	*vlres*	vo·li·tion	*vlj*
vit·ri·olic	*vlrelc*	vol·ley	*vle*
vi·va·cious	*vvas*	vol·ley·ball	*vlebl*
vivid	*vvd*	volt	*vll*
viv·idly	*vvdl*	volt·age	*vllj*
vo·cabu·lary	*vcblre*	volt·ages	*vlljs*
vocal	*vcl*	volts	*vlls*
vo·cal·ize	*vclz*	volu·ble	*vlB*
vo·ca·tion	*vcj*	vol·ume	*vol*
vo·ca·tional	*vcjl*	vol·umes	*vols*
vo·ca·tion·ally	*vcjll*	vo·lu·mi·nous	*vlms*
vo·ca·tions	*vcjs*	vol·un·tarily	*vlntrl*
vo·cif·er·ous	*vsfrs*	vol·un·tary	*vlntre*
vogue	*vq*	vol·un·teer	*vlntr*
voice	*vys*	vol·un·teered	*vlntr-*
voiced	*vys-*	vol·un·teer·ing	*vlntṛ*
voice·less	*vysls*	vol·un·teers	*vlntrs*
voices	*vyss*	vomit	*vᴸ*
void	*vyd*	vom·it·ing	*vᴸ*
void·ing	*vyd̲*	vo·ra·cious	*vras*
voids	*vyds*	vote	*vo*
vola·tile	*vll*	voted	*vo-*

voter		wa·fers	
vot·ers		waf·fle	
votes		waf·fles	
vot·ing		wag	
vouch		wage	
voucher		wager	
vouch·ers		wages	
vow		wagon	
vowel		waif	
vows		wail	
voy·age		waist	
vul·gar		wait	
vul·gar·ity		waited	
vul·ner·abil·ity		waiter	
vul·ner·able		wait·ing	
vul·ture		wait·ress	
vying		wait·resses	
		waive	
		waived	
W		waiver	
		waiv·ers	
		waiv·ing	
wad		wake	
wade			
wafer			

wak·ing		want·ing	
walk		wants	
walked		war	
walker		ward	
walk·ers		war·den	
walk·ing		ward·robe	
walk·out		wards	
walks		ware	
walk·way		ware·house (n.)	
walk·ways		ware·house (v.)	
wall		ware·housed	
wal·let		ware·houses (n.)	
wal·lop		ware·houses (v.)	
wal·low		ware·hous·ing	
wall·pa·per		war·fare	
walls		war·head	
wal·nut		war·heads	
wan		warily	
wan·der		warm	
wan·der·ing		warmer	
wane		warm·est	
want		warmly	
wanted		warmth	

warn	_rn_	wash·ing	_4_
warned	_rn-_	wash·out	_4ol_
warn·ing	_rn_	wash·outs	_4ols_
warn·ings	_rn_	wasn't	_zM_
warp	_rp_	wasp	_sp_
warped	_rp-_	waste	_S_
warps	_rps_	waste·bas·ket	_Sbscl_
war·rant	_rM_	wasted	_S-_
war·ranted	_rM-_	waste·ful	_Sf_
war·ran·ties	_rMes_	waste·land	_SlM_
war·ran·tor	_rMr_	waste·pa·per	_Sppr_
war·rants	_rMs_	wastes	_Ss_
war·ranty	_rMe_	waste·wa·ter	_Slr_
wars	_rs_	wast·ing	_S_
wart	_rl_	wast·rel	_Srl_
wary	_re_	watch	_C_
was	_3_	watched	_C-_
wash	_4_	watches	_Cs_
wash·able	_4B_	watch·ing	_C_
wash·cloth	_4cll_	watch·man	_Cm_
washed	_4-_	watch·men	_Cm_
washer	_4r_	water	_lr_
wash·ers	_4rs_	wa·ter·fall	_lrfl_

wa·ter·front	*ᴵrfrℳ*	way·laid	*ald*
wa·ter·ing	*ᴵr̲*	ways	*as*
wa·ter·log	*ᴵrlq*	way·side	*asd*
wa·ter·mark	*ᴵr rc*	way·ward	*aw*
wa·ter·melon	*ᴵr ℓn*	we	*ℓ*
wa·ter·proof	*ᴵrprf*	weak	*c*
wa·ter·proof·ing	*ᴵrprf̲*	weaken	*cn*
wa·ters	*ᴵrs*	weak·ened	*cn–*
wa·ter·shed	*ᴵrsd*	weak·en·ing	*cn̲*
wa·ter·tight	*ᴵrlu*	weaker	*cr*
wa·ter·way	*ᴵra*	weak·est	*c8*
wa·ter·ways	*ᴵras*	weak·ness	*c′*
wa·tery	*ᴵre*	weak·nesses	*c″*
watt	*l*	wealth	*ll*
wat·tage	*ly*	wealthy	*lle*
watts	*ls*	wean	*n*
wave	*v*	weaned	*n–*
waves	*vs*	wean·ing	*n̲*
wav·ing	*v̲*	weapon	*pn*
wax	*x*	weap·ons	*pns*
waxes	*xs*	wear	*r*
waxy	*xe*	wear·abil·ity	*rBˡ*
way	*a*	wear·able	*rB*

Word	Shorthand	Word	Shorthand
weari·ness		weed	
wear·ing		weeded	
wears		weed·ing	
weary		weeds	
weather		week	
weath·ered		week·day	
weath·er·ing		week·days	
weath·er·ize		week·end	
weath·er·iz·ing		week·ends	
weath·er·proof		week·lies	
weave		weekly	
weaver		weeks	
weav·ers		weep	
weav·ing		weep·ing	
web		wee·vil	
web·bing		weigh	
web·bings		weighed	
wed		weigh·ing	
we'd		weigh·ings	
wed·ding		weighs	
wedge		weight	
wed·lock		weighted	
Wednesday		weights	

weird		west·ern	
wel·come		west·erner	
wel·comed		west·ward	
wel·comes		wet	
wel·com·ing		wet·land	
weld		wet·ness	
welded		wet·ting	
welder		we've	
weld·ers		whale	
weld·ing		whales	
welds		wharf	
wel·fare		wharves	
well		what	
we'll		what·ever	
well·ness		what's	
wells		what·so·ever	
went		wheat	
wept		wheel	
were		wheel·bar·row	
we're		wheel·chair	
weren't		wheel·chairs	
west		wheeled	
west·erly		wheels	

wheeze		whipped	
wheezes		whirl	
when		whirl·pool	
when·ever		whirl·pools	
where		whirl·wind	
where·abouts		whisker	
whereas		whisk·ers	
whereby		whis·key	
where·fore		whis·per	
wherein		whis·tle	
whereof		whis·tles	
where·upon		white	
wher·ever		whit·tle	
whether		who	
which		who·ever	
which·ever		whole	
whiff		whole·hearted	
while		whole·heart·edly	
whim		whole·sale	
whim·per		whole·saler	
whin·ing		whole·sal·ers	
whip		whole·some	
whip·lash		wholly	

whom		wig·gle	
whom·ever		wild	
whop·per		wild·cat	
whose		wil·der·ness	
why		wild·life	
wicker		wildly	
wide		will	
wide·band		willed	
widely		will·ful	
widen		will·fully	
wid·ened		will·ing	
wid·en·ing		will·ingly	
wider		will·ing·ness	
wide·spread		wills	
wid·est		wilt	
widow		win	
wid·ower		wince	
width		wind	
widths		winded	
wie·ner		wind·fall	
wie·ners		wind·ing	
wife		wind·mill	
wig		win·dow	

win·dows	*Nos*	wiper	*pr*
wind·pipe	*Npp*	wip·ers	*prs*
winds	*Ns*	wire	*r*
wind·shield	*Nsld*	wired	*r-*
windy	*Ne*	wires	*rs*
wine	*n*	wir·ing	*r_*
wines	*ns*	wis·dom	*zd*
wing	*q*	wise	*z*
wing·ing	*q-*	wisely	*zl*
wings	*gs*	wiser	*zr*
wink	*q*	wish	*4*
wink·ing	*q-*	wished	*4-*
win·ner	*nr*	wisher	*4r*
win·ners	*nrs*	wish·ers	*4rs*
win·ning	*n_*	wishes	*4s*
wins	*ns*	wish·ing	*4_*
win·some	*N*	wist·ful	*Sf*
win·ter	*Nr*	wit	*l*
win·ter·ize	*Nrz*	with	*—*
win·ter·ized	*Nrz-*	with·draw	*dra*
win·ters	*Nrs*	with·drawal	*dral*
wipe	*p*	with·draw·als	*drals*
wiped	*p-*	with·draw·ing	*dra_*

with·drawn	*drn*	woke	*c*
with·draws	*dras*	wolf	*lf*
with·drew	*dru*	wolves	*lvz*
with·held	*hld*	woman	*n*
with·hold	*hld*	womb	
with·hold·ing	*hld*	women	*m*
with·hold·ings	*hld̄*	won	*n*
with·holds	*hld̄s*	won·der	*Nr*
within	*n*	won·dered	*Nr-*
with·out	*ot*	won·der·ful	*Nrf*
with·stand	*SN*	won·der·ing	*Nr̄*
with·stand·ing	*SN*	won·ders	*Nrs*
with·stands	*SN̄s*	won·drous	*Nrs*
with·stood	*Sd*	won't	*N*
wit·ness	*l´*	wood	*d*
wit·nessed	*l´-*	wooded	*d-*
wit·nesses	*l″*	wooden	*dn*
wit·ness·ing	*l´_*	wood·land	*dlN*
witty	*le*	wood·lands	*dlNs*
wives	*vs*	woods	*ds*
woe	*o*	wood·work	*do*
woe·fully	*ofl*	wood·work·ing	*do̱*
woes	*os*	wool	*l*

word		work·men	
worded		work·out	
word·ing		work·place	
words		work·room	
wore		work·rooms	
work		works	
work·abil·ity		work·shop	
work·able		work·shops	
work·book		work·ta·ble	
work·books		work·week	
work·day		world	
work·days		worldly	
worked		worlds	
worker		world·wide	
work·ers		wormed	
work·flow		worms	
work·force		worn	
work·ing		wor·ries	
work·ings		worry	
work·load		wor·ry·ing	
work·man		worse	
work·man·like		wors·en·ing	
work·man·ship		wor·ship	

worst	_rs_	wrath	_rl_
worth	_rl_	wreath	_rl_
wor·thier	_rler_	wreck	_rc_
wor·thi·ness	_rle'_	wreck·age	_rcq_
worth·less	_rlls_	wrecked	_rc-_
worth·while	_rll_	wrecker	_rcr_
wor·thy	_rle_	wreck·ing	_rc_
would	_d_	wrecks	_rcs_
wouldn't	_dM_	wrench	_rnC_
wound (n. or v.)	_M_	wrenches	_rnCs_
wound (v.)	_oM_	wres·tling	_rsl_
wounded	_M-_	wring	_rq_
wounds	_Ms_	wrin·kle	_rql_
wove	_v_	wrin·kles	_rqls_
woven	_vn_	wrist	_rs_
wow	_o_	wrists	_rss_
wran·gle	_rgl_	writ	_rl_
wrap	_rp_	write	_ru_
wrap·around	_rparoM_	write-off	_ru = of_
wrapped	_rp-_	write-offs	_ru = ofs_
wrap·per	_rpr_	writer	_rur_
wrap·ping	_rp_	writ·ers	_rurs_
wraps	_rps_	writes	_rus_

write-up	$ru = p$	yachts	yts
writ·ing	ru	yam	y
writ·ings	ru	yank	yq
writs	rts	yard	yd
writ·ten	rtn	yard·age	ydj
wrong	rq	yards	yds
wrong·ful	rgf	yard·stick	ydsc
wrongly	rgl	yarn	yrn
wrote	ro	yarns	yrns
wrung	rq	yawn	yn
wry	ru	year	yr
		year·book	yrbc
		year·books	yrbcs

X

		year-end	$yr = n$
		yearly	yrl
xerox	zrx	yearn	yrn
xer·oxed	zrx-	years	yrs
xer·ox·ing	zrx	yeast	ys
x-ray	ra	yell·ing	yl
x-rays	ras	yel·low	ylo
		yes	ys
		yes·ter·day	ysrd

Y

yacht	yt	yes·ter·days	ysrds

yet	*yt*	you've	*u'v*
yield	*yld*		
yield·ing	*yld̲*	**Z**	
yields	*ylds*		
yoke	*yc*	zany	*zne*
yolk	*yc*	zeal	*zl*
yon·der	*yNr*	zeal·ous	*zls*
you	*u*	zebra	*zbra*
you'd	*u'd*	ze·nith	*znl*
you'll	*u'l*	zero	*zro*
young	*yq*	zest	*zs*
younger	*ygr*	zest·ful	*zsf*
young·est	*ygs*	zig·zag	*zgzg*
young·ster	*ygsr*	zinc	*zq*
young·sters	*ygsrs*	zip	*zp*
your	*u*	zip code	*zp cd*
you're	*u'r*	zip codes	*zp cds*
yours	*us*	zip·per	*zpr*
your·self	*usf*	zip·pers	*zprs*
your·selves	*usvs*	zippy	*zpe*
youth	*ul*	zips	*zps*
youth·ful	*ulf*	zir·con	*zrk*
youths	*uls*	zo·diac	*zdec*

zone	*zn*	zoo	*zu*
zoned	*zn-*	zo·ology	*zoloje*
zones	*zns*	zoom	*z*
zon·ing	*zn*	zuc·chini	*zcne*

SPEEDWRITING SHORTHAND PRINCIPLES

By System Category

Simple Sounds

1. Write what you hear.

   high   *hi*

2. Write   C   for the sound of *k*.

   copy   *cpe*

3. Write ⌢ for the sound of *m*.

   may   *⌢a*

4. Write ⌣ for the sound of *w*.

   way   *⌣a*

5. Write   *ᴧ*   to form the plural of any outline, to show possession, or to add   *ᴧ*   to a verb.

   books   *bcs*

   runs   *rns*

6. Omit *p* in the sound of *mpt*.

   empty   *⌣le*

7. Write   *↗*   for the medial and final sound of *x*.

   boxes   *bxs*

   tax   *lx*

8. Omit the final *t* of a root word after the sound of *k*.

   act   *ac*

Vowels

1. Drop medial vowels.

   build   *bld*

2. Write initial and final vowels.

   office   *ofs*

   fee   *fe*

3. Retain beginning or ending vowels when building compound words.

   payroll   *parl*

   headache   *hdac*

4. Retain root-word vowels when adding prefixes and suffixes.

   disappear   *Dapr*

   payment   *pam*

5. For words ending in a long vowel + *t*, omit the *t* and write the vowel.

   rate

   meet

6. When a word contains two medial, consecutively pronounced vowels, write the first vowel.

   trial

7. When a word ends in two consecutively pronounced vowels, write only the last vowel.

   idea

Vowel Blends

1. Write   O   for the sound of *ow*.

   allow

2. Write   *y*   for the sound of *oi*.

   boy

3. Write   *a*   for the initial and final sound of *aw*.

   law

   audit

Consonant Blends

1. Write a capital   C   for the sound of *ch*.

   check

2. Write   ⌣   for the sound of *wh*.

   when

3. Write a capital   *n*   for the sound of *nt*.

   sent

4. Write   ⫫   for the sound of *ish* or *sh*.

   finish

5. Write   *l*   for the sound of *ith* or *th*.

   them

6. Write   *g*   for the medial or final sound of any vowel + *nk*.

   bank

   link

7. Write   *q*   for the sound of *kw*.

quick   *qc*

8. Write a capital   *n*   for the sound of *nd*.

friend   *frn*

9. Write   *δ*   for the sound of *st*.

rest   *rδ*

10. Write   *3*   for the sound of *zh*.

pleasure   *plzr*

11. Write   *q*   for the medial or final sound of any vowel + *ng*.

rang   *rq*

single   *sgl*

12. Write   *m*   for the sounds of *ance, ence, nce, nse*.

balance   *blm*

Compound Sounds

1. Write   *m*   for the sounds of *mem* and *mum*.

memo   *mo*

2. Write   *m*   for the sounds of *men, min, mon, mun*.

menu   *mu*

money   *me*

3. Write   *k*   for the sounds of *com, con, coun, count*.

common   *kn*

convey   *kva*

counsel   *ksl*

account   *ak*

Word Beginnings

1. Write a capital   *a*   for the word beginnings *ad, all*, and *al*.

admit   *ad*

also   *aso*

2. Write   *n*   for the initial sound of *in* and *en*.

indent   *ndn*

3. Write a printed capital S (joined) for the word beginnings *cer, cir, ser, sur.*

   certain   *Sln*

   survey   *Sva*

4. Write a capital D for the word beginning *dis.*

   discuss   *Dcs*

5. Write a capital M for the word beginning *mis.*

   misplace   *Mpls*

6. Write a capital P (disjoined) for the word beginnings *per, pur, pre, pro, pro* (prah).

   person   *Psn*

   prepare   *Ppr*

   provide   *Pvd*

   problem   *Pbl*

7. Write a for the word beginning *an.*

   answer   *asr*

8. Write a capital S (disjoined) for the word beginning *super.*

   supervise   *Svz*

9. Write el for the word beginning *electr.*

   electronic   *elnc*

10. Write ⌒ for the initial sound of *em* or *im.*

   emphasize   *fsz*

   impress   *prs*

11. Write ╲ for words beginning with the sound of any vowel + *x.*

   explain   *pln*

   accident   *dN*

12. Write X for the word beginnings *extr* and *extra.*

   extreme   *X*

   extraordinary   *Xord*

13. Write U for the word beginning *un.*

   until   *ull*

14. Write S for the word beginning *sub.*

   submit   *sl*

15. Write a capital $\mathcal{N}$ for the word beginnings *enter, inter, intro*.

enterprise

interest

introduce

16. Write $\mathscr{sf}$ for the word beginning *self.*

self-made

17. Write T for the word beginnings *tran* and *trans*.

transfer

Word Endings

1. Underscore the last letter of the outline to add *ing* or *thing* as a word ending.

billing

something

2. To form the plural of any outline ending in a mark of punctuation, double the last mark of punctuation.

savings

3. To form the past tense of a regular verb, write a hyphen after the outline.

used

4. Write $\mathcal{m}$ for the word endings *mand, mend, mind, ment*.

demand

amend

remind

payment

5. Write ℓ for the word ending *ly* or *ily*.

family

6. Write q for the word ending *gram.*

telegram

7. Write a capital S (disjoined) for the word endings *scribe* and *script*.

describe

manuscript

8. Write *w* for the word ending *ward*.

backward   *bcw*

9. Write *h* for the word ending *hood*.

boyhood   *byh*

10. Write *1* for the word ending *tion* or *sion*.

vacation   *vcy*

11. Write *q* for the word ending *quire*.

require   *rq*

12. Write *'* for the word ending *ness*.

kindness   *cN'*

13. Write *B* for the word endings *bil, ble, bly*.

possible   *psB*

probably   *PbB*

14. Write *ι* (slightly raised and disjoined) for the word ending *ity*.

quality   *qlᶦ*

15. Write *sl* for the sound of *shul* and the word ending *chul*.

financial   *fnnsl*

16. Write *v* for the medial and final sound of *tive*.

effective   *efcv*

17. Write *f* for the word endings *ful* and *ify*.

careful   *crf*

justify   *jSf*

18. Write *fy* for the word ending *ification*.

qualifications   *qlfys*

19. Write *sf* for the word ending *self*

myself   *usf*

20. Write *svo* for the word ending *selves*.

ourselves   *rsvo*

Marks of Punctuation

1. Underscore the last letter of the outline to add *ing* or *thing* as a word ending.

billing   *bl̲*

something   *s̲*

2. To form the plural of any outline ending in a mark of punctuation, double the last mark of punctuation.

savings

3. To form the past tense of a regular verb, write a hyphen after the outline.

used

4. Write   /   for the word ending *ness*.

kindness

5. To show capitalization, draw a small curved line under the last letter of the outline.

Bill

6. Write   \   to indicate a period at the end of a sentence.

7. Write   ✗   to indicate a question mark.

8. Write   ＞   to indicate the end of a paragraph.

9. Write   !   to indicate an exclamation mark.

10. Write   ═   to indicate a dash.

11. Write   =   to indicate a hyphen.

12. To indicate solid capitalization, double the curved line underneath the last letter of the outline.

13. To indicate an underlined title, draw a solid line under the outline.

14. Write   ⨍ ⨍   to indicate parentheses.

INDEX OF BRIEF FORMS

Alphabetical Listing

a (an)		as (was)	*3*
able	*B*	associate	*aso*
about	*ab*	at (it)	*/*
accept	*ac*	be (been, but, buy, by)	*b*
accomplish	*ak*	been (be, but, buy, by)	*b*
acknowledge	*acf*	between	*bln*
administrate	*Am*	both	*bo*
advantage	*Avf*	business	*bs*
after	*af*	but (be, been, buy, by)	*b*
again (against)	*aq*	buy (be, been, but, by)	*b*
against (again)	*aq*	by (be, been, but, buy)	*b*
already	*Ar*	came (come, committee)	*k*
always	*a*	can	*c*
am (more)	*⌐*	character (characteristic)	*crc*
an (a)	*.*	characteristic (character)	*crc*
appreciate	*ap*	charge	*G*
appropriate	*apo*	circumstance	*Sk*
approximate	*apx*	come (came, committee)	*k*
are (our)	*r*	committee (came, come)	*k*
arrange	*ar*	complete	*kp*

congratulate	*kq*	firm	*fr*
consider	*ks*	for (full)	*b*
continue	*ku*	from	*fr*
contract	*kc*	full (for)	*b*
contribute	*kb*	general	*jn*
control	*kl*	go (good)	*g*
convenience (convenient)	*kv*	good (go)	*g*
convenient (convenience)	*kv*	grate (great)	*gr*
correspond (correspondence)	*cor*	great (grate)	*gr*
correspondence (correspond)	*cor*	had (he, him)	*h*
customer	*K*	has	*hs*
deliver	*dl*	have (of, very)	*v*
determine	*dl*	he (had, him)	*h*
develop	*dv*	him (had, he)	*h*
difficult	*dfc*	his (is)	*)*
direct (doctor)	*dr*	hospital	*hsp*
distribute	*D*	immediate	*⌢*
doctor (direct)	*dr*	importance (important)	*pl*
during	*du_*	important (importance)	*pl*
employ	*⌢p*	in (not)	*n*
ever (every)	*E*	include	*l*
every (ever)	*ε*	individual	*nv*
experience	*vp*	industry	*n*

is (his)	⟩	own (on)	o
it (at)	/	part (port)	pt
letter	L	participate	pp
manage	⌐y	particular	ptc
manufacture	⌐f	perhaps	Ph
market	⌐r	please (up)	p
more (am)	⌐	point	py
necessary	nes	port (part)	pt
next	nx	present	p
not (in)	n	property	prp
note	nt	prove	pv
of (have, very)	v	public	pb
on (own)	o	refer	rf
once	oN	respond (response)	rsp
operate	op	response (respond)	rsp
opinion	opn	sample	sa
opportunity	opt	satisfactory (satisfy)	sat
order	od	satisfy (satisfactory)	sat
ordinary	ord	several	sv
organize	oq	ship	⊀
other	ot	signature (significance, significant)	siq
our (are)	⌐	significance (signature, significant)	siq
over	O		

significant (signature, significance) — *sig*

situate — *sit*

specific (specify) — *sp*

specify (specific) — *sp*

standard — *sd*

success — *suc*

suggest — *sug*

that — *la*

the — ⌐

they — *ly*

those — *loz*

to (too) — *l*

too (to) — *l*

under — *u*

up (please) — *p*

us — *s*

usual — *uz*

very (have, of) — *v*

was (as) — *z*

we — *e*

well (will) — *l*

were (with) — ‿

why — *y*

will (well) — *l*

with (were) — ‿

work (world) — ‿

world (work) — ‿

would — *d*

your — *u*

INDEX OF ABBREVIATIONS

Alphabetical Listing

advertise	*av*	dollars (dollar)	$
agriculture	*agr*	east	E
America (American)	*a*	economic (economy)	*eco*
American (America)	*a*	economy (economic)	*eco*
amount	*amt*	enclose (enclosure)	*enc*
and	*+*	enclosure (enclose)	*enc*
attention	*att*	envelope	*env*
avenue	*ave*	especially	*esp*
billion	B	establish	*est*
boulevard	*blvd*	et cetera	*etc*
catalog	*cat*	example (executive)	*ex*
cent (cents)	¢	executive (example)	*ex*
cents (cent)	¢	federal	*fed*
Christmas	*Xmas*	feet	*ft*
company	*co*	government	*gvt*
corporation	*corp*	hour	*hr*
credit	*cr*	hundred	H
day	*d*	inch	*in*
department	*dpt*	incorporate (incorporated)	*inc*
dollar (dollars)	$	incorporated (incorporate)	*inc*

information	*inf*	question	*q*
insurance	*ins*	record	*rec*
invoice	*inv*	regard	*re*
junior	*jr*	represent (representative)	*rep*
literature	*lit*	representative (represent)	*rep*
merchandise	*mdse*	return	*ret*
million	*M*	second (secretary)	*sec*
Miss	*m*	secretary (second)	*sec*
month	*mo*	senior	*sr*
Mr.	*mr*	south	*S*
Mrs.	*mrs*	square	*sq*
Ms.	*ms*	street	*St*
north	*N*	superintendent	*S*
number	*no*	thousand	*T*
okay	*ok*	total	*tol*
ounce	*oz*	university	*U*
percent	*%*	vice president	*VP*
pound	*lb*	volume	*vol*
president	*P*	west	*W*
quart	*qt*	yard	*yd*

INDEX OF PHRASES

The following phrases are presented in alphabetical segments beginning with the pronouns *I*, *we*, and *you* plus a verb, followed by infinitive phrases (*to* plus a verb), high-frequency word combinations, and word combinations with words omitted.

I am	⌐	I was	⅓
I appreciate	*iap*	I will	*il*
I believe	*iblv*	I will be	*ilb*
I can	*ic*	I would	*id*
I can be	*icb*	I would appreciate	*idap*
I cannot	*icn*	I would be	*idb*
I could	*icd*	I would like	*idlc*
I do	*idu*	we appreciate	*eap*
I feel	*ifl*	we are	*er*
I had	*ih*	we are not	*ern*
I have	*iv*	we are pleased	*erp-*
I have been	*ivb*	we believe	*eblv*
I have had	*ivh*	we can	*ec*
I hope	*ihp*	we can be	*ecb*
I know	*ino*	we cannot	*ecn*
I look	*ilc*	we could	*ecd*
I shall	*isl*	we do	*edu*
I should	*isd*	we feel	*efl*
		we had	*eh*
		we have	*ev*
		we have been	*evb*
		we have had	*evh*

we hope	*ehp*	you were	*u*
we know	*eno*	you will	*ul*
we shall	*esl*	you will be	*ulb*
we should	*esd*	you will find	*ulfn*
we were	*e*	you would	*ud*
we will	*el*	you would be	*udb*
we will be	*elb*	you would like	*udlc*
we would	*ed*	to be	*lb*
we would appreciate	*edap*	to call	*lcl*
we would be	*edb*	to come	*lk*
we would like	*edlc*	to determine	*ldl*
you are	*ur*	to do	*ldu*
you can	*uc*	to get	*lgl*
you cannot	*ucn*	to give	*lgv*
you can be	*ucb*	to go	*lq*
you could	*ucd*	to have	*lv*
you do	*udu*	to have you	*lvu*
you had	*uh*	to have your	*lvu*
you have	*uv*	to hear	*lhr*
you have been	*uvb*	to keep	*lcp*
you have had	*uvh*	to know	*lno*
you know	*uno*	to make	*lc*
you need	*und*	to offer	*lofr*
you should	*usd*	to pay	*lpa*

to receive	*Lrsv*	have had	*vh*
to say	*Lsa*	have not	*vn*
to see	*Lse*	have you	*vu*
to send	*Lsn*	have your	*vu*
to use	*Luz*	in the	*nr*
to visit	*Lvzl*	it is	*s*
to work	*Lo*	of our	*vr*
and the	*+*	of the	*v*
as I	*zi*	of you	*vu*
as to	*zt*	of your	*vu*
as we	*ze*	on the	*o*
as well as	*zlz*	on you	*ou*
as you	*zu*	on your	*ou*
as your	*zu*	should be	*sdb*
at the	*s*	thank you	*lqu*
can be	*cb*	that I	*lai*
could be	*cdb*	that we	*lae*
fact that	*fcla*	that you	*lau*
for the	*f*	that you are	*laur*
for you	*fu*	that you will	*laul*
for your	*fu*	that your	*lau*
has been	*hsb*	to you	*lu*
have been	*vb*	to your	*lu*

will be	*ℓb*	nonetheless	*nnls*
will you	*ℓu*	thank you for	*lqf*
will your	*ℓu*	thank you for your	*lqf*
would be	*db*	thank you for your letter	*lqfL*
would like	*dlc*	time to time	*LL*
as soon as	*33*	up to date	*pda*
nevertheless	*nvrls*		

IDENTIFICATION INITIALS FOR UNITED STATES AND TERRITORIES

Alabama (AL)	*AL*	Maryland (MD)	*MD*
Alaska (AK)	*AK*	Massachusetts (MA)	*MA*
Arizona (AZ)	*AZ*	Michigan (MI)	*MI*
Arkansas (AR)	*AR*	Minnesota (MN)	*MN*
California (CA)	*CA*	Mississippi (MS)	*MS*
Colorado (CO)	*CO*	Missouri (MO)	*MO*
Connecticut (CT)	*CT*	Montana (MT)	*MT*
Delaware (DE)	*DE*	Nebraska (NE)	*NE*
District of Columbia (DC)	*DC*	Nevada (NV)	*NV*
Florida (FL)	*FL*	New Hampshire (NH)	*NH*
Georgia (GA)	*GA*	New Jersey (NJ)	*NJ*
Hawaii (HI)	*HI*	New Mexico (NM)	*NM*
Idaho (ID)	*ID*	New York (NY)	*NY*
Illinois (IL)	*IL*	North Carolina (NC)	*NC*
Indiana (IN)	*IN*	North Dakota (ND)	*ND*
Iowa (IA)	*IA*	Ohio (OH)	*OH*
Kansas (KS)	*KS*	Oklahoma (OK)	*OK*
Kentucky (KY)	*KY*	Oregon (OR)	*OR*
Louisiana (LA)	*LA*	Pennsylvania (PA)	*PA*
Maine (ME)	*ME*	Rhode Island (RI)	*RI*

South Carolina (SC)	SC	Washington (WA)	WA
South Dakota (SD)	SD	West Virginia (WV)	WV
Tennessee (TN)	TN	Wisconsin (WI)	WI
Texas (TX)	TX	Wyoming (WY)	WY
Utah (UT)	UT	Guam (GU)	GU
Vermont (VT)	VT	Puerto Rico (PR)	PR
Virginia (VA)	VA	Virgin Islands (VI)	VI

IDENTIFICATION INITIALS FOR CANADIAN PROVINCES AND TERRITORIES

Alberta (AB)   *AB*

British Columbia (BC)   *BC*

Labrador (LB)   *LB*

Manitoba (MB)   *MB*

New Brunswick (NB)   *NB*

Newfoundland (NF)   *NF*

Northwest Territories (NT)   *NT*

Nova Scotia (NS)   *NS*

Ontario (ON)   *ON*

Prince Edward Island (PE)   *PE*

Quebec (PQ)   *PQ*

Saskatchewan (SK)   *SK*

Yukon Territory (YT)   *YT*

INDEX OF CITIES

American Cities

City	Shorthand	City	Shorthand
Akron	*acrn*	Columbus	*clbs*
Albany	*Abne*	Dallas	*dls*
Albuquerque	*Abcrce*	Davenport	*dvnpl*
Allentown	*Anton*	Dayton	*dtn*
Atlanta	*allNa*	Denver	*dnvr*
Austin	*aSn*	Des Moines	*d yn*
Baltimore	*blt*	Detroit	*dtryt*
Baton Rouge	*btn rz*	El Paso	*el pso*
Birmingham	*br gh*	Flint	*flN*
Boston	*bSn*	Fort Lauderdale	*fl ldrdl*
Bridgeport	*brjpl*	Fort Worth	*fl rt*
Buffalo	*bflo*	Fresno	*frzno*
Charleston	*CrlSn*	Grand Rapids	*grN rpds*
Charlotte	*srll*	Harrisburg	*hrsbrq*
Chattanooga	*Clnga*	Hartford	*hrlfd*
Chicago	*scg*	Honolulu	*hnllu*
Cincinnati	*sNnle*	Houston	*hSn*
Cleveland	*clvlN*	Indianapolis	*Nenpls*
Colorado Springs	*CO sprgs*	Jackson	*jcsn*
Columbia	*clba*	Jacksonville	*jcsnvl*

Jersey City	_jrze sle_	Orlando	_orlNo_
Kansas City	_KS sle_	Peoria	_pera_
Knoxville	_nxvl_	Philadelphia	_fldlfa_
Lansing	_lNg_	Phoenix	_fnx_
Las Vegas	_ls vgs_	Pittsburgh	_plsbrg_
Little Rock	_lll rc_	Portland	_plN_
Los Angeles	_ls ajls_	Providence	_PvdN_
Louisville	_luvl_	Richmond	_rCmd_
Memphis	_mfs_	Rochester	_rCSr_
Miami	_me_	Sacramento	_scrmto_
Milwaukee	_lce_	St. Louis	_sN lus_
Minneapolis	_mepls_	St. Paul	_sN pl_
Mobile	_B_	St. Petersburg	_sN plrsbrg_
Nashville	_nsvl_	Salt Lake City	_sll lc sle_
New Haven	_nu hvn_	San Antonio	_sn alno_
New Orleans	_nu orlns_	San Bernardino	_sn brnrdno_
New York	_NY_	San Diego	_sn deg_
Newark	_nurc_	San Francisco	_sn frnssco_
Newport News	_nupl nz_	San Jose	_sn hza_
Norfolk	_nrfc_	Sarasota	_srsla_
Oakland	_oclN_	Scranton	_scrNn_
Oklahoma City	_OK sle_	Seattle	_sell_
Omaha	_oha_	Shreveport	_srvpl_

City	Shorthand	City	Shorthand
Spokane	*spcn*	Etobicoke	*etbcc*
Springfield	*sprgfld*	Halifax	*hlfx*
Syracuse	*srcs*	Hamilton	*hmltn*
Tacoma	*tcma*	Kitchener	*ctnr*
Tampa	*tmpa*	Laval	*lvl*
Toledo	*tldo*	London	*lnn*
Trenton	*trntn*	Mississauga	*Msga*
Tucson	*tsn*	Montreal	*mtrel*
Tulsa	*tlsa*	Oshawa	*osa*
West Palm Beach	*Wp bC*	Ottawa	*ota*
Wichita	*cta*	Quebec	*qbc*
Wilmington	*lmgtn*	Regina	*rjna*
Worcester	*Sr*	St. Catharines	*sN ctrns*
Youngstown	*ygston*	Saskatoon	*ssctn*
		Thunder Bay	*tNr ba*
		Toronto	*trNo*
		Vancouver	*vncvr*
		Windsor	*nzr*
		Winnipeg	*npq*
		York	*yrc*

Canadian Cities

Brampton	*brtn*
Burlington	*brlgtn*
Burnaby	*brnbe*
Calgary	*clgre*
East York	*E yrc*
Edmonton	*edmtn*

METRIC TERMS

	meter m (length)	liter l (capacity)	gram g (weight)
kilo	km	kl	kg
hecto	hm	hl	hg
deca	dam	dal	dag
deci	dm	dl	dg
centi	cm	cl	cg
milli	mm	ml	mg
micro	crm	crl	crg
nano	nm	nl	ng